Vivid Faces

R. F. FOSTER

Vivid Faces

*The Revolutionary Generation in
Ireland, 1890–1923*

W. W. Norton & Company

NEW YORK • LONDON

For information about permission to reproduce selections from this book,
write to Permissions, W. W. Norton & Company, Inc.,
500 Fifth Avenue, New York, NY 10110

For information about special discounts for bulk purchases, please contact
W. W. Norton Special Sales at specialsales@wwnorton.com or 800-233-4830

Manufacturing by Courier Westford
Production manager: Julia Druskin

ISBN 978-0-393-08279-1

W. W. Norton & Company, Inc.
500 Fifth Avenue, New York, N.Y. 10110
www.wwnorton.com

W. W. Norton & Company Ltd.
Castle House, 75/76 Wells Street, London W1T 3QT

1 2 3 4 5 6 7 8 9 0

For Jay Tolson

I have met them at close of day
Coming with vivid faces
From counter or desk among grey
Eighteenth-century houses.
I have passed with a nod of the head
Or polite meaningless words,
Or have lingered awhile and said
Polite meaningless words,
And thought before I had done
Of a mocking tale or a gibe
To please a companion
Around the fire at the club,
Being certain that they and I
But lived where motley is worn:
All changed, changed utterly:
A terrible beauty is born.

– W. B. Yeats, 'Easter 1916'

Contents

List of Illustrations

PLATES

TEXT ILLUSTRATIONS

Molly Childers (*left, holding rifle*) and Mary Spring-Rice running guns from Germany to Ireland aboard the *Asgard*, July 1914.

Introduction: The Ireland of Yesterday

The revolutionary era in Ireland during the early twentieth century was famously described by the historian F. S. L. Lyons as embodying 'an anarchy in the mind and in the heart, an anarchy which forbade not just unity of territories, but also "unity of being", an anarchy that sprang from the collision within a small and intimate island of seemingly irreconcilable cultures, unable to live together or to live apart, caught inextricably in the web of their tragic history'.[1] This bleak interpretation was strongly influenced by the views of W. B. Yeats, who had influentially identified the quarter-century from 1890 to 1916 as a 'long gestation', during which Irish opinions turned from political to cultural nationalism after the shattering fall and death of Charles Stewart Parnell, leader of the Irish Parliamentary Party at Westminster. Parnell had apparently brought the party's objective of Home Rule for Ireland to the edge of achievement, promising the restoration of a parliament in Dublin which would exercise autonomy within the framework of the British Empire, and – for optimistic 'advanced nationalists' at least – possibly lead to something more. In the Yeatsian view, Parnell's destruction after a divorce scandal, and the rending apart of his party for nearly a decade, set in motion an inexorable process of radicalization, polarization – and collision. This interpretation has been much interrogated since; strong arguments have been made for the persistence and strength of the established constitutional-nationalist Home Rule party, the speed and unpredictability with which a revolutionary scenario emerged by 1916, and the necessity to recognize the decisive importance of extraneous influences, such as the First World War. But the fact remains that during this era enough people – especially young people – changed their minds about political possibilities to bring about a revolution against the old order, which included not only government by Britain but the constitutional nationalism of the previous generation.

The Irish revolution was sparked into life (ostensibly) with the 'Rising', or rebellion of 1916, when a small group of extreme Irish nationalists, organized by the 'Fenians', or Irish Republican Brotherhood, mounted a week-long insurrection in Dublin, occupying public buildings and creating mayhem before the British Army regained control. The revolutionaries had originally expected substantial help from Germany, with which Britain (and therefore Ireland, officially) was at war; when this went astray, they went ahead anyway, in what became a gesture of sacrificial violence rather than a serious challenge to Britain's government of Ireland. That government was already, so to speak, under review, and a measure of Home Rule for Ireland had been passed by the British parliament in 1912–14, granting Ireland some self-government; this had been the achievement of years of dedicated campaigning and negotiation by the leader of parliamentary nationalism, John Redmond, the inheritor of Parnell's mantle. But the implementation of a Home Rule parliament had been postponed for the war's duration, and in any case had been blocked by resistance from Protestants and unionists in the north-east of the country, bringing Ireland to a point of threatened civil war just before the world war broke out in August 1914. As in Russia, a sense of dammed-up domestic crisis was released by international war; but the outbreak of hostilities also constituted, for a minority of Irish revolutionary purists, an opportunity they had been anticipating for a long time.

But when did the Irish revolution begin? The period that started with the Easter Rising of 1916 and ended with the Civil War of 1922–3 has been closely excavated, particularly since the emergence of illuminating new sources such as the witness statements of the Bureau of Military History. However, what might be called the 'pre-revolution' – the quarter-century between Parnell's death in 1891 and the insurrection in 1916 – has not been explored so intensively, though the broad frameworks of Irish constitutional politics and political mentalities have been suggestively profiled.[2] Regarding revolutionary mentalities, however, the coverage has generally been less extensive, and less interrogative. With occasional brilliant exceptions, the motivations that propelled a dedicated minority into revolutionary attitudes by 1916, bringing more than 2,000 rebels on to the streets of Dublin and instigating years of guerrilla war, have received less attention.

A new look at the pre-revolutionary period in Ireland is all the more necessary, because traditional approaches to understanding revolutionary change in terms of class or ideology seem inadequate today. We search now, instead, to find clarification through themes of paradox and nuance; we have become interested in what does *not* change during revolutions, as much as what does.[3] And recent analysis of revolution has tended to demote the centrality of ideological dynamics and interpret ostensibly 'political' impulses as reflections of ethnic antagonism, anti-imperial reaction, and what one historian has resonantly called 'the psycho-underground of masculinities and local community conflicts'. Indeed, the guerrilla campaign, civil war and post-revolutionary fallout in Ireland in some ways paralleled the bloody events over Central Europe after 1918.[4]

Nonetheless the idea of the Irish revolution is still in process of definition, and not just its duration. How far was it a 'revolution' in the generally accepted meaning of the word? Should it be seen in its own terms, or mapped against other upheavals in contemporary Europe? It is now an accepted cliché – though a spectacular exaggeration – that events in Ireland from 1916 to 1921 served as a model for later revolts elsewhere.[5] However, the Irish revolution did not leave a theoretical template for other dominions to act upon, and the record of its events remained for many years patchy and obscure, though much has clarified in recent years. For revolutions in other countries, scholars have tried to isolate a 'tipping point': the moment when substantive change becomes possible, building on an alteration of 'hearts and minds' as well as the 'presenting problem' of an immediate crisis. This is true, for instance, of many studies of the American Revolution. But, among Irish historians at least, it is less common to analyse the pre-revolutionary mentality across a broad front: to trace that gradual process of alteration which prepares the way for crisis. In the Irish case, apart from the brilliant short studies by Lyons and Tom Garvin some decades ago, and Senia Pašeta's pioneering work on Irish nationalist women, not much attempt has been made at analysing the backgrounds and mentalities of those who made the revolution.[6] Yet the life-stories of the people involved are as important as their theories and ideas. In other contexts, it has been demonstrated that revolutionary process can be observed through the biographies as well as the theories of individuals, as Franco Venturi did for the first Russian revolutionaries in his classic study, *Roots of Revolution*.[7] (Strikingly, Venturi judged the most illuminating work by the Populist ideologue Chernyshevsky to be his unfinished autobiography, *Prologue of the Prologue*.) More recent work on the Russian revolutionary generation, such as *Heralds of Revolution*, Susan K. Morrissey's study of the 1905 student revolutionaries of St Petersburg, bears out this emphasis on personal experience.[8]

How relevant is this to the Ireland of the same era? How far can we reconstruct the processes, networks, experiences and attitudes of the Irish revolutionary generation around the beginning of the twentieth century? What happened in 1916 drew attention to a change of mentality, a change in hearts and minds, whereby within two or three years Irish opinion would shift dramatically away from the old, constitutionalist Home Rule idea, and towards a more radical form of republican separatism, achieved if necessary by force of arms. Gradualism was replaced by revolution: it is in these years, especially from 1918, that a revolutionary vanguard appeared in an organized way, and sophisticated structures of subversion and rebellion emerged.[9] (Though these latter phenomena owed much to previous formations in Irish history.)

Nonetheless, the idea of a preceding sea-change in Irish opinion persists, and most of the book that follows is devoted to trying to trace it, at the personal level of individual lives. It attempts to recapture the voices of people from the era, rather than relying too heavily on later memories and rationalizations – and to do this by charting opinions evidenced in letters, reflections and diaries. Some of these voices became mainstream, and some marginalized. I have tried to profile a selection of the activities and influences which moulded the 'revolutionary generation' – a concept examined in the first chapter. The book also attempts to indicate the ways in which personal lives and predilections reflected and anticipated the larger, more seismic shifts that came into view during 1916 and its aftermath. The emphasis does not fall exclusively upon people who became prominent revolutionaries (though several of the cast of characters did). Rather, I am attempting to characterize the worlds of students, actors, writers, teachers, civil servants; often from comfortable middle-class backgrounds, and often spending part of their lives working in Britain. They were not, by and large, from families with a 'Fenian' or extreme separatist background; revolution (and, often, anti-British feeling) did not seem to be in their 'objective' interests; their radicalization came by degrees. Established politics, and the high culture of Yeats and his circle, are seen as less relevant than the experiences and ideas of more obscure people, expressed as far as possible in their own words. This involves sources such as diaries kept by the young Cork republican activist Liam de Róiste, forever starting up clubs, magazines and societies; his friend the playwright and eventual hunger-striker Terence MacSwiney; the radical Quaker Rosamond Jacob, determined to insert herself into the world of Gaelic and nationalist revival which she sensed happening around her; the Gaelic League organizer Piaras Béaslaí, migrating from Liverpool to Ireland in search of some kind of romantic destiny; and the Trinity law students Kevin O'Shiel and Diarmuid Coffey, whose journals chart their cautious shift from moderate to 'advanced' nationalism. Large collections of letters, journals and unpublished autobiographies, through which similar trajectories can be traced, exist in a number of Irish locations. Several old revolutionaries had devoted their mature years to amassing material on the fabled years of the struggle, collecting accounts, documents and memories from their contemporaries – much of it now in the invaluable archives of University College, Dublin.

Many of the sources for the revolutionary period reflect a very self-conscious process of memorialization on the part of the revolutionary generation – the subject of the last chapter of this book. This happened through official channels, such as the Bureau of Military History, a government agency which, from 1947, started collecting the memories of those active in the revolution – a huge, though not unproblematic, source, only recently opened to historians.[10] The Military Service Pensions Collection will similarly form a rich testimony of autobiographical exegesis, but should equally be approached with caution as a repository of history 'as it actually happened'. There were also – as will be seen in the last chapter of this book – individual enterprises on the part of ex-revolutionaries such as Ernie O'Malley and Richard Mulcahy. The impulses behind these projects have much to do with politics: the traumatic split and civil war that followed the Treaty in 1921 entailed upon survivors the necessity of gathering material to prove their side was the right one, and their actions consistent with the principles of the revolution. But there were other impulses, including disillusionment, nostalgia and a certain air of disbelief. Did we do that? How did it happen? How did we end up here?

The records thus accumulated advert more often to the experience of revolutionary activity after the 1916 Rising than to the networks, preconditions and processes of the 'pre-revolution' – the ways whereby people, often unlikely people, became radicalized. This is more profitably approached by examining the individual lives of the revolutionaries, several of whom were, like Liam de Róiste, vaguely conscious, even at the time, that their lives reflected a larger reality. Letters, diaries and other contemporary reflections have not been misted by hindsight, and can reflect the way that young dissidents saw themselves making history. There are visual indications, too, such as the posed publicity pictures from a strange venture in the summer of 1914. A famous photograph shows two women in a yacht, the *Asgard*, proprietorially guarding boxes of armaments marked 'Hamburg'. One is the 34-year-old Mary Spring-Rice, Anglo-Irish daughter of the second Baron Monteagle, of County Limerick, and cousin of the prominent Anglo-Irish diplomat Sir Cecil Spring-Rice (who wrote, inter alia, the words of 'I Vow to Thee My Country', by which he did not mean Ireland). The other woman is Molly Childers, Bostonian wife of Erskine Childers, thriller-writer, civil servant, soldier, Home Rule supporter and eventually hard-line republican. They are pictured illegally running guns from Germany, in the summer of 1914, to arm the Irish Volunteers, a militia set up formally to defend Home Rule in the face of Ulster opposition, but also embodying a more secret agenda. Others on this enterprise were equally unlikely figures (they include the young cultural nationalist Diarmuid Coffey, whose diaries and reflections we will encounter again). None of them was really a 'revolutionary' at that point: how did they end up appearing to be so? Some answers may be found in the kind of individual experiences which this book attempts to trace.

The approach is thematic rather than chronological, looking at the activities embraced by young, politically interested people in the pre-revolutionary period before moving on to the events of the revolution itself, and the subsequent fallout. The lives of various people are threaded through the book, recurring in various ways; the last chapter charts some post-revolutionary lives to their conclusion. A wide cast of characters is introduced, in different contexts; the key facts of their careers will be found in the Biographical Appendix at the end of the book. Nonetheless the book sustains a kind of chronology in the themes chosen, which track the development of the revolutionary generation through successive stages of activities and conditioning. These include education, journalism, agit-prop theatre, relations with their families and each other, and the dramas of their personal lives. This approach perhaps reflects historiographical changes since 1978. The Olympian, assured, decisive tone of Lyons's path-breaking work no longer comes easily; themes of fracture, paradox, change and unreliable memory have come into focus, along with the sense of an unforeseeable future. The simple dualities of the nationalist impulse to separatism were complicated by various forms of ambivalence and antagonism, which were culturally and even ethnically inflected – as has been indicated in brilliant work on the revolutionaries by Tom Garvin, David Fitzpatrick, Peter Hart, Senia Pašeta, Frances Flanagan and others. This book builds on such work in its attempts to delineate the way a generation is 'made' – and often made retrospectively. The Irish radicals studied here saw themselves, like their Russian contemporaries, as building and inhabiting a different world from that of their parents. The previous generation was often the perceived enemy every bit as much as the British government.

Following the revolutionaries through their overlapping circles of activity – from schoolrooms to draughty rehearsal-halls to university lectures to Dublin cafés to newspaper offices – I have tried to trace networks of interests and preoccupations which reflected new currents of thought, in personal relations as well as abstract commitments to radical principles. Such identifications coexisted with the more predictable preoccupations of cultural revival, the Gaelic League, drama clubs and summer-schools where Irish was learnt from native speakers. To draw a group portrait, or to construct a group biography, of a generation requires delving below the striking of political attitudes, and attempting to reconstruct the way life was lived in student societies, Gaelic League dances, and the front rooms of houses on those Dublin streets where comrades found lodgings close to each other and sat up late at night talking. The more one reads the accounts, letters, diaries and reflections of this generation, the more one gets the sense of an intimate but complex city, with certain areas defined by political subcultures. But there were also circles of like-minded people experimenting with new ways of life in Waterford, or Cork, or Belfast, and they have their place here, too.

What emerged from this world was a generation who became alienated not only from British rule but from the values and ambitions of their parents, and finally from the alternative offered by the constitutional Irish Parliamentary Party, apparently on the edge of delivering Home Rule by 1912. In his leitmotif poem 'Easter 1916' Yeats also interrogated the extent to which the revolutionary generation was 'bewildered' by 'excess of love' – and of hate. For many of them disillusionment came with age; others kept the faith till they died. In either case, their memories are not always the most reliable guide – which is why this book is weighted towards contemporary diaries, letters and journalism. The picture that emerges owes much to the work of recent scholars of the revolutionary period – as will be clear from the footnotes. But it also tries to convey the thoughts, attitudes and expectations of the revolutionaries themselves, along with the extraordinary events which they helped precipitate, and the results with which they lived.

The treatment of the revolution by historians has usually concentrated on the larger narrative, and individual biographies tend towards simplistic hagiography. That moment of irreversible change, that elusive 'tipping point', remains unestablished. The patterns behind the revolutionary split over the Treaty in 1921–2 raise a whole range of uncomfortable questions, which reflect in turn the complexity of revolutionary commitments among individuals. These questions may be illuminated by addressing and exploring the unexpected lives of that extraordinary generation, using the wealth of sources recently uncovered. We may now decode complex networks of influence, operating through education, through mentoring, through reading, through

The search for a tipping point remains – well, a search.

family, through theatre, through journalistic co-operatives and through love. Large questions, such as the nature of Irish anti-imperialism and the short-circuiting of socialism and feminism, still loom unanswered. The mature revolution was far more monocultural, and more ethnically defined, than the pre-revolution. The theme of generational conflict raises European echoes too. In an earlier era Ivan Turgenev wrote *Fathers and Sons*, reflecting on the way radicalization happened within the family as well as in society at large. Thirty years on, a cohort of people emerged in Ireland who, like Basarov in that novel, were determined to destabilize the worlds they were born into: believing, like their contemporary José Ortega y Gasset in early-twentieth-century Spain, that they were a generation 'without fathers in the spiritual order', whose duty was to create a transformative sensibility in the minds of their contemporaries.[11] The parallels with other countries experiencing disruption at a time of war are worth bearing in mind, and the intersections between religion, nationalism and revolution, so potent then, remain vividly present elsewhere in the world today.

Perhaps the Irish revolution can be explored anew by summoning up those 'vivid faces' described by Yeats, getting behind those counters and desks and into their lives and minds. 'Ireland of yesterday,' wrote the politician and *littérateur* Stephen Gwynn in 1918, 'was Ireland before the revolution . . . We may well envy those who lived more easily and quietly in the Ireland of yesterday, and held with an unquestioning spirit to the state of things in which they were born.'[12] But the 'Ireland of yesterday' contained a vital minority of people who did *not* hold with an unquestioning spirit to the inherited state of things. Studying their world and how they conceived it, both at the time and later, may show in turn how a revolutionary generation comes to be made, rather than born.

'John Bull's Famous Circus', a cartoon by Robert Lynd for Bulmer Hobson's short-lived newspaper the *Republic*, 11 April 1907, indicates the contempt felt by the younger generation for the world of constitutional nationalism.

I

Fathers and Children

*You see, my parents are not quite like myself. I think I am
rather characteristic of a certain section in Ireland. The younger
people of Ireland have been thinking in a way that some of the
older ones have not.*
     *– Muriel MacSwiney, Testimony to American
Commission on Conditions in Ireland, 9 December 1920*

I

The men and women who made the Irish revolution knew that they
were different from their parents. The way that the constitutional-
nationalist Irish Parliamentary Party lost its grip on Irish opinion
reflected a generational shift; the fracture between old and new broke
along lines of age as well as of ideology. Older people, such as the
Fenian Tom Clarke – who had served his time in British prisons for
republican activities before returning to Ireland in 1907 and was
fifty-eight years old in 1916 – were recognized as exceptional by their
acolytes. 'To all the young men of the Separatist movement of that
time he was a help and an inspiration,' recalled the passionate young
Cork nationalist P. S. O'Hegarty. 'And he was surely the exception in
his own generation, the one shining example.'[1] For radical nationalists of O'Hegarty's age (he was born in 1879), the previous generation
had sold the pass to craven constitutionalism, by deciding that the
Fenian agenda of achieving separation from Britain through physical
force was outmoded, and opting for parliamentary agitation instead.
For them the world of secret revolutionary societies, spectacular

dynamitard gestures, and doomed risings like the damp-squib Fenian insurrection of 1867, were a thing of the past. O'Hegarty used his ample spare time, during his employment as a British civil servant in the Post Office, to write a great deal of journalism intended to prove that this analysis was wrong.

But the older generation continued to see things differently. A year and a half before the Easter Rising of 1916 the parliamentary nationalist leader John Redmond made a speech at Wexford which described modern Ireland as the Irish Parliamentary Party saw it:

> People talk of the wrongs done to Ireland by England in the past. God knows standing on this holy spot it is not likely any of us can ever forget, though God grant we may all forgive, the wrongs done to our fathers a hundred or two hundred years ago. *But do let us be a sensible and truthful people.* Do let us remember that we today of our generation are a free people (*cheers*). We have emancipated the farmer; we have housed the agricultural labourer; we have won religious liberty; we have won free education ... we have laid broad and deep the foundations of national prosperity and finally we have won an Irish parliament and an executive responsible to it (*cheers*).[2]

This reflected a number of key reforms won by the Home Rulers through the machinery of the Westminster parliament, culminating in the Home Rule Bill, which gave the projected Irish parliament fairly wide powers of autonomy, while firmly retaining imperial supremacy.[3] Nonetheless, Redmond was a figure scornfully regarded by most young radicals, who believed that he and his parliamentary colleagues lived an indolent and corrupted life among the fleshpots of London – a rather unfair image of the existence of the average Irish Parliamentary Party member. More profoundly, to the minds of O'Hegarty and his friends in the advanced-nationalist clubs of Cork, Dublin and London, the constitutional achievements itemized by Redmond were neither relevant nor accurate. It is worth remembering that Redmond's claims would have chimed with the opinions of the majority in Ireland in 1915; the radicals were still a minority. At the same time, many of the attitudes and beliefs which they embraced so fervently were echoed, if in a diluted and perfunctory form, by the rhetoric of constitutional nationalism. That Fenian pedigree which

Tom Clarke represented was often invoked from Irish Parliamentary Party platforms. In the later memories of those who participated in the 1916 Rising, a hereditary Fenian indoctrination would be the predominant feature of their pre-revolutionary conditioning.[4] And – without the benefit of hindsight – O'Hegarty's young friend Terence MacSwiney, writing his diary in 1902, recorded proudly that he was an 'extremist'.

> There is something very ironical in the fact of this term [extremist] being applied by those Irish politicians who are known as 'constitutional' if we only examine the matter closely enough. The 'extremist' so-called is one who has an ideal and strives to the best of his ability to aid in the realization of that ideal ... And so the 'extremist' keeps the ideal of nationality unsullied and adopts for his watch-word – No Compromise ... But the Constitutionalist's idea of our rights is a home parliament under the English flag; and if you attempt to explain to him that this is not the full measure of our rights but that in reality our country should be raised to a position of Sovereign Independence, he will in all probability tell you that you are an 'extremist'.[5]

For some 'extremists', like MacSwiney, the notion of a righteous war of liberation was a desideratum from early youth; the idea pulses through his personal writings in the early 1900s, supplying a romantic counterpoint to his daily life working as a clerk and studying at night-school. This belief was founded in imbibed ideas of history, from mentors at school as well as at home, which will be discussed later in this book; it was also founded in a fervent and mystical devotion to Catholicism.

But extremism could flourish in other seed-beds too, and the beliefs embraced by MacSwiney were also articulated by radicals from very different backgrounds. Feminism, socialism, anti-imperialism, anti-vivisectionism were among the anti-establishment beliefs appealing to young people in the Edwardian era, in Ireland as in Britain. Several of them also embraced secularism, as O'Hegarty, writing from London in 1904, tried to explain to his old Christian Brothers schoolfellow:

> you will be surprised to hear that I am an anti-cleric. I don't hold that the priests are our natural enemies but I do think strongly that they

3

have acquired the habit and that nothing but strong determined action will break them of it. They ruined every movement – directly or indirectly – since the passing of the Maynooth Grant in 1795 and we have to put them in their places if we are going to do anything. Even today the U[nited] I[rishman] is an 'atheistic' paper and daren't be sold outside the towns. There's no use shutting our eyes to the fact that the hierarchy are governed indirectly from London through Rome ... The Catholic Church in Ireland wants reform root and branch quite as much as it did on the Continent prior to the Reformation. We have no true religion in Ireland for our religion is alien not national. Most of the fellows here are anti-cleric to a greater or less degree ... It is only when a man leaves Ireland that he begins to see straight on some things, this amongst them.[6]

This echoed the anti-clericalism professed by some Fenians in the 1860s, but it also suggests the impatience of young radicals with the power of Catholicism in Irish life by the early twentieth century. While removal to London could accentuate this reaction, other radicals, especially from Protestant backgrounds, needed no encouragement to see the Catholic Church as one of the main obstacles to liberation – along with the Irish Parliamentary Party. The two were often jointly identified through the Ancient Order of Hibernians, the Catholic political and social association founded in Ulster, led by the Belfast politician Joe Devlin and routinely denounced by 'extremists'. To the revolutionary generation, such institutions represented a corrupt old order which had to be exorcized.

As the new century dawned, these feelings were not restricted to the political extremists alone; W. B. Yeats, writing in the *United Irishman* in 1901, conjured up an undercurrent of revolutionary initiates bent on overthrowing a decadent modern civilization, working among the multitude as if 'upon some secret errand'.[7] But, at this point in his life, Yeats expected the new age to be one of spiritual revelation, rather than political transformation. Fourteen years older than MacSwiney and O'Hegarty, he had been through his Fenian period, and his own relations with many of the future revolutionaries were – to say the least – problematic. He soon became a supporter of Redmond's Home Rulers, along with the majority of nationalist Irish people; the radical and separatist agenda of the nationalist ginger-groups that came together under the name 'Sinn Féin' ('We Ourselves') in the early 1900s seemed alien to him. But when he witnessed the fallout of the 1916 Rising, he realized he had seen 'a world one has worked with or against for years suddenly overwhelmed. As yet one knows nothing of the future except that it must be very unlike the past.'[8] The poem in which he interrogated the revolutionary act, and those who made it, became canonical. The reality of the Rising jolted his assumption that Ireland had settled into an everyday mode. In 1914 he had told an American audience that the age of heroics was past:

> There was a time when every young man asked himself if he were not willing to die for his country. Ireland was his sweetheart, his mistress, the love of his life, for whom he faced death triumphantly. That is the theme of my [1902 play] 'Kathleen ni Houlihan'. And it is not over-drawn, as those who know Ireland may attest. But Ireland has changed. The patriotism of the Irish is the same, but the expression of it is different. The boy who used to want to die for Ireland now goes into a rage because the dispensary doctor in County Clare has been elected by a fraud. Ireland is no longer a sweetheart but a house to be set in order.[9]

Two years later, his poem 'Easter 1916' recalled that anti-heroic mood before the insurrection, when people lived 'where motley is worn', denoting the style of the clown in *commedia dell'arte*: a world of exaggeration where no one really means what they say. But the people invoked in the poem, the makers of revolution, turn out to inhabit a different, internal world, expressed in their 'vivid faces'. As it happens, Yeats knew many of them, some since his Dublin youth twenty years before. He had debated with them in the Arts Club, quarrelled with them in the columns of the nationalist press, even been involved in a jealous love-triangle with one of the leaders, John MacBride. Several of the leading revolutionaries were middle-class intellectuals like himself, at home in the slightly Bohemian circles of Dublin's literary and theatrical world. The fact of the attempted revolution, for which the leaders paid with their lives, had changed them utterly; but Yeats was as astonished as most moderate nationalists that it had come to this. That feeling of astonishment has, in a sense, persisted.

'Easter 1916' is also a poem about biography, providing thumbnail sketches of several people whose names will recur in this book, including the upper-class rebel Constance Markievicz, the poet and university lecturer Thomas MacDonagh, and the schoolteacher and revolutionary ideologue Patrick Pearse. But to recapture the sense of a generation at a time of flux, we need to look at the minds and attitudes of a wider range of actors. For many young, obscure Irish people in the opening years of the new century shared a sense that change was afoot, and that their generation would embody it. In 1905 yet another young Cork nationalist in MacSwiney's circle, Liam de Róiste, confided to his diary:

> I often wonder whether there has been an actual, objective change of affairs, or of general ideas in Ireland during the past decade that makes things seem different to me now from what they did three, four, five years ago. Or, is it a change of ideas within myself, the inevitable change from boyhood to youth, from youth to manhood? I presume both are working. I am changing and things around me change.[10]

Along with many of his generation, de Róiste sensed that he was living at a time of flux, of transformation that could take place both personally and nationally. (He had, for one thing, already changed his name to its Gaelic version, having been born William Roche: many like-minded people in this era did the same.) And it is now possible to look at the making of revolutionaries, often from unlikely material, or in unlikely locations – the way that they become a 'revolutionary generation'.

The concept of a 'generation' is both fertile and troublesome, especially when linked to a change of political consciousness.[11] Rather than simply defining a twenty-five or thirty-year cohort, occurring in immovable chronological order, the notion has become a more fluid concept: a group or groups, not necessarily made up of people born at the same time, who conceive of themselves as bonded together by cultural mentality and social circumstance. And, following the fashions of historiography as well as changes in the wider world, we may now be coming to see the notion of 'generationism' challenging or even replacing class as an organizing principle of analysis: conceiving of age groups as carriers of intellectual and organizational alternatives to the status quo, acting under the constellation of factors prevalent at the time of their birth. Significantly 'the problem of generations' was decisively rethought in the decade after the First World War; it has since been applied to the Risorgimento generation in Italy, and a 'generation of 1914' across Europe. Similarly we might perhaps discern a 'generation of 1916' in Ireland, reacting against their fathers. To become a revolutionary soldier in the Irish Republican Army, Ernie O'Malley later recalled, was in its way a revolt against 'the wise domination of age, to some hard and harsh in the soul as the cancer of foreign rule'. Throwing off the traces was 'an adventure and a relief'.[12]

This was recognized very early on – as was the opposing strength of ancestor-worship. An astute observer noted in 1919:

> The revolt of the new generation against the supremacy of the old, which has become the stock theme of the later English dramatists, is still on the other side of the Irish Sea a revolutionary doctrine almost as subversive as Bolshevism. A man's duty is not only to do what his parents wish, but to think as they think, not necessarily because it is right, but because it is a command ... It is difficult as yet to say in what degree the victory of Sinn Féin represents a triumph of youth over crabbed age, and whether the clash of opinion will affect other than political issues.[13]

The history of the revolution and its aftermath suggests that this did not happen, and a reassertion of traditional attitudes would be – in Ireland as elsewhere – a powerful theme in the history of the 1920s.

The danger of generalization across a generation must be guarded against; even a self-conceived generation can contain within it so-called 'generation-units' which are in apparent disagreement in some ways, but linked by affinities of response to their social and historical circumstances. Still, there is at least one way in which these larger European frameworks can be applied to Ireland. Generations are largely recognized in retrospect: this is the sense in which they are 'not born, but made'.[14] And a generation is made not only by conscious processes of identification and rejection in the lives of the protagonists, but also retrospectively, in their memories, and in their control of the larger territory of official and social memory.

Move to "generation own"

[Handwritten margin note: To Foster, cultural change is produced by intellectual work, etc. Worth calling this book a work of intellectual biography.]

II

The changes that convulse society do not appear from nowhere; they happen first in people's minds, and through the construction of a shared culture, which can be the culture of a minority, rather than a majority. In Ireland, as elsewhere, discontented and energetic young men and women, whose education often left them facing limited opportunities with a sense of frustration, turned their attention to critically assessing the status quo. Out of such material a vanguard may be created, uniting several 'generation-units'. There is also the important factor of geographical concentration, notably in Dublin. The accounts, letters, diaries and reflections of the revolutionary generation conjure up an intimate but complex city, with certain areas defined by political subcultures: a geography of radical Dublin. Radicals encountered each other in certain small shops and restaurants around Sackville (now O'Connell) Street and Rutland Square (now Parnell Square), radiating from Nelson's Pillar. Such places sold radical newspapers and afforded meeting places, in close proximity to the premises which Yeats's celebrated friend and muse Maud Gonne rented in North Great Georges Street to house her radical women's organization, Inghinidhe na hÉireann ('Daughters of Ireland'), as well as the Fenian-inspired Dungannon clubs.

It was a narrow circuit. On a brief jaunt to Dublin from her Waterford home in January 1911, the 23-year-old nationalist Rosamond Jacob first made her way to her Quaker relations, the Webbs, in Brighton Square, Rathgar, where she met the radical-artistic *bon ton*, including the painter Sarah Purser and the academic Charles Oldham. Later she set off with Elizabeth Somers to the Inghinidhe rooms – six flights up, piles of the radical feminist journal *Bean na hÉireann* on the floor, pin-ups of Maud Gonne and 'John Brennan' (the journalist Sydney Gifford) on the walls, the latter in narrow skirts and smoking a cigarette. Jacob went on to inspect Hugh Lane's new gallery for modern art in Harcourt Street, and dined at the vegetarian restaurant in Westland Row (there were at least two such establishments in Edwardian Dublin). Later she met her friend Edith White, a schools inspector and Gaelic enthusiast, at the Café Cairo in Grafton Street, and ordered some cream hopsack material at Kellett's drapery store to make herself a 'national costume'. Evening entertainments included a *soirée* at the Vegetarian Society, with harp music, and a Gaelic League *céilidh* (an evening of Irish dancing and music).[15] On a later visit that same year she stayed with Constance Markievicz, bought cigarettes at Tom Clarke's paper-shop in Great Britain Street (the drop-off point for most IRB activity in Dublin; now Parnell Street), went to a lecture by Patrick Pearse, and was smitten with the Irish Republican Brotherhood organizer and newspaper manager Seán MacDermott ('very young and distinctly handsome, with black hair and large dark eyes').[16] All these people would play leading parts in 1916.

With similar immediacy, the unpublished autobiography of the republican activist and academic Michael Hayes delineates a network of like-minded nationalist families living around the Clanbrassil Street area of the south city, extending into Harold's Cross, and the local church halls and pub rooms where IRB-related organizations met, and infiltrating the notably nationalist Christian Brothers school in the area. Further up the social scale, there were certain respectable streets in the southern suburbs of Rathmines, Rathgar and Ranelagh where middle-class radicals clustered, such as Belgrave Road, with the journalists Francis and Hanna Sheehy-Skeffington, the doctor and medical campaigner Kathleen Lynn and her partner Madeleine ffrench-Mullen; or Oakley Road, with the Pearse family, Éamonn and Áine Ceannt, Thomas MacDonagh and his wife Muriel; or Harcourt Terrace, where the cultural and artistic literati such as the Coffey family, Sarah Purser, the librarian Thomas Lister, the writer and Gaelic League founder Douglas Hyde and the republican solicitor and writer Ned Stephens lived side by side.

In his unpublished memoir, the republican activist and lawyer Kevin O'Shiel discerned 'five different Dublins' around 1910, besides the world of studentdom which he inhabited as an (unusual) nationalist at Trinity College, Dublin. There was 'Castle Dublin', with its government officials, police and law officers, and so on, which he saw as 'a ruling caste', living an Olympian and largely exclusive existence – though under the Home Ruler Viceroy and Vicereine, the Marquis and Marchioness of Aberdeen, some grappling-hooks were thrown out to middle-class Catholics. Then there was the professional world of lawyers, doctors and university people; the 'intelligentsia' of writers and artists, 'a powerful though limited Bohemia, radiating much influence on national and metropolitan thought and politics'; the commercial world; the world of local ward politics; and, surrounding them all, the vast and hardly known world of proletarian Dublin in tenements and narrow streets. There may have been many more Dublins, but they all intersected in a smaller space, and overlapped perhaps more than O'Shiel may have recognized or remembered.[17] Nonetheless, radical nationalists sustained themselves in a self-referencing world which conceived of itself in opposition to all of the above.

III

But, with the exception of the imposing neoclassical bulk of the General Post Office, dominating Sackville Street and its immediate environs, where the first act of the 1916 Rising would be unveiled, the city is not where the remembered, iconic revolution was imagined and re-enacted afterwards. The conventional image of the Irish revolution is preserved in Seán Keating's paintings from the 1920s on, where Soviet realism meets Gaelic idealization: peasants with rifles. The Irish landscape itself played a powerful part in radical-nationalist consciousness, echoing a theme long implanted in romantic sensibility. When Rosamond Jacob searched for wildflowers in the woods above the Suir Estuary and walked in the Comeragh mountains, or when Terence MacSwiney cycled to the mountain lake at Gougane Barra and recalled every impression in the trembling and exalted prose of his diary, or when F. J. Bigger filled his motor-car with excited antiquarians and explored the Antrim Glens, they recorded a high-voltage connection with landscape which was at once sensual, romantic and – in a real sense – ideological. As with Ernie O'Malley's later memories of bivouacking on Tipperary mountainsides, or William Bulfin's much read *Rambles in Eirinn*, they invoked a sense of authenticity and belonging. This access to a pre-lapsarian Irishness, through immersion in an unspoilt landscape, was also a vital part of the revolutionary generation's experience at Gaelic League summer-schools, as will be seen below. And those who appreciated it most passionately were usually radicalized in urban contexts, and often nurtured a sense of outsider status, by descent, class or religion.

These middle-class revolutionaries may have had more in common with their Russian contemporaries than is usually imagined, different though their ideologies were. Both Irish and Russians represent a generation bent on self-transformation; both had a sense of deep differentiation from their parents' generation; both were affected by currents of religious purism which became diverted into other channels; both would move from an era of artistic, social and sexual experimentation into one of repressive conservatism. However, this comparison should not be pushed too far. In a valuable study of Ireland published in English in 1911, and closely read by the revolutionary generation, the French sociologist L. Paul-Dubois reflected on the differences between revolutionary Irish nationalism and its nineteenth-century Continental predecessors.

> Of Continental Anarchism [the Irish Physical Force Party] has no strain, except in those desperate moments in which it has practically lapsed into anarchism. It has not for psychological basis the spirit of revolt against fact, nor the primitive design of destroying everything to make room for the Utopia of a new world which should proceed by spontaneous generation from the ruins of the old. Faced with the social miseries of the time, it has not, like Revolutionary Socialism, acquired the desire to substitute for an egoistic and bourgeois society a communistic and humanitarian one. It does not, like Russian Nihilism, represent the effort of an intellectual proletariat to destroy an autocracy. Nothing is further from its national aspirations than the Federalist doctrines of the Paris Commune. Nothing is more foreign to it than that first principle of Continental Socialism, the Class War ...[18]

In a sense, this restrained approach to socio-economic change is borne out by the diaries, letters and reflections of the Irish revolutionary generation. The shy and punctilious young engineer Richard Mulcahy, born in 1886, emerged rather unexpectedly as a celebrated revolutionary in 1916–22 and later became a controversial general in the Free State Army. He preserved in his archives a comment by his more high-profile revolutionary comrade Michael Collins, reflecting on the outcome of the Anglo-Irish War and the Treaty of 1921:

Revolutions and political movements mostly end in disappointment and utter wreck. Ours, a difficult combination of the two, has succeeded hitherto in a manner unique in history, and for the reason that it was based on something more than mere revolutionary and political impulses – something finer, deeper and more worthy to succeed – the impulse to a nobler life, not of the meaningless, abstract, non-human kind which is all that is looked for by revolutionaries and social reform[er]s, but a human consciousness of the vital indestructible Gaelicism within us struggling to life and expression. It was this which carried us to success where previous movements failed.[19]

By this reading, rather in line with Paul-Dubois, racial identity trumped more abstract ideological commitments and ensured unity and success. But two thoughts occur at once. The first is the factual correction that unity was *not* ensured, since, with the achievement, in 1922, of the Anglo-Irish Treaty, the revolutionary movement broke bitterly apart, precipitating a violent civil war. Moreover, there was also the unwelcome fact that the revolution had turned, in some areas, into a struggle between communities as well as between republicans and the British state. This too had its European parallels.

The second difficulty with Collins's claim is suggested by the diaries, letters and reflections of a range of middle-class revolutionaries. Some testaments, notably the diaries of young Gaelic League and separatist activists such as Piaras Béaslaí, Terence MacSwiney and Liam de Róiste, and the copious correspondence of Roger Casement, are strikingly similar in tone. They invoke not only James Clarence Mangan's incantatory early-nineteenth-century poem of Irish national deliverance, 'Dark Rosaleen', but also Byronic heroes, Werther and Hamlet. They declare their ambition to 'live and die greatly' and make a mark in the world. Béaslaí, who grew up comfortably in a middle-class Irish community in Liverpool (son of the editor of the *Catholic Times*), even has a section of draft memoirs, written in his early twenties, called 'My Boyhood: Early Deeds'. In 1904, aged twenty-three, after suffering reverses in the Bootle branch of the Gaelic League, he tells his diary:

I will assert myself! I will make my presence felt. Life is full of fields for me. Here I am a man with such an education, such a wide knowledge, and I have no value or esteem while any fool or churl or clodhopper from this to London is able to look down on me. Oh God! Can I endure it. Shall I be despised? Shall I live a poor weak puny life – I who have strength and will and a fire within me which will not rest.[20]

The answer, clearly, was to get to Ireland, which he fervently idealized from his childhood holidays. 'I shall wake up the Gael, appeal to him, trust in him.' He actually did this, working as a Gaelic League organizer, becoming known to the police and taking a prominent part in the 1916 Rising. The passionate and puritanical Terence MacSwiney, writing in the early 1900s while a commercial clerk and part-time student at the Royal University, is even more grandiloquent:

When I picture myself thus, never a truant to the fair world of the Ideal pursuing a monotonous round of study and gaining perhaps University Honours – to come forth like the other 'geniuses' and to go at once into obscurity and remain there, when I consider myself there in the dull grey of life with a ray from [. . .] to lighten me the fair Land of Dreams in which I love to roam, then it is I get a conception of what a misery [it] would be for me if I were not gifted with imagination, or being gifted with it disciplined it into death, for to reap its flowers one must go with it lovingly and tend it and not let it run altogether wild . . . I read and read again with pleasure undoubted much of the verse I have written. It moves me as much almost as [if] all the dreams and hopes wrapped up in it were born in reality – God grant the dearest of them may be – I do not bear to think of Life without some of them.

I cannot proceed further with this now – as I am due at the Gaelic League in an hour's time and must have tea first.[21]

His friend de Róiste, a teacher at Skerry's Commercial College, Cork, though a more equable and less high-flown character, strikes the same note – in between turning out unpublished poetry and plays, and dreaming of writing the great unwritten novel of Irish Catholic life. 'And where is this Ego within a man? I pity myself at times, flatter myself at times. I have moods heroic, moods sublime, moods dismal and moods – blank!' But Ireland, he believes, will redeem him.[22] Such confessions, however pretentiously they read to later eyes, chime closely with young European contemporaries of the 'generation of

1914'. And the flyer circulated by de Róiste for a meeting of one of
the many societies which he organized in early-twentieth-century
Cork declares a manifesto for disaffected youth:

> YE WHO THINK and Ye who work; Ye who are tired of the old
> ideas, the useless and effete, and long for the new, COME to the Public
> Meeting in the Municipal Buildings tomorrow, Sunday, January 21st
> 1906, at 1 p.m., AND HEAR what the New Policy for Ireland, to be
> expounded by the Celtic Literary Society, is.[23]

Other personal documents indicate a slate of ideological preoccupations which extend beyond 1848-style romantic nationalism, powerful
though that impulse is. Secularism, socialism, feminism, suffragism,
vegetarianism, anti-vivisectionism pulse through the Bohemian circles of Dublin, and even of Waterford and Cork, in the decade before
1916. Sometimes these impulses coexist with sacrificial ultra-
Catholicism and old-style Fenianism, but they may also compete or
conflict with them. Rosamond Jacob was delighted by the unabashed
Fenianism of speeches delivered by the IRB activists Patrick McCartan and Michael O'Rahilly (who styled himself 'The O'Rahilly', like a
Gaelic chieftain) at a Waterford demonstration against a royal visit in
May 1911. 'It must have been a great surprise to the audience – I suppose the younger people present had never heard real nationalism
talked on a public platform in their lives before, and they seemed to
appreciate it.' But at a private meeting afterwards her good impression of O'Rahilly (elegant, dark good looks, simple delivery) was
torpedoed by his self-importance and above all his violently racist
beliefs about American blacks. 'It was awful. I suppose he is an
anti-democratic Griffithite sort of Sinn Féiner.'[24]

O'Rahilly would later be one of the most celebrated combatants in
the 1916 Rising, and thus placed beyond criticism. But there were
other radical attitudes, and other revolutions, that never reached fru-
ition. Whether they could have, or not, is not the point; the objective
here is to recapture the expectations of that 'pre-revolution', if the
'real' revolution is taken as having started in 1916 (Ireland's 1789).
The few works that have episodically tried to do this tend to approach
the revolutionaries in terms of occupational structure and geographical background.[25] What comes through in these more personal profiles

of the future revolutionary elite is disentitlement; frustration; provincialism; self-dramatization; and the pervasive influence of education in a profoundly Catholic manner, which involves an equally profound nationalism.

Such feelings could sometimes be mobilized by the religious organizations and orders woven deeply into the fabric of Irish life, such as the Christian Brothers, the dominant religious order in Irish education. Terence MacSwiney, educated by the Brothers, preached violent sacrifice in his writings fifteen years before he died on hunger-strike, and spent much of the time while he was attempting to lead the Easter Rising in Cork absorbed in an Irish-language edition of Thomas à Kempis – a medieval religious writer also inspirational for de Róiste and Béaslaí.[26] Inside the Church, as inside the family, the turn of the century saw a conflict between generations, the younger priests embracing nationalism, to the discomfiture of their elders.[27] The struggle between the generations was also reflected within the ranks of the Irish Republican Brotherhood, and lies behind the restructuring of that movement in the early 1900s through the exertions of young men such as the enthusiastic Ulster activists Bulmer Hobson and Denis McCullough.[28] The fault-lines of conflict that run through Irish society and erupt at critical moments – such as the Land War of 1879–82, when tenants wrested control over their farms from landlords by means of boycott, intimidation and mass organization – have also been connected to later outbreaks of violence. But these approaches perhaps underestimate the radical mindset and contribution of students, women, intellectuals, journalists and émigrés.

The biographies of the revolutionaries suggest the need to accommodate such class and educational profiles. A middle-class or privileged background is often glossed over afterwards, notably in the cases of women, who could – and did – feel imprisoned by the limitations and expectations enforced by gender. The violently revolutionary Sighle Humphreys and her O'Rahilly cousins went to exclusive schools and lived in large Ballsbridge houses with servants and motor-cars, but chose to separate themselves from their unionist neighbours. The parents of Geraldine Plunkett and her brother Joseph, one of the ringleaders of 1916, were extremely well off and moved eccentrically between a series of large houses with plenty of servants, a lifestyle buttressed by a considerable rental income. Under Countess Plunkett's rule, home life was erratic and often violent: Geraldine recalled 'we always spoke under our breath, as though we were in jail', and the children relentlessly plotted their escape.[29] Reading the papers of nationalist radicals like Alice Milligan or Máire Comerford or Mabel FitzGerald (born McConnell), the sense of stultifying family background is palpable. Milligan, a Northern Protestant who edited radical journals, pioneered consciousness-raising drama and influenced several leaders of the revolution, notably MacSwiney and de Róiste, referred to herself as being 'an internal prisoner' of her own family. Máire Comerford, journalist and indefatigable republican hunger-striker, moved far away from a Catholic-gentry childhood of ponies and tennis parties in County Wexford. Mabel McConnell, a strong-minded and markedly attractive young Northern Protestant in full flight from her *haute bourgeoise* family, became radicalized at university in Belfast and then London, worked briefly as secretary to George Bernard Shaw and George Moore, and eloped with the young poet Desmond FitzGerald; she privately reflected: 'I seem to base all my friendships in nationalism; other things are as important, but not nearly as much so.'[30]

Escape, for people like Mabel, could be facilitated by foreign travel. Many of the revolutionary generation followed well-established Irish routes to Continental Europe, for purposes of education, work or leisure, as well as travelling regularly across the Atlantic. Mobility, and access to faster and cheaper transport in the Edwardian age, created new opportunities for evading the world of their parents. Others, such as Rosamond Jacob, questioned the assumptions of their background while still trapped in it. The plain, intense, uncompromising child of free-thinking parents, she wrote copious diaries recording her frustration with bourgeois provincial life, a powerful sense of thwarted sexual longing, alienation both from her Quaker background and from the dominant Catholic ethos, and her implacable determination to break into another world. A passionate cult of Irish republicanism and Fenianism provided one route, and the cultural and social sphere opened up by membership of the Gaelic League another. In classic back-to-the-people mode, Jacob records her attempts to learn Irish, to seek out like-minded people, and to make the contacts which would bring her from sleepy Waterford, where 'anything Irish spells disaster', into revolutionary nationalist circles in Dublin, and the glamorous ambience of Constance Markievicz and Maud Gonne.[31] In this world, she searched for similarly secularist thinkers, though she was often disappointed: her robust if rather reductionist belief that 'the Catholic church is one of the greatest influences for evil in the world', and that it was 'incomprehensible how any sane person of any intelligence could be a Catholic', did not always meet with approval among her new nationalist companions.[32] Certainly not among the MacSwiney family in Cork – Terence, and his sisters Mary and Annie. The fervent devotion of Terence's diaries is exceptional even for the time. He seeks advice about the propriety of reading Tolstoy because of the Russian's religious unconventionality, and records his anxious hopes and speculations as to which of his friends might have a religious vocation. A total abstainer, he avoided mixed company except for patriotic purposes, and inveighed against 'beastly sensual passion'.[33] Yet he also believed in the transformative power of radical theatre and worshipped Ibsen.

A decade later, Terence would become celebrated as a nationalist martyr, dying on hunger-strike in 1920; his sisters remained irreconcilable republicans all their lives, while his widow, Muriel, a daughter of the hugely wealthy brewing and distilling Murphy dynasty, followed a yet more radical course, moving to Germany and then France, and embracing communism with all the fervency with which she had espoused republican nationalism. Her testimony to an American commission on conditions in Ireland in 1920 emphasized her sense of being part of a special generation:

> my parents are not quite like myself. I think I am rather characteristic of a certain section in Ireland. The younger people in Ireland have been thinking in a way that some of the older ones have not . . . They wished to belong to England. They were well off and quite comfortable and thought only of themselves. That is dying out now. The younger members of such families are Republican . . . I am only characteristic of a great many who were brought up shut up at home. And still the Irish spirit comes out of them in spite of everything.[34]

The large family of Ryan sisters from Tomcoole, County Wexford, who will recur in this story, came from a different background from

Muriel, and stayed close to their parents, but they too struck out on a new path. The high-spirited daughters of a 'strong-farmer' family which believed fervently in education for girls as well as boys, they travelled abroad, worked as teachers, scientists and university lecturers, and shared the sense of making a new world. Like many of the revolutionary elite, they had become radicalized when living and working in England; other examples include Mary MacSwiney, P. S. O'Hegarty, Michael Collins and Mabel FitzGerald. Yet what linked these disparate people was – and here we might remember the observations of Paul-Dubois – Anglophobia. Rosamond Jacob on visits to England wrote contemptuously of everything from the landscape to the faces of people in the street, and in 1913 violently disagreed with the argument of the Labour leader Jim Larkin that the interests of the working classes of both countries were the same; this implied, she thought, 'a revolting unwholesome Englishness'.[35] Diarmuid Coffey, far from a revolutionary, told his girlfriend Cesca Trench that the point of independence was 'to be able to hate the English comfortably from a position in which they can't look d—d superior and smile'.[36]

Mabel FitzGerald, after sojourns in London and Brittany, returned to Ireland and became deeply involved in the separatist cause. She wrote to her ex-employer George Bernard Shaw in 1914, from the wilds of County Kerry. Here, she told Shaw, she was bringing up her son to speak Irish, and to adopt 'the sound traditional hatred of England and all her ways; you should just hear him say "Sasanach" [Englishman], the concentrated hate in his voice is worthy of Drury Lane.' Shaw riposted with an affectionate but hard-hitting reply. 'As an Ulsterwoman, you must be aware that if you bring up your son to hate anybody except a Papist, you will go to hell … You must be a wicked devil to load a child's innocent soul with a burden of old hatreds and rancours that Ireland is sick of … You make that boy a good International Socialist – a good Catholic, in fact, in the true sense – and make him understand that the English are far more oppressed than any folk he has ever seen in Ireland by the same forces that have oppressed Ireland in the past.'[37]

Shaw also told Mabel that 'he who is master of the English language is master of the world', and jeered that Gaelic revivalism 'is not Irish; it was invented in Bedford Park, London, W' (a palpable hit at his old adversary W. B. Yeats). Mabel's sense of the Irish zeitgeist in 1914 was more acute than his, but his accusation that she was 'a born Orange-woman who is also a bit of a spoilt beauty' and 'an educated woman trying to live the life of a peasant' must have struck home. There is indeed something very *narodnik* about the life she and many of the 'generation of 1916' were trying to lead at the time – searching, like Russian radicals, for authenticity in rural life and hoping that the uncorrupted values of the Irish peasantry would somehow rub off on them.[38] As will be seen in the next chapter, the Gaelic League's summer-schools in Irish-speaking parts of the country (Ring, County Waterford, Cloghaneely, County Donegal, Ballingeary, County Cork) provided a transformative function for young people from city suburbs and acted as forcing-houses for separatist beliefs. As Shaw saw, the revolutionary mindset characteristic of educated and intelligent people repudiating the prejudices of their upbringing required several kinds of repudiation (which might, he warned Mabel, rebound against her when her own son rebelled: 'nothing educates a man like the desire to free himself by proving that everything his parents say is wrong'). The Russian exile Alexander Herzen, who knew about revolutions, remarked some time before: 'To be the scourge, the executioner of God, one needs naive faith, the simplicity of ignorance, wild fanaticism, a pure, uncontaminated, childlike quality of thought.'[39] This characteristic can be discerned in Rosamond Jacob's friend Edith White: 'a most extraordinary person, far the most interesting Gaelic Leaguer I ever met, not that that is saying much.' White was a schools inspector who believed in fairies, earth-spirits and vegetarianism as well as Gaelicism; she had left behind her glum Methodist background but hated the Catholic Church and believed that priests were trained in techniques of mass hypnosis.[40] Edith had been a 'rebel in everything from her birth', and when her mother burned her Irish texts, she retaliated by rechristening herself Máire; but when Edith/Máire discovered Theosophy, she dropped nationalism as a parochial irrelevance, to Jacob's lasting disillusion-ment. Similar figures, such as the mystic-minded writer of fairy stories Ella Young, kept the faith, along with the belief in earth-spirits (though, in her case, moving to California probably helped).

Crucially, the revolutionary generation was bent on self-transformation, sometimes achieving it quite spectacularly. In 'Easter

1916' Yeats apostrophizes a woman who, in his opinion, spent her days in ignorant goodwill and her nights in argument. This was Constance Markievicz, born Constance Gore-Booth to an aristocratic family with a great house – Lissadell – near Sligo, where Yeats met her and her sister, Eva, in the early 1890s. But in later years she followed a track that strongly recalls those Russian revolutionaries that Venturi describes as 'repentant gentry'. She went to art school in London and Paris, where she met and married a Polish painter, Casimir Dunin Markievicz, who may or may not have been a count.[41] Back in Dublin, she moved into the worlds of agitprop theatre and radical politics, eventually becoming a socialist. That is where Rosamond Jacob, torn between fascination and disapproval, encountered her: she features hilariously in Jacob's diaries, presiding over a dishevelled household, dressed theatrically and smoking like a chimney. Markievicz easily espoused the idea of physical violence, telling Jacob impatiently that shooting was easy – 'if you can shoot straight with an air-gun you can do the same with a rifle.'[42] Her main contribution to the pre-revolution was to found a movement of military boy scouts, the Fianna, many of whom would later handle rifles in the Irish Volunteers, rechristened during the revolution the 'Irish Republican Army', or the 'IRA'.

In some ways Markievicz seems like a one-off, and her eccentricity and stridency were mocked by others besides Yeats; even her comrades in arms referred to her as 'the Loony'. Some elements of her Ascendancy background adhered. Diarmuid Coffey's diaries record Constance and Casimir hosting annual shooting-parties at Lissadell right up to 1916 – when she went after bigger game and allegedly shot a policeman. But Markievicz was a more serious person (and politician) than is often remembered. She is also representative of a small band of Ascendancy rebels – often women, whose reaction against the Establishment they were born into is partly compounded of guilt, and partly of feminist frustration (many of them were also involved in the contemporary suffrage movement). Albinia Brodrick, sister of the Earl of Midleton, is another; she rechristened herself 'Gobnait ní Bruadair' and became a stalwart of the most irreconcilable wing of Sinn Féin.[43]

As one looks at the revolutionary generation, these figures recur. Very often, like Markievicz, they had been to art school – which seems to have had a distinctly radicalizing effect. It certainly affected four sisters from Dublin's upper middle class, the Giffords. Coming from a strict unionist background, they all became revolutionaries: Rosamond Jacob's diary describes the way they used their parents' absences to smuggle 'contraband friends' into an impeccably unionist house in Temple Villas, Rathmines.[44] One sister, Sydney, was an influential journalist, writing revolutionary propaganda under the name 'John Brennan'. Grace was an accomplished political artist, whose cartoons recorded the conflicts and personalities of the revolution; the artist William Orpen, who taught her, painted a dazzling portrait of Grace as emblematic of 'Young Ireland' in 1907, and she went on to marry the 1916 revolutionary Joseph Plunkett in his condemned cell. The husband of another sister, Muriel, was Thomas MacDonagh, who would also be executed in 1916, and who had taught in the influential nationalist school founded by Patrick Pearse, St Enda's. Like Constance Markievicz, both men feature in Yeats's poem about 1916. Pearse, a fascinating and divisive figure, came late to revolutionary politics, but had long been at the forefront of cultural politics – as editor of the Gaelic League's journal, and a powerful advocate of the revival of the Irish language. He also wrote poetry and plays, mostly in Irish, of a propagandist bent. Charismatic, inefficient and driven by complex personal urges, he focused his energies on education, adopting some radical child-centred ideas but also creating a kind of *madrasa* of revolutionary nationalism in his school. Here, Pearse preached the necessity of personal sacrifice, using as his models the heroes of Irish sagas and the theology of Christian mysticism. His work not only magnetized the children of nationalist intellectuals, but also built up a cadre of unconventional young teachers such as MacDonagh (who repudiated conventional Catholicism in favour of a sort of Neoplatonic mysticism). Pearse and MacDonagh represent vital aspects of the radicalization process: education and language, which will be considered later in this book. And the accusatory opening sentence of Pearse's 1915 essay 'Ghosts' is quintessentially 'generation of 1916', in claiming that the old men had failed both Ireland and their inheritors. 'There has been nothing more terrible in Irish history than the failure of the last generation.'[45]

The final person held up in Yeats's poem as emblematic of revolutionary transformation does not, like the others, come from the middle-class intellectuals or the repentant gentry; but the choice of John MacBride has its own resonance, especially in personal terms.

> This other man I had dreamed
> A drunken, vainglorious lout.
> He had done most bitter wrong
> To some who are near my heart,
> Yet I number him in the song;
> He, too, has resigned his part
> In the casual comedy;
> He, too, has been changed in his turn,
> Transformed utterly:
> A terrible beauty is born.

MacBride – a Fenian, from a small farming and shopkeeping Mayo background, who had fought against the British in South Africa – had married Yeats's great unattained love, Maud Gonne, in 1903, a year when she was also received into the Catholic Church. (Called on to renounce all heresies, she told Yeats, 'I said I hated nothing in the world but the British Empire which I looked on as the outward symbol of Satan in the world . . . In this form I made my solemn Abjuration of Anglicanism & declaration of hatred of England.'[46]) After this marriage of ideological conviction, in which two revolutionaries came together to swear confusion to the British Empire, they briefly became a poster couple for radical Irish nationalism before the marriage collapsed in bitter recrimination in 1906. MacBride represents, like Tom Clarke, the Fenian beliefs and attitudes of nineteenth-century tradition. Somewhat at odds with ideologues such as Plunkett, Pearse, MacDonagh and even Markievicz, he had more in common with the IRB architects of revolution who do not appear in the 'Easter 1916', Tom Clarke and Seán MacDermott. Yeats's poem profiled the renegade aristocrat, the charismatic mentor of the young, the literary intellectual and the violent man of action: symbolic figures in every classic revolution. But the 1916 insurrection owed at least as much to Fenian conspirators like MacDermott and to the brilliant socialist ideologue James Connolly – a combative, volatile autodidact, radicalized in an impoverished Edinburgh youth and, like many other activists, an incomer into the crucible of Irish politics at the turn of the century. The part played by socialist beliefs and labour activism in the pre-revolutionary mindset can too easily be forgotten, given the drastic restabilization of politics in a Catholic-nationalist mould during the War of Independence and after.

IV

The culture of pre-revolution may be explored through these emblematic figures and their intersections. There are structures of intermarriage, drawing networks of friends, lovers, sisters, cousins even closer.[47] The Ryan family, Douglas and Madeleine ffrench-Mullen, Terence MacSwiney and his sisters, the Plunkett brothers and sisters, the Giffords, Robert and Dulcibella Barton (reacting against their Wicklow Ascendancy family), and Rosamond and Tom Jacob in Waterford – all supported each other as siblings as well as fellow separatists. They reflected that enclosed, self-referencing, hectic world which the revolutionaries inhabited; it is one of the reasons why the split over the Treaty was particularly traumatic. Such linkages penetrated unlikely sectors of Dublin's upper middle class such as the Plunkett family, resident in grandest Fitzwilliam Square, with servants living in the attics and working in the basements, French governesses and holidays abroad. Their dilettante father – a papal count and director of the National Museum – was sustained by the riches of a great Dublin building fortune; the children, Joseph and Geraldine, set up house together in another Plunkett property, on suburban Marlborough Road, and turned it into a kind of revolutionary cell, printing a radical magazine from their front drawing room and later stockpiling weapons and ammunition. Their mother owned a farm on the edge of Dublin, in Kimmage, which became a combination of radical commune and armed camp for Constance Markievicz's troop of nationalist boy scouts, the Fianna. The atmosphere of these places was vital to the process of revolutionary indoctrination, but it should also be remembered that they were established by moneyed privilege. Yet bizarrely, in an unpublished draft memoir, Geraldine recorded that in Ireland before 1916 the metaphor of 'slavery' to describe Ireland's position 'was not a poetic fiction; it was an actual fact'.[48] There are other sorts of compensation mechanisms than those born of economic and social frustration. Elsewhere Geraldine Plunkett recalled how her experiences at medical school in 1910 led her away from the 'shabby-genteel professional people' that she despised, and into the circles of young men and women up from the country: their manners and accents were strange to her, 'but they were alive, they were the coming generation'.[49] As discussed later in this book, the student world of the National University embodied many radicalizing influences and connections.

The nationalist culture of Terence MacSwiney and his family was grounded in a less entitled and more aspirant ethos. Living in Cork, though from a partly English background, they found their social and career expectations baulked by their father's early death, and their preoccupation with education, self-betterment and a desire for a public role pulses through Terence's diaries and his sisters' correspondence. He went to night-school, and his sisters became teachers or nuns. The same desire for educational self-betterment similarly drove the career of Terence's friend Liam de Róiste, from a small farm on the shores of Cork Harbour; he worked for the Cork Industrial Development Association, teaching Irish at night-school while devoting every spare minute to nationalist clubs and societies in Cork. (Like de Róiste, many of the revolutionaries came from families with a dead or absent father, including Terence MacSwiney, Seán and P. S. O'Hegarty, Éamon de Valera, Erskine Childers and Patrick Pearse). Provincial autodidacts such as MacSwiney and de Róiste were fascinated by theatre and were obsessive readers, but their reverence for Shakespeare and Ibsen, and a taste for amateur dramatics, did not extend to unqualified approval of Yeats and the Literary Revival – an antipathy which, strangely, united many of the revolutionaries. The hieratic, didactic and elite elements of Yeats's literary persona grated on them, and so did the metropolitan cultural revivalists' repudiation of simplistic nationalist rhetoric; Yeats tried to exclude such reductionist dogma from his Abbey Theatre. Freethinker as she was, Rosamond Jacob hated J. M. Synge's explosively subversive plays, and Geraldine Plunkett wrote menacingly: 'It would require a large and brutal book to explain the mentality of the Abbey directorate.'[50] Yet theatre, as will be seen later, was a recognized and vital forum for the cultural propaganda of nationalism.

Drama could also unleash excesses of conventional religious reaction, but the religious consciousness of the revolutionary generation was not a straightforward matter. The notion of sacrifice recurs insistently in Terence MacSwiney's diaries, often expressed in baroquely religious imagery. When the real revolution was set in motion and claimed lives, the language of religion came naturally to its supporters. The executions of the revolutionary leaders are generally held to have begun the shift towards endorsement of revolutionary violence among a wider sector of the population; but Máire Comerford disagreed, holding that it was the initial sacrifice of the individuals concerned that affected public opinion, even before their execution. Reading contemporary accounts suggests that she may be right.

When Yeats completed 'Easter 1916' in the September of that year, the next phase of the revolution still hung in the balance; but by the beginning of 1919 a guerrilla war had sputtered into life, and until the truce and Treaty of 1921 the Irish countryside would be racked by violence between IRA gunmen and the forces of the police and army, while those quiet Dublin streets conjured up at the beginning of Yeats's poem would be 'changed utterly' in their way. This will be outlined in the closing chapters of this book. What happened in Ireland during these years is not very often instanced in general 'revolutionary theory' – perhaps because it took place on a small scale and, though largely successful in displacing the established order, replaced that order with a socially and politically conservative ethos. This is, however, part of the general pattern: revolutionaries, having symbolically killed their fathers, become 'founding fathers' themselves. The conclusion of a recent book about generations and political culture is apposite. 'Founding fathers, itself a generational concept, play a critical role in constructing a generational consciousness that seeks to impose cultural unity on disparate groups and constructs a national consciousness that tends to be exclusionary towards latecomers or women.'[51] This statement, very relevant to Ireland, was anticipated more pithily by Kevin O'Higgins, one of the dominant politicians of the new order. 'We were probably the most conservative-minded revolutionaries that ever put through a successful revolution.'[52]

What had their revolution been about, regarding objective interests? As the leader of constitutional nationalism John Redmond had pointed out in his 1915 speech, by 1900 the struggle over the land was effectively won, and it could be argued that the form of British government was neither unduly oppressive nor unrepresentative: indeed, the prospect of Britain granting self-government, or 'Home Rule', to Ireland seemed inevitable.[53] The government's pusillanimous response to Ulster's resistance from 1912 changed things; but a revolutionary mindset existed well before 1912–14 and presented the makings of a revolutionary opportunity. In Ireland, as in other pre-revolutionary cultures, attention should be paid – as Yeats knew – to the radical potential of the 'middle strata' of society. We do not have a contemporary Irish source such as the survey of young people's attitudes conducted by Massis and de Tarde in France in 1912, on which so many ideas about the 'generation of 1914' were based.[54] But it is possible to try to recapture how they thought. More attention might also be paid to the portfolio of radical causes taken up by middle-class Irishwomen in the 1890s and afterwards: the associational counter-cultures that tended to be written out of Irish history in the period of post-revolutionary stabilization, but that clearly provided a conduit into radical politics, as the diaries and letters of militant Irishwomen in the pre-war era show beyond doubt. Nor do we have a source such as the questionnaire circulated among St Petersburg students in 1907–8 about sexual behaviour and attitudes; but sex was not absent from pre-revolutionary Ireland (though the founding fathers made a determined effort to control it in the post-revolutionary state). People ran away with each other to start communist communes in Donegal;[55] the lesbianism of several key figures was surprisingly unabashed; and, by 1919, Rosamond Jacob was enthusiastically reading Freud on dreams and sex, and attending a series of lectures which linked sexual repression and revolutionary violence.[56] By 1921, alas, that lecturer was thrown out of Dublin – a pointer for the future.

Dreams matter, if not always in the manner suggested by Freud. 'We lived in dreams always,' wrote the old revolutionary Denis McCullough to his comrade-in-arms and brother-in-law General Richard Mulcahy many years later; 'we never enjoyed them. I dreamed of an Ireland that never existed and never could exist. I dreamt of the people of Ireland as a heroic people, a Gaelic people; I dreamt of Ireland as different from what I see now – not that I think I was wrong in this.'[57] The Irish revolution, like the histories of its perpetrators, bristles with ironies, reversals and unanswered questions. In an unpublished memoir Michael Hayes unwittingly echoes Shaw's riposte to Mabel FitzGerald by daringly suggesting that, for all the talk about the Gaelic League, his generation was radicalized through the *English* language. This is borne out by much of the journalism and correspondence of the revolutionaries, as well as by the arguments over language and identity that lasted on into the independent Irish state.

Karl Mannheim's influential definition suggested that a political generation became 'an actuality only where a concrete bond is created between members of a generation by their being exposed to the social and intellectual symptoms of a process of dynamic destabilization';[58] and we can see this happening in Ireland from the last decade of the nineteenth century. The policies of the British government between 1890 and 1912 certainly provoked dynamic destabilization and a revolutionary response, but by a sort of law of unintended consequences – not because they were oppressive, but because they were the reverse. It should be remembered that one reason why the revolution eventually took a conservative rather than an expropriating course was that the inequities of the Irish land system had already been addressed, by the application of government money through cumulative Land Acts from 1881 to 1909, enabling tenants to buy out their holdings. Reflecting on the revolution, Sean O'Faolain made the point that, by 1916, the panoply of Irish historical grievances, used as the rationalization for armed resistance, had become 'purely emotional impulses'.[59] But the revolutionary generation did not see it like that.

In a paradoxical outcome, when it was all over, the dispensation they had helped to bring into being was in some respects not so very different from that of their parents. In the 1920s Arthur Balfour – forty years earlier a draconian Chief Secretary of Ireland ('Bloody Balfour'), now a philosophical retired British Prime Minister – remarked that the Ireland of today 'is the Ireland *we* made'. Some of that Ireland indeed endured, and was endorsed by the post-revolutionary regime.

In many important aspects, the radicalism of the pre-revolutionary era was accordingly suppressed and became a distant memory. But, from around 1900, to those who embodied the Irish radical imagination, British government seemed to be imposing on Ireland a grubby, materialistic, collaborationist, Anglicized identity, with the collusion of their parents' generation; and that is what they fought to eradicate and replace with a purer new world.

The Gaelic Leaguer Claude Chevasse taking an Irish class on Achill Island, 1913, drawn by Cesca Trench.

2

Learning

His Majesty's Commissioners of Education had taken every precaution to keep from us the bitter, ancient memories of our race. From various unguarded sources the ancient memories nevertheless escaped through – in a phrase, or a word from a teacher, or no more than an inflection in his voice, or in an uncensored passage in a history book about the bravery of Irish soldiers in the Jacobite or European wars, until, drop by drop, the well-springs of my being became brimful, and finally, when I was sixteen, which was the year of 1916 and of the last Irish Rebellion, it burst in a fountaining image of the courage of man.
– Sean O'Faolain, Vive Moi! (1964)[1]

I

Education in Ireland, like literature and a number of other cultural phenomena, has always taken on a political and religious complexion; preserved, as so much else, in sharp relief in Northern Ireland, but sustaining a low-level intensity throughout the rest of the island. By the later nineteenth century the structure of schooling was essentially denominational, with Catholic teaching-orders dominating secondary education for the majority, while the Protestant minority attended their own schools (or, in the case of the Anglo-Irish Ascendancy, went to elite 'public schools' in Britain). At primary level, the government's attempt to introduce a secular system in the 1830s rapidly mutated into a sectarian pattern too. The question of education continued to bedevil British government policy throughout the nineteenth century, providing an active battleground where the Catholic Church could square up to centralizing or secularizing tendencies on the part of their rulers, and helping also to institutionalize enduring divides in Irish social life. Those who would eventually embrace revolutionary politics often remembered an early conditioning by a Fenian schoolmaster, or the equivalent; several influential figures in 'the movement' themselves went on to be connected with the profession of teaching. But the educational world of the period was not quite as straightforward as might be assumed; nor did the schooling received by future revolutionaries always follow predictable paths.

This did not stop contemporary sociologists from sweeping judgements. Paul-Dubois's influential survey *Contemporary Ireland*, mentioned in the last chapter, described the effects of the national system originating in 1831, and the doomed attempt to avoid a system divided on religious lines.

> The new system was dominated by two principles, both of which are inspired by those doctrines of so-called 'liberalism' and 'neutrality', which England rejected for herself and yet wished to impose on the Sister Isle. The first principle is that the schools shall be 'mixed', that is to say, shall be attended by pupils of all denominations. Very soon, however, this first principle became inoperative, Presbyterians and Episcopalians refusing to be bound by it no less positively than Catholics. Almost everywhere the schools organized themselves according to distinct denominations, a circumstance which has led to an excessive multiplication of small and inefficient schools.

This was a fairly accurate picture, and, as Paul-Dubois noted, it helped to negate any idea of 'neutrality'.

> The second principle is that of 'neutrality'. Religious instruction is given only outside school hours, and given separately to members of each denomination. This second principle has survived in spite of the check sustained by the first; consequently, in exclusively Catholic or Protestant schools it is forbidden, even now, to teach religion in school hours, to read the Bible, or to hang crosses or crucifixes on the walls. Be it Protestant or Catholic, in fact, the school must remain officially neutral, and hence we find on the part of the teachers an inclination to

subterfuge and compromise, and on the part of the pupils a tendency to scepticism and indifference.[2]

The sympathy Paul-Dubois felt for Irish nationalism, and his antipathy to British government in Ireland, clearly trumped any native French inclination towards *laïcité*; his book, well researched and armoured with a heavy battery of footnotes, became something of a bible for nationalist intellectuals in early-twentieth-century Ireland, and was responsible for converting at least one to revolutionary beliefs.[3]

But the extent to which Irish education produced 'scepticism and indifference' among their pupils, by the time Paul-Dubois was writing, is highly questionable – and not only in religious terms. He was, of course, referring to primary education. Secondary education was decisively influenced by the 1878 Intermediate Education Act, which directed new funding opportunities to both Catholic and Protestant schools.[4] Like the 1831 legislation described by Paul-Dubois, the system allowed for effective denominationalism of educational control; it also imposed a utilitarian but effective system of payment by results and hugely increased the number of Catholic children completing secondary schooling, even if it did so by utilizing 'the Victorian commercial code applied to education'. The radical educationalist and nationalist zealot Patrick Pearse condemned it as a 'murder machine', but the system might be seen as an effective response to Catholic denominational claims rather than a grotesque Saxon imposition.[5] Within the strictures of the system, teaching-orders such as the Christian Brothers were enabled to create a powerful educational mechanism which has often been credited with inculcating an ethos of robustly anti-British values and endorsing radical nationalism. Some certainly felt that it created a 'large body of malcontents' among Catholic youth, who became, according to the lawyer Christopher Palles, 'an idle discontented lot, picking up a precarious livelihood by occasional journalism and by their discontent, filling the press with that underspirit of disloyalty and hatred of England which all self-respecting Irishmen deplore'.[6] But whether this adequately explains the shift towards revolution among the generation of 1916 is another matter.

And then there was the vexed question of university education.

Palles was a conservative Catholic who had been to Trinity College, the bastion of the Irish establishment, and largely Protestant. But most Irish Catholics laboured under a sense of being second-class citizens, fobbed off with the examining structures of the Royal University – an examining body which awarded degrees via the 'Queen's Colleges' set up in mid-century at Cork, Galway and Belfast, and the small Catholic University run by the Jesuits in Dublin. The campaign for a university 'of their own' finally succeeded with the establishment of the National University of Ireland in 1908. Before this celebrated victory, Catholics at all three levels of Irish education shared a sense – often noisily articulated – that the structures in place were not serving the purposes of Irishness, as conceived by the coming generation. This would change – as would so much else – in the crowded years of the early twentieth century. The way that education operated in Ireland for the revolutionary generation (those born, roughly, between the 1870s and the 1890s) is an important element in the process of political radicalization. And it showed, among other things, that radical critics of the established order could emerge from some unlikely places.

Paul-Dubois and Palles were not alone in noting the importance of education and its psychological effects during the first decade of the twentieth century in Ireland. As elsewhere in Europe, some radical ideas were in the air. Patrick Pearse's educational experiments at the progressive schools he founded, St Enda's and St Ita's, are celebrated, pursuing the development of the individual child in an atmosphere fervently dedicated to Gaelic ideals and Irish nationalism. Other educational experimentalists with a radical-nationalist agenda included Louise Gavan Duffy, who taught at St Ita's and later at St Bride's School and tried to perpetuate the Pearsean values and approach for girls. In Cork, Mary MacSwiney's progressive Scoil Íte, founded in 1916 after she was fired from the Ursuline convent for her political beliefs, appealed to parents very far from sharing her uncompromising republican values, simply because it was a good school.[7] There were also new foundations such as Mount St Benedict near Gorey, founded with the Sweetman family's money and attracting the children of nationalist intellectuals much in the way that St Enda's did, if less militaristically. The atypical Anglo-Irishman Shane Leslie, during a particularly fervent period of nationalist conversion in 1910, taught Irish history there and wrote rhapsodically to the Ulster antiquarian F. J. Bigger that it was 'the most delightful of schools, in fact the only school besides Scol Enna [*sic*] where I shd care for Irish boys to go . . . the principles are Sinn Féin'.[8]

Leslie, a prolix and emotional writer who ricocheted between England and Ireland, could qualify as a member of the Irish intelligentsia, if an unusual one; but the relationship between Irish intellectuals and the growth of nationalism is complex, and not easily assimilable to the wider theoretical literature on the subject.[9] Schools such as Pearse's and Gavan Duffy's were very small, and those future radicals influenced by a new approach to education among a nationalist intelligentsia determined to move outside the old structures of Irish education remained a minority. Equally important was the persistence of the old system, its pervasive denominationalism, and – in the schools run by certain teaching-orders – its determinedly nationalist ethos. Paul-Dubois attacked the National schools for inculcating Anglicization, scepticism and indifference, but the testaments of revolutionaries contain many direct contradictions. In his unpublished autobiography, the republican activist (and future academic) Michael Hayes remembered the emphatically nationalist beliefs among his schoolfellows at the Christian Brothers' school in Synge Street, Dublin:

> National schools had entirely failed to make these people English, but had opened to them the world and the English language. It was in that language that Separatist or Republican Irish nationalism found expression in verse, in prose and in speeches from Wolfe Tone to Patrick Pearse. Irish was and remains a token of separateness, of our instinctive nationhood, but more political nationalism is an Anglo-Irish product and its medium is English.[10]

Thus the National schools run by the Brothers were nationalist (as well as Catholic) in ethos long before the emergence of more experimental institutions in the early twentieth century; this is confirmed by their textbooks. The recollections of Hayes and others make it clear that the language of Catholicism was a central element in the inculcation of nationalist belief; the rhetoric of 1916 would enshrine it in a particularly mystical and sacrificial form, preserved at its most supercharged in Pearse's late political rhetoric and Joseph Plunkett's overheated poetry. But to project this back as the general orientation of the education of the revolutionary generation is to give only part of the picture. Several influential radicals followed James Joyce's dictum that it was as important to fly by the nets of religion as by those of British domination; given the well-established hostility of the Catholic Church to Fenianism, it could even be a necessity, as P. S. O'Hegarty instructed Terence MacSwiney. MacSwiney's Catholicism remained intense and perfervid, as did that of Patrick Pearse; but radical circles could also contain the agnosticism of Hanna Sheehy-Skeffington and the Gifford sisters, and the self-confessed 'paganism' of Constance Markievicz (before her late conversion to Catholicism). Thomas MacDonagh, after an early period of fervent religiosity, avoided attending religious services and followed a pantheistic bent; and the young Northern Fenians Denis McCullough and Bulmer Hobson prided themselves on having educated Seán MacDermott out of his excessive piety.[11] The attitude of several radical activists towards the Church was distinctly hostile – not to mention the feelings of those from Protestant backgrounds, such as Rosamond Jacob, whose experiences in Gaelic League branches did much to reinforce their robust opposition to clerical interference and, indeed, to the Catholic religion itself. Jacob and others joined the League, in fact, precisely to escape the sectarian frameworks of social life in which they had grown up. They were therefore sharply sensitive to the efforts of priests to brand Gaelic activities with a specifically Catholic identification, and stressed the inclusive and specifically secular and unpolitical ideals with which the League had begun in 1893.

Much of this would be forgotten after the revolution. So would the efforts and achievements of teachers who were neither mystics nor Christian Brothers. The number of women in the teaching profession escalated sharply in this period; low pay, variable status, gender prejudice and insecurity of tenure were emphasized by the Irish Women's Graduate Association, which was itself composed mainly of teachers, and a sense of injustice motivated politically minded women

graduates such as Hanna Sheehy-Skeffington in other radical directions too. Injustice propelled the Irish National Teachers' Organisation
(INTO) to near rebellion against the authorities in 1898.[12] The
Association of Secondary Teachers of Ireland (ASTI) was also established in this period, starting with a spin-off meeting from the
Association of Intermediate and University Teachers (AIUT) in
1907 and representing – as in several other areas of radical activity at
this time – the dissatisfaction of Cork activists with what they saw as
a Dublin-centred organization. A whiff of anything resembling
trade-union organization was guaranteed to raise the hackles of the
Church, which relied on Catholicism acting as a cultural vaccine
against socialism, or even labourism. This became rapidly apparent
when the national teachers' union actually came under ecclesiastical
ban in two provinces in 1899.[13] Much needed to be done regarding
standardization of qualifications, adequate remuneration and security
of tenure, none of which was addressed or systematized by the Intermediate Education Act, but the Catholic Church's intense suspicion
regarding anything that looked like Continental-style secularization,
or government interference, imposed a heavy brake on progress. It
also may have goaded certain members of the teaching profession
into adversarial and radical political attitudes.

Nonetheless the social position of teachers in Ireland was interesting and almost unique: at once symbiotically involved with the local
clergy, and caught in a kind of intellectual competition with them. The
Fenian schoolmaster is a fixture in provincial novels such as Canon
Sheehan's oeuvre, and also in anecdotal sociology such as Terence
McGrath's *Pictures from Ireland* (1880) and George Birmingham's
An Irishman Looks at His World (1919). The memories of many
revolutionaries bear it out, preserved in their testimonies in the Bureau of Military History. Marie Perolz recalled that the Presentation
nuns 'made a rebel of me'; Joseph Furlong of Wexford was just one of
many who gave the same accolade to the Christian Brothers who
educated him.[14] 'When men and women in such a position,' Birmingham reflected, 'are underpaid, insecure and goaded into a position of
profound discontent, they are likely to become active agents of revolution, none the less powerful because they cannot act openly. It is
impossible to estimate, though it is interesting to guess, how far the

present condition of Ireland is due to the influence of National School teachers.'[15]

An analysis of IRA membership around the same time (1919) emphasizes the number of men who had been through teacher-training courses.[16] Several teachers prominent in the secondary teachers' union from 1909 onwards would also be prominent in the revolution: they include two future rebel commanders in 1916, Thomas MacDonagh and Éamon de Valera, as well as the firebrand republican Mary Mac-Swiney (who would be unsuccessfully defended by the union after her dismissal by the Ursulines in 1916). Many other notable teachers and union members were committed Gaelic Leaguers, nationalists and future revolutionaries, including P. J. Kennedy, who kept St Colman's College in Fermoy 'Gaelic to the spine', and Michael Hayes, Frank Fahy, Tomás Ó Deirg, Margaret Browne and Annie McHugh.[17] De Valera would emerge into prominence after the Rising and go on to dominate twentieth-century Irish politics, but before 1916 he was active in the world of education rather than revolutionary organiza-tion. Chairman of the secondary teachers' union's Leinster Provincial Council in 1910, he taught at Blackrock, Rockwell and Belvedere colleges before being appointed Lecturer in Mathematics at Carysfort in 1906, while keeping up a bewildering number of part-time duties in other educational institutions.[18] The union's conflict with the pri-orities of Catholic management came into sharp relief with Augustine Birrell's legislation of 1912, instituting a Teachers' Salaries' Grant, providing £40,000 annually for intermediate education, distributed according to careful criteria of payment and conditions. This was sup-ported by the teachers and predictably opposed by the Church, always afraid of losing influence to the British state in educational matters. The early history of the union and the variety of its membership (christened 'unlikely radicals' by their historian) should remind us that Irish education during the pre-revolution was not entirely a mat-ter of 'faith and fatherland' values disseminated by the Christian Brothers on the one side, and Castle Catholicism proselytized in upper-class boarding-schools such as Clongowes on the other. The organization of teachers across the profession operated as a radical-izing process in its own right.

II

Nonetheless, the influence on the revolutionary generation of the Christian Brothers is undeniable. Since its foundation in the early nineteenth century the Order had spread widely outside Ireland, but its ethos remained powerfully nationalist and fundamentalist, as well as harshly disciplinarian. In a striking passage of his autobiography, Todd Andrews declared that the 1916 Rising and all that followed would simply not have been possible without the Brothers. 'Without the groundwork of the Christian Brothers' schooling it is improbable that there would ever have been a 1916 Rising, and certain that the subsequent fight for independence would not have been successfully carried through. The leadership of the IRA came largely from those who got their education from the Brothers, and got it free.'[19] An examination of the educational backgrounds of the rebel leaders tends to confirm this. Several schools catering for the middle classes, such as Castleknock and Newbridge, had no former students who took part in the Rising in 1916. Two other elite institutions, Clongowes and Rockwell, had one spectacular combatant each – Michael 'The' O'Rahilly and Thomas MacDonagh. MacDonagh, it is fair to assume, was more radicalized by his teaching at St Colman's, Fermoy, and especially at St Enda's, than by his education at Rockwell, where he lost his sense of religious vocation and – for a while – much of his faith. Of other boarding-schools, Mungret College boasted two recorded 1916 revolutionaries – Frank Fahy and Seán Brady. Blackrock College mustered six, including Éamon de Valera (a scholarship boy who was idyllically happy there). The Jesuits at Belvedere could claim five. But this is nothing compared with the overwhelming number who had been through the Christian Brothers' institutions.[20]

It is not surprising that the most exclusive schools failed to produce large numbers of revolutionaries; the prospectuses of Blackrock and Tullabeg specifically promised 'a sound English education' and 'an English mercantile education' respectively, to the fury of D. P. Moran, the deeply nationalist and Anglophobic editor of the *Leader*.

The Irish 'highly respectable' class did not grow up in a night, it did not grow up of its own volition, but it is a development and a creature of several generations of national muddle. It is now trying to be both English and Irish, with the more decided leaning towards the former ... It is then farewell to common sense, independence, reality and nationality, and all hail to shams. The culmination of all this is that educational institutions vie with one another in offering to the *Irish* nation what they call a 'sound *English* education'; and the sons of the high-falutin' and treason breathing nationalists and the traders of 'rebel' Cork and 'Gallant' Tipperary are reminded of the various facilities offered for making their sons *English* gentlemen, and of getting them into the Home and Indian service of that great world institution which, when they are speaking at some local meeting, they love to call 'that foul, nefarious and bloodstained Empire upon the crimes of which the sun never sets'.[21]

Moran also castigated the Benedictine boarding-school in Wexford, Mount St Benedict, for having the temerity to teach its pupils French and send them abroad on cultural trips.

The numbers of identifiable rebels educated in the very different atmosphere which hung about the Christian Brothers reached many dozens. Even a cursory roll-call of the better-known combatants, whose ideas and lives feature in this book, would enlist Todd Andrews, Robert Brennan, Éamonn Ceannt, Con Colbert, Seán Connolly, Michael Hayes, Seán Heuston, John McBride, Denis McCullough, Terence MacSwiney, Richard Mulcahy, P. S. O'Hegarty, Ernie O'Malley, Patrick and Willie Pearse, Desmond Ryan, Austin Stack and Éamon de Valera. MacSwiney's obsessive and verbose early diaries probably spoke for many of them. Apparently constructed to leave the full materials for a later hagiography, his journals detail his eight years with the Brothers, from 1886 to 1894, as the formative experience of his educational life. But they also show that his nationalism was clearly inculcated first of all at home, and then through the Young Ireland Society and the Celtic Literary Society, meeting in the lanes of Cork.[22] Some further caveats might be entered. There is the simple fact of numbers: so many people passed through the Christian Brothers' tutelage, especially in comparison with the small numbers attending smart boarding-schools, that it is inevitable that far more of those 'out' in 1916 would be alumni. Those involved in the Fianna, the Volunteers, the Citizen Army and the other organizations which provided the revolutionary combatants came from exactly the *couche sociale* catered for by the Brothers.

But the actual planners and leaders of the 1916 enterprise tended to come from more elitist or less predictable educational formations. The exclusive Jesuit boarding-school Clongowes Wood ('the eminent Tommy Atkins college', as D. P. Moran called it, implying a corrupt connection with the British Army) was better represented than might appear.[23] Dick Humphreys, however, had previously been indoctrinated by Pearsean influence at St Enda's and was sent to Clongowes by his nationalist mother to operate as a kind of 'sleeper', if we can judge by a rather pathetic letter he sent home. 'You talk about my going to Clongowes and starting a Gaelic League and a hurling team, that may be all right in theory but not in practice, and even supposing you could change a few of the boys' spirit and start an Irish game, who would pay for the hurleys and balls and the hundred other things necessary – not the priests.'[24] This is borne out by the picture of Clongowes in the early 1900s drawn by Francis Hackett in his autobiographical novel *The Green Lion*. Both teachers and pupils 'steered clear of pronounced nationalists, whom they regarded as extravagant, besides being unpalatable to their wealthier friends. Thus the Greater Glory of God became in effect the Greater Glory of Suburbia, and a nervous titter the younger Jesuits' answer to those rude forces that primary education had already begun to release among the common people.'[25]

However, some processes of education steered clear of suburban values. The sophisticated and theatrical young Joseph Plunkett, besides short sessions at a Paris *lycée*, Catholic University School and Belvedere College, was educated at home and (for a year aged eighteen) in the Philosophers' Class, Stonyhurst. His education was bound to be patchy at best, given the erratic, eccentric and sadistic regime imposed by his unbalanced mother in what her daughter Geraldine described as 'the hellhole of our family life', which involved horsewhippings and botched amateur operations on his tubercular glands.[26] Stonyhurst can also claim the republican lawyer George Gavan Duffy (similarly the radical child of a distant, if more balanced, upper-class parent). Liam Mellows, later a formidable guerrilla supremo, went to military schools at Wellington Barracks, Cork, Portobello Barracks and the Royal Hibernian Military School in Dublin. (Meeting him in Waterford a few years before the Rising, Rosamond Jacob noted how his education had given him a fascination with military activity and strategy.) The energetic and imaginative young Ulsterman Patrick McCartan, who would become influential in revolutionary circles on both sides of the Atlantic, went to a local Latin school in Tyrone, Trumague Academy, where he was taught by the local secretary of the National League, a strong nationalist. Perhaps because of this, McCartan found St Patrick's College, Armagh (which banned Gaelic games until 1917), insufficiently patriotic. At his next port of call, St Macartan's, Monaghan, he was exposed to the full force of the 1898 commemorations of the United Irishmen rebellion of 1798, which, he recalled, 'raised a nice little spirit among the boys'; they were given Alice Milligan's life of the 1798 revolutionary Wolfe Tone to read, and discussed Fenianism and revolutionary tactics. He ended his odyssey at St Malachy's, Belfast, where the 'lack of nationalism' disappointed him – though it also produced John MacBride and Seán MacEntee.

The leading players in the 1916 drama came from more varied educational backgrounds than might be inferred from the recurrent motif of some time spent with the Christian Brothers. Seán MacDermott, who would play a key part in reorganizing the IRB and planning the Rising, grew up in a tiny farm cottage on the side of a windy hill in Leitrim, and educated himself by correspondence courses and night-school in Cavan. Tom Clarke had not gone much further than Dungannon National School. The precocious Bulmer Hobson, who would also play a potent part in reviving separatist values in culture and politics from the turn of the century, went to the Friends' School, Lisburn; always counter-suggestible, he emerged from its Quaker conditioning as a physical-force nationalist. The De La Salle Brothers in Ardee and Waterford educated the 1916 commanders Éamonn Ceannt and Thomas Ashe respectively; the Brothers in the Waterford College subscribed to Gaelic League journals on a large scale, and were prominent supporters at nationalist demonstrations in the city, according to the beady-eyed Rosamond Jacob.

Máire Comerford's brothers went to the gentler Mount St Benedict, along with several other prominent middle-class nationalists. It was set up in 1907 near Gorey, County Wexford, by a Benedictine, Dom Francis Sweetman, officially under the patronage of Downside Abbey. However, it always had an edgy relationship with that institution, due to the opinionated and controversial character of its founder, whose cousin John Sweetman, the well-off Sinn Féin supporter and some-time President of the movement, had put a considerable sum of money into the venture. Dom Francis had served as a Forces chaplain in the Boer War, and in early days apparently encouraged boys to join the British Army, but by 1916 his views had become strongly republican; and, as we have seen from Shane Leslie's testimony, the school was considered a nationalist hotbed well before that. It also taught Irish (unlike Clongowes, where Gaelic was thought to be 'the language of the kitchen'), which was why Stephen Gwynn sent his sons there.[27] He may have been disappointed. Irish was taught by an English convert to nationalism, Victor Collins, who had lived on the Irish-speaking Aran Islands. 'He used to tell us,' an ex-pupil sardonically remembered, 'that the islanders were amazed that anyone could stay there so long and learn so little Irish. Their amazement was fully justified.' At the time of the Rising the terrifying Matron, Aileen Keogh, who cropped her hair, smoked cheroots and for relaxation felled large trees with an axe, cycled to Dublin, threw herself into the fray and was arrested; apparently her guarding officer was an old Mount St Benedict boy who at the sight of her turned tail and fled.[28]

But the educational institution which most clearly acted as the nursery of the revolutionary generation was St Enda's, founded by Patrick Pearse in 1908. No other school so deliberately indoctrinated and recruited students to be revolutionaries. More than thirty of the revolutionaries in the GPO had been there at some stage, and five of the fifteen executed leaders had taught there. It is worth pointing out that St Enda's set out to be the very opposite of the Christian Brothers. Pearse, like his sister Margaret, wanted to create a progressive, child-centred educational experiment, and saw this as a de-Anglicizing process; it was effectively a Gaelic League stratagem. 'The Irish-speaking boy is more beautiful than any flower, more graceful than any wild creature of the fields or the woods.'[29] Pearse saw the

Christian Brothers approach to these potential blossoms as brutally utilitarian, satanically preparing pure Irish boys for the corrupt British civil service, and he attacked the Order for this on several occasions. In his earlier career, Pearse could in fact be notably anti-clerical, at least in educational matters; the mystic Catholic note became predominant only after the school moved to the Hermitage at Rathfarnham, a country house in the foothills of the Dublin mountains, in 1912. Here the cultic atmosphere took over, with the spirits of Gaelic heroes and nationalist martyrs regularly invoked. The St Enda's ethos in any case represented rather unconventional Catholicism, though the school did host an Arch-Confraternity of the Sacred Heart. Pearse was preoccupied with early Irish Christianity, a faith that was pre-Invasion and pre-lapsarian, and kept clerical interference in its place. (Some Irish Protestants shared this identification, ironically enough.) He was also preoccupied by master–boy relationships, as reflected in his works *An Rí* (*The King*), *The Master* and *Eoin*. From 1913 on, this went with an indoctrination through rituals, tableaux, pageants and the heroic fantasy-playground of Eamhain Macha, Pearse's imagined homosocial world of the original Fianna Éireann – a blood-brotherhood of mythic Gaelic heroes, led by the warrior-king Fionn mac Cumhail.[30] This was actualized in pageant form, and infused throughout the enclosed world of the Hermitage.

Pearse's own early teaching experience in University College and (of all places) the Protestant girls' school Alexandra College opened his eyes to the possibilities of the teacher as guru, with teaching filling the place of fosterage in the ancient Gaelic tradition; creativity, heroic inspiration and commitment to a master-figure were the ends of education, while family ties were to be left behind. Not every prospective parent found this appealing. The prominent Irish parliamentary politician John Dillon decided to send his children to Mount St Benedict after arriving to view St Enda's and finding, to his disgust, 'boys playing hockey in skirts'.[31] Actually it was hurley, in kilts. The word 'modern' kept recurring, albeit in rather reactionary dress, and the staff included several well-known intellectuals, while many more visited to give inspirational one-off lectures.

All this could not have been more different from the Christian Brothers. But the number of boys who were exposed to it remained very small. With the move to the Hermitage in the foothills above Dublin, St Enda's school-roll dropped from 130 to 70. In 1915–16 there were only 28 in the senior school. The ethos by then had become more like a sect, with the PT master Con Colbert routinely swearing senior boys into the Irish Republican Brotherhood. Those who went on to University College stayed en bloc, forming a St Enda's University Group, keeping in close contact with the school, returning there to teach and often continuing to live on the premises. The atmosphere of dedication, and the powerfully charismatic presence at the top, is suggestive of Benjamin Britten's later music-school establishment at Aldeburgh – except that the St Enda's boys were by this stage also making bombs under the supervision of their chemistry master.

The education of revolutionary women seems to have been even less conventional and predictable, but then women's education was less predictable by nature. Middle-class revolutionaries such as Máire Comerford and Muriel Murphy, who would later marry Terence MacSwiney, were educated at home by governesses, as well as in smart convents, often in England – the Holy Child, St Leonards-on-Sea, for Muriel, and a French convent at Farnborough for Máire: they cannot have been typical alumnae. Muriel later claimed that she had been denied any formal education, but this may have been part of her lifelong animus against her rich upper-class family.[32] The orphaned Brigid Lyons Thornton went to a middle-class convent school in Longford, but her nationalist family constantly denigrated the nuns for their slavish attitude towards the royal family and the gentry; when she went to the Ursulines in Sligo in 1911 she found a far more accommodating atmosphere, where nationalist politics could be openly discussed. (Rosamond Jacob, on the other hand, identified the Waterford Ursulines with the most conventional values of the *seoinín*, a word denoting aspirational pro-British snobbery.) Geraldine Plunkett, also in revolt against her parents, hated her time with the Sacred Heart nuns at Mount Anville and rejected their 'useless ornamental education', insisting on a year's self-schooling before taking her matriculation exam.[33] Then she went to Loreto on Stephen's Green to study Fine Arts, as the National University was not yet ready, and in 1910 proceeded to the medical school at Cecilia Street, acquiring a political education along the way. Áine O'Brennan (who would marry

45

the future 1916 leader Éamonn Ceannt) and her equally radical sisters Kathleen and Lily went to the Dominicans in Eccles Street, where de Valera also taught. Louise Gavan Duffy arrived there in 1907, having been brought up, like her brother George, with very little knowledge of Ireland – although their aged and rather distant father was Sir Charles Gavan Duffy, the Young Ireland veteran of 1848. Louise, already fervently nationalist, found Eccles Street a very stimulating environment.

> It was an exciting place for me in a very new life: there were crowds of girls from all parts of Ireland – there were whiffs of politics – we had lectures from some very fine women, to whom we owed more than we knew, and who, as well as giving us outstanding teaching in their subjects, let in for us a little outside air. I have never forgotten Miss Mary Hayden, Mrs Sheehy-Skeffington, Mrs Macken, Mary Elizabeth Byrne – and at last I began to learn Irish seriously with Sile Ní Chinnéide.[34]

This radical conditioning enabled her to teach for Pearse and to start her own school; she would later join her St Enda's companions in the GPO in 1916.

Female rebels, like their male counterparts, came from a wide range of educational backgrounds. The formidable Ryan sisters from Wexford (who would also play a part in 1916) went to Loreto in Gorey, and Terence's sister Mary MacSwiney to the Ursulines in Cork. Protestant nationalist women, often part-educated at home, sometimes went to England (the Trench sisters, Cesca and Margot, to Malvern School and Manor House, Brondesbury, respectively). Others, including the medical pioneer Kathleen Lynn, attended Alexandra College in Dublin, under the influential Isabella Mulvany. Though 'Alex' was generally very Protestant-establishment, its college-level education was a vital step in women's education, and the nationalists Mary Hayden and Alice Oldham profited from it; the republican historian Dorothy Macardle also taught there. Other Protestant schools were equally unlikely to nurture rebels – though Rosamond Jacob was anxious to go to the Quaker school at Mountmellick, as she found 'Miss Smith's' in Waterford, which she was constrained to attend, 'sickeningly loyal'.[35] She had a low opinion of the national credentials of the local Quaker school, Newtown, though several nationalists would later teach and study there, and the headmaster's wife was a cousin of the notoriously republican Bulmer Hobson, who came to speak at Newtown, to the horror of many. (Jacob claimed that the headmaster, Dr Clark, had to be carried out afterwards but this may have been wishful thinking.) Rosamond's brother Tom, oddly, went to the Christian Brothers at Waterpark College: perhaps her parents, being registered agnostics, took a casual view about doctrinal difference. In Cork, the Grammar School had some nationalists on its staff, and the Farrington family who attended it were, like the Jacobs, Sinn Féiners from an early stage and devotees of Irish republican history.

Nor was Bulmer Hobson the only Ulster Protestant nationalist. Born into a wealthy Protestant unionist family, the independent-minded Mabel McConnell (later FitzGerald) went to Victoria College in Belfast and Queen's College, Belfast, and thence to St Mary's Training College, Paddington – but Queen's was where she really became a nationalist, joining Sinn Féin and the College's Gaelic Society. The nationalist journalist and dramatist Alice Milligan, a generation older, similarly benefited from her middle-class Methodist upbringing in Belfast. Methodist College ('Methody') pioneered equal education opportunities for women, and Milligan had a brilliant career there, though she later affected to believe that she learnt far less from her Methodist teachers than from conversations with Irish-speaking country people in rural Ulster.[36] The poet and activist Susan Mitchell, who also became a passionate Sinn Féiner, went to the respectable Protestant girls' school Morehampton House in Dublin and later regretted the lack of Irish history on the curriculum, which insulated her from 'the remarkable intellectual change' happening around her. She later wrote of 'that pathetic longing to be like the herd, that the uniformity of a girl's education indicates to her as the proper path for those who aspire to belong to what I had hitherto known as society'.[37]

For Mitchell and several others, both Catholic and Protestant, an identification with nationalist tradition offered a gateway into another, freer society: a hope which would later be severely disappointed. Overall, it seems clear that radical-nationalist opinions could be inculcated through various kinds of teachers, operating outside such obvious locations as the Christian Brothers' schools or St Enda's. It should also be remembered that among strong-minded young *refuse-niks*, revolutionary opinions could be the outcome of exposure to influences intended to produce exactly the opposite effect.

III

Nor was the process of learning restricted to the classroom and lecture hall. Where women such as Cesca Trench and Susan Mitchell really received their radical education was in Gaelic League classes, and the same was true of many of their male counterparts.[38] In Ireland, as elsewhere in Europe, the sense that reclaiming a threatened national language was an essential part of asserting a distinct cultural identity developed through the later nineteenth century. The modernization and commercialization of the Irish economy, and the seismic social and demographic effects of the 1840s Famine (above all, mass emigration from the West of Ireland), had combined to reduce Irish-speaking communities to a minimum, largely concentrated on the western seaboard. Nationalist orthodoxy believed that this was, on more than one level, the result of a deliberate British policy. The Gaelic League had originated in the early 1890s, determined to reverse the process, and under the leadership of academically minded zealots such as the Gaelic scholar and folklorist Douglas Hyde and the historian Eoin MacNeill its objectives were formally non-political. 'Revival' at first stood for a purely cultural and educational enterprise. But the threatened loss of the language was seen as a British initiative, and for most of the League's adherents, learning the Irish language was a necessary prelude to an independence which was implicitly political, as the Reverend P. F. Kavanagh told a Listowel audience: 'What nation in Europe can boast a language superior to our own – a language so venerable for its antiquity, so admirable for its structure and for the copiousness and extensiveness of its vocabulary, a language in which alone the Irish mind – *perfervidum ingenium Scotorum* – finds its most perfect utterance?' If the revolutionary nationalists Tone, Emmet, Fitzgerald and Mitchel were alive today, he added, they would all be Irish-speakers; and the restoration of the language was 'a happy presage of the uprising of the race itself, of the coming of the time when the long-oppressed Gael, speaking his own beautiful language, shall rule in his own fair land'.[39]

Few dared disagree, apart from the reliably awkward socialist Frederick Ryan, who decided by 1904 that learning Irish had become a sort of opium of the people:

> I confess when I see the young men and women rushing to acquire the rudiments of Irish (and it seldom gets beyond that) in order to show they are not as other nations, the phenomenon seems to me to have something of pathos in it ... The desire for political independence is admirable; that counts for real manhood. Only a nation of slaves would contentedly resign themselves to be governed by another nation. But the mere desire to speak another language does not of necessity at all correlate with the active desire for political freedom.

In fact, Ryan suggested, the language movement 'acted as a soothing rather than a stimulating influence'. Nor was he convinced that being English-speaking necessarily hindered the progress of Irish people towards political liberty.[40] Future events would do much to prove him right.

But, for most young zealots, an attempt to learn Irish was inextricably bound up with the assertion of an identity independent of Britain. Certainly the diaries of Terence MacSwiney and of Piaras Béaslaí, the latter a young Irish revivalist growing up in Liverpool, suggest as much. MacSwiney's friend and schoolfellow P. S. O'Hegarty experienced an epiphany on the South Mall in Cork in 1902, when he heard the strains of Irish music from a *feis* (a mixture of concert and festival) organized by the League.

> Something in the songs – though I could understand only a few of the words – something in the music – something in the atmosphere gripped me, and I seemed to be put in touch with something far back in the Race. Unknown depths in me were stirred and across the centuries I seemed to be in touch with the days when Irish speech and Irish manners and traditions were in every valley and on every hill and by every river. Is this mysticism? Oh no. It is actual fact. I understood, accepted, and felt myself to be one with the Gael. For the first time I saw the

whole of Ireland. It was a revelation, and one which in the fifty years that have since elapsed, has not faded.[41]

More prosaically, in Dublin, Michael Hayes remembered his Fenian father taking him in 1897 'to the parish hall in Lower Clanbrassil Street where St Kevin's Branch met'. His father told him the League was 'a separatist organisation', which the youthful Hayes did not understand; but he settled down to learning Irish from Séamus Downey, a National teacher from the Irish-speaking district around Ring, County Waterford.[42] Richard Mulcahy similarly recalled how the Gaelic League came to Thurles when he was at school there (with the Christian Brothers). A new teacher, Seán Ó Cearbhaill, arrived and started classes; Mulcahy had already tried to learn Irish at Mount Sion in Waterford, but Ó Cearbhaill's method was different, combined as it was with hurling, cultural awakening and nationalist politics.[43] The institution of summer colleges to learn Irish, particularly at Ring and at Ballingeary, County Cork, was endlessly influential. Significantly, though the subscription was around £2, there were usually free places for teachers. Ballingeary was the first, established by the notoriously 'political' Keating branch of the League in 1904; seventeen others, providing evening classes and summer-schools for Irish teachers, had followed by 1912, and were publicized relentlessly in the nationalist press. Patrick Pearse fondly imagined they resembled 'the Bohemian university life of early Christian Ireland'.[44]

More realistically, the MacSwiney siblings, Liam de Róiste, Daniel Corkery and other young Cork nationalists saw Ballingeary as a way of connecting with Gaelic purity by escaping from a city corrupted by materialism and dominated not only by a celebrated merchant-prince caste but also by the looming presence of British Army barracks and naval fortifications. But to achieve purification took an effort. Liam de Róiste agonized in 1906 over his inability to learn Irish, after years of attempted immersion. 'I find difficulty in speaking Irish; I find myself dull. I teach it indeed, as well as I can, but I cannot say, with honesty, that I know the Irish language. I am very conscious that native speakers, in their hearts, laugh at my attempts.'[45] His correspondence and private writings continued to employ English almost exclusively – including his letters to his wife, though she had been one of his pupils and taught the language herself. This was not, however, the point. Two years later he recorded the bliss of a fortnight at Coláiste na Mumhan, Ballingeary – 'a time of pure delight, of unmixed pleasure ... a breathing spell, in oblivion of all distorting things, of the city, of the many vexatious problems in my life; [it] has helped me in my spiritual warfare, thank God.' But what meant most to him was not trying to speak Irish but the contact with fellow souls, the daily Mass and Rosary 'as the shadows deepened around the little chapel', 'journeys to spots of sacred and historic memory'. Annotating his diaries thirty-two years later, he noted more prosaically that his memories of Ballingeary were now principally of depression and unending bad weather.[46]

The importance of such places lay in bringing together the like-minded and suggesting the possibility of a new way of life. For the hard-working and rather solitary Richard Mulcahy, who spent his early life cramming for Post Office examinations and engineering qualifications, Ballingeary was a liberation, and introduced him to kindred spirits: in 1910, Piaras Béaslaí was lecturing there along with Cathal Brugha, both IRB stalwarts, and the Gaelic scholar Osborn Bergin. Just after the Easter Rising, the seventeen-year-old Sean O'Faolain went to Ballingeary and found that 'the language acted both as a matrix to the tissues of our political faith and as its sign and password; our zeal to speak Irish bound us into a community, a new, glowing, persecuted, or about-to-be-persecuted political sect.'[47] Cycling there along the grass-grown country roads, he felt he was obliterating time and migrating into an ancient world. Other Irish colleges embodied similar connections and associations. The Gaelic League school at Omeath, on the shores of Carlingford Lough, was held to occupy a particularly symbolic position – in Leinster but connected to the ancient feats of the mythic Fianna. Overseen by a founder of the Gaelic League, Eoin MacNeill, it seems to have been less political than Ring or Ballingeary. Roger Casement's correspondence records a parallel enthusiasm about Cloghaneely in Donegal (run by Agnes O'Farrelly), where Geraldine Plunkett and her brothers also had a blissful time. At Ring, learning Irish through Fenian stories, Michael Hayes felt a similar sense of connection with a purer vision of uncorrupted Irishness – though he objected to the backward-looking approach of the teacher, Reverend Dr Richard Henebry, who wanted to bring Ireland back to 'an old way of life'. Hayes thought the object-ive should rather be to bring Irish into the modern world.[48]

Rosamond Jacob found Ring a revelation. She met there Dublin radicals, as well as teachers from De La Salle and other Waterford Catholic establishments, whom she would never have encountered normally in the endemically stratified social life of the city. She shared a house with Jennie Wyse Power, a formidable networker whose Irish Farm and Produce Company shop on Henry Street in Dublin was a key meeting place for radical suffragists and nationalists; thus yet another contact was made which drew Jacob into the world of revo-lutionary politics. Ring provided other opportunities too. The beauty of the surroundings, the likeable eccentricities and outspokenness of the local farmers and fishermen, the freedom to meet and talk with people far removed from the circles of polite Protestant society in Waterford – all combined into an intoxicating liberation.[49] This mat-tered more than speaking Irish fluently, which remained an obstacle for her, as for de Róiste, Alice Milligan and many other activists. For Jacob, Ring was a rite of passage into an idea of Irish authenticity – though she also felt that women were not treated sufficiently as equals and that here, as in other Gaelic League endeavours, the influence of Catholic clerics was becoming pervasive.

She had a point. The attitude of the Church towards Gaelic revival-ist circles, as those circles became increasingly politicized, was notably ambivalent. The clerical membership of the League remained small in the early years, though its clericalization proceeded apace from the late 1890s. National teachers and priests were prominent in local branches, re-creating the two professions' symbiotic but sometimes hostile relationship with each other. The educational heft of the League's summer-schools and evening classes soon became heavily clerical, dominated by the enormous influence of Father Eugene O'Growney (Professor of Irish at Maynooth, and author of the sem-inal *Simple Lessons in Irish*). The almost equally influential Irish-language activist Father Peter O'Leary's unequivocal statement that the Gaelic League was a Catholic organization and that alle-giance to the Church 'should override all other associations' was widely resented, given the part played by Protestants such as Douglas

Hyde in establishing the movement.[50] Increasingly, the Church enlisted Irish-language education as part of its campaign against the influence of English 'gutter literature' and popular entertainments. This coincided with the repulsion felt by nationalist ideologues towards cultural Anglicization in a secular sense – a feeling ostentatiously endorsed by Protestant nationalists such as Cesca Trench, Rosamond Jacob, Kathleen Lynn and Bulmer Hobson – people for whom Anglophobia and Gaelicization were a way of demonstrating national credentials and annoying or rejecting their parents, without having to embrace Catholicism. Diarmuid Coffey, a young lawyer and writer from Dublin's Catholic *haute bourgeoisie*, wrote repeatedly to the fervent nationalist Cesca Trench, whom he would later marry, about her sense of Protestant apartness. 'I have been thinking about what you said about not being really Irish and I am sure you only get that feeling because you have been so long in Sasanac [English] society in India and England and that the moment you land on Irish soil you will feel quite differently about it'; he assured her that he had plenty of 'non-Irish blood' but felt completely Irish.[51] The point that he was securely Catholic and she was railing against a Protestant background went tactfully unmentioned. 'Blood' was often a signifier for religion.

Similarly, for Irish people living abroad, the Gaelic League helped to reinforce national identity in a way that implicitly declared a religious solidarity too. Pamphlets produced by the Gaelic League of London in the 1890s suggest a strong clerical input, condemning the 'vulgarities and veiled indecencies' of popular English literature and declaring that the Anglicization of Irish communities was 'injurious alike from moral, religious, national and industrial standpoints'; living in England exposed the Irish to 'contact with a form of civilization from which the Deity is gradually being eliminated'.[52] Joining the League and learning Irish would enable 'the revival of Irish industries (as in other countries where similar circumstances have occurred), increased religious faith and fervour, a higher moral tone and standard, and a general improvement in national character'. Founded in October 1896, the Gaelic League of London grew apace; its committee members included old Fenians such as Dr Mark Ryan and future republican activists such as Art Ó Briain and Fionán MacColuim, as well as genteel intellectuals. MacColuim moved to Ireland to work as the League organizer in Munster, but his efforts in the London Gaelic League remained legendary.[53] As in Ireland, the League organized classes, singing lessons and dances, and instantly appealed to the London-Irish community. A music festival in Queen's Hall during 1901 attracted nearly 3,000 people and helped to raise money to send back to the League in Ireland. Lessons in nationalist history formed a staple of the classes.[54]

The expatriate League's annual reports, as well as journals such as *Féile na nGaedheal*, were mostly written in English, and they issued constant appeals for qualified Irish teachers; but it seems likely that the real point of proceedings was to create a sense of national solidarity among Irish immigrants, rather than to extend the knowledge and use of the Irish language among the Irish abroad. Ó Briain indefatigably addressed school audiences in areas of London with large Irish populations, preaching about his own conversion as a boy at school in England. This came via a Duffy's book catalogue which led him to O'Reilly's Irish–English dictionary, and Archbishop MacHale's translations of Thomas Moore poems into Irish. From such sources he learnt for the first time of the 'mutilation' of the Irish mind by the National School system in Ireland, making it 'more unnatural and more degenerate . . . Better a thousand times life without any organized system of education at all than continue this evil and poisonous anti-national humbug that passes for education today.'[55] Radical nationalism was part of the package; MacColuim was only one of the 'London Gaels' who would return to fight for the republican cause.[56]

A few years after his epiphany on the South Mall, the intellectually ambitious young Cork nationalist P. S. O'Hegarty came to London as a clerk in the Post Office, joined London-Irish organizations such as Cumann na nGaedheal and the Gaelic League, and found himself teaching Irish-language classes as well as giving lectures in Irish history. O'Hegarty was just one of many Irish nationalists who took their civil service examinations, obtained jobs in England and bonded with each other through a sense of exile as well as through a commitment to cultural regeneration and political nationalism. He put the easygoing conditions of his employment to good use, and used his office-time to become a formidable journalist, as he recalled long afterwards.

I am a natural born civil servant. I have never yet discovered any civil service work that I couldn't do with one tenth of my brain and in about a third of the time the ordinary civil servant takes ... When I think of it now in cold blood it astonishes me what generous treatment the English always give the Irish individually. I spent 11 years in the London GPO and never experienced anything but kindness, almost indulgence. I was allowed to do the most unheard-of things ... Of course in their hearts the English in those days regarded all Irishmen as being a bit mad, and mad people must be indulged.[57]

A striking number of young people from Irish rural backgrounds also emigrated to London, gained college qualifications and entered the employ of the Post Office; the most celebrated would be Michael Collins.

Back in Ireland, the public rhetoric of the League was less openly politicized and less confessional, but the ideal of non-sectarianism and inclusivity was hard to live up to, and Protestants within the League showed an increasing self-consciousness and restiveness.[58] The prominence of Catholic clerics such as O'Growney, Richard Henebry and Michael O'Hickey in the educational structures of the League's schools implied a certain tension, though O'Growney, for one, consistently emphasized the cross-community potential of the Gaelic movement. Reporting on the Gaelic League Feis at Wexford in 1910, the *Irish Nation* reported that 'the finest feature' was the presence of so many priests. 'They worked like Trojans to make the Feis a success. Young and old were there.'[59] This assumption of clerical authority was predictably disapproved of by Rosamond Jacob (who attended the Feis) and other secular-minded nationalists. Nonetheless, they continued to come. Many never became adept at the language – joining the League as nowadays people might take out membership in a gym, full of good intentions but rapidly falling off. But as a mechanism for meeting like-minded people and forming networks, the League was unrivalled; the law student Hugh Kennedy, for instance, went to Gaelic League lectures in Irish history at 46 Rutland Square, and there met the devout Gaelic Leaguer Éamonn Ceannt, the teacher Sinéad Flanagan (who would marry Éamon de Valera), and others of a more radical stamp than his college friends. Once again, it hardly mattered that the lectures were given in English.[60]

By the turn of the century Gaelicism was entrenched in the educational system, especially with the movement for bilingual education in Irish-speaking districts; Catholic-school managers endorsed this strongly. Simultaneously, the number of League branches with priests as officers grew exponentially, reaching three quarters by the turn of the century.[61] The League's journal *An Claidheamh Soluis* ('The Sword of Light') was sharply conscious of the need to bring the language movement into the educational system via sympathetic school managers – who were, in the vast majority of cases, Catholic religious. The journal gave the Christian Brothers particularly high marks for introducing Irish-language courses, at least in their secondary schools; but many bishops, and those in charge of girls' schools, were accused of conniving at an Anglicizing approach instead. Where the League's own classes and summer-schools were concerned, however, tension between clerics and the educational organization could flare up – especially where the issue of co-education was concerned. The social atmosphere of Gaelic League classes during the summer at Ring or Ballingeary or Cloghaneely or Achill was relaxed and informal; the diaries of Rosamond Jacob and Cesca Trench record moonlight walks, swimming, dancing and flirting; Piaras Béaslaí went a lot further, as will be seen later. Escapes to the *Gaeltachtaí* (Irish-speaking areas) in the summer set a tone and built relationships which would be sustained through winter evening classes.

Such behaviour was bound to raise confrontation with priests involved in the movement as officers, and often did. They levelled the accusation of anti-clericalism against elements of the League – an assertion that sometimes lapsed into the language of sectarianism. The Rory O'More branch in Portarlington was convulsed in 1905 by the issue of clerical dictation regarding co-educational classes: the parish priest, Father E. O'Leary, himself a committed *Gaeilgeoir* (Irish-language enthusiast), denounced the practice of teaching men and women together as morally iniquitous. The row spiralled into splits, boycotts and sustained campaigns of personal invective; the local League was supported by influential journalists such as Patrick Pearse and W. P. Ryan, while Church authorities supported Father O'Leary against the League leader P. T. MacGinley. In July 1906 the turbulent priest entered forbidden territory by specifically denouncing the inoffensive Douglas Hyde, founder of the League, who supported the local branch, as a Protestant. The 'mongrel organization' favoured by the godless Hyde, O'Leary claimed, was deliberately and mischievously spreading dissension among Catholics. The Rory O'More branch had already upped the stakes by denouncing 'the unlimited control of the schools, and, we may add, of the teachers, now exercised by the clergy' as 'a menace to public liberty in Ireland'.[62] O'Leary's attempts to form a purified and exclusively Catholic version of the League in his parish did not win the day, and at the national Ard-Fheis (annual general meeting) of the League the following month a significant number of priests endorsed MacGinley and the Rory O'More branch, ensuring that the 'battle of Portarlington' slipped into the background.

But the issues raised, particularly over clerical control of education, simmered below the surface. MacGinley was one of those League activists who had cut his teeth in the London organization before returning to Ireland, and *Inis Fáil*, the journal of the Gaelic League in London, strongly supported him, arguing that O'Leary was to blame for improperly invoking priestly authority. 'Nobody can be allowed to obstruct Irish-Ireland. Priests and bishops have their rights in national and secular affairs like other people, but they cannot be dictators ... The layman who resists intolerance and dictation is not only a true friend of Ireland but a good friend of the Church in the long run.'[63] However, few were robust enough to proudly claim the banner of anti-clericalism as unequivocally as P. S. O'Hegarty:

> when we are called anticlerical, it really means that we are insisting for the nation as a whole and for every individual in it that the Church should confine itself to such matters as come within its province, and that secular matters remain secular. And we are anticlerical, all of us, in that sense, and rightly so.[64]

Other secular-minded nationalists like Pat McCartan, the Sheehy-Skeffingtons, Rosamond Jacob and W. P. Ryan warmly endorsed this view, but they were never more than a small if vocal minority. Nonetheless, in these conflicts and tensions can be traced the background to the controversy over introducing compulsory Irish for matriculation in the new National University of Ireland in 1908. This pitted the League against senior bishops, and led to internecine struggles of intense savagery. The battle even produced its own martyr in the violently nationalist Dr Michael O'Hickey of Maynooth, whose conflict with his superiors over the issue led to his being forced out of Maynooth and marginalized; a fruitless fight to gain support for his case at Rome, and his early and exhausted demise, earned him the sobriquet 'the man who died for the language'.[65] It is significant too that many younger priests supported compulsory Irish, rather than following their bishops' belief that the National University should rather be encouraged to attract English Catholic students and even refugees from Trinity, an agenda which would be stymied by making Irish essential. And the Irish Parliamentary Party was seen by young extremists to be hopelessly divided and pusillanimous on the issue of compulsory Irish; thus Redmond's party lost much of the credit which it could have claimed for bringing about the university legislation in the first place.

In this, as in other areas, we see the inter-generational antagonism that was so marked a feature of the pre-revolutionary period. Patrick Pearse scornfully dismissed the eminent Jesuit Dr William Delany, President of the Catholic University College, on the grounds of age as much as conservative anti-nationalism. 'He is an old man and we have no hopes of converting him to our ideas; he was old when the Gaelic League was born.'[66] Advanced-nationalist journals enthusiastically reported that the students of University College had set themselves against their teachers, who cared more about 'generously allocating chairs and salaries amongst themselves' than creating an independent Gaelic-speaking Ireland; *Sinn Féin* gave wide and approving coverage to student demonstrations on behalf of compulsory Irish.[67] Pearse's rhetoric and O'Hickey's public letters and pamphlets also infer a connection between political radicalization and the language issue in education. Unsurprisingly, out of over a hundred tested variables in one pioneering study of Irish nationalism, the percentage of National schools in which Irish was taught for fees in 1911 is one of the most significant indications of a later centre of revolutionary activity.[68]

IV

The row over compulsory Irish in the new National University during 1908 to 1909 not only indicated the high voltage of political feeling where Irish-language, educational and clerical interests were brought into conflict; it also suggests the part played by university politics in the conditioning of the revolutionary elite. The new institution was the result of a long campaign by Catholics, pressed hard by the Irish Parliamentary Party, and eventually brought into being by the sympathetic Liberal Chief Secretary Augustine Birrell. The aim was for access to a properly funded university institution that would reflect the ethos and religion of the Irish majority. The 1908 legislation accordingly set up a new National University, elevating Queen's College, Belfast, to university status, and leaving Trinity College where it stood. Thus Queen's continued to cater for the Northern Protestant bourgeoisie, and Trinity for the Protestant elite and 'Castle Catholics'; while a new federal National University was invented, with constituent colleges in Dublin (known as University College, Dublin), Cork and Galway. This abolished the old Royal University, with its second-class status as an examining body. More influentially, just as at other levels of the Irish education system, it effectively constructed a denominational university system without using denominational language.

Much of the ethos of the old Catholic University College, run by the Jesuits on Stephen's Green, was transferred into University College, Dublin. But besides an overwhelmingly Catholic atmosphere, the new university (which would eventually occupy an impressive building just off the Green, on Earlsfort Terrace) also embodied a robust subculture of political debate, largely centred on the Literary and Historical Society, which became the arena within which nationalist politics were discussed. Many 'L & H' debates focused on the inadequacies of the Irish Parliamentary Party and the need for cultural renewal. The inaugural meeting of the L & H at UCD featured a paper entitled 'The Rise of the National Movement' read by the Society's Auditor, Michael Davitt, son of the great Land League leader; subsequent meetings declared their nationalist colours by voting against federal Home Rule, condemning the British occupation of

India and deciding that Dickens was a seriously overrated novelist.[69] Nonetheless the overwhelming ethos of the student politicians, in the first years of the new institution, was in favour of Home Rule. The recurrent demonstrations against singing 'God Save the Queen' at the annual conferral ceremony (most famously in 1905) were remembered in retrospect as a flashpoint of change, but at the time would not have been out of line with constitutional nationalism of a Parnellite tinge: it probably represented anti-Trinity College emotion as much as anti-monarchical feelings, and a determination to cock a snook at the President, Delany, who was seen as a 'Castle Catholic'. For nationally minded students, however impatient they were with the older generation of constitutional nationalists, and however interested in the Gaelic League and Sinn Féin, the future seemed – up to 1914 – a Home Rule future. University graduates and students were not over-represented among those 'out' in 1916.

At the same time the culture of the National University in the years before the Rising was lively, politicized, co-educational and notable for setting up connections and networks that would be exploited later in life. The recollections of nationalist students who later became influential public figures, such as Michael Hayes, J. J. O'Connell, Agnes O'Farrelly, Arthur Clery and Hugh Kennedy, make this clear. C. S., or 'Todd', Andrews, arriving at the university from a lower-middle-class background in 1919, was scathing about this networking:

> The L & H was run mainly by the sons of Castle Catholics and the detritus of the Irish party. The whole proceedings seemed to me to lack seriousness (as of course it was intended to do) and to be downright frivolous in character. What I did not understand was that the L & H was a training ground for lawyers and careerists who were poised in waiting for the coming of Home Rule and who, in the event, reaped the benefit of the IRA struggle and embraced joyfully the advent of the Free State as providing for their talents something even more advantageous than Home Rule.[70]

There were also young academics attached, or partly attached, to the university who mixed with the undergraduates in political as well as educational circles: figures such as Tom Kettle, Francis Sheehy-Skeffington and Francis Cruise O'Brien were past-masters of critical attack on the status quo but not, in political terms, advanced nationalists; they formed the nucleus of the Young Ireland branch of the United Irish League, attempting to infuse new life-blood into the increasingly sclerotic arteries of the Home Rulers. But there was also a radical-nationalist presence within the University, and ideas circulated from outside. The future Volunteer leader Eimar O'Duffy, the rebellious product of a bourgeois 'Castle Catholic' background, became an ornament of the L & H and later drew a vivid picture of student culture in the pre-revolutionary era in his autobiographical 1919 novel, *The Wasted Island*: in all university discussions, his hero and alter ego finds 'Nationalism was taken for granted and all Irish questions were approached on that basis.'[71]

This was true beyond the halls of UCD. The student National Literary Society, approvingly noted for its radical-nationalist and Irish-Ireland rhetoric, was not confined to University College: 'its ideal is to bring the students of the various colleges together on the common ground of nationality.'[72] At its inaugural meeting, the majority of students in fact came from the Cecilia Street Medical School.[73] Papers read at its meetings included subjects such as 'The Treatment of Political Prisoners in Ireland', and Geraldine Plunkett was surprised to find that it dealt far more with politics than with literature. University College was conveniently situated in the centre of Dublin, town and gown were not widely separated, and 'real' politics rapidly found their way into the student forum. Not only were the journals of the radical nationalist Arthur Griffith read, but Arthur Griffith himself spoke at L & H meetings. UCD students warmly responded to Griffith's political movement, at this stage a loose grouping of culturally separatist organizations which had come together under the umbrella name 'Sinn Féin' ('We Ourselves'). In May 1906 a self-consciously internationalist student manifesto warmly welcomed the Sinn Féin policies of national self-reliance in economic matters and native cultural revival:

Hungary, Poland, Finland, a section of Russia, Ireland, India and China have partly struck together on this new policy, just as great scientific generalization dawns not on one but on many countries at the same time. The Swadeshi movement in India is the most recent example, and we are glad to see that our class are playing their part. Our own Sinn

Féin movement is therefore practically identical with the general policy which has been taken up in most countries somewhat similarly situated to us. We seek to hit England, (a) Through anti-enlistment and the subsequent crippling of her army, (b) Curtailment of the drink traffic and the consequent diminution in her revenue, (c) Through the boycott of her industries, following the example of China and India.[74]

The irrepressible Bulmer Hobson, involved in a wide spectrum of radical-nationalist activities but with no formal connection to the University, nonetheless proselytized there and later sold the IRB journal *Irish Freedom* on the campus. Though he used another of his newspapers, the *Republic*, to claim that nationalism was flourishing in Queen's University, Belfast, he knew where the possibilities were really located.[75]

His companion in the Irish Republican Brotherhood and the nationalist Dungannon clubs movement, Seán MacDermott, also infiltrated UCD. Their ally Pat McCartan, now a medical student at the Royal College of Surgeons, issued a manifesto to 'the whole students of Ireland' and began a short-lived and extremely 'advanced- nationalist' journal, *Irish Student*. This came out in May 1910, published from his digs at 18 Belvidere Road and sold – inevitably – from Tom Clarke's shop at 75A Great Britain Street, which acted as a meeting place for nationalists and a centre of distribution for their writings. The journal argued that the new university should be national rather than Catholic, reflecting McCartan's anti-clericalism; it was intensely anti 'West Briton' and pro the Irish language, and advocated confrontational tactics, praising Romanian and Indian student radicals. McCartan preached that students could be 'Ireland's best stewards. They can strike a telling blow. The day has passed for argument and reason, and now our watch-word must be – prepare.' The *Irish Student* did not last long. 'I got abuse for starting it,' McCartan later reflected, 'and more abuse for stopping it but only one man backed up his opinion with a subscription in aid of it. There is no doubt it hit home in the quarter for which it was intended . . . many wanted to know who was behind it. Many were quite complimentary as to the writing in it though they themselves are West Britons. But down deep the Irish spirit is someplace even in the worst of them.'[76]

A certain amount of West Britonism was detectable in the much more successful magazine *National Student*, full of advertisements for dress shops round Grafton Street and carrying accounts of sporting prowess, club events, parodies, jokes about Loreto girls and sarcasms about the poor attendance at Gaelic societies. When the magazine and its readers were satirized in *An Claidheamh Soluis* and the *Leader*, the editors responded that they were not obliged to publish only 'true-blue national articles'.[77] But the *National Student* also carried rhapsodic articles about Ring and advertisements for Irish colleges such as Ballingeary, with the editor assuring his clients that their establishment would be drawn to the attention of exactly the kind of clientele they wanted to reach. And since the editorial team included Patrick McGilligan, J. J. ('Ginger') O'Connell and others later to make their names in the republican movement, the increasingly radical direction of the magazine should not come as a surprise. O'Connell's editorials ringingly called for the new university to be 'the centre of cultured nationalism' and for it 'to combat the forces of Anglicization and national indifference wherever they are to be found in the student world'.[78] This consciously differentiated University College from Trinity, with its traditionally Protestant and Ascendancy ethos: though here too a Gaelic Society was founded in 1907, securing 'the services of a native Irish-speaker' for classes, building up a library and inviting speakers such as the Gaelic League supremo Eoin MacNeill, who proposed on 17 November 1908 the motion 'that Irish studies deserve deeper attention than hitherto accorded them'. The seconder was the irredeemably Anglophone W. B. Yeats.[79]

But as radical nationalism intensified, so did the current of feeling among the student body of the newer university. In late 1913, an article in the *National Student* by Louise Gavan Duffy firmly identified the student body with the language movement, with a strong implication of its political undertow: 'those who join the race now may have every hope of being in at the finish.'[80] In the same month, the foundation of the Volunteers was hailed with a celebratory editorial about the need for 'the knowledge and discipline of arms'. By June 1914, the editorials on Ireland's claim to nationality were emphatic, and included a powerful attack on the idea of Partition.

Judged from many aspects, political events, profoundly concerned with Ireland, present a dramatic picture, as of an amazing army deploying before a final, decisive conflict. The drift of them seems to make for a great trial of the whole morality of Irish Nationalism. And there seems to be developing a powerful, and in many respects a final struggle, in which as it were the honour and the personality of Ireland is at stake in which the ideals already tried and nurtured in all kinds of sufferings are to be offered yet another violence . . . The only political status for their country that Irishmen will accept . . . will be fought for to the last and shall not be alienated.

Degradation could be faced down; they must fight. The days of expedience and juggling were over. 'The set of politicians who try these things will be the first to learn that – Ireland can do without any one of us; none of us can do without her. They will learn in violence.'[81] Four years on from McCartan's short-lived *Irish Student*, general opinion in the university was catching up with him.

Those students most amenable to such 'advanced' rhetoric were probably not from the upper echelons. Michael Hayes, a carpenter's son originally destined to be a solicitor's clerk, owed his distinguished academic career to making the most of his Christian Brothers education and profiting from the opportunities offered under the Intermediate Education Act. He excelled in Irish and French, and his exam results in 1905 won him a scholarship of £50 p.a. to Trinity, which his father rejected, fearing he would be subjected to Protestant proselytism. The following year Hayes won a full scholarship to University College, plus a Bishops' Scholarship, totalling £104 p.a. – at sixteen, he was earning well above the average for a skilled workman's wage. He entered university at a significant time – though he continued to teach part time for the Christian Brothers at Synge Street, and it was through teachers' union meetings that he first encountered a shy, gauche and rather cadaverous young mathematics teacher called Éamon de Valera. Though a committed Gaelic Leaguer, de Valera was unfamiliar with the other venues where young nationalists congregated, such as the Cairo and DBC cafés, the pubs around Stephen's Green or L & H debates; only later, through the Volunteering movement, would he enter nationalist political circles. At college in

1906 Hayes met students more fully engaged with Sinn Féin sympathies, though his autobiography attests to the general expectation of Home Rule. And it was at an Éire Óg ('Young Ireland') meeting in Camden Street, off College grounds, that he first met Harry Boland and Seán MacDermott, 'an extremely attractive person, not in the slightest way resembling the traditional picture of the revolutionary, but he was the great organizer of the Irish Revolutionary Brotherhood and the most important organizer of the Rising'.[82]

University life had a notably radicalizing effect on women, whose education up to that point had been less exposed to political influences. Geraldine Plunkett recalled this particularly strongly. She first heard physical-force tactics detailed at the University's National Literary Society, whose principal aim, she realized, was not to raise literary consciousness but 'to nationalize the students and subsequently the professions'. 'It was only in the students' hour late at night, walking home through the deserted streets, that we learned what was happening and the correct revolutionary point of view.'[83] The Ryan sisters, from Wexford, were also politicized in this new world. Out of twelve children born to a 150-acre farm, nine got university degrees. Money was short, but Min (Josephine Mary), Agnes and Nan managed to travel to Europe, sometimes working as governesses, and for some years moved between teaching jobs in England and Ireland. The Ryan girls went to Loreto College at 77 Stephen's Green, where another sister, Johanna (Sister Stanislaus), played a powerful role, and then to University College, around the corner at Earlsfort Terrace. The most intellectual of them, Mary Kate, became Hayes's colleague in the French department at UCD. A brother, James, went to medical school at UCD (and was sworn into the IRB by Seán MacDermott). As will be seen, the Ryans would go on to play roles in radical-republican politics, and to marry several key revolutionary figures, creating something like a dynasty in the new order.

The correspondence of the Ryan sisters vividly conjures up the liberation, fun and intellectual excitement of UCD in the years before 1916. Mary Kate ironically described the whole family as 'never content to accept people as they are'; hypercritical, challenging, 'confoundedly conceited'.[84] The family traditions were nationally minded rather than nationalist; teaching in England from 1905 (first in Bedford, then in LCC schools in London), she wrote letters that were cheerfully satirical about 'the English' but not notably political. The eldest sister, Nell, who remained at home in Wexford, was ardently nationalist, and slightly mocked for it by her siblings. In 1907, however, Mary Kate joined the Gaelic League of London and things began to change. At that point Min was moving from Fulda in Germany to Rouen, Agnes was in Belgium, and Nan was working as a governess in San Sebastián. Mary Kate was plotting to get Min back from France to a job in London, a plan which succeeded in 1909, but this was not the ultimate objective. 'When all comes to all what is the great good of our arriving at living in London. I know some people who won't like that at all. Let us look to something better – to Ireland. You would be surprised or will be when you come home to see the difference in Irish politics since you left. Sinn Féin was barely mentioned then. Now it is written about in English papers even ... The Sinn Féiners are gaining ground every day. The parliamentarians are losing and making asses of themselves with silly speeches. Their cause is weak if not gone.'[85]

Mary Kate had an axe to grind; she was in the throes of a complicated relationship with the starry young UCD graduate and Irish Parliamentary Party MP Tom Kettle, who in 1909 would marry Mary Sheehy, daughter of another Irish MP, David Sheehy. Mary Sheehy was also one of a formidable sisterhood; her sister Kathleen would marry the journalist Francis Cruise O'Brien (whose sister married Eimar O'Duffy), while the feminist Hanna Sheehy married the radical Francis Skeffington, joining and hyphenating their names. Around the turn of the century the lively Sheehy household at 2 Belvedere Place was a magnet for hopeful young intellectuals from University College, including James Joyce; but, though David Sheehy's family came from a radical and even Fenian tradition, he now represented solid Irish Parliamentary Party values, against which his daughter Hanna would rebel. The Ryan girls did not like the Sheehys, whom Mary Kate blamed for persuading Tom Kettle not to throw in his lot with Sinn Féin; as farmers' daughters, they also felt looked down upon by the *haute bourgeoise* Sheehys. At a party in the Irish Club in London in 1908, meeting 'a section of humanity that I ought to know more about', Mary Kate was infuriated. 'To hear Mary [Sheehy] saying we'll be getting Home Rule ... is very pathetic. To hear her condemn the Irish language – show a coldness and indifference for Irish manufacturing question – speak of Gaelic Leaguers as low class – ah well – I am not surprised that the Sheehy girls are not very popular after all.'[86]

By 1909 Mary Kate was writing on Gaelic-headed notepaper; though still impatient with her sister Nell's excessive 'piety in the Irish cause', she was becoming more radical in her own politics. This was crystallized when she returned to Dublin in 1910 to become University Lecturer in French at UCD, where her younger sisters Chris and Agnes were students (they too would become teachers). Mary Kate was stylish and attractive, and her first lectures caused a certain sensation among male students; she became close to her sister Nell's friend Seán T. O'Kelly and his inseparable companion Seán Forde; she gave tea parties at her flat in Leeson Park Avenue and held court in the DBC café on Sackville Street, where O'Kelly described her 'surrounded – as usual – by a host of her worshippers ... dispensing smiles with tea and cakes with her usual queenly dignity'.[87] But the Ryan sisters' letters also record going to Gaelic League *feiseanna*, plays at St Enda's and *céilidhe* organized by the Students' National League in Rutland Square; by 1911 Kate was regularly attending the historian Alice Stopford Green's nationalist parties at her house on Stephen's Green. Later Kate would establish her own nationalist salon at 19 Ranelagh Road.

Hayes records that women naturally entered into student societies such as Éire Óg and other Gaelic League spin-offs (which was where Richard Mulcahy met his future wife, Min Ryan, when Mulcahy was attending night classes at the technical college in Bolton Street, for the purposes of taking the Post Office Engineers' examinations).[88] Another subset of students where radical nationalism seemed to thrive involved medical students – at the Royal College of Surgeons as well as at UCD. The future IRA commander Ernie O'Malley began his brief student life as a medical student, before history took over, as did James Ryan and Eimar O'Duffy. Cathal Brugha was similarly destined and Kathleen Lynn, Dorothy Stopford, Brigid Lyons Thornton and other women doctors shared their advanced-nationalist beliefs. Radical opinions also flourished at the College of Surgeons, where Pat

McCartan and Daniel T. Sheehan from Kerry set up a Dungannon Club in December 1905 (an IRB ginger-group which had started in Belfast the previous March). Thirty-one members rapidly joined, making it 'successful beyond all expectation'. 'All from the highest down are getting afraid of the Dungannon Club,' McCartan wrote proudly in 1905, though two years later his ally Bulmer Hobson was lamenting 'it is hard to wake up Dublin but we will do it yet.'[89] McCartan was ambitious for his student society, inviting older intellectuals such as Yeats, Hyde and Alice Milligan to lecture to them. His manifesto to students appealed to them to do 'what the students of other countries do', suggesting that he was aware of the part played by St Petersburg students in the Russian revolution earlier that year. He also made 'a strong appeal to Protestant and Catholic students to join hands and be Irish true and brave and neither Rome's nor England's slaves', adding privately, 'the Protestant student is not the "ungettable" man one is led to imagine.'[90]

McCartan is another of those revolutionaries whose anti-clericalism was later rather lost to view; his correspondence of this time speculates, among other things, whether Archbishop Healy was responsible for two illegitimate children recently born to servants in his household. Two years after founding the Dungannon Club at the College of Surgeons, ever the optimist, he believed 'for the first time since Emmet was expelled from Trinity we have the students aroused though we have some hostile.'[91] The radical medical-student subculture again suggests echoes with pre-revolutionary Russia at an earlier period: those uncompromising revolutionaries Basarov in Turgenev's *Fathers and Sons* and Vera Pavlovna in Chernyshevsky's *What is to be Done?* are medical students, and so were many of the student revolutionary generation of St Petersburg in 1905.[92] The Irish student generation in the pre-revolutionary era did not develop a fully fledged radical culture of *studentchestvo*, as happened in St Petersburg. But they were equally moved by images of martyrdom, religious imagery (rather than formal religious practice), and the moral and aesthetic advantages of dying young. There are of course enormous differences of context. Government repression in both countries, for one thing, is not comparable: the whole university of St Petersburg was shut down for over a year after 1905, mass expulsions were common, and a military response was always on the cards; whereas the most that middle-class radicals in Dublin had to put up with was the Irish-Edwardian version of repressive tolerance and the disapproval of priests. Still, in both countries, student revolutionary movements looked to joining forces – with 'the streets' in Russia and with the 'hillside men' in Ireland. Both believed in transforming the inadequate reality bequeathed by the last generation. Both experienced a radicalization in the city that could be diffused back into the provinces when they went home (or, in the Russian case, were exiled). And when revolution again came to Russia, in 1917, the student generation in Dublin took a close interest.[93]

Another sector of third-level education where nationalist influences were imbibed was in the art colleges, particularly Dublin's Metropolitan School of Art. As a branch of the government's Department of Agriculture and Technical Instruction, charging low fees and teaching evening classes, it was a less elite institution than the Royal Hibernian Academy schools. Roughly speaking, the Metropolitan trained art teachers, while the RHA trained artists – though there were plenty of exceptions to both rules. Connections in art schools and artistic circles generally linked together high-profile nationalists such as Maud Gonne, Constance Markievicz and Ella Young, all dilettante artists in their way; more relevantly, professional artists such as Patrick Tuohy, Seán Keating, Willie Pearse, Cesca Trench and (earlier) Oliver Sheppard seem to have absorbed nationalist beliefs during their training. However, since Tuohy, like Willie Pearse, came there from St Enda's in 1909, he was already radicalized. He would be one of those St Enda's boys who occupied the GPO in 1916, while Keating became the iconic painter of the revolutionary experience – regretting always that he had never been an activist himself, like his friend Seán Moylan, whom he used as a model for his heroic studies of revolutionaries.

There were other routes to a radical education. The Ryan sisters' friend Seán T. O'Kelly, born in 1882, was the son of a boot manufacturer in Berkeley Street. At the Christian Brothers schools in St Mary's Place and later North Richmond Street, his interest in the Irish language was ignited by a brilliant lay teacher. O'Kelly did not go to university, but in 1898 became an assistant in the National Library in Kildare Street – a temple of learning for many autodidacts, including – a decade earlier – the young W. B. Yeats. The legendary librarian Thomas Lyster took O'Kelly under his wing, sent him to night courses at the Royal Dublin Society, and introduced him to late-Victorian Irish intellectuals such as William Magee ['John Eglinton'], R. I. Best, Edward Dowden and John Kells Ingram – a conservative Trinity don who in his hot youth had written the iconic nationalist anthem 'Who Fears to Speak of Ninety-Eight?' (O'Kelly was delighted when Ingram told him that, contrary to rumour, he did not repudiate it: 'I stand over every word of that ballad.'[94]) O'Kelly enjoyed many arguments about nationalism and the Irish language with his seniors. While still on the Library staff he took part in demonstrations against the Boer War, joined the IRB in 1901, was part of Arthur Griffith's lunching circle at the Irish Farm and Produce Company restaurant in Henry Street, and wrote for Griffith's *United Irishman*. But, affected by Griffith's *diktat* that working for the civil service was as bad as joining the British Army, he resigned from the Library in 1902, to Lyster's annoyance, and went to work for the Gaelic League. In January 1906 he became (at twenty-three) a Sinn Féin member of Dublin Corporation, and an indefatigable committee man in advanced-nationalist circles. He was set on the path that would eventually make him, in another age, President of Ireland.

V

In the overall process of radicalization, how important is formal education likely to be? The life-stories of many Irish revolutionaries in this era, as confided to the Bureau of Military History in the 1940s and 1950s, emphasize just as strongly a family member who provides a powerful nationalist conditioning: Michael Hayes's father, or, in the case of Michael O'Rahilly and Kathleen Clarke, a spinster aunt. This kind of influence, however, may create a general nationalist cast of mind rather than precipitating a conversion to 'advanced' organization and the endorsement of violence. As Richard Mulcahy later put it to Hayes, 'You were reared in a nationalist atmosphere but nevertheless in common-sense surroundings and you got into the University atmosphere and the Gaelic League atmosphere without having any military tendency in your bones or your marrow at all.'[95] Influences from home continued to resonate even after transmigration to school or college, especially among large, close-knit families like the Ryans: Agnes noted that at one of Mary Kate's UCD parties, the guests could be classified as 'Wexford-born, Wexford-connected, Wexford-patronized, Wexford-borders, Wexford-obsessed (Seán Forde), Wexford-possessed (Seán T. O'Kelly), Wexford-weakness (R. Lynd), etc.'[96]

Above all, radicalization happened in specific groups and activities ancillary to school or college, such as classes in the *Gaeltacht*, dramatic societies and acting groups, and student journalism and societies. Again, as with the Ryans, a sojourn in England at school or college could predispose young people to extreme opinions. Piaras Béaslaí's copious diaries, recording *Gaeilgeoir* activities in Liverpool around the turn of the century, vividly profile the development and mindset that would eventually send him 'back' to Ireland to search for a republican role in the revolution. Kevin O'Shiel, like Eimar O'Duffy, was brought up in an upper-middle-class Catholic home where politics were rarely discussed. Both became converts to nationalism at exclusive boarding-schools in England. O'Shiel devotes many pages of his unpublished memoir to describing the process: it seems to have happened as a combination of reaction against local prejudice and occasional encouragement from politically minded mentors.[97] Mary MacSwiney's experience at school in England was also decisive; and it was in England too that Máire Comerford and Muriel Murphy, later MacSwiney, were brought to realize how far they dissented from the bourgeois values of their upper-class Catholic backgrounds.

From 1914, as the Ulster crisis deepened and the First World War threatened, outside events provided their own momentum for radicalization. As will be seen in a later chapter, the Volunteering movement, above all, militarized a large sector of advanced nationalists, creating a decisively 'Machiavellian moment'.[98] But even Volunteering built on the foundation of the Fianna boy-scouting movement, pioneered by Hobson and Markievicz, and its rhetoric drew on the imagery of independence nurtured in Irish classes and the Christian Brothers' history lessons. It is hard not to see, among lower-middle-class Catholics, a general sense of exclusion being mediated and reaffirmed through

71

Irish education. But one should also note other *couches sociales*: the independent-minded children (often daughters) of the Catholic *haute bourgeoisie* (the Comerfords, the Plunketts, the O'Rahillys, the Humphreys); and the middle- and upper-class Protestant nationalists in revolt against their backgrounds (Roger Casement, Cesca Trench, Rosamond Jacob, Kathleen Lynn, Bulmer Hobson, Herbert Pim, the Gifford sisters, Robert and Dulcibella Barton, Erskine Childers). Like the better-known (and slightly older) Maud Gonne, Constance Markievicz and Alice Milligan, they seized on advanced nationalism and Irish-Ireland values as part of a general rebellion, partly fuelled by a sense of guilt and compensation. Alice Milligan, writing to the young Terence MacSwiney, described herself as 'an internal prisoner' of her own family. It might also be speculated whether women, often educated at home, had less oppressive structures to rebel against than their brothers or cousins, who had to shake off the accumulated conditioning of upper-class schooling in the imperial age. And sexual dissidence, as we will see later, could be another alienating factor.

The range of middle-class revolutionaries in Edwardian Ireland runs a fascinating gamut of types and backgrounds, but they were united by some marked affinities. One was a robust Anglophobia. Another was a dedication to the bomb and bullet that may not always have taken on board what the policy actually entailed. Min Ryan admitted afterwards that when Tom Clarke told her in 1916 that most of them would be 'wiped out', it brought her down to earth with a bump. 'I got an awful shock because I was living a most unreal kind of life as if nothing could happen to anyone; I could hardly believe that we would take up arms at all and then I began to believe that we would come out of it alright.'[99] The five years from 1916 to 1921 would provide a steep learning curve. But the conditioning influences of the twenty years or so before then, which constructed these expectations, were often mediated through educational institutions where the like-minded found each other and established an *esprit de corps*.

The First World War altered everything and created the conditions for an IRB insurrection, planned with German aid. But the mentality that this appealed to had been set over the previous decade or so, and not just from the pure-milk Fenianism preached by the IRB. Behind the rapid polarization set in motion by the guns of August 1914 there lay a potent mélange of careers and prejudices and orientations, imbibed through education and peer-groups as much as through family influence – and, indeed, often acting in direct and deliberate contradistinction to family tradition. Once again, the radical potential of the middle classes should be remembered, often bringing down on their heads more than they anticipated. A political education took many forms, then as now. It could embrace processes operating outside the classroom and the lecture hall, such as sexual radicalism, feminist agitation or agit-prop theatre. Nationalist radicals bonded together within closed worlds such as Pearse's Hermitage, or the Plunkett children's armed encampment at Larkfield, or the Gaelic League Oireachteas (annual festival), or lunches at the Irish Farm and Produce Company, or the summer-schools at Ring and Ballingeary. 'Among my new friends,' Máire Comerford recalled, 'in our lovely new world of revolt, were many who had no more personal grievance against life than I had. We were from various strata of society, but we were rank and file republicans in love with the new freedom we hoped to make secure.'[100] This was one more love-affair doomed to disillusionment – an inseparable part of the life of a revolutionary generation.

A poster by Grace Gifford for the 4–9 January 1915 programme at the Irish Theatre in Hardwicke Street, run by Joseph Plunkett and Thomas MacDonagh, which ambitiously put on contemporary international work as well as new Irish plays by Eimar O'Duffy and others.

3

Playing

Writing is a bubbling forth of the revolution of the soul . . .
practically all the Abbey plays – to specify the particular point
at issue – are revolts . . . The plays are nearly all revolts against
something or other, something which we may not like but which
a lot of us are not prepared to face. The artist faces it; and even-
tually the people follow.

– P. S. O'Hegarty, 'Art and the Nation',
Irish Freedom *(March 1912)*[1]

I

Writing about Irish theatre in *Sinn Féin* in 1906, Kathleen O'Brennan
asserted confidently that drama was a 'nationalizing force'. 'In the
countries struggling for precedence or rights of nationhood, the
drama has its honoured place. Behind the political struggles in Japan,
Hungary, Finland and Denmark, were the great national dramatists;
though to the majority of us in Ireland the names of those men are
unknown, yet the result of their work has had its stimulating effect
even here.'[2] O'Brennan went on to argue that drama was the 'art of
the people', the quickest way to galvanize the emotions of the crowd
into energy, the most democratic of the arts. 'Through the drama
our people can be taught the history of our country, and how that
history has affected the present condition of Ireland; they can also be
taught that what we most need is the power of concentrating through
ourselves.'

O'Brennan's belief was shared by many fellow nationalists, but by the time of her article the function of a national drama was already controversial. A year later, in January 1907, the explosive potential of Irish theatre was tested to the full, when John Millington Synge's *The Playboy of the Western World* caused riots in the Abbey Theatre and precipitated a frenetic public debate in which the Sinn Féin movement was well to the fore. The play, in which a country boy gains sexual allure and the admiration of his community by claiming to have killed his father, was seen by nationalists as traducing the very values of uncorrupted Irishness which they were so assiduously fostering. (The saturnine and complex Synge was already notorious for his portrayal of a loveless Irish marriage in an earlier play, *In the Shadow of the Glen*.) Above all, the row over *The Playboy* brought into question what the objectives of a self-consciously Irish dramatic movement should be: a matter of profound interest to many of the revolutionary generation.

The issue had been looming since the turn of the century. By 1907 the national theatre movement begun in 1899 by W. B. Yeats, Augusta Gregory and Edward Martyn had split and re-formed. On one hand, there was the Abbey Theatre, founded in 1904 under the firm grip of Yeats, Gregory and their star playwright, Synge, which deliberately put art above politics. On the other, there was a burgeoning number of small companies which maintained a more directly political intent. Dramatic controversy provided the backdrop to a continuing argument about art and propaganda. Martin Esslin's reflection that the theatre is where a nation 'thinks in front of itself' is sharply illustrated by this era in Ireland's theatrical history; Yeats repeatedly paraphrased O'Brennan by misquoting Victor Hugo: 'in the theatre the mob becomes a people.' After the inauguration of revolution in 1916, more than one commentator would point to the choreographed nature of the event, as if the theatre had taken to the streets.[3] Those famous photographs of Dublin streetscapes shattered by rebellion look like a stage-set. This perspective came naturally, after a decade and a half of dramatic ferment.

The politics of theatrical activity in early-twentieth-century Dublin has usually been seen in terms of the emergent Abbey Theatre and the preceding phenomena of the Irish Literary Theatre and the Irish National Theatre Society. However, the connection of the Abbey to nationalist politics is an ambiguous and thorny subject, reflecting in part Yeats's political reorientation over the first decade of the twentieth century. During the decade that saw the theatre emerge from its Irish Literary Theatre origins in 1899 into an independent, director-controlled stock company in 1909–10, Yeats was himself mutating from a passionate young Fenian fellow traveller and demonstrator against royal jubilees, magnetized by Maud Gonne, to a sceptical nationalist moderate, supporting Redmond and Home Rule. Nonetheless, the same era was punctuated by key moments when the drama on the Abbey stage projected into the political consciousness of the audience, with far-reaching effects. One was the first production of Yeats and Gregory's nationalist allegory *Cathleen ni Houlihan* in early April 1902, mounted by Maud Gonne's feminist-nationalist organization Inghinidhe na hÉireann, with Maud herself playing Ireland.[4] The play presented the idea of a sacrificial struggle for Ireland's freedom, renewed from generation to generation. An old woman comes to a farmhouse preparing for a wedding and calls the bridegroom away to fight for the restitution of her 'four green fields'; when he follows her bidding, she is miraculously transformed into 'a young girl with the walk of a queen'. As with the row over *The Playboy* five years later, when Sinn Féin led disruptions from the audience, the Abbey can be seen as a crucible for the preoccupations of the revolutionary generation. The young Lennox Robinson speaks for many. Sitting with fewer than fifty people in the Cork Opera House on a hot August afternoon in 1907 and watching the Abbey players in a programme of short plays by Yeats and Gregory – *Cathleen ni Houlihan*, *The Hour Glass*, *The Jackdaw* and *The Rising of the Moon* – he experienced 'a magical effect . . . certain national emotions and stirrings hidden from my good Unionist parents were crystallized for ever.'[5]

But the Abbey was only part of the story, and far from the most radical part. Despite the origin-myth sedulously cultivated by the principals, the theatre of national consciousness did not start with Gregory, Yeats and Edward Martyn meeting on a rainy summer day in 1898, at a house at Duras on the Claregalway shore, and planning a literary theatre to proclaim Ireland's artistic and cultural identity. There was already a tradition of radical Irish nationalism which was intensely theatrical, focused on public display and ritual performance. Symbolic funerals, such as that of the exiled Fenian Terence Bellew MacManus in 1861, were theatrical events in their own way; his body, banned from Dublin's Pro-Cathedral by a Church establishment nervous about endorsing extreme nationalism, was appropriately placed on the stage of the Mechanics' Institute in Abbey Street, site of the later theatre, and incorporated in a ceremonial public performance. Commemorative ritual took other forms too, retrospectively deifying martyrs and mobilizing people en masse for subversive purposes: 'becoming a people', as Yeats would have put it. The tableaux, pageants and demonstrations which are such a feature of the pre-revolutionary era, at Patrick Pearse's school or the Gaelic League Oireachteas, took their place in a long tradition of performance.

Nor did Irish theatre with a national and nationalist perspective begin new-minted in 1899, though several people connected with the early Abbey enterprise liked to give that impression. In 1902 the *Freeman's Journal* reminded its readers of the pre-existing tradition:

> The Irish Literary Theatre appealed to a limited audience because it was literary. At the other end of the Irish theatrical world we have had for many years an Irish drama that was not literary in either the modern or the Elizabethan acceptation of the term but which – as we know it in the Queen's Theatre – appealed very powerfully to the mind of the average man in Dublin, and especially the average working-man. Superior people sneer at what they consider the crude and melodramatic pictures of '98 and other periods of Irish history which from time to time are presented in the oldest and most historic theatre in Dublin. For the most part they are critics who have never witnessed the wonderful influence which even a very plainly-told story of Irish patriotism has on the minds of the honest working-men and working-women of Dublin.[6]

Recent re-evaluations of the melodramatist Dion Boucicault, notably his hit play *The Shaughraun* of 1874, stress a political and even pro-Fenian idealism wrapped up in the blarney – apparently popular with British as well as Irish audiences.[7] There was also an established taste for more demanding fare. Notwithstanding the Abbey founding myth, Dublin theatres in early 1899 were showing not just silver-fork frivolities but plays by modern and experimental Europeans such as

Sudermann, Maeterlinck and Pinero. The seismic effect of Ibsen in London during the 1880s also transferred rapidly to Dublin – deeply influencing the Irish experiments in realist drama by Edward Martyn, and affecting Yeats's theories of dramatic innovation and national identity. (Though whether he caught the subversive irony of *Peer Gynt* as frequently as he invoked it is another matter.)

Moreover, there was a lively theatrical culture of nationalist drama in Cork and Belfast. Hubert O'Grady's Irish National Drama Company mounted plays with titles such as *The Fenian* and *The Famine*, featuring themes of eviction, emigration and national sacrifice; Dublin audiences were well used to plays dealing with the 1798 Rising, long before *Cathleen ni Houlihan*.[8] The titles of the plays presented by the Kennedy Miller Combination, an outfit closely connected with the Queen's Theatre in Dublin from 1889, are suggestive: *The Irishman, The Nationalist, Lord Edward, Theobald Wolfe Tone, Rory O'More, The Insurgent Chief, The Ulster Hero, Sarsfield*. Following the model of Boucicault's *Robert Emmet*, J. W. Whitbread produced a cycle of plays commemorating heroes of 1798, and playing to popular appeal with Irish audiences, though they also toured all over the British Isles into the early 1900s. An Englishman, he was praised by the *Irish Playgoer* for 'turning the attention of many a previously indifferent young Irishman to the history and literature of his country'; he also funded a prize of £100 in 1902 for 'the best Irish drama written by an Irish man or woman born of Irish parents and residing in Ireland'.[9] These enterprises are forgotten now, and ignored in the theatrical history constructed by Yeats and his collaborators as well as by many later theatre historians, but clearly suggest a nationalist and historical bent; many later Abbey stalwarts cut their teeth acting at the Queen's.[10] The connection between theatrical performance and Irish nationalist rhetoric was well established by late-nineteenth-century Irish melodrama, and the original National Theatre Society did not come out of nothing.

However sententious and declamatory, popular drama could pack a nationalist punch and make direct connections with contemporary politics. Hubert O'Grady's *The Eviction* was first played in 1881, at the height of the Land War; several of his productions, like those of J. W. Whitbread and J. B. Fagan, were seen as overtly and undesirably political by Dublin Castle, though they passed the Lord Chamberlain's Office in England (whose writ did not run in Ireland). Fagan, unlike Whitbread, was Irish, educated at Clongowes; he later became an influential figure on the London stage. His 1798 play *The Rebels* opened in London but played at the Gaiety in September 1899. In 1902 the proceeds of a run of *The Insurgent Chief* paid for the erection of a nationalist monument in County Wicklow. Yeats, unlike his colleagues Frank and William Fay, sometimes acknowledged this tradition. In his occasional theatre magazine, *Samhain*, he wrote of 'the National Players, whose representation of *Robert Emmet* in St Cecilia's Hall some years ago, interested me and touched me. It was frankly propagandist, had the dignity of a long national tradition, and carried my imagination to Davis and to Mitchel. All work which is done without selfishness for something beyond one's self has moral beauty.'[11] By this time – 1908 – he was firmly set against drama that carried an overt political message, but the fact that at the *fin de siècle* these plays were sustaining an audience bred on nationalist narratives had not escaped him.

But if there was a politicized audience, the theatre they were exposed to was not experimental or avant-garde up to the start of the new century; and nor were the people producing, writing or acting in it. From the early 1900s, however, the development of the Abbey Theatre was accompanied by challenging alternatives, spearheaded by political activists. They included breakaway groups such as the Theatre of Ireland and provincial initiatives like the Ulster Literary Theatre and the Cork Dramatic Society. In Dublin the Irish Theatre Company, which occupied the Hardwicke Street Hall, appropriated the Abbey's original idea of cosmopolitan theatre and mounted plays by radical young nationalist intellectuals like Thomas MacDonagh, Joseph Plunkett and Eimar O'Duffy. And Gaelic League enthusiasts attempted to create a travelling company producing plays in Irish for country audiences. Through these activities, radical nationalists tried to find an audience. This met with mixed success; but they certainly found each other, as Sydney Gifford remembered when recalling nationalist life before the revolution. 'It was a feat of endurance for any amateur society to produce a play in those days. It meant that boys and girls, who had worked hard all day, gave up their evenings through the winter months to rehearsing in ice-cold basements, so that they might give one or two performances in a tiny hall.'[12]

The dramatic activities of Inghinidhe na hÉireann mobilized the energies of Maud Gonne, Alice Milligan, Ella Young and many other women through pageants and plays; Gonne later remembered Molly and Sara Allgood, Máire nic Shiubhlaigh, Mary Quinn, Marie Perolz and Helena Molony as learning their craft at dramatic classes arranged by Inghinidhe in the York Street Workman's Club.[13] Many actors played an active part in later revolutionary activities, while those involved in writing and producing agit-prop drama in a number of formats and locales include not only MacDonagh, Plunkett and O'Duffy but other soon-to-be celebrated revolutionaries such as Terence MacSwiney, Constance Markievicz, Patrick Pearse, Bulmer Hobson and Helena Molony. All of them saw their theatrical activities as an integral part of nationalist consciousness-raising.

II

One way or another, most of these people were reacting against what they saw as the insufficiently political nature of the Abbey Theatre, especially after Yeats and Gregory asserted their control, backed by money from the domineering English philanthropist Annie Horniman. Yet politics had been part of the warp and weft of the enterprise from the beginning; Yeats's early pronouncements in the theatre's house magazine *Samhain* suggest as much, even if his language is prophetically *de haut en bas*. In 1903 he wrote of the need to transform history through personal emotion, as an essential step in creating a national theatre; but already his attitude to 'propagandizing' work had aligned him against the powerful nationalist ideologue Arthur Griffith. 'If we think that a national play must be as near as possible a page out of *The Spirit of the Nation* put into dramatic form,' he wrote in *Samhain 1903*, 'then we may be sure that this generation will not see the rise in Ireland of a theatre that will reflect the life of Ireland as the Scandinavian theatre reflects the Scandinavian life.'[14] A national theatre, he argued, had to accept the contradictions and ambiguities of life, and reject the simple-minded heroics of patriotism.

From this point Yeats began arguing that J. M. Synge was the most authentically 'national' of Irish writers because the most challenging – an argument which was a red rag to Arthur Griffith. In 1903 Synge's play *In the Shadow of the Glen*, with its Ibsenite theme of a woman's escape from a loveless rural marriage into a liberated wandering life with a tramp, had driven Maud Gonne, Douglas Hyde and several actors out of the Irish National Theatre Society, denouncing the Society's abandonment of 'national and propagandist work'.[15] Griffith's paper the *United Irishman* had violently attacked Synge's drama too, supported by much of moderate middle-class nationalist opinion. The young nationalist student Hugh Kennedy went to *In the Shadow of the Glen* on 8 October 1903 and recorded in his diary that it was a composite of Ibsen and Boucicault, written 'by a fellow named Synge, a Protestant & socialist'. In Kennedy's view it revolted against all the criteria of art, and by ignoring religion it provided an inauthentic and squalid picture of Irish life. 'Some representative of Liffey-street socialism near me shouted "Liberty" when I hissed ... Yeats in a speech expounded some nonsense intended to convey that religion is only second or third or nowhere after literature.'[16]

In fact Yeats liked to claim, then and later, that the other-worldly and quietly mischievous Synge harboured no political agenda whatsoever: the pure artist in search of a theme, whose radical innocence simply saw things anew, while Irish audiences were unable to bear the reality. This drastically over-simplified both Synge's world-view and the effect of his extraordinary plays, but it suited Yeats's larger purpose. By 1905 he was declaring that as long as he had any control over the National Theatre Society (effectively, the Abbey), 'no plays will be produced at it which were written, not for the sake of a good story or fine verses or some revelation of character, but to please those friends of ours who are ever urging us to attack the priests or the English, or wanting us to put our imagination into handcuffs that we may be sure of never seeming to do one or the other.'[17] The reaction of Griffith's *United Irishman* was to argue, by a brutally reductionist logic, that any cultural broker who declared that politics were the curse of Ireland (and of Irish theatre) was, objectively speaking, a unionist.[18] It was clear that people who wanted Irish theatre to perform the function of political consciousness-raising would have to look somewhere other than Abbey Street.

Yet to concentrate on Yeats skews the picture. In all his polemics for *Samhain* denouncing propagandist art, he rarely missed a chance to invoke his authorship of *Cathleen ni Houlihan* as an unassailable assertion of his credentials as national playwright. Even the moralizing Hugh Kennedy admitted in his diary that he found this play 'always delightful'.[19] But this iconic 1902 work, proclaiming the need to sacrifice home, family, love and life itself to redeem Ireland's national soul, was in many ways a late flowering of the 1798 drama pioneered by O'Grady and Whitbread. It was also at least as much Gregory's child as Yeats's. For all its hallowed status, it was in nearly every way atypical of the Abbey's work. Rosamond Jacob significantly found it 'miles above Yeats's ordinary level' when she saw a revival in 1909.[20] The symbolic politics in Yeats's own *Countess Cathleen* in 1899 might seem almost as powerful, considering that the central character is a great lady who offers to give up her eternal soul as a sacrifice to save her people. But in that play the enemies of the starving Irish peasantry are neither English oppressors nor local landlords, but satanic soul-gatherers and bourgeois materialists; it summons up Wagner rather than Thomas Davis, and one can only regret that it never became a fully fledged opera (though the effort was made). In the early days of Yeats and Gregory's enterprise, Arthur Griffith's radical press devoted many approving columns to the theatre, before he repudiated the Abbey and all its works in 1903.[21]

The *United Irishman* also ran playwriting contests, and its first drama critic, Frank Fay, became a key figure in the Abbey as actor and adviser – as did his brother William. From a lower-middle-class Dublin background (his father was a government clerk), Frank went to Belvedere College and then became an accountant, but was obsessed with the theatre from his youth. Frank was at this stage of his career a highly political animal, denouncing parasitic 'West Britonism' in Irish culture. His expansive early ideal was a nationally conscious theatre, infusing enthusiasm and political vigour into its audiences, preaching anti-commercialism and anti-capitalism, ideally through the Irish language. But this uncompromising approach would be diluted with time, and exposure to the Abbey's more rarefied atmosphere. As early as the controversy over Synge's 1903 play, Fay's career was set on a path which exactly countered Griffith's. It is not surprising that he was disappointed, nor that he changed his priorities; but others would continue to keep the faith.

After giving up hope of the Abbey's national credentials, the *United Irishman* remained preoccupied with the potential of drama: it made a feature of printing the text of new plays, the majority having nothing to do with the Abbey (an exception was Yeats's Nietzschean *Where There is Nothing*, rapidly put in print in order to retrieve the project from his enemy George Moore). Griffith also published Frederick Ryan's substantial slice of realism about local politics and corruption, *The Laying of the Foundations*. By contrast, many of the plays publicized by the *United Irishman* were pietistic exercises, 'fragrant of holy water and mouldy costumes';[22] others were direct exhortations to political action, such as Maud Gonne's *Dawn* (29 October 1904), a static and didactic piece about eviction, emigration and redemption through resistance.[23] Gonne declared in the *United Irishman* that national drama had to be written for, and comprehensible to, 'the people', not an over-educated elite. But since such plays sustained most of their existence on the printed page rather than on the boards of a theatre, it might be asked how far theatre could be a vehicle for plays whose dramatic effect was sacrificed to propagandist priorities. They certainly had no place in Annie Horniman's vision, after she paid for the new Abbey Theatre formally established in 1904. The story of Horniman and Irish theatre could make a Shavian drama in itself, pulsing with the manipulations of possessive love and the economics of indebtedness. As she saw it, Yeats (for whom she nourished a devouring but unrequited passion) was to be her Wagner or Goethe, rather than a D'Annunzio, and Dublin was to become a Bayreuth or Weimar – certainly not the capital of a new and independent nation. In the end she drew the same conclusion as Arthur Griffith, but for opposite reasons: the words 'Irish' and 'national' were irrelevant to Abbey productions.

Yeats would have disagreed, but his interpretation of these loaded terms was very different from Griffith's. By the autumn of 1905 he was determined 'to put an end to democracy in the theatre', which damped down the nationalist politics which had been an essential part of the original players' ethos. The young actors who came in with the Fay brothers epitomized 'the solidarity and intensity of a sect, and the high spirits of a social club'; they were at once 'a nest of families, a workshop of amateurs, a cell of political revolutionaries'.[24] Some would be seduced, suborned or cowed by the excitement of the early Abbey years – the tours in England and Scotland, Yeats's glamour, Gregory's 'terrible eye' (as Arthur Symons put it). Others would transfer their thespian energies into more directly political theatre.

Not that the Abbey was devoid of political content: in pace with her own developing nationalism, Gregory's allegorical history plays such as *Kincora* (1905) and *Dervorgilla* (1907) carried a distinct political message about the corruption of English domination, and the need to recapture and nurture a Gaelic independence. Though Arthur Griffith was no friend to Gregory, whose Ascendancy *hauteur* never left her, these stories of the mythic background to Ireland's oppression by a foreign power, involving betrayal and collaboration, suggested clear parallels with Sinn Féin's call for psychological as well as political autonomy. This is especially true of *Dervorgilla*, where the eponymous Irish princess responsible for inviting the Normans to invade Ireland lives out a lonely old age in fear of exposure. A decade later, after the 1916 Rising, Yeats's plays *The King's Threshold* (rewritten from its original form) and *The Dreaming of the Bones* (1919) also preached political independence and challenged authority. *The King's Threshold* highlighted the theme of self-starvation in a political cause, and *The Dreaming of the Bones* linked Dervorgilla's adultery and betrayal (again) with the story of a present-day revolutionary on the run. The Abbey also kept its lines open to more radical operators such as Thomas MacDonagh and Constance Markievicz, and in 1920 would put on Terence MacSwiney's *The Revolutionist* when he was dying on hunger-strike.

But this was when everything had changed utterly. In the pre-revolutionary period, the disillusionment of radical nationalists can be traced in the columns of D. P. Moran's paper the *Leader* and Arthur Griffith's *United Irishman* and *Sinn Féin*, which puffed Markievicz's Theatre of Ireland constantly while labelling the Abbey a 'plague house'.[25] Alice Milligan, more impressive as a pioneer of nationalist *tableaux vivants* than as a literary critic, tried to make the case for the Abbey's political potential in 1906: '*Kathleen ni Houlihan* [*sic*] is worth an infinity of such volumes as *The Wind Among the Reeds* and in *Countess Cathleen* the tragedy of the famine era finds ample expression.'[26] But, by then, battle lines had been drawn and a general antipathy towards the enterprise of Yeats and Gregory pervaded the private reflections of the revolutionaries.[27] They attended the Abbey almost religiously, as the diaries of young nationalists like Diarmuid Coffey and Rosamond Jacob show. But for a political illumination they looked elsewhere.

III

Many involved in the early Abbey enterprise had been drawn into the world of political theatre through the dramatic presentations – part tableau, part magic-lantern show, part didactic narration – staged by Alice Milligan for various cultural organizations around the *fin de siècle*. Her 'living pictures' were projected through the Gaelic League, which appointed her as travelling lecturer in 1904. They were also adopted by organizations such as Maud Gonne's Inghinidhe na hÉireann and educational institutions with a penchant for nationalist propaganda. The productions travelled to England, and a Milligan pageant at the Liverpool Gaelic League inspired the youthful Piaras Béaslaí with the possibilities of dramatic propaganda.[28] The diminutive and indefatigable Milligan had already made her mark by editing the nationalist journal *Shan Van Vocht*, along with Anna Johnston, and her literary output continued unabated, as will be seen in a later chapter. However, static pageant-plays such as *The Wearing of the Green* (1898), *The Last Feast of the Fianna* (1899) and *The Deliverance of Red Hugh* (1901) never transcended the limitations of the genre; 'tawdry' was the damning verdict of Augusta Gregory on *The Last Feast*, though it was played by the Irish Literary Theatre as well as the Theatre of Ireland.

But Milligan never spurned a cliché. Themes from Irish history (heroic legends derived from Standish O'Grady, the wars of the Gael and the Gall, seventeenth-century confrontations, the heroics of 1798) were recycled and presented with maximum pietistic uplift. And she was not out to impress Lady Gregory. Milligan's impact and influence was felt not in the little theatres of radical Dublin but in community theatre, Christian Brothers schools and local groups. Her dramatic interventions affected young nationalist activists in the provinces: celebrating amateur theatre at local level and in rural districts, they also popularized instructions for do-it-yourself Irish drama in undemanding but widely read journals such as *Ireland's Own* and the *Irish Weekly Freeman*. Ancient Irish chariots could be made out of rocking-chairs, Gaelic crosses out of bits of brown paper, royal costumes out of scraps of tapestry; she directed her readers to shops where Ristona lustre paint and gold tissue gauze could be obtained. Her correspondence suggests the range of interests aroused, but also the determinedly unsophisticated nature of the productions involved. Milligan's conviction that plays should be constructed from 'ancient, historical and legendary themes' was buttressed by the belief that in the 'fortunate era' of olden times, 'all garments, including those of royalty, were home-made.'[29] So, in a sense, were the plays.

Back in the metropolis, if the Abbey had become the Established Church by 1905, what were the dissident congregations? They made up a network of little companies, sometimes overlapping each other. The Theatre of Ireland was staffed by refugees from the Abbey as well as by Constance and Casimir Markievicz, Helena Molony and other radical Sinn Féiners; Padraic Colum was their best playwright. Though disaffected with the Abbey, they still occasionally used their premises; that was where they produced Thomas MacDonagh's *When the Dawn is Come* in 1908. They overlapped with Casimir Markievicz's Independent Theatre Company from 1908 to 1912. Both enterprises were contemptuously attacked by Yeats in *Samhain*, the Independent Theatre Society for having shown 'little sign of work or purpose' and the Theatre of Ireland for exposing Markievicz's 'struggles with a strange language and strange circumstances'.[30] This was a low blow at Markievicz, a large, bear-like Pole whom Constance Gore-Booth had met at art school in Paris and subsequently married, returning to Dublin with him in 1903. Like his wife, Markievicz was a natural Bohemian in the process of rejecting an upper-class landed background, though at first they both frequented Dublin Castle circles as well as those of the artistic avant-garde. A writer as well as a painter, he became a fixture on the Irish artistic scene in the early years of the new century, and a heavy-drinking and combative member of the Arts Club. Drama would replace painting in his life, and he later worked in theatre circles in Kiev, Moscow and Warsaw.

Markievicz and his wife contributed a gamey flavour to theatrical society in Edwardian Dublin. Rosamond Jacob ventured up from her respectable Quaker home in Waterford to stay with Constance Markievicz and Helena Molony in their Mount Street flat in July 1911. They had moved there after an unsuccessful period trying to run a commune involving 'Fianna Éireann', an unruly troop of nationalist boy scouts founded and organized by Constance. This had required taking up residence, along with an agricultural expert who was to teach them co-operative farming, in a large North Dublin house called Belcamp Park, inspired by John Vandeleur's early-nineteenth-century socialist colony at Ralahine. (Bulmer Hobson had lent the Countess a book about it.) After its predictable failure, both Markieviczes were back in Central Dublin, and much involved in theatrical rather than economic experiments. Jacob was fascinated by the Bohemian atmosphere: no carpets, lovely oil sketches by both Markieviczes leaning negligently against the walls, an old skull beside a bronze bust of the nationalist martyr Robert Emmet on a table, portraits of patriots tacked up beside Russian icons, meals eaten casually in the kitchen. 'As for the Countess, she is a good deal what I expected, very lively and talkative and intense – very intense – and with a very tony accent which I suppose she can't help. She is tall and very slight with pretty thick brown hair and rather a pretty, finely cut, pink and white face, but it's too thin. She had on rather a narrow high-waisted grey linen dress and very swagger shoes, and she says damn and My God every now and then.'[31] Theatrical in everything, Constance subsequently appeared at breakfast in a white alpaca knee-length coat worn over bright pink stockings and high-heeled shoes. Later Jacob would spot the Count drunk and excitable at a Dublin party, singing seditious songs in a strong Polish accent and unable to swear fluently in English.[32]

But he had a serious side too. After acting in various comedies and charity performances, Markiewicz set up the Independent Dramatic

Company in 1908 as a professional venture, changing its name to the Independent Theatre Company in 1911. His first Irish plays feature clumsy social comedy and obscure allegory – 'thesis-dramas with no revelation of the thesis', according to one harsh reviewer.[33] But by 1907 the Markieviczes were involved with Theatre of Ireland people – seceders from the Abbey such as Máire nic Shiubhlaigh, a radical nationalist who had been a founding member of Inghinidhe na hÉireann, and the poet–playwright Séumas O'Kelly. From 1908, in keeping with his wife's increasingly radical stance, Markievicz's plays veered into nationalist politics – notably *The Memory of the Dead*, put on by his Independent Dramatic Company both at the Abbey and at the Gaiety in 1910 and probably a collaborative work by both Markieviczes. The themes of heroic patriotism suggest a throwback to the late-nineteenth-century fare at the Queen's Theatre. Set in Sligo and Mayo during the 1798 Rising, it deals with two rebels (one cautious, one hot-headed) in love with the same girl. Unlike in *Cathleen ni Houlihan* (where a bridegroom prefers to fight for Ireland rather than consummate his marriage), a wedding does take place, to mislead the authorities about the planned Rising. The husband disappears and is suspected of betraying the rebels, but is revealed as a hero after his return in disguise and noble death. His child is consecrated to set Ireland free, as the curtain falls.[34] The cast included, besides Constance Markievicz, future revolutionaries such as the young Fenian doctor Patrick McCartan and the charismatic Seán Connolly, who would later join the Abbey, and die on the roof of the City Hall during the 1916 Rising. Delia Cahill, reviewing the play from a nationalist and feminist perspective, declared her relief at seeing 'a man shouldering a pike, to go out to fight the English, and to see a woman send him. We want more plays of that style in Ireland of today – rousing, Nationalist plays. Art, not for art's sake, but for Ireland's.'[35]

Appearing in *Sinn Féin*, this was preaching to the converted. Less indulgently, the breakaway groups, whose productions were often amateurish as well as declamatory, were vulnerable to the particularly violent and moralizing tone of Dublin's theatre critics, such as W. J. Lawrence of the *Evening Telegraph* and 'Jacques' (J. J. Ryce) of the *Evening Herald* and *Irish Independent*. Nothing daunted, Markievicz was also involved in the Dublin Repertory Theatre, with Evelyn

Ashley, from 1913 to 1914: their ambition was for more commercial work, but a bitter split developed between Ashley and the Markieviczes over Constance's involvement in labour politics.[36] Small dramatic companies continued to form and split like amoebae in the years up to the First World War; there were also several amateur companies centred on colleges and societies, as well as Delia Larkin's Irish Workers' Dramatic Society, attempting to put on didactic plays with social themes from 1912. *Sinn Féin*'s reference to 'the dramatic life that is surging all around' Dublin was well founded.[37]

As the Markieviczes demonstrate, those active in this world were often also involved in radical political agitation – even if their repertoire did not always reflect their political preoccupations. Patrick Pearse's brother Willie started up yet another company, the Leinster Stage Society, in 1910, but the plays mounted there tended to concern – as the *Irish Times* mordantly put it – 'our old friends the fairies, who seem to have fallen on evil days since the introduction of railway trains'.[38] Regarding political content, the briefly active Cumann na nGaedheal Theatre Company is more relevant, arising as it did directly from Arthur Griffith's line-up of political societies that morphed into Sinn Féin; it soon merged with the National Players Society, which was recruited from the Keating branch of the Gaelic League, an organization notoriously infiltrated by the IRB. Their repertoire, often played in the Molesworth Hall, tended to revolve around Irish translations and lumpen historical pageant-dramas by the relentless Alice Milligan. Arthur Griffith loyally puffed their productions: 'The members of Cumann na nGaedheal Theatre Company are putting their best into [their repertoire] and not alone will there be given a due interpretation of their artistic merits, but the political and social lessons will receive an additional emphasis from the enthusiasm, wholehearted and sincere, of the actors.'[39] This was not enough: the dedicated playgoer Joseph Holloway confided sadly to his diary in September 1906, 'they seem to become worse and worse each time I see them.'[40]

But the company certainly acted as a forum for political ideas and discussion. So did the Theatre of Ireland, which reconstituted itself as Na Cluicheoirí or Cluithcheoirí na hÉireann ('Ireland's Players') in order to appear at the annual Oireachteas of the Gaelic League. This suggests that they could strike an Irish-Irelander note, though their membership represented a broader church than that.[41] Their great 1909 success, Séumas O'Kelly's *The Shuiler's Child*, deals with the adoption of a child whose mother is a workhouse inmate, and its message is socialist and feminist rather than nationalist. Máire Nic Shiubhlaigh produced a legendary and harrowing performance, and her success provided a useful stick to beat the Abbey with, but *The Shuiler's Child* was not emblematic of the kind of political theatre which the revolutionaries were seeking to mount, which perhaps accounted for the play's success. The same is essentially true of the best productions which the Theatre of Ireland produced, which tended to be Ibsenite problem-plays addressing the domestic oppression of creative spirits. Ibsen's pervasive influence is also evident in Ryan's *Laying of the Foundations*, which combines a socialist message with a plot reminiscent of *An Enemy of the People*. Yeats liked it, despite declaring at just this time that 'the reign of the moralist is the reign of the mob' – the beginning of his onslaught on propagandist art which would be responded to by the revolutionary generation with reviews like Delia Cahill's, quoted above.[42] The trouble was that the political plays mounted by the radicals were manifestly unsuccessful with audiences. Thomas MacDonagh's *When the Dawn is Come* is a good example.

MacDonagh was a soulful and intense young teacher; he had first worked at St Kieran's College, Kilkenny, where he experienced a Damascene conversion to nationalism via the Gaelic League, before moving to the more congenial St Colman's College, Fermoy. By 1908 he had written a great deal of bad poetry and moved from conventional Catholic faith to a kind of Neoplatonic mysticism; he had also moved to Dublin and was teaching with Patrick Pearse at the experimental and radically nationalist school St Enda's, which he helped to found. And he had his sights set on becoming a playwright. The title of his first produced play suggests a nationalist allegory in the mode of *Cathleen ni Houlihan* – or, indeed, Maud Gonne's *Dawn*. But *When the Dawn is Come* is an allegory about compromise, betrayal and foreign rule, set in the near future; MacDonagh began writing it in 1907 and it may have been inspired by discussions over the Irish Councils Bill of that year, whereby radical nationalists thought that the Liberals were trying to buy off the Home Rule demand. The Abbey rather unwillingly co-operated in the production (Synge apparently helped with its construction and Yeats was persuaded to accept it, against his will). At the climax of the play a redeemed deliverer dies, having taken up arms against the invader, liberating his nation. The critical reaction was uncertain, a confusion which must have also affected the playwright. When the play ended, Douglas Hyde, in the audience, abused the play to everyone around him and then loudly called for the 'author', who appeared to applause. When Hyde was asked why he had done so, he said, 'because I had never seen him and wanted to see what he looked like'.[43] Unsurprisingly, one of the very few positive reviews appeared in the journal published by Patrick Pearse's school. *An Macaomh* recorded that the boys who saw it went home 'yearning for rifles'.[44]

MacDonagh's attempts to produce a more effective revised version, called 'The Victor', seem to have fizzled out. However, he migrated up the academic scale, and in 1911 was appointed Assistant Lecturer at the National University. By 1914 he was once more immersed in theatrical ambitions. This was the year that yet another combination of players emerged, the Irish Theatre Company – bankrolled by the irrepressible Edward Martyn, a survivor from the Irish Literary Theatre of 1899–1902, where so much had begun. He worked uneasily with MacDonagh, his brother John, and the excitable and theatrical young poet Joseph Plunkett – whose wealthy mother owned the Hardwicke Street Hall in which they produced their experimental plays.[45] This ramshackle theatre in a run-down street north of the Liffey was a kind of playground for the headstrong Plunkett children. Domestic life among the Plunketts resembled a dystopian version of the unconventional family sagas being written by E. Nesbit in England at this time. Joseph, Geraldine, George, Jack and Mimi Plunkett, freed from their erratic education and at odds with their dictatorial mother and ineffectual father, used the family's far-flung property empire to further their own subversive enterprises. One instance was the farm-building complex at Larkfield in the Dublin suburbs, which they ran as a mixture of commune, training-camp and bomb factory, and another was the theatre. For Hardwicke Street, Countess Plunkett provided velvet curtains, a rebuilt stage, various props and much of the production costs, though 'her idea of a really good play was Town-ley's eighteenth-century farce *High Life Below Stairs*'.[46] The enterprise was, like everything to do with the Plunketts, riven by violent rows and family stand-offs. Her children were more inspired by the Moscow Arts Theatre: *Uncle Vanya* and *The Cherry Orchard* were part of the repertoire as well as *Pillars of Society* and *An Enemy of the People*.

MacDonagh had by now written a short fantastic comedy about the transmigration of souls, called *Metempsychosis*, published in the *Irish Review* (which he co-founded) in 1912. Briefly and unsuccessfully staged by the Theatre of Ireland in the new Hardwicke Street Theatre later that year, it is spectacularly unpolitical, except insofar as it seems to parody the beliefs of Yeats and AE (George Russell). Mac-Donagh's last play, *Pagans*, was more accomplished, and exemplified the kind of modern European drama which the Irish Theatre Company wanted to project through the new premises: an Ibsenite treatment of unfulfilled marriage played against a starkly modernist backdrop. Significantly, the play then veers into nationalist politics, with the hero unexpectedly joining a revolt against British rule. In the context of the time, this gesture reads like an *acte gratuit*; four years later it would look very different.

MacDonagh wanted to lure Frank Fay, England-based since his quarrel with Yeats, back to Ireland and the new theatre. He failed, but the correspondence with Fay shows that MacDonagh envisaged a young, radical, experimental dramatic co-operative, using Martyn's money but avoiding putting on the patron's own plays; he and Plunkett were at one in this. They had, however, to accommodate Martyn's inclination towards a clumsy variety of satirical fantasy, such as *The Dream Physician*, which incorporated thinly disguised portraits of George Moore, Yeats, Shane Leslie and James Joyce. (Radical playwrights were united by a dislike of Yeats and a wish to ridicule him before sympathetic Dublin audiences.) It was easier to agree with Martyn that Chekhov (new to Dublin), Maeterlinck and Ibsen should also be part of the fare. So was *The Dance of Osiris*, a mystical essay in Egyptology by Plunkett 'to try out some Gordon Craig ideas on a small scale'.[47] Hardwicke Street would also eventually put on the first plays by yet another clever young man in revolt against his solidly middle-class Dublin background, Eimar O'Duffy – who later ungratefully satirized the enterprise as 'the Eclectic Theatre Company' in his novel *Printer's Errors*. This was the kind of thing that made O'Duffy unpopular, but it reflects the incestuous and mutually critical nature of Dublin theatrical life.

But Hardwicke Street also provided a stimulating forum for Mac-Donagh's and O'Duffy's experiments – which included the latter's *Walls of Athens* (1915), directed by Plunkett and using ancient Greece as a metaphor for destroying the union between Ireland and Britain. In the same year O'Duffy also wrote an absurdist fable called *The Phoenix on the Roof*. This dealt with the arrival of an extraordinary revelation to an unbelieving bourgeois family in present-day Dublin, when a miraculous bird nests above their house. Diarmuid Coffey found it 'very badly acted ... might be good but I didn't think so'.[48] However, the idea of a mythical destiny being reborn in fire would look distinctly prophetic within a very few months.

IV

Outside Dublin, radical and experimental drama fulfilled a similar function in Cork and Belfast. Cork, a port city with strong connections to the British Army and the British Empire, had an established tradition of conventional drama and music-hall, vividly recaptured in the autobiography of the writer Sean O'Faolain. Living on Half Moon Street near the Cork Opera House, O'Faolain's mother (the wife of a policeman) took in theatrical 'artistes' as lodgers during the early years of the century, creating a rich cast of characters to people her son's budding imagination. Looking back, O'Faolain realized that the melodramas and romances which brought these people to Cork represented 'the English theatre at its lowest ebb since about 1699'. 'Plays and actors, good or bad, they introduced me to art and to England, they made London my capital, they inflamed my imagination and fanned my senses, they doped me and benzedrined me; I was their willing Trilby, a name that names them and their age, Edwardian in all its blissful somnambulism.'[49] What woke him up, appropriately, was a play by Lennox Robinson, who had himself been galvanized by the Abbey Players' visit to Cork a decade or so before. In December

1915 Robinson's play *Patriots* was produced at the Cork Opera House, and O'Faolain found himself seeing recognizable Irish country people on stage, speaking an authentic language of Fenian memories and contemporary political frustrations; the shock of recognition was profound and played a strong part in making him a writer. It also helped make him a 'rebel'.[50]

O'Faolain was just fifteen then, and did not realize that, outside the precincts of the Opera House, Cork had been experiencing its own theatrical revolution over the previous decade. The Cork Dramatic Society was less eclectic than the Theatre of Ireland or the Hardwicke Street Theatre, partly because it was dominated by the personalities of Daniel Corkery and Terence MacSwiney. But it too displayed a strong interest in Chekhov and Ibsen, both of whom influenced the work of Corkery – a gloomy, frustrated schoolteacher, whose impressive 1917 novel about the limitations of provincial life, *The Threshold of Quiet*, took as its epigraph Thoreau's dictum that 'the mass of men lead lives of quiet desperation'. Corkery, a devout cultural nationalist, believed profoundly in the power of drama, and was a moving spirit in the formation of a nationalist drama group in Cork in 1908, along with the zealous Terence MacSwiney and the indefatigable joiner and organizer Liam de Róiste – both in their twenties and both frustrated by the intimate enmities of Cork nationalist politics.[51]

The slightly older Corkery, unmarried and austere, was a guru to younger men; his circle of acolytes would later include the writer Frank O'Connor and O'Faolain himself. Besides writing his own plays, he produced swingeing dramatic criticism for the *Leader*. Corkery was interested in abstract and simplified stagings, such as Yeats was experimenting with at the Abbey; the emblem of the Cork Dramatic Society – a mythological Irish warrior leaning forward in dramatic pose – strongly evoked the famous Abbey logo of a woman and hound. In Corkery's opinion (as in Yeats's) the new Dramatic Society should put on 'original work and translations from such languages as French, German, etc.', but not all of his colleagues agreed, and during its five-year life the Cork Dramatic Society restricted itself to plays specially written for it.[52] De Róiste wrote a number of plays with titles such as *The Road to Hell: A Realistic Drama of Irish City Life* (1908). This was a teetotal manifesto postulating that 'the drunk army is the army that really keeps our nation enslaved'; unsurprisingly it did not reach production. Nor did his Pearsean symbolic drama, *Fodhla*, where a dying Irish queen has to be saved from 'the Gall' (foreigners). De Róiste later decided that his plays were 'really an expression of ideas that might have been better in other form'.[53] This may have been true of several of the Cork Dramatic Society's productions, but they filled a recognized need.

The membership numbered teachers, shop assistants, clerks and a few medical students; they all seem to have been men. What brought them together in An Dún, the Gaelic League Hall in Queen Street, Corkery later recalled, was a desire 'to see the life of the nation, of our own people, made vivid on the stage'; he sent his colleagues long, thoughtful letters analysing their work and advising them to emulate Molière.[54] His own most successful play, *The Embers* (1909), deals with the compromises of Irish politics, the decadence of ideals and the latent power of old-style Fenian idealism to radicalize the youth of today. 'A country without fools is a country without heroes,' declares the new recruit as the curtain falls on the death of his republican mentor. 'I'll be timid no more – look, I kneel at your feet. I'll set my soul on fire kissing your cold hand.'[55] Corkery also tackled labour politics in a hard-hitting 'slum play' about a strike called *The Labour Leader*, which provides a wordy but powerful delineation of early-twentieth-century Cork, as well as a Nietzschean argument for the liberating force of violence; it migrated to the Abbey. In more sardonic mode, he wrote a short play called *The Epilogue* (1911), dealing with the failure of a dramatic society. 'Neither critics nor audience understood it,' according to the *Cork Tatler*, but he knew what he was writing about; performances at An Dún never ran for more than two or three nights, audiences peaked at fifty or sixty, and receipts for a production never exceeded £9.00.[56] But the experience would be formative for a far more famous revolutionary than Corkery.

This was the 29-year-old Terence MacSwiney, the other dominating personality in the Cork Dramatic Society, and a more forceful and political animal than Corkery. MacSwiney was the only member at the first meeting to put 'B.A.' after his name, a designation that mattered to him and was hard won. As we have seen, he was an autodidactic, obsessive, introspective youth, from a family who had come down in the world; there was an absent father, a martyred mother and powerful sisters. After the Christian Brothers he educated himself through night-school, held down a job as a clerk and taught 'business methods' at Cork Municipal School of Commerce (full time from 1912). Incapable of relaxing or taking a holiday, and sleeping very little (often arising at 2 a.m. to write, and then going to 7 a.m. Mass), he poured out his soul into immense diaries. Here he analysed his intellectual opinions, his wish to make his name in the world outside Cork and the state of his soul. Histrionic, frustrated and ambitious, he resembled a character drawn by Corkery, who indeed used him as inspiration for several (including the young Daly in *The Embers* – the son of a parliamentarian, obsessed with bringing idealism back into Irish politics and reversing the present decadence). Like his sisters Mary and Annie, Terence was both a convinced physical-force nationalist and a devout Catholic, preoccupied by the corruption and materialism emanating from England like a poisonous miasma. MacSwiney wrote screeds of pious and fervent poetry, uniformly derivative and repetitive; he also produced a number of plays for the Cork Dramatic Society.

The rule of the Society was that no writer could act in his own play, which was no hardship to MacSwiney; Corkery described him as uninterested in direction or scenery, and incapable of acting, but preoccupied with learning the craft of playwriting: though he refused to submit work to the Abbey on principle. ('I would not agree for example to put my work before the English public and seek English criticism and support as the Abbey people do.'[57]) MacSwiney was preoccupied by the need to rediscover (or invent) a native style of Irish drama, and even of Irish opera, uninfected by English influence – a subject which brought out his most sententious and humourless side.[58] (Italian and German influences were acceptable, which explains why he thought there was a possibility of operatic developments.) He wrote blank-verse historical pastiches such as *The Last Warriors of Coole*; a prosy and sentimental drama about childlessness and domestic violence called 'The Eternal Longing'; a lengthy dialogue discussing political expediency versus republican purism called *The Breamers*; and a more successful political play called *The Holocaust*, which fiercely denounced Irish political lethargy.[59] Writing shortly after

MacSwiney's death on hunger-strike in 1920, and thus with a certain hindsight, Corkery recalled that the martyr's comrades knew that he belonged with 'the great ones of history and literature; of late years we never had any doubts that he would die tragically, nor that the end would crown his life'. More interestingly he compared him to Ibsen's Brand in his energetic, obsessive, driven nature, 'tortured by his desires'. MacSwiney revered Ibsen and possessed a full set of his plays. 'Synge he did not like,' added Corkery, 'but then Synge's outlook on life and his own were frankly opposite.' In Corkery's words, 'He was right, he knew it; he had the key of things; there were waverers every-where, but they could be gathered in, straightened up and set marching – they could even be taught how to die.'[60]

This was the message MacSwiney preached in *The Holocaust*, and also in his later play, a five-act polemic called *The Revolutionist*. The dramatic instructions read: 'Time, contemporary; certain political reforms are assumed.' But if these reforms amount to Home Rule, the play's protagonist, Hugh O'Neill, is clear that it is only 'partial'; he preaches the necessity of 'friction' and denounces compromise and reconciliation. As a revolutionary purist, he also despises conspiracy and secret societies; the implicit message is that the representatives of the Fenian tradition have been corrupted by evasiveness and bragga-docio. In reaction to them, an uncompromising younger generation asserts itself against the collaborationism and hypocrisy of their elders. 'If we go violently against them,' says one of the older gener-ation, 'they will prevail in the end. They have youth on their side. What they say now will be said in Ireland when we are in the grave.'[61] The hero, an idealized portrait of MacSwiney himself, sacrifices love, health and eventually life to the pure ideal. The Ibsenite theme of the charismatic purist set against a world of conventional compromise recurs again and again in Irish political theatre. MacSwiney would reprise it in real life and his greatest dramatic success would be post-humous, created by the theatrical spectacle of his own public death.

The other chief centre of radical dramatic activity outside Dublin was Belfast – where drama was intrinsically political, and a visit to the theatre often meant taking part in rows among the audience, as they declared their adherence or opposition to the presumed political mes-sage being played out on stage.[62] In the attempt to make the theatre a forum for more progressive activity, the key figure was the idealistic and energetic young Quaker Bulmer Hobson, brimming with ideas in this sphere as in others. Hobson was inspired in 1902 to try to do for his native city what the Irish Literary Theatre had done for Dublin – though he was irritated when Yeats's response to his request to play *Cathleen ni Houlihan* in Belfast was distinctly unencouraging. Viewing matters from distant Belfast, Hobson did not realize that the Irish Literary Theatre was coming to the end of its life, to be replaced by the Irish National Theatre Society and eventually the Abbey. However, his charm, enthusiasm and gusto carried him far. On his visit to Dublin the youthful impresario stayed with Maud Gonne (who interceded on his behalf), met the actors associated with the new movement and returned to Belfast enthused with the potential of drama to bridge old divides and inspire new commitments. Hobson's original wish was to set up a Belfast branch of the Irish Literary Theatre, but, after another disagreement with the Dublin management about playing AE's *Deirdre*, they reconstituted themselves as a separate entity: the Ulster Literary Theatre.

Hobson, as a fervent nationalist and Irish-Irelander, wanted to provide an art theatre for the Belfast *lumpenbourgeoisie*, but he also wanted to sound a political rallying-call; the Ulster Literary Theatre was very much part of the initiative which set up the nationalist Dungannon clubs around the same time, and was rooted in the dramatic and cultural events around the 1898 commemoration of the United Irishmen's rebellion against British rule in 1798. This drew in energetic and *simpatico* young Northerners like Denis McCullough and Patrick McCartan. Hobson precociously founded a 'Protestant National Association' in that year, and was deeply influenced by Alice Milligan's nationalist history-pageants, mounting *tableaux vivants* in his Ulster Debating Club while still in his teens.[63] As with Milligan a few years before, Hobson's Ulster Protestant background made his conversion to nationalism a matter of almost religious translation; her dawning realization of a new faith, reflected in her diary when studying in Dublin from 1891 to 1893, was an important precedent for Hobson. Like her, he sustained an ambition to spread the word within his native province, using an idealized version of its history in the 1798 Rising to make the point. Milligan's experience in magic-lantern and photography techniques had already pioneered the presentation of pious theatrical pageants, following her initiative in popular nationalist journalism; Hobson looked to a more intellectual enterprise.

And the time seemed ripe. The emergence of a specifically Ulster Theatre came at a moment when various regional movements were attempting to challenge the predominance of Orange and unionist identifications among the province's Protestant majority and to replace it with a new, inclusive nationalism. This was the great hope of Hobson and his Ulster Catholic contemporaries McCartan and McCullough, and a message constantly preached by Hobson in the *Nationist* around 1905, as well as in many Dungannon Club meetings faithfully reported by *Sinn Féin*.[64] 1898 had galvanized memories of the imagined Protestant nationalism of 1798, mediated energetically by Alice Milligan through her editorship of the *Shan Van Vocht* and her own plays and windy sub-Fergusonian poetry; Thomas MacDonagh fancifully judged her in 1909 as 'the most Irish of living poets and therefore the best'. As the more ironic and detached Padraic Colum pointed out, Milligan's historical world-view managed to eliminate all the obstacles between her own Protestant tradition and Gaelic Ulster – 'no Plantation, no John Knox, no industrial Belfast'.[65] Paradoxically, some of the Ulster Literary Theatre's most resonant successes, by Gerald MacNamara, would later revolve around satirical treatments of these very themes. But this was a far cry from the romantic nationalist agenda preached by Hobson and friends in the early 1900s.

This was summed up by Hobson's own play *Brian of Banba*, published (like so many didactic national dramas) in the *United Irishman* on 2 August 1902. An allegory of noble resistance against a Saxon invader, its first performance inaugurated the new theatrical company in early December 1904, along with *The Reformers* by 'Lewis Purcell' (the *nom de plume* of Hobson's ULT colleague David Parkhill).[66] In contrast with Hobson's Milliganite fervour, Purcell's play was yet another astringent treatment of local politics, with an Ibsenite tinge. Simultaneously with the first ULT productions, Hobson began to publish *Uladh*, an opinionated literary and dramatic journal which began as a kind of imitation *Samhain*, but soon asserted an

interestingly regional perspective, arguing for both a distinct Northern identity and the breaking down of sectarian barriers. 'We aim,'
declared the first editorial, 'at building a citadel in Ulster for Irish
thought and art achievements such as exists in Dublin ... We shall
have our own way, though the differences will always be within the
generous circle of one nationality, just as local idiom may be, or the
different character of the country and the coast, North, South, East
and West may be, and still be, Irish.'[67]

The question whether these aims were compatible hung uneasily in
the background, as the editor of *Uladh* admitted:

> Frankly, the performances given so far by the Belfast company of play-
> ers have been creditable, but, at the same time, very bad. What do I
> mean?
>
> In order to understand our difficulty it is necessary to remember that
> we live in Belfast, that we are Presbyterian, or that we are Catholic, or
> Episcopal, with a hard layer of Presbyterian crudeness and repression
> upon top of that; and crudeness and repression are not good for the
> stuff out of which actors are to be made.
>
> Where every national impulse has been dried up at its inception, all
> gaiety eyed with suspicion, all good-will withdrawn lest it commit one
> to a little generous feeling, and all forms and ceremonies deemed
> unprofitable and vain, how can the necessary forgetfulness and self-
> abandonment exist that mimicry and pantomime demand?[68]

The Ulster Literary Theatre kept its flag flying, while Hobson happily ricocheted around his various political organizations and
initiatives. His tendency to start up something, and then move on
while it languished in his wake, was becoming evident. Its dramatic
rationale remained emphatically regional, though the players made
odd uneasy sorties out of Belfast.[69] In March 1907 they occupied the
Abbey (still reeling after the riots provoked by Synge's *The Playboy of
the Western World*) and presented new Northern plays to Dublin
audiences. This was accounted a success, and they returned a year
later.[70] They also lost some of their personnel to the more blatantly
nationalist Theatre of Ireland. But the ULT's real success came later,
with Gerald MacNamara's gleeful parodies of revivalist themes and
tropes, such as *The Mist That Does Be on the Bog* (a direct challenge

to the Abbey ethos) and indulgent mockeries of adamantine unionist beliefs, like *Suzanne and the Sovereigns* and *Thompson in Tir-na-nÓg*. Here, hard-nosed Northern values and native wit were used to deflate the warring monoliths of Catholic nationalism and Protestant Orangeism; while the pretensions of misty Gaelic never-never-lands were reduced to farce by tough Ulster scepticism. It was all a long way from Alice Milligan.

More had originally been hoped for by the ULT. In 1905 *Uladh* announced that a real advance was represented by the reception of the Ulster Literary Theatre.

> New forces and strong forces are at work among us, and to those who knew Ulster the applause that greeted *The Reformers* and *Brian of Banba* was redolent of much. Ten years ago, it is odds that the mimic riot in the last act of *The Reformers* would have been followed by a very real riot amongst the spectators; five years ago a manager would not have been surprised to find a body of policemen on duty in the hall to keep the peace; but now the spectacle is cheered by men who, though they still label themselves with the old party designations, have begun to realise that they are Irish in something more than name.[71]

The idea that theatre could perform miracles of reconciliation, and infuse national feeling into a hitherto divided audience, took the idea of 'a mob becoming a people' into new and fantastic realms. But plays such as Lewis Purcell's *The Enthusiast* (1905), focused on farming life and co-operative societies, struck a more sardonic note in dealing with intercommunal tensions in Ulster; the play ends with Protestants retreating to their tribal drums, and suggests a move on the ULT's part from Milliganite propaganda to regional consciousness.[72] Hobson's final defection south to Dublin, where the nationalist living was easier, exacerbated the process; the ULT would continue in a comfortable groove until 1934. It clearly had not created a post-sectarian nationalist avant-garde in Ulster. And Hobson, like his mentor Milligan, remained an Ulster Gaelicist and Fenian who refused to become Catholic, and would be correspondingly alienated from much of the ethos of post-revolutionary Ireland. James Power, writing about the Ulster Literary Theatre in *Uladh* as early as 1905, had forecast as much:

North is North, and South is South, irrevocably, and though the line of demarcation be not so firmly drawn as between the Occident and the Orient it nevertheless demands recognition ... It seems to me that if Ulster be true to its instincts it must necessarily have a somewhat different view from the rest of Ireland. And, at a time when the more genuinely Celtic provinces are casting off the intellectual misfits of generations to clothe themselves in native thought, it is surely unreasonable to ask that the North should continue to cloak its individuality with alien modes of expression.[73]

The story of the ULT, as its few commentators implicitly if unwillingly admit, is essentially about a partition of the mind.

V

People felt differently in Dublin. In 1907 Padraic Colum, currently star playwright for the Theatre of Ireland, wrote to W. G. Fay urging him to bring the Abbey into line with patriotic feeling: 'Be National. Put yourself in the way of that great wave that is certainly breaking across the country. If we are not with it, we will be of no account. I have been living in the country and I feel that Ireland is full of life. We have achieved the nation and the Nation is about to become self-conscious.'[74] The varieties of dramatic experience in pre-revolutionary Ireland reflected the position of theatre in Irish life, and the relation of audience to players in Ireland – a particularly intense conjunction, often with a political edge. George Bernard Shaw, never unduly anxious to compliment his fellow countrymen, nonetheless described the Irish audience as 'the most sensitive and, on provocation, the most turbulent audience in the world'.[75] Yeats's invocation in 1899 of 'an audience uncorrupted and imaginative ... trained to listen by its passion for oratory' was not entirely far from the mark. It is, therefore, significant that Arthur Clery, writing from a Sinn Féin perspective for the Leader in 1903, forecast that the new form of Irish drama would be 'political allegory'.[76] At the same time this reflected some wishful thinking, and the dramatic sensation of that year, Synge's In the Shadow of the Glen, is hard to read as a political allegory; a dissatisfied wife leaving an elderly miser husband for the freedom of the roads with a seductive tramp was not an obvious parallel to Ireland's achieving freedom from British rule. It may, however, be seen as sociological rather than political propaganda, like the first version of Yeats's *The King's Threshold* in the same year, where a poet threatens to starve himself to death as a gesture against philistine royal authority. And the audiences who went to theatres other than the Abbey were certainly conscious that they were often implicated in a political exchange. Sinn Féin itself made an attempt to found its own theatre at the rear of its Harcourt Street premises, hoping thereby to control the direction of radical Irish drama; a Building Fund was organized, but nothing came of it.[77]

The auditorium at the Abbey, or the Plunketts' Hardwicke Street Theatre, or the small halls where the various Irish companies played, were often only half full, but young nationalists attended them regularly and fervently, confiding to their diaries their impressions afterwards, and remaining acutely conscious of the theatrical modes which could be utilized for their own propagandist activities. They were sharply attuned to the 'theatre of revolt' breaking out on stages across Europe;[78] not for nothing was Ibsen such a pervasive presence in the Irish dramatic imagination. Yeats and Synge had attended the Théâtre de l'Œuvre and the Théâtre Libre in 1890s Paris, and the former had come reeling out of Jarry's *Ubu Roi* with a sense that more than one kind of revolution was on the way. And the youthful James Joyce, after attending a performance of Hermann Sudermann's play *Heimat* in Dublin in 1895, had told his parents that its theme was revolution against the world of his elders. 'The subject of the play is genius breaking out in the home and against the home. You needn't have gone to see it. It is going to happen in your own house.'[79]

But themes of public rather than private dissent still monopolized the stage. The ritual and repetitive nature of nationalist resistance (at least as retailed through the traditional Story of Ireland) lent itself readily to theatrical and performative presentation, especially in an era when all plays might be seen – in P. S. O'Hegarty's words – as a revolt against something or other. Moreover, ambitious and politically minded young people were not only desperate to get their plays performed; they were highly conscious of the connection between theatre and propaganda. When Yeats declaimed in *Samhain* against the limitations of a purely political approach, Terence MacSwiney responded with 'The Propagandist Playwright'.[80] He agreed that didactic, humourless patriotic fare with clichéd characters was counter-productive, and called for emotion, truth and passion in drama rather than special pleading. But MacSwiney also denounced the pretensions of an 'art theatre', and called for grand themes and characters 'great in heart and soul', in order to 'give utterance to the Irish revolution'. The inevitable, if implicit, target was his *bête noire*, John Millington Synge.

The controversy over Synge's masterpiece *The Playboy of the Western World* in January 1907 was central to the issue of generational conflict as well as of theatrical politicization in the pre-revolutionary era, though the issues at stake were social, cultural and psychological rather than conventionally political. The idea that Christy Mahon might become admired, celebrated and sexually successful in a rural Connacht community because people believe he has killed his father, and then be repudiated in disgust after old Mahon turns up alive, was electrifying. When the audience rioted on the opening night at Synge's supposed slur on the character of the native Irish, the Abbey management added fuel to the flames by calling in the police to quell the outburst. The *Leader*, when condemning Synge's controversial theme, made an astute point about politically acceptable and unacceptable crime in Ireland.

> In so far as 'crime' is condoned by the Irish people, the attitude of mind is to be explained by plain historical causes. A large amount of the 'crime' of Ireland has been associated with the endeavours of Ireland to combat the tyranny and injustice of England, and the officers and trappings of 'justice' have got inextricably mixed up with English tyranny and injustice in this country. Everybody who knows Ireland from the inside understands this attitude of the mind. Mr Synge comes along, and whether from malice, stupidity, or desire for cheap notoriety, he puts up a common parricide, a man who believes he has committed the awful and unnatural crime of murdering his father, into a position that might be occupied by, say, one who had participated in the rescue of [the Fenian leader] James Stephens, and who was being hunted down

by the police . . . Is not that suggesting that parricide, and a low, sordid order of parricide at that, is a cause of great popularity in Mayo . . . and when an outraged people protest, Mr Synge calls in the police.[81]

In the eyes of Sinn Féin ideologues, who choreographed much of the public protest, the Abbey was now irretrievably tainted: not only because it endorsed a scabrous, cynical and even obscene presentation of the native Irish in the sanctified West, but because it protected itself by calling in the police, representing the mailed fist of British government in Ireland. This outrage almost overwhelmed the issue of the play's content; Yeats and Gregory's theatre, so far from symbolizing a Trojan Horse to infiltrate subversion into the courts of power, now seemed like an outpost of the garrison itself.

This meant that elements within radical nationalism who were not, in principle, hostile to Synge's work had to align themselves against the Abbey on the grounds of its reliance on the coercive powers of the British state. Bulmer Hobson was one prominent example. Himself a prentice playwright, with a realistic apprehension of Irish country life, he probably appreciated Synge's genius. But, since he was currently absorbed in allying his Dungannon clubs to Sinn Féin, he had little choice but to take a high line, though in the end he opted for freedom of expression. Here, as elsewhere, Protestant nationalists probably retained an uneasy memory of Cardinal Logue's attempt to censor *The Countess Cathleen* in the interests of Catholic probity; Yeats certainly did. The organ of the Gaelic League, *An Claidheamh Soluis*, edited by Patrick Pearse, read a stern lesson:

> Whether deliberately or undeliberately [Mr Synge] is using the stage for the propagation of a monstrous gospel of animalism, of revolt against sane and sweet ideals, of bitter contempt for all that is fine and worthy, not merely in Christian morality but in human nature itself . . . The Anglo-Irish dramatic movement has now been in existence for ten years. Its net result has been the spoiling of a noble poet in Mr W. B. Yeats, and the generation of a sort of Evil Spirit in the shape of Mr J. M. Synge . . . It is the beginning of the end.[82]

This was over-optimistic on Pearse's part; within a few years *The Playboy* would be a standard of the Abbey repertoire, though it retained its capacity for shock-value in Irish America. The future was with Synge, though he did not live to see it, dying of Hodgkin's disease at thirty-eight in 1909. Above and beyond the bogey of the police in the theatre and the alleged satanism of the playwright, *The Playboy* might be considered as yet another reflection of Oedipal conflict: the war of the generations of which Joyce had warned his parents. In this sense, the play was political in content as well as in its unintended effect. W. P. Ryan, writing in the *Irish Nation and Peasant* after Synge's death, decided that Synge's 'fantastic demoralization' in *The Playboy* showed that he was really thinking of Irish politics, paralleled in 'that topsy-turvey drama': the 'da-destroying loy [spade]' was about to be wielded against parental authority by the new generation.[83] (Sociological rather than political propaganda, again.)

At the time of its production, three years earlier, critical opinion had been less certain. 'Perhaps it is an allegory,' wrote one journalist, 'and the parricide represents some kind of nation-killer, whom Irishmen and Irishwomen hasten to lionise . . . [But] if it is an allegory it is too obscure for me; I cannot stalk this alligator on the banks of the Liffey.'[84] By 1910, however, the beast was in clearer view. Much more recently, the play has been read as a decolonizing text about psychological liberation. But for contemporary opinion to adopt this interpretation, Christy would have had to kill a policeman, thus aligning himself with what the *Leader* defined as politically acceptable violence. The day for that would come.

VI

Much more directly, *The Playboy* also focused attention on the issue of authenticity and representation. If the portrait of Irish life in the West presented by Synge was unacceptable and inauthentic, the obvious riposte from true Irish nationalists was to show the alternative; and the purest way of representing uncorrupt Irishness was through the Irish language. Several ideologues optimistically decided that the stage was one way of presenting this to the public. One of the Gaelic League's original agendas was to 'restore traditional Irish drama', which rather begged the question of what this tradition was. Early on,

Douglas Hyde mounted little Irish-language plays in the Dublin drawing-rooms and back gardens of sympathetic Gaelic revivalists. These became staples of Gaelic League festivals, along with similar one-acters by Father Peter O'Leary (Peadar Ua Laoghaire) and Father Dinneen; but their amateurism and mediocrity were privately admitted by more ambitious operators, including Patrick Pearse.[85] Enthusiastic reviews in the nationalist press did not disguise the small scale of the enterprise, and the reliance upon audiences already safely converted to the cause. Milligan-style pageants were another staple – moralizing tableaux from Irish history, such as Shane O'Neill kneeling to Queen Elizabeth, or Geoffrey Keating writing his history of Ireland while on the run in the Wicklow glens; or, more pointedly, scenes contrasting exploited emigrants in English slums with contented Irish-Irelander farmers, happy and morally superior at home.

But these presentations did not fulfil the desideratum of a genuine Gaelic drama, which might raise consciousness through the medium of the Irish language itself. Attempts at Irish-language plays were mounted in Belfast, and even London; an optimistic reviewer claimed 'it was quite evident that everyone present could follow the sense with ease, and the fixed attention of the faces showed how strong a propagandist and educative factor the drama can be – it is the old victory of the concrete over the abstract.'[86] Occasionally Gaelic drama even breached the Abbey stage, but, for all Yeats's lofty and vague declarations, the Irish National Theatre Society, despite its name, was not going to risk losing its audiences by exposing them further to the Irish language. Douglas Hyde's *An Tincear agus an tSidheog* (*The Tinker and the Fairy*), produced for the Abbey by Nugent Monck in February 1910, was the first, and the last for another twenty-six years.

Given Hyde's and Pearse's interest in dramatic production, it was logical for the Gaelic League to persist with Irish-language plays, putting productions on at (for instance) the 1901 Pan-Celtic Conference in Dublin and the Galway Feis. In both cases they were guaranteed specific audiences of the converted, and the political message was clear; the Feis also included dramatized pageants representing 'Driving Back the Demon of Anglicization' and 'No Surrender to the GPO' – a reference to the campaign to make the postal services accept letters addressed in Irish.[87] But the effort to propagandize a wider audience was problematic. Drama was usually part of the annual Gaelic League festival, the Oireachteas. The radical-nationalist dissidents in the Theatre of Ireland, always alert to propagandist potential, played their great success *The Shuiler's Child* yet again at the 1913 gathering, along with a play in Irish, *Bairbre Ruadh*, under their alternative banner of Na Cluicheoirí – though the programme thoughtfully provided synopses in English.[88] Earlier, the National Players Society, Gaelicizing themselves as Cumann na hAisteoirí Náisiúnta ('Company of National Actors'), put on an Irish-language version of *Robert Emmet*, written for the 1898 centenary by Henry Connell Mangan in October 1903.

In 1907, the idea of a Gaelic Dramatic Society putting on touring programmes was floated in *The Irish Peasant*, backed by the inevitable (and munificent) Edward Martyn. 'As a means of stimulating an interest in the language among the people of the districts where it is still generally spoken it certainly ought to prove very effective, and besides this, it would bring a much-needed variety and amusement into the undeniably monotonous lives of the hard-working *Gaeilgeoiri* in the country districts.'[89] But the only specifically Irish-language theatrical company to see the light of day was Na hAisteoirí ('The Actors'), established in October 1912. The ubiquitous and deep-pocketed Edward Martyn was yet again involved as Chairman, but the moving spirit was the Manager, Piaras Béaslaí.

Béaslaí, born Percy Beazley to a middle-class Irish immigrant family in Liverpool, was a passionate *Gaeilgeoir* and nationalist who, after years of Gaelic League activity in Britain, had fulfilled his ambition of coming to live in Ireland. As seen earlier, his copious diaries, like those of MacSwiney and de Róiste, record his fervent wish to play a great role in the national story, to strike a blow for freedom, and to drive the usurper from the shores of Inis Fáil; as with his Cork contemporaries, this was expressed in elaborate Victorian rhetoric, which slowly morphed into Irish as he painstakingly learnt the language. Like them too his daily reflections swoop from glorious highs to despairing lows. A rather melodramatic personality, Béaslaí had protested violently and publicly against the *Playboy* and ended up in court, where Yeats testified against him. In Gaelic League circles in England he had pioneered amateur dramatics, and later, working as a Gaelic League organizer and teacher in Cork, he was influential in setting up Na hAisteoirí.

> It is far easier to induce three hundred people to come to a hall and witness a play in Irish than it is to induce three hundred people to purchase and read a book in Irish. Even persons who do not understand a word of Irish can come to a play in that language and criticise the acting; while those large numbers of Irish-speakers who cannot read their own language can only be reached by the medium of drama.[90]

It was also, he reflected in his diary, a useful way of meeting girls.

The strolling players who toured south Munster in the summer of 1914 were all Volunteers, as well as members of the famously politicized Keating branch of the League (when not rehearsing, some of their spare time was spent in rifle practice).[91] Most were teachers or civil servants. Terence MacSwiney helped with lodgings and a venue in Cork; they went on to Macroom, Inchigeela, Ballingeary and Skibbereen, ending in Killarney. As Béaslaí remembered it, they encountered crowded houses and wild enthusiasm everywhere.[92] Béaslaí's papers include touching descriptions of pulling hand-carts of props up mountain roads, travelling by bicycle and donkey-cart, before alighting in some small town or village to produce a play for the delectation of the inhabitants, 'in their own language'. Bookings were arranged through local clergy, and performances took place in village halls, with all the attendant limitations:

> In Inchigeela there was an excellent village hall, but no stage. We contrived to overcome this difficulty. In a field in the neighbourhood there had been some festivities and a platform for dancing had been constructed by stretching planks across empty porter barrels. We transported the planks and barrels to the hall and made a fair enough stage. Then we constructed curtains, fixed up our parlour scene, and finished it by borrowing furniture from the local hotel where we were staying. The inhabitants gazed with amusement as we passed backwards and forwards through the street carrying stage 'flats', chairs, tables and couches.[93]

They also made it to Dublin, borrowing the Abbey stage. Though Béaslaí frequently threatened resignation (as in most of the organizations he joined), it must have been all he ever dreamt of during his apprenticeship in the Bootle Gaelic League. But how effectively it advanced the cause of radical nationalism must be doubted.

The same judgement might be applied to Ernest Blythe's efforts in the Dingle peninsula. Living outside Ventry and trying to perfect his Irish, he started a Dramatic Company among the locals, putting Abbey staples (*Cathleen ni Houlihan* and *The Pot of Broth*) into Irish. The local Christian Brothers school provided a premises and Blythe's Kerry neighbour Desmond FitzGerald reported to Michael O'Rahilly that the impresario was 'very pleased with everything so far'.[94] But the plant did not take root – perhaps fortunately, since he does not seem to have sought permission from the plays' authors.

Far more directly effective Irish-language or bilingual interventions were mediated thorough Patrick Pearse and his experimental school St Enda's. Pearse, a histrionic and charismatic personality, like so many of his generation, was preoccupied by theatre, which played a large part in the activities of his school. From early on, legendary pageants with a national theme were central.[95] The dramatic events at St Enda's, such as a performance of Standish O'Grady's 'The Coming of Fionn' in March 1909, attracted large audiences from the cultural-nationalist *bon ton*: including Yeats, who remembered it all his life.[96] Between 1908 and 1915 five of Pearse's plays were produced at St Enda's, sometimes transferring to central Dublin venues; these tended to be morality-tales revolving round the figure of the 'redemptive boy', but beyond their religious or homoerotic echoes a message of liberation from foreign corruption could be easily detected. They were widely publicized by postcards depicting scenes from the plays, and by advertisements in the nationalist press. *Íosagán*, about the death of a child saint, was played at the Abbey in 1910 and at Hardwicke Street in 1915, as well as at St Enda's in 1909; *An Rí* and *The Master* also reached Central Dublin audiences. All dealt with redemption through a sacrifical youth, revolving around Pearse's belief in the concept of the *macaomh*, or holy boy warrior; there are echoes from Wagner as well as from the Cuchulain cycle. Edward Martyn, Wagnerite and lover of boy choirs, was yet again involved as a patron. *Íosagán* is probably the ur-version of Pearse's boy-sacrifice plays, but most of his oeuvre invokes the rejection of the family for an idealized male community dedicated to a higher cause. Death comes as both transfiguration and solution. *An Rí* is particularly militaristic, but *The Master*, which played at the Hardwicke Street Theatre in 1915, further developed this sacrificial and violent theme. It climaxed in *The Singer*, where a beautiful and charismatic young poet offers himself in a Christ-like sacrifice against 'the foreigner': he leaves the stage to go to his death, 'pulling off his clothes as he goes'. This homoerotic fable was finally acted in late 1916, some months after Pearse's own execution by the 'Gall'. In the same enterprise of Easter 1916 many of the boys who had acted in these productions, such as Eunan McGinley, star of *Íosagán*, or Pearse's favourite Cuchulain, Frank Dowling, had fought as well.

The conflagration of Dublin 1916 would also envelop other passionate thespians: Constance Markievicz, Máire nic Shiubhlaigh, Joseph Plunkett, Thomas MacDonagh, Eimar O'Duffy, Terence Mac-Swiney, Piaras Béaslaí, Helena Molony, and the Abbey actors Charles Wyse Power, Michael Conniffe, Arthur Sinclair and Seán Connolly. Even the Marxist ideologue and labour leader James Connolly was a part-time playwright; in 1915 the drama group of the socialist militia, the Citizen Army, mounted his history-play about the 1867 Fenian Rising, *Under Which Flag?* The Rising is often called a revolution of poets; in fact playwrights and actors were far more prominent. Appositely, when the insurrection broke out, several people mistook the manoeuvres for street theatre; Constance Markievicz was asked by passers-by at Liberty Hall if she was rehearsing a play for children, and Joseph Holloway, encountering a copy of the 'Proclamation of the Irish Republic', took it at first for a playbill.[97]

This climactic performance was in some ways the result of intense rehearsals conducted since the turn of the century. What happened on the fringes of the Abbey, in Milligan's portentous *tableaux vivants*, within the Theatre of Ireland, on the fit-up stages of Na hAisteoirí, at the Hardwicke Street Hall, in the Cork Dramatic Society or in St Enda's school productions, was an intense and potent form of national consciousness-raising. Exiled in England in 1909, Frank Fay wrote disconsolately to a friend: 'We are a nation of actors in real life. Even in Gaelic circles they were playing at "nation-building" (and other miserable phrases) when I knew them.'[98] That play continued, and built up momentum towards 1916. If the plays were sometimes only allegorically political, they were played to audiences who could read behind every word; they were well used to political theatre. Perhaps this is one reason why, in post-revolutionary Ireland, the stage continued to be a political arena, and the government paid close attention to controlling it.[99] And at the height of the revolution in 1920, with Terence MacSwiney dying in Brixton Gaol, the Abbey (adroitly rediscovering its nationalist roots) would at last mount a production of his unwieldy five-act play *The Revolutionist*. Life had overtaken Art, with a vengeance.

When she gets it, what will she do with it?

The ominous implications of female emancipation, as seen by the
Leprechaun, 1913.

4

Loving

In many and sometimes surprising ways, family romances, both conscious and unconscious, helped to organize the political experience of the Revolution; revolutionaries and counter-revolutionaries alike had to confront the issues of paternal authority, female participation, and fraternal solidarity. They had to tell stories about how the republic came to be and what it meant, and those stories always had an element of family conflict and resolution. Some of the elements of the stories were perennial – the relations of fathers to sons, husbands to wives, parents to children, men to women – but their particular configurations were contingent on the social and political patterns produced by the revolutionary process.

– Lynn Hunt, The Family Romance of the
French Revolution *(1993)*[1]

I

As the last chapter suggests, pre-revolutionary Ireland was an important location for the 'theatre of revolt', in a literal sense. But one central aspect of that revolt more or less absent from the drama written and acted by the future revolutionaries concerns the world of sex. Synge was, as usual, the exception. Not only did he allow (in *The Shadow of the Glen*) a sexually frustrated wife to escape into an adventurous life with a tramp, leaving her materialist husband to his cottage and his cronies; *The Playboy of the Western World* could be seen as a parable illustrating the need to throw off patriarchal authority and find sexual liberation. The play makes no bones about the physical magnetism between Pegeen and Christy, or the sexually ravenous dispositions of the Widow Casey and the Widow Quin. This contrasts diametrically with the sexual refusal at the centre of *Cathleen ni Houlihan*, and the way that homoeroticism is safely diverted into servitude and death in the plays of Patrick Pearse. But the revolutionaries were part of a generation which explored other forms of liberation besides the political and national, and one of these concerns the drama of loving. This may be explored through patterns of family relationships among revolutionary coteries, and also the sexual identities of some key figures in that remarkable generation.

The extent to which radical-nationalist political attitudes inferred sexual radicalism too is often questionable; *social* radicalism and sexual radicalism present a closer overlap, though even in that conjunction one kind of liberation does not necessarily imply the other. It is generally assumed that this was particularly true for Ireland, as the revolutionary Todd Andrews recalled much later: 'the absence of sexual relations between the men and women of the movement was one of its most peculiar features. I suppose all revolutionaries are basically Puritanical, otherwise they wouldn't be revolutionaries.'[2]

This is, however, not the whole story. From diaries, letters and private reflections it is clear that many of the female generation who made the revolution were frustrated by the expectations held out for them by their seniors, and were prepared to embrace alternative relationships to that of the heterosexual marriage. Nor were alternatives unknown in male revolutionary society either: one of the most celebrated revolutionaries also left for posterity the most detailed record of homosexual adventures imaginable. The men and women we are considering were, after all, the generation of Edward Carpenter, and some at least read Freud. Part of recapturing their world must involve prospecting the ties of affection, and the patterns of tension, between families, friends and lovers.

Without imposing a crudely Freudian framework upon the lives of the revolutionary generation, individually or collectively, it is worth considering – as Lynn Hunt does in relation to France – the idea of a 'family romance'. This might mean a fantasy of reordering the family one inherits, and replacing it with a new, liberated entity, reflecting 'a creative effort to reimagine the political world, to imagine a polity unhinged from patriarchal authority'.[3] Naturally this did not apply to all of the revolutionary generation. Some Irish revolutionaries came from families which had 'kept the faith' from Fenian times, and saw themselves as carrying on an inherited tradition – or so they would fondly recall later on, illustrated by many recollections preserved in the Bureau of Military History. It is striking how often the figure of a spinster aunt of powerful nationalist opinions hovers behind a youthful consciousness, like Dante Riordan in Joyce's *Portrait of the Artist*. Kathleen Daly, later Clarke, grew up with such a mentor, as did the young O'Rahillys. Both families were from the well-off rural bourgeoisie; a solid adherence to respectable commercial values was compatible with celebration of a Fenian tradition in the family, a pronounced distaste for Anglicized, or 'shoneen', standards, and a dislike of England itself.

But other radicals decided autonomously to challenge the assumptions with which they had grown up. Terence, Mary and Annie MacSwiney in Cork, Rosamond Jacob in Waterford, Mabel McConnell in Belfast, Piaras Béaslaí in Liverpool, Roger Casement (though he had initially left Ballycastle to make a career in the Empire), the Gifford sisters in Rathmines, the Plunkett family waging war on their mother in Fitzwilliam Place, and Hanna and Francis Sheehy-Skeffington – all imagined a new post-imperial world. Some of them, like the Sheehy-Skeffingtons, also attempted to lay down the lines of a new kind of marriage in a socialized society, and many desired to destabilize the familial order which they had inherited. In some cases at least, there was also a conscious impulse to challenge the even more pervasive patriarchalism of the Church.

This is not always obvious, for a number of reasons. One is the sharply conservative aftermath of the revolution, when nascent ideas of certain kinds of liberation were aggressively subordinated to the national project of restabilization (and clericalization). Another restraining influence is the powerful familial bond asserted by the Irish family, perhaps most particularly the Irish mother, who often wielded overwhelming authority even in an ostensibly patriarchalist dispensation. Terence MacSwiney's dedication to his 1914 play *The Revolutionist* reads: 'TO MY MOTHER'S MEMORY, for the heritage of her great faith, the beauty of her living example, and the ecstasy of her dead face.' But other members of his generation felt very differently about their mothers, and about the home itself. A striking number of radical revolutionaries were at an angle to family life in another way, having a dead or absent father: Bulmer Hobson, Patrick and Willie Pearse, MacSwiney and his sisters, Roger Casement, Éamon de Valera, the O'Hegarty brothers, Liam de Róiste; while Denis McCullough, in a gesture worthy of Synge's Christy Mahon, ejected his own father from the IRB cell to which he was introduced, on the grounds of drunkenness. Embracing the path of radical nationalism, if you were from a unionist family, obviously entailed a repudiation of parents and sometimes siblings, as is clearly demonstrated by Muriel Murphy (later MacSwiney), the Gifford sisters, the Bartons and Alice Milligan. But there were less obvious patterns of rejection too. The reader of Liam de Róiste's diaries only discovers several volumes in that he has brothers – whom he hardly ever mentions. The reason becomes clear: they are serving soldiers in the British Army. And, though Kathleen Daly came from a well-known nationalist family in Limerick, her parents raised strenuous objections when she decided to marry Tom Clarke, a friend of her uncle, who had been gaoled for IRB activities. Their opposition, it seems, was founded on his age, his inferior class and his poverty. It was not only ideological objections that were raised in the way of young Irish radicals trying to build a new life.

The four Gifford sisters did so decisively, escaping from their comfortable Rathmines background, memorably delineated by Sydney.

> Our family home in Dublin was on the South side, in what was called a 'good residential district', which meant, in those days, a stronghold of British imperialism. More than anything else the district resembled a waxworks museum. The people who surrounded us were lifelike but inanimate models of distinguished English people. It was a deadly atmosphere, in which any originality of thought or independence of action was regarded as eccentricity or lawlessness.
>
> You have guessed it! It was Rathmines: butt of local humour for a couple of generations because its residents seemed to typify the flunky Irishman; with their strange, synthetic English accent, their snobbery, and their half-hearted desire to be a ruling caste. Rathmines was a

phenomenon. It was not a racial group, not a political stronghold, but a spiritual condition. Its people were castaways, wrecked by mischance on this island called Ireland, and ever scanning the horizon for a ship that would take them and their families away to some of the British colonies.[4]

The Gifford girls jumped ship and 'married out' in spectacular fashion: Muriel to the schoolteacher Thomas MacDonagh, the radical art student Grace to Joseph Mary Plunkett (in his condemned cell, after the Rising), Sydney (briefly) to Arpad Czira, a Hungarian she met in New York. Nellie remained unmarried. All were passionate nationalists. Their brothers remained respectable unionists, but it seems clear that the girls reinforced and sustained each other in their taking up a republican commitment and membership of several radical organizations. There are several other cases where siblings bonded together in revolutionary beliefs. Terence MacSwiney's sisters Mary and Annie were just as extreme nationalists as he was, even before his death on hunger-strike left them with a flame to guard for the rest of their lives. Geraldine, Joseph, George, Jack and Mimi Plunkett supported and reinforced each other's radical politics, partly as a strategy in the continuing war against their mother, who is presented in Geraldine's copious autobiographical writings as sadistic and partly deranged. The Ryan sisters and brothers in Tomcoole, County Wexford, reinforced each other's nationalist beliefs, which were maintained most rigorously by Nell, the eldest; the correspondence of her younger sisters mocked her affectionately at first, but they grew into radicalism together through joining Sinn Féin and other organizations. Their parents seem to have remained moderate Home Rulers, while supporting their headstrong children in their revolutionary careers.

Upper-class radicals similarly formed alliances against their parents' values. Robert and Dulcibella Barton's father was a Wicklow Tory gentleman, owner of the beautiful Glendalough House and estate, who had been a youthful friend of his neighbouring landlord and contemporary Charles Stewart Parnell but never spoke to him again when he entered Home Rule politics. Barton's children made up for this by becoming inveterate Sinn Féiners (in Robert's case, after a rather chequered course), as did their cousin Erskine Childers.

Constance Markievicz and her sister Eva Gore-Booth, though they came from a more liberal gentry background, similarly bonded together against family traditions, embracing socialism as well as republicanism. Roger, Nina and Tom Casement, growing up in an erratic Northern unionist family (father a peripatetic retired army captain who died when Roger was twelve, mother an alcoholic), bonded together in a fiercely sentimental nationalism. Among the Quaker middle classes of Waterford, Rosamond Jacob and her brother Tom both became Sinn Féiners and Gaelic Leaguers, while their parents remained moderate Redmondites. Cesca Trench and her sister Margot, born into a well-known Church of Ireland family of conventional unionist beliefs and imperial affiliations, Gaelicized their names, joined Sinn Féin and denounced their family's traditions, though with a sort of rueful affection. Renaming was a powerfully symbolic act, often taking the form not merely of finding the nearest Irish version to one's English name but of adopting a queenly or mythic identification such as Emer (Helena Molony) or Lasairfhíona (Elizabeth Somers).

As already outlined, the Ryan sisters also exemplified the opportunities for new worlds afforded by education for women. As students and teachers, they travelled and worked in England, France and Germany, but eventually centred on Dublin and political involvements – which were often romantic entanglements too. They not only embraced the coming vogue, but eventually married influential figures in the republican movement. Chris married Michael O'Malley, Agnes married Denis McCullough, and the UCD academic Mary Kate married the revolutionary (and future President of Ireland) Seán T. O'Kelly; when she died, her sister Phyllis married him in turn. Josephine, or Min, was in love – like many – with the charismatic Seán MacDermott; after his execution she would marry another long-term admirer, Richard Mulcahy, who would be a long-serving minister in post-revolutionary governments and an indefatigable recorder of the revolutionary experience. (Min, who charmed men but was disliked by some of her female revolutionary comrades, seems to have had the sense of survival of a Balzacian heroine: when Hanna Sheehy-Skeffington lost her teacher's job for political activities in 1912, Min's unsisterly reaction was immediately to try to get it for herself.)

This ploy failed, but Mary Kate was determined to bring her sister back from London, into the exciting world of pre-war Dublin. The Ryan sisters' correspondence profiles a lively existence of parties, flirtation and romance, revolving around Mary Kate's Dublin circle. In her London days she had been unhappily attracted to Tom Kettle MP, but even before he became engaged to her *bête noire* Mary Sheehy, Kate had decided he was not what she was looking for in a man – though the experience left her jaded and inclined to cynicism. After a recuperative trip to Paris in 1908, she mused on the relative straightforwardness of French people. 'I am sure the Irish are the most tricky affected people under the sun now. Even the French have no idea of that kind of playing with people which the Irish practise and which *we* are perfect at.' Above all, she felt she had had enough of men – 'their childishness & stupidity & gullibility & at the back of all that their conceit – their delusions about themselves and in rotation about you, about women.'[5] But Kettle continued to fascinate her, and she wrote long letters to her sisters claiming unconvincingly that he no longer attracted her (except for his eyes and his smile) – finally denouncing him because he had no sense of fun, unlike favoured Wexford friends such as Robert Brennan. 'Finally about T Kettle – he has not enough of the Devil about him at all. Men ought to have a spark of the devil about them.'[6] Her devoted admirer, the diminutive ex-librarian Seán T. O'Kelly, may have had an unsuspected devilish streak, since he was capable of sending her sister Nell flirtatious letters at the same time as pursuing Mary Kate. (Begging Nell to tell him about a dream she had had in which he featured, he asked, 'How did you interpret it? I am quite certain it was not in a dream you made the discovery that I could be (and frequently am, I may say) a disagreeable and very discontented soul.'[7])

Mary Kate resisted marriage, enjoying her life as a university lecturer and monitoring her sisters' admirers as well as manipulating her own. In 1911 she remarked to Min, after meeting various 'newly married ladies', 'I prefer the Bohemian life by far, only can it go on for ever? There is something very undignified in not knowing when one is old, when youth is over. I wonder about myself.'[8] However 'Seán T', as he was universally known, pressed his suit from Kate's return to Dublin in 1910 until their marriage eight years later, in a world that was changing beyond recognition. The next time she visited Paris would be in 1919, when she and her new husband represented the 'Provisional Government of the Irish Republic', attempting to influence the peace treaty negotiations at Versailles.

I I

The exciting lives of the Ryan sisters remind us, however, that these were young people, thrown into each other's company, often in circumstances which were by their nature unchaperoned and 'daring'. It is difficult to recapture the love-lives of the past, at least when they were consensual; one of the disadvantages of most histories of sexual behaviour is that so much of the evidence has been gathered from criminal records, or from the experiences of the poor, the violent and the marginal. But one of the attractions of the Gaelic League, especially its summer-schools and *céilidhe*, was the opportunity it provided for romantic and sexual contact. The younger Ryan sisters, while living at the Loreto Convent residence for women students, were technically not allowed to go unchaperoned to cafés and dances with young men in Dublin; Agnes's letters to her sisters from the Gaelic League summer-school at Ring clearly indicate a sense of welcome liberation. This was swiftly noted by the authorities. J. J. Sheehan's *A Guide to Irish Dancing* (1902) warned dancers: 'Don't hug your partner round the waist English fashion. When swinging, hold her hand only. A bow to your partner at the end would not be amiss, but be careful to avoid any straining after "deportment". Leave that to the Seoinini [socially ambitious imitators of the English]. In short, be natural, unaffected, easy – be Irish and you'll be alright.'[9]

The corruptions inherent in undisciplined dancing continued to exercise the guardians of revivalist culture. The 1903 Gaelic League Oireachteas produced a report on the subject, with detailed taking of evidence on the propriety of jigs and reels, the dangers of 'stamping' and the decadence of polka-steps. The possible derivation of reels from eighteenth-century quadrilles was a very sensitive question, raising the issue of the purity of national tradition; but other kinds of purity were clearly in mind as well. A major controversy also developed over teaching men and women together in Gaelic League

Irish-language classes, which was violently opposed by some priests. This and other attempts to impose Catholic moral policing upon the activities of the supposedly non-sectarian League infuriated people such as Rosamond Jacob. She and her brother also campaigned, fruitlessly, against sending League representatives to 'the immoral literature committee which is a Catholic affair and no business of the Gaelic League anyhow'.[10]

Jacob, for her part, was determined to read as much immoral literature as she liked. It is clear from her diaries that she also relished the opportunities for touching men and responding to the moves of her partners in Irish dancing. Cesca Trench's diary records the long summer nights on Achill Island, where she went to Gaelic college: swimming, flirting, sleeping out of doors wrapped in cloaks.[11] The diaries of Piaras Béaslaí record much fairly indiscriminate hugging, kissing and cuddling in the Bootle Gaelic League during the early 1900s, though he also records his snobbish disapproval of several of the girls he meets there, on social or educational grounds. He subscribed to some feminist principles nonetheless, condemning Coventry Patmore's view of women as sentimental and exploitative, admiring George Meredith's feminist novels and appreciating Ibsen's *A Doll's House*.[12] His visits to Ballingeary Gaelic College in Cork as a part-time teacher afforded more spectacular opportunities than Bootle, enabling him to smuggle the local priest's young sister, Bridie Fitzgerald, into his bedroom at night. He confided to his diary, 'I always wound up the night by carrying her upstairs to bed,' and hiding her in his room. She had, he believed, 'a kind of fearless innocence, not ignorance for she spoke openly and fearlessly on the most forbidden topics. Never before had I been in such intimacy with a female.' Bridie came to his room every night, and returned in the morning before he got up. He felt extreme guilt afterwards, but 'time eventually solved it'.[13]

The actual sexual behaviour of the radical generation is hard to track, but sexual unconventionality was not unknown. In 1916 Geraldine Plunkett believed, and recorded, that her sister-in-law Grace Gifford was pregnant when she married Joseph in his prison cell, and had a miscarriage shortly afterwards; in an extraordinary passage of her memoir, she describes in unflinching detail the visit to her widowed sister-in-law where this became clear.

Various friends kept telling me that I must not let her go [to America] because if she had a child it would make a greater scandal . . . I thought that was rubbish but they were very sure of it. Grace said or did nothing either way & I just carried on. The Castle thought that she was pregnant but that Joe was not the father. One day I went to Larkfield & on asking for her I was told she was still in bed – I went up to her room. She was in bed & a big white chamberpot was full of the remains of an abortion etc. I said nothing & she said the same. I went away a good deal relieved. [Marie] Perolz knew & agreed with me. We could not make her out. Perolz did not know whether Grace had induced it or not.[14]

Geraldine also claimed that both Grace Gifford and her sister Nellie shocked the republican hero Rory O'Connor by demanding that he spend a night with them. When Geraldine herself got married just before Easter 1916, her mother Countess Plunkett characteristically went around telling people that her daughter was pregnant.

This was not in fact the case, but some took such situations in their stride. The decisive Mabel McConnell, born in 1884, fell in love with the young poet Desmond FitzGerald in 1910, when she was working in London and enthusiastically involved in the Gaelic League, Sinn Féin, and the Women's Social and Political Union. Four years younger, Desmond was a less zealous nationalist at this stage (his love-letters to her are entirely, if self-deprecatingly, in English). He admired her passion and vehemence, and tried not to resent her Sinn Féin commitments coming between them, though his letters are sometimes unable to resist irony ('forgive the non-Irish manufacture of the paper. Yours was most edifying').[15] For his part, he was more involved in the fringe circles of Imagist poets, and apologized for boring her with friends like T. E. Hulme, Florence Farr and Ezra Pound.[16] Having returned unwillingly in early 1911 to her rich family in Belfast, Mabel discovered she was pregnant. She escaped (out of a window, late at night) and fled back to London. She and Desmond were married in May 1911 and decamped to live an artistic life in Brittany. This may have spared her family some embarrassment, though the fact that they were married in a Catholic ceremony cannot have pleased such pillars of unionist orthodoxy (her father was the managing director of the Craig family's whiskey distillery). Independent-minded to the end,

Mabel deferred her own conversion till much later in life ('I always wanted to be a Catholic but suspected that I did not want it enough'[17]). The FitzGeralds subsequently moved from Brittany to Kerry, where Desmond's opinions radicalized in tune with Mabel's and he turned into a committed if sometimes despairing evangelist for the Irish language. He moved on to become a leading republican propagandist, closely monitored by the police, fought in the GPO in 1916 and played a leading part in the establishment of the Free State.

Like the FitzGeralds, P. S. O'Hegarty and his wife Mina Smyth represented a union between South and North, marrying two very different backgrounds. He was a nationalist and a firmly unbelieving ex-Catholic, she a Belfast Presbyterian. Like Mabel, she was a university graduate and similarly came from a family where the girls became nationalist while the boys stayed unionist (and also tended to follow a military profession). The O'Hegartys, like the FitzGeralds, met in London, where they were both involved in the suffrage movement, though in later days P. S. would turn violently against the influence of women in politics, believing that political involvement released their capacities to be 'unreasonable' and 'dangerous'.[18] Ironically, this opinion was one of the few which he would continue to hold in common with his comrade and future adversary Éamon de Valera – another revolutionary who found love through Gaelic League activities, marrying his Irish teacher, Sinéad Flanagan (four years older than him), after a romantic summer at Irish College in Tourmakeady.

For one well-known revolutionary, sexual allure was inseparable from her reputation. Maud Gonne – born English but a fierce convert to Irishness – had been celebrated in the lovelorn poetry of W. B. Yeats throughout the 1890s and early 1900s, and figured inevitably in anti-British demonstrations and organizations. By then in her forties (she was born in 1866), her speeches, journalism and demonstrations had made her an icon of resistance and romance for many of the younger generation. Her commanding presence, great height and legendary good looks made her much sought after for platform events; she was also well known to the police for her IRB connections and the leading part she had played in the campaign against the Boer War as well as opposing the Jubilee and royal visit. Above all, her energies were thrown into the nationalist women's organization Inghinidhe na hÉireann and its attendant theatrical enterprises. Much of this activity was enabled by her personal wealth, and the independence it conferred also allowed her to live an unconventional private life. A long affair with the right-wing French politician Lucien Millevoye in Paris had produced two children, one of whom – Iseult – survived. Her identification as Gonne's adopted 'cousin' deceived few in Dublin, but a public scandal erupted only after her mother's brief union with John MacBride, an IRB member who had come to prominence fighting alongside the Boers. He and Gonne married in 1903, against strenuous warnings from friends and family on both sides. Arthur Griffith put it sharply: 'For your own sake and for the sake of Ireland to whom you both belong, don't get married. I know you both, you so unconventional, – a law unto yourself: John so full of conventions. You will not be happy for long.'[19]

He was right, and the question of conventionality came sharply into focus during their separation case in 1904–5, not long after the birth of their son Seaghán (later Seán). The court hearing brought many allegations of sexual misconduct into public notice and split nationalist opinion. MacBride's shock at his wife's 'evil life before our marriage' was amply recorded: '"Woman", it is a disgrace to womanhood to call her by that holy name.' Gonne's charges against MacBride – that he was an uncontrollable alcoholic who had sexually abused Iseult and other women in her household – made the separation and custody case long and complicated. The case also had a seismic impact on political life in Dublin, rehearsing details of the couple's personal life in public and fuelling frenzied gossip.[20] Gonne's reputation certainly suffered, and she was famously hissed by some of the audience on an appearance at the Abbey Theatre – though it seems that her major perceived sin was her assault on the character of a republican hero, rather than her own transgressions against conventional morality. 'Advanced nationalists' closed ranks around MacBride and refused to give credence to Gonne's allegations – or even to admit MacBride's legendary drinking habits. Gonne wrote disconsolately to her one-time champion, the old Fenian John O'Leary: 'I was blameless as regards my married life. My husband has wronged me deeply . . . I think if you knew the whole story you would understand that I must safeguard my little son from the example of his father. I have hidden from everyone what I have suffered from John MacBride's drunkenness during our married life.' But male nationalist opinion preferred not to listen, taking the view that objecting to drunkenness was 'a morbid peculiarity' and that a wife's part was to put up with it; as Yeats put it: 'the trouble with these men is that in their eyes a woman has no rights.'[21] In sexual matters also, Gonne's testimony was discounted, and her reluctance to bring Iseult into a French court to face MacBride was taken as proof of the flimsiness of her case: an interpretation oddly echoed by MacBride's defenders in recent years.[22] (In his rambling testimony MacBride himself referred to the nine-year-old Iseult as 'the perfect speciment [*sic*] of a decadent'.[23]) Gonne was attacked not only for her life-style but for her background and 'Englishness', which hurt her to the quick; after the legal separation was formalized in 1906, she spent most of her time in Paris, where she had sole custody of her son.

From that date up to 1916 her Irish involvements tended to be humanitarian rather than political, though Inghinidhe na hÉireann stayed loyal to her. The Rising, and MacBride's subsequent execution, would give her a new role, but the trauma of her rejection by old comrades, and the misogynistic feelings unleashed by the episode, left an enduring scar. As late as 1918 republican widows like Áine Ceannt still fiercely disapproved of her because of what they inaccurately called her 'divorce'.[24] Even before this, when she visited nationalist circles in Cork and dazzled the young Liam de Róiste, he was warned by a priest that she was a woman of immoral life; he bravely 'took this as the usual malice of enemies against Irish republicans; I told him that she was not a Catholic: hence not to be judged by our standards.' Meeting MacBride later, and not yet knowing who he was, de Róiste 'immediately got a peculiarly bad impression. It was as if some inward voice said to me, "Beware!"'[25]

Todd Andrews's recollection that there were no sexual connections between the young puritans of this era seems unlikely. Much later the feminist and republican Marie Perolz similarly told the Bureau of Military History, 'we did not think about sex or anything else. We were all soldiers and I was only bothered about what I could do for Kate Houlihan', but this may reflect the atmosphere of the 1940s and 1950s rather than the situation at the time. Annie O'Brien recalled that, though she was deeply attracted to Con Colbert from St Enda's, and went to parties and Irish dances with him, to her disappointment 'he was not at all interested in girls; he was entirely engrossed in his work for Ireland.'[26] However, Kevin O'Shiel, as a Catholic nationalist student at Trinity in 1910, remembered that the topics discussed at night in College rooms were, in order of importance: 'sex, sport, religion, literature, medicine (gynaecological and forensic, mainly), law, history, politics'.[27] The priority is interesting: sex first, politics last. He also vividly describes the prostitutes advancing on to the streets as the shops closed and the lights dimmed, though he adds that relationships with girls of his own class were chaste. Liam de Róiste's diaries also suggest as much: reviewing them much later from the vantage of 1943, he described his friends and himself as 'puritans'.[28] He records his feelings for Nora O'Brien, his wife-to-be, in purely patriarchalist terms: in his letters to her she is 'my Baby' or 'Banban', a child to be treasured, protected and jokingly threatened with chastisement. But he also records, with a shudder, his exposure to temptation, apparently in the streets of Cork, and how nearly he fell. 'A horrible temptation presented itself to me this evening. Thank God, I finally overcame it. But, it left me thinking there are potentialities for evil within my soul which, if not crushed by religion and reason, would whirl me to I know not where. It is dreadful to think one may be overcome by wicked temptations and evil thoughts and emotions. God guard me from them.'[29] A long exegesis follows, on the 'incitements to the indulgence of the brute in my nature', and the constant temptations presented around him; the 'baser passions' are destroyers, and must be repressed. Again and again, he dreaded 'sinking to the level of the beasts, unreasoning. Of all things, I desire my thoughts to be pure. Despite my desire, impure thoughts will come. They are utterly hateful, and they annoy.'[30] Yet he could not help asking himself whether it was essentially wrong to live with a woman before undergoing the sacramental ceremony of marriage.

Nor did de Róiste's scruples stop him borrowing a copy of Zola's *Nana*, though reading it left him 'dragged down, confined, imprisoned'; he felt first revulsion, then indifference, and 'pity that any man should write as this Zola writes of the swinish, brutish passions of our human nature. Even though "the trail of the serpent is over us all", why should we glory in, or fondly dwell upon, ponder over, or write glowingly of, the signs of that trail? Why do writers of talent and genius love to wallow in the mire?'[31] One exact contemporary, also born in 1882, could have told him. This was, after all, exactly the era when James Joyce wrote his astonishingly frank love-letters to Nora, full of specific erotic instruction and revelling in obscene language.[32] Such written evidence is rare, if not unique; and, unlike their contemporaries in St Petersburg, the student radicals of Edwardian Ireland did not take part in sociological surveys about their sexual lives and attitudes. But not all were as agonized as de Róiste. The charismatic young IRB organizer Seán MacDermott remarked merrily on his 1911 census form that he was 'heartbroken for being single', and few women remembered him without describing his looks. Men were not immune either: Richard Mulcahy remembered him fifty years later as 'an extremely handsome boy, a beautiful head and a sallow complexion that had a certain beauty of its own, you know, and lovely outline of face'; his wife Min concurred, adding that MacDermott walked with a stick after a bout of polio, but 'otherwise he was absolutely perfect'.[33] The beautiful Mary Maguire, who taught at St Ita's and later married Padraic Colum, was pursued aggressively by Thomas MacDonagh before his own marriage to Muriel Gifford; Maguire found his refusal to take no for an answer, and obsessive behaviour, distinctly alarming.

Rosamond Jacob's diary is notably frank about her sexual longings; she frankly apprises the physical qualities of the young Gaelic Leaguers who came to her parents' house, and reserved for a special volume of her diary her sexual obsession with Tony Farrington, whose sister Dorothea (or Queenie) married Rosamond's brother Tom. Rosamond was 'ravished with Tony's beauty', as she put it, making every excuse to touch him and to see him unclothed; 'it is getting almost impossible not to catch hold of him and kiss him', 'the lovely set and make of him, the beautiful lines and curves', and she wrote obsessive love-poems to him, never sent.[34] The Farringtons, a middle-class Quaker family from Cork, struck her initially as soulmates: nationalist, unconventional, free-spirited and remarkably handsome. The boys, Ben and Tony, talked knowledgeably about sexual taboos and relationships, remarking casually that women did not have to get married in order to have babies, and she found she could talk about sex with her sister-in-law Dorothea and discuss whether most women were 'oversexed'. Dorothea revealed that she 'admired young German women because they had so much sex in them'.[35] She also railed against the practice of not telling girls enough about sex before they married, with which Jacob's mother emphatically agreed (though her daughter thought privately that girls must be 'illiterate or imbecile' if they didn't find out for themselves).[36]

She would come in time to dislike her sister-in-law intensely, but her longing for Tony lasted many years. She would subsequently transfer her sexual obsession to the much younger – indeed, adolescent – Owen Sheehy-Skeffington, son of her friend Hanna ('he is well made and I should like to see him stripped'[37]). Plain and intense, Jacob feared that her powerful character and vehement opinions would always repel men. When she shared her worries with Dorothea, 'she was stumped by my contention that if it's want of sex in me that makes me unable to attract, why can I care so much about them. She admitted that feeling sex so much ought to have an effect, and said I should go to a hypnotist.'[38] Later in life, aged forty-one, she would have a passionate but secret physical affair with the republican activist Frank Ryan, which was described in unflinching physical detail in her diaries. ('I got him into the other room & into bed – kept his shirt on, but when I was naked he took me in his arms, standing & then got into bed & I cd feel his lovely skin all over – but he's still inexperienced & I couldn't get right, except once when he hurt like hell.'[39])

In an arresting passage of her 1915 diary, Jacob discussed her own sexuality:

> I certainly am in some ways a man in disguise. My love for Tony is more masculine than feminine. I love him, not spiritually & patiently & unselfishly as a woman is supposed to love a man, but physically and impatiently & selfishly, as a man loves a woman. The idea of his being happy apart from me has no charms for me at all, I'd rather have him unhappy near me than happy far away. It's more a craving & a passion for him than proper love. And the very act of picking someone younger than myself to love is like a man.[40]

She particularly appreciated her Dublin Sinn Féiner friend Ned Stephens (a nephew of J. M. Synge) because they could talk about sex. 'I told Ned I was tired of politics and he said *buideacas* [*sic*] *le Dia* ["Thanks be to God"] & we soon got on to sex. He was very interested in my difficulties, when I said could it be unnatural in me to admire female beauty more than male because most [wo]men did, he said they must be homosexual – it was such a new idea to him that most women are like that.'[41] In 1919 Stephens was responsible for another revelation. 'He had a book on dreams that looked very interesting, by some German professor. Ned said it held that all dreams were products of the subconscious self & showed what it wanted & was like when scientifically examined – & that most dreams are connected with sex – inhibited sex desires chiefly. Comparatively few of mine are, as far as I can see.'[42] Stephens felt a kind of duty, according to Jacob, to enlighten his more repressed friends about their sublimated sex drives, a habit which was not universally popular; but she 'loved the straightforward simple way' he discussed subjects such as birth control. He told her that 'sex feelings are to be expressed as freely as any other kind & more harm is done in the world by repression of them than almost anything else. People may love others of the opposite sex to any extent, whether they are married or not.'[43] Her own reading soon embraced Freud on dreams, Jung's *Psychology of the Unconscious*, and *Sex* by Thompson and Geddes, as well as books on sexual perversion lent by another Sinn Féin friend.[44] Attending a lecture on sexual fixations a year later, she learnt that 'the Irish suffer from a frightful sex repression (so they certainly do) & *that's* why they are so given to violence & fighting . . . & the English have a gastro-intestinal complex, which is worse.'[45]

Jacob, from an agnostic and intellectual Protestant family, may have been exceptionally advanced in her opinions, but, like many feminists, she felt that men should behave more chastely, reading Christabel Pankhurst's polemic on venereal disease *The Great Scourge* with fascination.[46] On birth control, she was infuriated by a Catholic maternity nurse who told her family planning was 'against the laws of God and the churches' while admitting that working-class women should have fewer children. 'Men in that class were such passionate brutes that they would half-kill women who resisted them. A fine result for 19 centuries of the Church!'[47] The attitudes revealed by Maud Gonne's legal proceedings against her husband, and her subsequent ostracism, could not have surprised Jacob or her friends. Discussing gender roles with Madeleine ffrench-Mullen and Helena Molony, she 'held that the natural Irish feeling of both sexes has some contempt for women in it'. Molony agreed; ffrench-Mullen was more doubtful, though having lived on the Continent, she admitted that French and Belgian husbands would share housework in order to allow women to attend political meetings. They agreed that this would never happen in Sinn Féin circles.

Nonetheless Jacob disapproved of the ethical stance in Strindberg's *There are Crimes and Crimes*, and found *The Picture of Dorian Gray* 'a vile book' for moral reasons. But she also believed that 'promiscuity in both sexes is better than the double standard of morals',[48] and in this she was at one with many of her generation. Constance Markievicz, with her hard-drinking and erratic Polish husband, may have been allowed a similar licence (Bulmer Hobson later told his son Declan of his surprise when she demanded to warm herself, on night manoeuvres with her Fianna boy scouts, by getting into bed with them). However, though they behaved more conventionally, the marital correspondences of Éamonn and Sinéad de Valera,[49] and Tom and Kathleen Clarke, are unabashed in their passionate endearments, and sense of physical deprivation when they were apart (which was often). Writing to Sinéad from the West of Ireland, where he was teaching in a Gaelic League summer-school, de Valera sent her a translation of an erotic poem in Irish ('I couldn't go into the meaning with the mixed class ... but I wished you were with me till we discuss it'). Retailing the poet's descriptions of his beloved's 'unfastened breast' and her 'three jewels, the nicest in the world', he added: 'The word "beal beosac" came into a poem a few days ago. We translated it as "nectar lipped" – but I understood what the poet meant. Those wild kisses.'[50]

III

Other marriages operated at a lower temperature. Rosamond Jacob was interested in the distinctly unsensual bond between Francis and Hanna Sheehy-Skeffington, who maintained separate bedrooms – 'the most civilized way', according to Hanna. 'She said she was glad to be through with sex & regarded it as rather a nuisance & a hindrance in life. There is a kind of coldness and asceticism about her. She said she had imagined me, like Dr Lynn & Madeleine. Having no use at all for men' – a judgement which, Jacob added, also applied to Dorothy Macardle (usually dressed in 'shirt and trousers, looking very nice') and Ella Young, preoccupied by fairylore and romantic sisterhood.[51] How far such feelings implied a consciously lesbian lifestyle (which was embraced by many of their contemporaries in feminist circles in England) is another matter. The mystic-minded Young, later prominent in lesbian communes in California, combined her sexual proclivities with a form of goddess-worship, and an obsession with Maud Gonne; her papers are now divided between Ballymena Library and the Centre for Lesbian, Bisexual, Gay and Transgender History in San Francisco. Cesca Trench's sister Margot, who was involved in radical-nationalist movements while working in Belfast and remaining a strong Anglican, was also lesbian, conducting a passionate affair with an English feminist, Judy Withers.[52] Kathleen Lynn, a radical Protestant doctor, and Madeleine ffrench-Mullen, lived together all their lives in a relationship with all the marks of a marriage; Jacob records going into their bedroom and finding them breakfasting in bed together, as was their custom;[53] their letters to each other when imprisoned for republican activities express passionate love. Rosamond's friend Edith White, the ex-Methodist who rechristened herself Máire and took to Gaelicism and earth-spirits, confessed to an overpowering desire to dress as a man and go around Dublin in that guise; she appears as an emotional and argumentative friend in the diary of Alice Milligan as well as that of Rosamond Jacob.[54] Besides Lynn and ffrench-Mullen, female couples were well known among socialist and radical circles, such as Louie Bennett and Helen Chenevix, and Elizabeth O'Farrell and Julia Grenan; to a certain extent, lesbians may have been drawn to such organizations in order to meet each other.

With the obvious exceptions of Roger Casement, F. J. Bigger and Patrick Pearse, it is harder to track same-sex desire among the men of the revolutionary generation, but the diaries of Piaras Béaslaí and Terence MacSwiney suggest powerful homosocial bondings. In Béaslaí's case this takes the form of blinding crushes on Gaelic League friends, followed by shattering disillusionments: pages of his diary are taken up by his jealous resentment when a beloved male friend takes up with an unworthy girl. 'From the very first he caught my eye & dwelt in my mind: yet I cdn't bear to let him see how much I thought of him ... I am diving very deep into psychology & I must leave it again.'[55] Thomas MacDonagh temporarily lost his faith at Rockwell after what his biographer describes as a 'complicated' relationship with another seminarian, the subject of long and fervent poems which their author later wisely repudiated. MacSwiney's friendships were equally heartfelt but more sublimated; he avoided relationships with girls, though he obsessively tracks in his diaries the chances of one or other of his female acquaintances becoming a nun. He would eventually marry the much younger Muriel Murphy, to the disapproval of his powerful sisters. MacSwiney apparently saw himself as devoted to the coming revolution in a monk-like way, especially after he had spent all the money he had (including the proceeds of the sale of his beloved library) to start a journal, *Fianna Fáil*. This sacrifice, he felt, ruled out marriage; he prayed 'that I might subordinate my personal desires to the service of Ireland, and never fail in my duty ... When friends criticised and blamed me for not getting married, they never realised how they touched the most intimate part of my feelings; and that sympathy rather than abuse would have been more to the point.'[56] But he retained his idiosyncratic principles:

> The feeling took shape definitely that if I was to be married, the girl should make the approach to me rather than I to her. That was so much the reverse of the natural course of things that it seemed to remove the possibility of marriage for me altogether. But the more unusual the point of view seemed, the more fixed I became on it. It was as clear a thing as ever felt. Because it looked that anyone united to me would have to follow the hard path. I wanted her to advance to that path, rather than I should ask her to come to it.[57]

Muriel, a zealot in her own way, proved up to the challenge. Determined to escape from the gilded cage of her parents' grand house in Tivoli, she read MacSwiney's polemics and plays and went to some trouble to arrange a meeting in late 1915, overcoming his reluctance. When she saw him she was magnetized by his dark looks, olive skin and strangely light blue eyes, 'which though perfectly sane and quiet were inspired and inspiring'.[58] They married in 1917, the day after her twenty-fifth birthday, when she had come into control of some of her own money; their few years together were punctuated by his frequent periods of imprisonment for republican activity, but their letters suggest a close and tender relationship. Others, such as Bulmer Hobson and Seán MacDermott, were probably too busy organizing theatre initiatives, publishing little magazines and running Fianna groups to give any immediate thought to marriage, though MacDermott considered himself engaged to Min Ryan by 1916 and Hobson would marry his fellow republican Claire Gregan after 1916.

Another form of suppression was adopted by Patrick Pearse. Like many charismatic teachers, his fascination with boys seems to have had a sublimated sexual component, as evidenced in the erotic verses he wrote to them, and his romantic descriptions of his favourites, such as Frank Dowling, on whom Pearse published a rhapsody in the June 1909 issue of the school magazine: 'in face and figure and manner, my own high idea of the child Cuchulain; that "small, dark, sad boy, comeliest of the boys of Éire", shy and modest in a boy's winning way, with a boy's aloofness and a boy's mystery, with a boy's grave earnestness broken ever and anon by a boy's irrepressible gaiety; a boy merely to all who looked upon him, and unsuspected for a hero save in his strange moments of exaltation, when the sevenfold splendours blazed in his eyes and the hero-light shone about his head.'[59]

There is an apparent innocence about these frank declarations, and though biographers concur about Pearse's sexual orientation, it has never been suggested that it found expression in exploitative behaviour towards his charges. There is, however, a disturbing implication in the final verses of his controversial poem 'Little Lad of the Tricks', where the poet addresses a 'child of the soft red mouth', forgiving him for a childish act of mischief and offering him a kiss.

> There is a fragrance in your kiss
> That I have not found yet
> In the kisses of women
> Or the honey of their bodies.

This homoerotic admiration is complicated and darkened by the final verses:

Lad of the grey eyes
That flush in thy cheek
Would be white with dread of me
Could you read my secrets.

He who has my secrets
Is not fit to touch you;
Is not that a pitiful thing,
Little lad of the tricks?

Although loyal admirers later constructed the story of Pearse's engagement to Eibhlín Nicholls, a Gaelic Leaguer who drowned young, this
seems to have been a fiction, and no other relationship with a woman
ever emerged.

The Northern nationalist F. J. Bigger also maintained a cult of boyhood, in his case in a more recognizably Uranian mode. Bigger was
one of the most colourful and influential figures in early-twentieth-
century Ulster cultural life.[60] A rich amateur scholar, and a pioneering
antiquarian and folklorist, he was obsessed with the restoration of
Gaelic modes of dress and architecture, and expressed this in various
flamboyant ways. At Ardrigh, his large house overlooking Belfast
Lough, where he lived with his adored mother and entertained an
impressive roll-call of cultural revivalists, or in the medieval 'Shane's
Castle', a restored tower house at Ardglass, he organized archaeological expeditions, *feiseanna*, pageants and dances, featuring boys in
kilts or more elaborate costumes that he lovingly designed himself. He
was kept under police observation because of the republican company he kept, but politics were not always at the top of his mind.[61]
These overwhelmingly homosocial occasions, his aesthetic preoccupation with 'lads', his adopted Anglo-Catholicism, the obsessive
dressing-up and the interest in sacrificial boy-warriors are all very
suggestive of contemporary homoerotic cults in Britain, but, as with
Pearse, Bigger's activities seem to have remained sexually sublimated.
The boys, remarked a male friend and frequent guest of Bigger, 'are a
dear lot of youngsters, although I think Mr B is a bit foolish over
some of them, but he is a boy himself and that's all to the good'.[62]
This indulgent friend was Roger Casement, whose homosexual

1. Constance Markievicz
in her acting days,
dressed to kill.

2. Rosamond Jacob.

3. Grace Gifford (later Plunkett) with William Orpen, who taught (and painted) her at the Metropolitan School of Art.

4. Arthur Griffith, speaking beside Nelson's Pillar in Sackville Street.

5. Alice Milligan (*left*) and Anna Johnston, bent on converting Belfast to nationalism in the 1890s.

6. Members of the Dungannon Club pose with a copy of Bulmer Hobson's paper the *Republic* in 1907. Though they are unidentified, Denis McCullough is probably the tall figure in the second row with his hands on Seán MacDermott's shoulders.

7. Maud Gonne (*behind the banner, wearing a hat*) surrounded by members of Inghinidhe na hÉireann, wearing Tara brooches, *c.* 1905–6.

8. A performance of *An Pósadh* (*The Wedding*) by Douglas Hyde at the Gaiety Theatre in 1904, by members of the Gaelic League. *From left to right*: Seán T. O'Kelly (later President of Ireland); Peadar Macken (killed at Boland's Mill in 1916); Sinéad Flanagan (later de Valera); Michael O'Hanrahan (executed after 1916); Douglas Hyde (later President of Ireland).

9. Éamon de Valera in
his schoolteaching days.

10. Roger Casement,
aged about twenty-five.

11. Seán MacDermott.

12. Patrick McCartan.

13. Bulmer Hobson.

14. A pageant at St Enda's. Usually identified as *The Coming of Fionn*, 1909, it is more likely to be the 1914 performance *Fionn: A Dramatic Spectacle*, featuring Willie Pearse (*centre, in winged helmet and tunic*).

15. F. J. Bigger (*lying on the grass*) at Ardrigh, with his chauffeur, the 'Orange boy', Tommie Jones.

16. One of Bigger's young friends dressed in a 'traditional' Gaelic costume, with goose-wing head-dress, designed by Bigger.

17. Fianna Éireann, the nationalist boy-scout movement headed by Constance Markievicz, practise first-aid; many of them would later need the real thing as 1916 combatants.

feelings were not sublimated. An Ulsterman like Bigger, born in 1864 into an insecure and dysfunctional family, Casement left school at fifteen and pursued a career in the Empire, first in commercial shipping and trading companies and then as a British consul in Africa and South America. Here his unremitting and heroic campaigns against the exploitation of natives employed in the rubber industry earned him a deserved reputation as a great humanitarian, as well as a knighthood. By 1904 his feelings had turned against the Empire, and he was embarked on a passionate pilgrimage into advanced nationalism via cultural revival. Tall, dashing, slightly histrionic and extremely good-looking, he rapidly became something of a cult figure in nationalist and Gaelic League circles; he made particular friends of the young IRB members who congregated at Bigger's house, notably Denis McCullough, Seán MacDermott and Bulmer Hobson. Casement offered Hobson, always on the edge of a financial crisis, a large loan to buy a farmhouse, with a room where Casement could stay with him, and also suggested making Hobson his financial agent when abroad; his disjointed, emotional, idiomatic letters to Hobson are signed 'my love to you, a cara'.[63] To Hobson, a fellow Protestant, he could also confide some unreconstructed ancestral prejudices which survived his conversion to nationalism. 'The Irish Catholic man for man is a poor crawling coward as a rule. Afraid of his miserable soul and fearing the Priest like the devil. No country was ever freed by men afraid of bogies. Freedom of Ireland can *only* come through Protestants because they are not afraid of any Bogey.'[64]

The expression of Casement's feelings for Hobson, McCullough and others was kept within conventional bounds, but he was pursued by his own bogies, in the form of a secret sexual life. Bigger's nephew would later claim that his uncle's response to reading some of Casement's personal diaries, left with him for safekeeping, was immense shock and the rapid consigning of them to the furnace. If true, this was hardly surprising. After the Rising, Casement's diaries would feature as a sulphurous instalment in the long tale of perfidious Albion and betrayed Hibernia: reasonably enough, since the use made of them by the British authorities was indeed perfidious in the extreme, when extracts were circulated among influential people in order to torpedo the campaign to have his death sentence for treason commuted. The damage to his reputation was all the greater since the diaries record his sexual relations with native boys and men in the countries where he worked so hard as a humanitarian, as well as his energetic cruising in various European cities. The belief that the diaries thus used were forgeries became an article of faith for most Irish nationalists, but it has not survived forensic examination, handwriting tests, analysis of possible interpolation and cross-checking references with other sources about Casement's life.[65] The consensus is that Casement kept an extraordinarily full record of his compulsive sexual adventures and desires in a series of so-called 'Black Diaries', several of which survive – notably that for 1911. The other volumes surviving cover the years 1903 and 1910. (He also kept a simultaneous 'White Diary' recording the respectable and professional side of his life, as consular official, increasingly passionate nationalist, and courageous campaigner in the Congo and the Amazon basins.) The intention of the secret sexual record was probably for use as a kind of auto-gratification in itself, and there may have been a certain amount of fantasy involved. But the diaries also stand as a record of outlawed sexual activity, carried on obsessively not only in Italy, Brazil and other far-flung places, but also in London, Dublin and Belfast, and beginning at the latest when he was twenty.[66] His partners were much younger men (sometimes teenagers), and money or presents often changed hands, but Casement saw these arrangements as consensual and seems to have been privately unabashed about his sexuality. The only reflection in his available diaries about homosexuality as a condition comes when he records the suicide of Sir Hector MacDonald, a popular and eminent general, after a scandal involving a teenage boy; Casement, expressing compassion for the dead man, refers to his homosexuality as 'a disease' to be treated rather than a crime to be punished, which is possibly how he would have argued his own case.[67] Nonetheless his own experiences seem to have brought him more pleasure than pain or self-reviling; though most of his encounters were passing, he had a sustained sexual relationship with a young Belfast man, Millar Gordon.[68] A diary entry for May 1910 sharply evokes his secret life. 'Left for Warrenpoint with *Millar*. Boated & *Huge* Enjoyment. Both Enjoyed. He came to lunch at G. Central Hotel. Turned in together at 10.30 to 11 after watching billiards. Not a word said till – "Wait – I'll untie it" & then "Grand". X Told many tales & pulled it off on top grandly. First time – after so many years & so deep mutual longing. Rode gloriously – splendid steed. Huge – told of many – "*Grand*".[69]

As with Pearse, there is no evidence of any romantic interest in women; and, as with Pearse, loyal comrades later invented such a connection, posthumously enlisting Casement's older friend Ada MacNeill as a potential wife. But, though she may certainly have had ideas about the glamorous Casement, he fled from her pursuit, writing to his cousin Gertrude that he wished 'the poor old soul would leave me alone . . . I have very strong feelings of friendship for her, and good will and brotherly Irish affection, but I wish she would leave other things out of the reckoning.'[70] Casement, like Bigger, sustained comradely and affectionate friendships with strong-minded women nationalists to whom he wrote elaborate and rather camp letters; they included Alice Stopford Green, Ada MacNeill, his sister Nina and his cousin Gertrude Parry. His ideas for publicizing Green's book *Irish Nationality* in 1911, shared with Hobson, are striking: 'I want sandwich boys in Irish kilts with a beautiful poster announcing the book, to stalk magnificent down O'Connell Street – two fine, big-eyed soft-faced innocent-faced Dublin urchins with the blessings of God on their lips and their healthy cheeks washed clean and rosy fair.'[71] The picture that emerges from the two most substantial biographies,[72] as well as from the diaries and his profuse correspondence, is of a nervous, occasionally manic personality, capable of great acts of bravery and of pushing himself to the limit and striking extreme attitudes – while living a secret life of compulsive homosexual cruising, which, along with unfulfilled yearnings, clearly brought him moments of immense enjoyment and release.

One reason why the question of Casement's homosexuality remained electric was that on at least two high-profile occasions previous homosexual scandals in Ireland had involved officials in Dublin Castle, in 1882 and 1907; the other famous case was of course that of Oscar Wilde's prosecution in 1895. The assumption could be made, in puritanical Irish nationalist circles, that homosexuality was a vice peculiar to imperial rulers, or to those corrupted by predatory aesthetes in decadent London. Accepting that a nationalist hero could be as passionately committed to pursuing young men as to Cathleen ni Houlihan was not going to come easily. Clearly Casement's illegal sex life had to be strictly secret; but it is also clear that he saw no contradiction, and little guilt, in the combination of this activity with a commitment to the rights of colonized nations and to the freedom of Ireland. (His cult of Germany, which he often cited admiringly as a virile power which could teach the decadent British a lesson, might seem illogical but fits consistently with his rather febrile and hero-worshipping temperament.) It might also be supposed that, even if few of Casement's nationalist friends engaged as vigorously in transgressive sex as he did, the instincts of at least some of his companions may have been as unconventional as his own. The desire of young people, often from fractured or troubled home backgrounds, to reject patriarchal and colonial authority, and to make a new untrammelled world in a brotherhood or sisterhood of like-minded souls, may also have carried a strong if unspoken charge of homosocial bonding.

IV

This would carry over into the years of overt revolutionary activity after 1916; one of the most traumatic aspects of the Civil War that followed the Treaty was the sundering of bonds between people who had forged close relationships in the brotherhood of guerrilla campaigns. The revolution and its aftermath brought other changes, too. The indications of a freethinking, sexually adventurous aspect to the revolutionary temperament before 1916 seem to disappear with alacrity afterwards. Some of the young romantics, like Thomas MacDonagh and the heart-throb Seán MacDermott, died by execution. So did Joseph Plunkett, after the famous gesture of marriage to Grace Gifford in his condemned cell. The hostility of his sister Geraldine towards Grace continued unabated, and, as we have seen, she believed not only that Grace was pregnant, but that the father was probably not Joe; she stresses the utter surprise of Joe's family when he announced his engagement to Grace, not hitherto regarded as a likely prospect.

However, his love-letters, now available for consultation, cast doubt on this: their authenticity is fully attested by their excitement, ecstasy, passion, occasional recrimination, repetitiousness and banality. The letters also prove that the couple were secretly engaged in December 1915, and that the engagement was common knowledge among their associates by January 1916.[73]

Joe Plunkett's letters to Grace, in their very normality, humanize this rather odd and affected figure. As will be demonstrated in the last chapter of this book, other young romantics, who survived 1916, did not find their hopes and expectations of personal liberation fulfilled. Grace Gifford Plunkett never remarried; her sister Muriel, the widow of MacDonagh, drowned in mysterious circumstances shortly afterwards; Sydney Gifford emigrated to America. Cesca Trench, shocked and saddened by 1916, did get married, to Diarmuid Coffey, but died shortly afterwards in the influenza pandemic of 1918. Rosamond Jacob, like many, lacerated herself with fury for having missed the 1916 Rising. Shortly afterwards she moved to Dublin and a life of political commitment, but her love-affair with Frank Ryan did not bring her happiness. Her friends Kathleen Lynn and Madeleine ffrench-Mullen remained together for life, yet, like many independent-minded women, found that the post-revolutionary regime offered no respite from patriarchal values – rather the opposite. Terence MacSwiney would die on hunger-strike in 1920; his widow Muriel soon opted for a liberated life on the Continent, and, though she had at least one serious relationship (and bore another child), she never remarried. The flame of Casement's memory was kept alive by his devoted cousin Gertrude and his erratic sister Nina, but the inauthenticity of his diaries remained a cornerstone article of faith. Hanna Sheehy-Skeffington, whose pacifist husband was murdered by a British Army officer during the Rising, also spent a life of political agitation, and also found the new dispensation as antipathetic to feminism as it was to sexual freedom. In any case, as Rosamond Jacob remarked after talking to a puritanical American feminist at an international suffrage congress in 1916, 'women's rights means right to free love in some countries much more than in others.'[74]

This should not come as a surprise. Todd Andrews's belief that revolutionary activists are puritans by nature may be close to the mark; it has been noted by others too.[75] For better or worse, the Robespierres generally dominate the Dantons, and so it would prove in Ireland, where reading Freud remained a distinctly minority taste. Nor did the Irish revolution produce a radical sexual theorist on the lines of Wilhelm Reich, though some of his ideas would have appealed to Rosamond Jacob. The local tendency towards reaffirming puritanism was encouraged by other factors. In Ireland, the process of post-revolutionary restabilization also took a markedly religious form – partly the result of a long tradition of faith-and-fatherland identification, but more directly because many elements in the Catholic Church in the years after 1916 rapidly aligned themselves with the rhetoric of extreme nationalism.[76] In the process, there was little room for those whose pre-revolutionary activity had prioritized feminism, anti-patriarchalism and the breaking down of sexual conventions; while the youthful high spirits and romantic attachments of many young republican nationalists were transmuted into more sober, and conservative, commitments after the fighting actually broke out. But this makes it all the more important to recapture the pre-revolutionary world, when, for some activists at least, liberation from British rule would also – they hoped – mean the institution of a new order of relationships. Whether this new order was based on the ideal of a new kind of family unit, or of equal male–female roles in work and marriage, or of the homosocial bonding of Pearse's and Bigger's reborn version of Red Branch and Fianna brotherhoods, or of female partnerships in a social organization friendly to feminism, did not matter – they were all doomed to disappointment.

Sigmund Freud would not have been surprised. In 1921 Rosamond Jacob read his book *Totem and Taboo* and recorded her own interpretation of it. 'It derives all religion from the boys of a primeval family joining to murder their da. It was great stuff, so reasonable and stimulating.'[77] We seem to have come back, yet again, to Synge's *Playboy of the Western World*. In fact, *Totem and Taboo* is more directly about Freud's version of the origins of the social contract, and the evolution of civil society. It posits a post-revolutionary situation where the band of brothers, having killed their father, had to rationalize a new order which would preserve the organization that had made them strong. This involved the subordination of women as well as a reconciliation with the values and image of the dead father, mimicked through systems of rank and status. If Rosamond Jacob found Freud's theory of social development 'reasonable and stimulating' in 1921, for many Irish ex-revolutionaries who lived on into the Free State set up by the Treaty in that year, it would have rung a very loud bell indeed.

VOL. I.—No. 2.   BELFAST, 7TH FEBRUARY, 1896.   PRICE TWOPENCE.

America.

America! America!!
Hearken! oh, mighty foster-land,
 A harp-note peals across the sea
From the green hills whereon we stand
 Waiting with hearts that shall be free.

When Ireland's sons upon your shores
 Were famine-driven, and fever-flung,
You stretched, amid the tempests' roar,
 The helping hand to which they clung.

And in your day of dire distress,
 When all that loved you leapt to war
Against the red flag pitiless ——
 You called the exiles near and far.

You did not call to them in vain
 Who found a home upon your breast,
They rose to rend your galling chain,
 And dying gave to you their best.

Over a hundred years have gone
 Since, Queen triumphant of your fate,
You stood in the glow of Freedom's dawn,
 And England crouched before your gate.

And records of your trials tell,
 As North alert, met South awake,
How Irishmen poured shot and shell
 Against each other for your sake.

Now, on the verge of war's alarm,
 In our expectancy we crave
The strength of your indignant arm,
 The counsel of your wise and brave.

In memory of old times, that were,
 Of those who fought, and fell, and died,
Your rapture or your grief to share,
 Let not our pleading be denied.
  America! America!!

The Captain's Daughter.

"In comes the Captain's daughter, the Captain of the yeos,
 Saying, 'brave United men we'll ne'er again be foes!'"

HER father was not captain of the yeos, but late of an
 infantry regiment in her present Majesty of
England's service, retired and living on his Irish estate;
they were mere moonlighters, not "brave United men"
at all, not then at least, but they have learned better
ways since, and the quotation strikes just the right note
for my story, so in spite of petty inaccuracies you have
it there to begin with. Here then is a true account of
how she met them, I need not tell you who told me.

The second issue of the *Shan Van Vocht*, 7 February 1896, featuring the work of the editors, Anna Johnston and Alice Milligan.

5
Writing

The first real foundation I got for my national faith or instinct was a little 'Life of Wolfe Tone' by Alice Milligan ... We separatists saturated ourselves with writings by & about the men of 1798, 1848 & 1867.

– Patrick McCartan to
William Maloney, 13 November 1924[1]

One must have lived in Ireland to understand the spell cast, in the long run, by the endless repetition of gratuitous statements.
– Sylvain Briollay, Ireland in Rebellion *(1922)*[2]

I

The twenty years or so before the Irish revolution witnessed a great upward curve in Ireland's remarkable literary history. These are the years that saw Yeats's arrival as the supreme poet of the Celtic Revival, with the work collected in *The Wind Among the Reeds* in 1899, and then the hardening and refining of his poetic voice into the sardonic eloquence of *Responsibilities* in 1914, along with a great flood of plays, literary criticism, stories, essays and polemic. Yeats's books, in their beautiful bindings designed by Althea Gyles and Thomas Sturge Moore, suggest the innovation and sophistication of the high culture of the age. So do the plays of J. M. Synge, whose small but dazzling oeuvre left a comet trail across the first decade of the century, while the London stage had already welcomed Wilde's great success and the beginning of Shaw's. Moreover these are also the years of James

Joyce's apprenticeship, with the long gestation of *Dubliners* and *Portrait of the Artist* climaxing in their publication in 1914–15. The fiction and (unreliable) memoirs of George Moore also stand as landmarks in the period, demonstrating that Joyce was by no means the first Irish novelist to explore the interaction between sexual identity and personal fate.[3]

Late-Victorian and Edwardian Ireland also bred a host of other original and idiosyncratic writers such as AE, John Eglinton, Somerville and Ross, Augusta Gregory, Padraic Colum, Standish O'Grady, Daniel Corkery, Joseph Campbell, George Birmingham and James Stephens. At more populist levels, Irish novelists such as Katharine Tynan, Rosa Mulholland and Katherine Cecil Thurston catered for extremely large markets in Britain and Ireland, a world of Irish literary production rather cast in the shade by the stars of the Revival, but recently resuscitated.[4]

But the books read by the young revolutionaries were not necessarily those that would mark their era for posterity. The generation who came to maturity between 1890 and 1916 lived in a world where Irish writing in the English language was not only innovative, powerful and sought after by English and American publishers; it was also immersed in the political and cultural debates of the day. This was especially so in the case of Yeats, though Russell, Eglinton, Gregory and O'Grady also entered the lists. However, the print culture that galvanized the imaginations and opinions of young radicals was not, principally, that of the novels, short stories, plays and essays produced by the landmark writers who dominated the high culture of this period. It was more potently represented by the traditions of popular history mediated through journalism. The little newspapers and magazines of the nationalist fringe sometimes helped to inject the work and influence of elite writers into the general consciousness. But they more often excoriated them as politically unacceptable or counterproductive. Hard-nosed journalistic polemic rather than poetry and fiction, disseminated in a culture that was highly literate as well as politically engaged, created the influences most directly brought to bear upon the revolutionaries.

It is worth remembering that two of Yeats's great subjects for poetry, Maud Gonne and Constance Markievicz, were much more centrally involved in the world of radical journalism than in the more rarefied circles of literary production. Tough-minded young Fenians such as Seán MacDermott or Richard Mulcahy had little time for reading Yeats or Moore, though they did go to the Abbey Theatre; the correspondence of the Ryan sisters or Seán T. O'Kelly, highly educated though they were, presents a similar picture. The same is true for Liam de Róiste and Terence MacSwiney, who looked on the Yeats circle with extreme suspicion. Their friend P. S. O'Hegarty, a passionate *littérateur* and bibliophile from his youth, is one of the few exceptions to this rule; unconsciously Anglophile, he believed the great poets to be 'Shakespeare, Milton, Browning, Tennyson, Swinburne, Meredith and Yeats'.[5] Synge's drama was considered suspect by many advanced nationalists; and middle-class radicals like Hanna Sheehy-Skeffington and Rosamond Jacob found such work insufficiently political, or downright anti-national. Long afterwards, when Hanna was told of Yeats's death in 1939 by her 22-year-old nephew Conor Cruise O'Brien, he was struck by her response.

> I tried to tell her something of my generation's sense of loss by Yeats's death. I was genuinely moved, a little pompous, discussing a great literary event with my aunt, a well-read woman who loved poetry.
>
> Her large, blue eyes became increasingly blank almost to the polar expression they took on in controversy. Then she relaxed a little: I was young and meant no harm. She almost audibly did not say several things that occurred to her. She wished, I know, to say something kind; she could not say anything she did not believe to be true. After a pause she spoke:
>
> 'Yes,' she said, 'he was a Link with the Past.'[6]

So he was; but the extent to which he was central to the history of many of the revolutionary generation remains a rather moot point.

Hanna had been an influential radical journalist and was thus representative of what was essentially an alternative culture. Communication between the radicals and the outside world ran along streams of printers' ink; and the same can be said for the vectors of communication that linked the revolutionaries to each other. When Rosamond Jacob walked down the hill from her family's comfortable suburban terrace above Waterford city into the little streets of the town, she directed herself to the small paper-shops where she knew she could buy the *United Irishman*, or later *Sinn Féin*, or the *Spark*. Another young Waterford radical later itemized them: 'Ned Cannon's in O'Connell Street – Mrs Clancy's, Colbeck Street, and Mrs O'Reilly's, Parnell Street. In these shops one could obtain copies of "Nationality", "Young Ireland" and the other papers which had long or short lives before being banned by the British.'[7] In Dublin, Sydney Gifford found her path of conversion through a newspaper:

> My music teacher, a mild nationalist, gave me a copy of a weekly Nationalist paper which I smuggled home and read secretly, for nothing with a Nationalist tone was allowed in our house. Shortly afterwards the well-known poet Séumas O'Sullivan, seeing me carrying the paper, offered me his copy of Arthur Griffith's paper *Sinn Féin*, as something better worth reading. I began to buy *Sinn Féin* every week, and was soon on fire with a desire to write for it.[8]

She followed through this ambition, becoming a successful and influential journalist; Rosamond Jacob also became a contributor to the papers she read, and the part women played in creating radical propaganda was decisive. The theme of the contraband newspaper recurs. Richard Mulcahy, working for the Post Office in Thurles, similarly smuggled in copies of the *United Irishman* from 1903, and later the *Republic*, keeping them out of sight of his civil servant father.[9] And when he came to Dublin, like so many others, his path to radicalization lay through Tom Clarke's shop at 75A Great Britain Street, where Mulcahy knew he could buy copies of the papers with which he agreed. Sydney Gifford, though she had written for *Sinn Féin* for several years, had not heard of Tom Clarke until she passed its door in 1910 and noticed 'a daring display of placards', which, 'defying the usual custom of newsagents of that period . . . appeared to be publicly proclaiming that he sold such papers as *Sinn Féin*, the *Gaelic American* and the most dangerous of all, *Irish Freedom*'. She subsequently discovered that the shop also supplied 'a rendezvous where people went to discuss topical events, to argue on controversial subjects, or to leave messages'; it was an address, Bulmer Hobson assured F. J. Bigger in 1911, which 'will always find me'.[10]

The papers edited and managed by revolutionaries such as Arthur

Griffith, Bulmer Hobson and Seán MacDermott were not circulated on a *samizdat* basis; they took their place in a culture which fostered and harboured a vast range of journalistic products, operating over a varied market. As so often, this can be profiled for 16 June 1904 by looking at James Joyce's *Ulysses*. The winding and interpenetrating quotidian journeys of Leopold Bloom and Stephen Dedalus take them through pubs where journalists are encountered and newspapers discussed, down streets where ubiquitous newsboys shout the names of their wares, into the editorial offices of the constitutional-nationalist *Freeman's Journal* and the pink-paged *Evening Telegraph* (where they nearly meet), and on to the National Library, where George Russell, John Eglinton and others discuss the content of the magazines which they edit, such as the *Irish Homestead* and *Dana*. In the National Library too we are reminded that this is where Irish history is laid down, in newspaper records, as Bloom arrives to check the files of the *Kilkenny People* for the past year.[11]

This is all very much as it was: Aeolus, the wind-god, blew news around Dublin, and further afield, through the daily, weekly and monthly press. As we have seen in the play-going subcultures of radical Dublin, debate and controversy were fought out gladiatorially in the press; it was where Yeats learnt his youthful abilities as a polemicist.[12] The world of periodicals sustained a culture of literary and political discussion, a tradition that goes back to the 'reading-rooms' of the Repeal movement in the 1840s, when scarce but closely conned periodicals were dispersed through discussion groups meeting in provincial towns. From the mid-1880s, the revived Young Ireland societies were promoting this approach; significantly, radical political ginger-groups called themselves the 'Celtic *Literary* Society' or the 'Cork *Literary* Society'.[13] Literature signified politics, as Geraldine Plunkett found to her surprise at UCD. The literary 'economy' was a vital agency of modernization in nineteenth- and early-twentieth-century Ireland; it was also a vital carrier of Anglicization, in the literal sense of using the English language flexibly and influentially. This was no less true when the message preached by a journal was specifically, even vitriolically, anti-English. The Irish-language input was generally kept to token columns, and the medium remained an implicit part of the message. The revolution would be conducted in English.

II

The tradition of wordy polemic addressed through a profuse periodical literature did not originate at the turn of the century, although the early 1900s saw a proliferation of new titles across the spectrum. A powerful and self-reinforcing relationship existed between newspapers and nationalism, from the mid-nineteenth century on.[14] The Home Rule machine under Parnell had elevated journalists to positions of influence, notably through William O'Brien's racy and widely read *United Ireland*. The movement also harnessed idiosyncratic provincial newspaper editors, as well as the support of the more sober *Freeman's Journal*, and the services of indefatigable scribbler-MPs such as T. P. O'Connor, Justin McCarthy and J. J. O'Kelly. By the late 1890s Parnell was a tragic memory, but his ageing lieutenants still dominated the newsprint columns. Over the next generation they would be contradicted, challenged and eventually displaced by new and more radical writers and editors. But they all took their place in a tradition of literacy, wordiness and dramatic assertion; it is reflected not only in the public press but in the police reports of the time, often marked by pleasingly complex punctuation, elegant phrasing and a sense of dramatic narrative.

It has been calculated that 332 newspapers were circulating in Ireland between 1900 and 1922 (not including news-sheets or papers that originated in Britain).[15] Irish demotic politics were conducted in a process of public yet intimate dialogue and exchange. With the outbreak of the First World War and the advent of the 'mosquito press' of subversive and satirical journals, this became almost manic, and the rhetoric reached new heights of extremism – as many establishment figures bemusedly noted. But even before this, the proliferation of titles is striking, and so – intermittently – were the circulation figures. Well-off backers (including Maud Gonne) came and went, ingenious loans were set up, advertising revenue was extracted from firms emphasizing their commitment to Irish-made produce, contributors worked for nothing, and titles succeeded each other with bewildering ease.

Sympathetic printers were no less essential than generous funders and committed journalists: Griffith's *United Irishman* campaigned with especial bitterness against the Dublin printers Browne & Nolan for employing staff from Britain instead of native compositors. Seán T. O'Kelly was inducted into the IRB in 1901 by a printer, Patrick Daly, and noted how many republican initiates were connected to the trade.[16] Radical periodicals and posters bore the imprint of Patrick Mahon in Yarnhall Street, or Joe Stanley's Gaelic Press in Liffey Street, or the same proprietor's retail 'Art Depot' in Mary Street, or the Irish Printing Depot, Lower Abbey Street (which also produced Ancient Irish vellum notepaper, Irish-made wrapping-paper, art calendars and so on).[17] These businesses tended to operate just north of the Liffey, within easy reach of the editorial offices they served.

Alice Milligan, the pugnacious Northern pioneer of tableau theatre, was also a trail-blazer with the journal she edited with Anna Johnston ('Ethna Carbery') in the late 1890s, the *Shan Van Vocht*. The title, meaning 'Poor Old Woman', refers to yet another female personification of Ireland, expressed in a patriotic ballad of 1798. A vivid photograph captures the pair of young Ulsterwomen at this stage of their lives; there is a distinct air of looking for trouble. Their paper set out the classic mixture of stories, reportage, polemic, Gaelic revivalism, exemplary biographies of famous Irish people, exhortations to buy Irish-made goods, and popular history. The formula was not particularly revolutionary in itself, but this was Belfast. And the paper contained revolutionary potential: the range and vitality of advanced-nationalist journalism helped to prepare the way for the shift into open subversion from 1912.

The *Shan Van Vocht*, like other radical journals, often employed themes and tropes from the unpolitical press, notably romantic fiction. This afforded another avenue to those would-be contributors languishing in bourgeois households, like Rosamond Jacob, who spent many years of the pre-revolutionary era working on her novel 'Callaghan' and sending off stories to generally unreceptive editors. More commercially successful authors such as Katharine Tynan and Nora Hopper produced reams of stories in which love conquered across sectarian, political and national divisions (a tradition stretching back to the more substantial 'national tales' pioneered by Irish novelists after the Act of Union). Milligan's tales appeared under titles such as 'The Outlaw's Bride', invariably dealing with rebellious girls from privileged unionist backgrounds getting it together with sexy Catholic freedom-fighters, and daring damsels foiling bumbling British officers. These present a combination of disguised autobiography and wish-fulfilment, and articulate a poignant contrast with her own long life, full of disappointments.

Milligan has been hailed as an underrated pioneer of radical-nationalist journalism and – as seen in an earlier chapter – agit-prop drama. This is true in some ways, but her low profile in the cultural history of the period reflects the derivative and banal nature of her writing, and a congenital weakness for bathos ('O Ireland dear, of my whole life's love for thee/O Ireland dear, thy redemption come to thee!'[18]). Her work sustained a resolutely orotund Victorian flavour while contemporaries were defining new territory. Another reason for Milligan's subordinate position in the Irish historical record may be that she adhered to the Protestant faith of her youth and was disillusioned by the clericalism and narrow-mindedness of the post-revolutionary dispensation.

But in the 1890s and early 1900s she was a key influence upon literary-minded young nationalists such as Bulmer Hobson, Patrick McCartan and Terence MacSwiney. During the 1890s she was a neighbour of F. J. Bigger on the Antrim Road, and became closely involved in the expansive cultural and political activities centred on Ardrigh. Here she met the dashing separatist Roger Casement, the revolutionary socialist James Connolly, the actor-musician Cathal O'Byrne and others. She also played a prominent part in the 1898 project of commemorating the 1798 Rising, in which Bigger was a central figure; there was a special room at Ardrigh dedicated to 1798 memorabilia, and he indefatigably searched out the graves of forgotten rebels. The Rising played an essential part in the self-definition of Northern Protestant radicals, as proof positive that their native culture held within it the potential for all-Ireland nationalism – a clear rejoinder to contemporary encouragement of Ulster unionism by the Conservative Party in Britain.[19] Milligan advanced these arguments during her editorship of the *Northern Patriot* from October 1895, often in verses that could have come straight from Thomas Davis's *Nation* in the early 1840s:

And now, when Ascendancy closed its foul reign,
And the notes of the Angelus peal o'er the plain,
Shall we suffer disunion to raise its vile head
In the long-suffering land where our fore-fathers bled?
Oh, no, 'neath the old flag united we'll stand,
In a peaceful endeavour to lift up our land
To her long vacant place 'mid the nations again,
Nor look with distrust on the Northern Men.[20]

She projected the thesis more aggressively in the *Shan Van Vocht*, and kept up the pressure through lectures, historical discussions, plays and fiction.[21] The *Shan Van Vocht* folded in 1899 because of financial troubles, and perhaps also because it tried to tread an editorial line of non-sectarianism and high-minded proto-Fenianism without endorsing party or factionalist politics. When Arthur Griffith took over its subscription list to begin his own paper, he would make no such mistake.

The profusion of journals read by aspiring radicals around the turn of the century did not subscribe to identical ideas. The *Shan Van Vocht* indicated as much by instituting a column called 'Other People's Opinions', giving house-room to agendas such as James Connolly's socialist republicanism without necessarily endorsing it. Maud Gonne was never particularly open to other people's opinions, but she printed socialist dispatches from Connolly in *Irlande Libre*, dealing with social conditions in Ireland, and referred to him as 'notre collaborateur', while herself remaining suspicious of socialist economics – as befitted someone much involved in French radical right-wing politics. By contrast Alice Milligan inveighed against 'anarchical methods' and 'bomb throwing and blowing up buildings without aim or reason' in the *Shan Van Vocht* during the 1890s – clearly seeing developments on the Continent as presenting an awful warning for Ireland. Nonetheless, while 'not at liberty to preach revolution', the paper promised to report the doings 'of revolutionaries, insurgents, conspirators in Matabeleland, Johannesburg, Cuba, Canada'.[22] Romantic Fenianism dictated the tone of her magazine (and was probably the commitment which terminated Milligan and Carbery's other employment as editors of the *Northern Patriot*). The language of soldierly preparation was frequently employed, and used to advance the idea of achieving discipline and drill through sport: 'It is the bounden duty of every man, of every body, who dares to dream of freedom, to make himself in every way that lies in his power a soldier fit for Ireland's service,' declared Milligan in 1896.[23] This too was prophetic.

After Milligan, many of the people who dominated the radical press in the early years of the new century are the familiar names who would come to prominence later. They include Arthur Griffith, Bulmer Hobson, Helena Molony, Seán MacDermott, P. S. O'Hegarty, Terence MacSwiney, Hanna Sheehy-Skeffington, Patrick Pearse and Maud Gonne – though some, such as Fred Ryan or D. P. Moran, would fall into obscurity or take themselves elsewhere. By far the most prominent figure was Griffith, an enigmatic man whose eventual emergence as President of the new Free State after the War of Independence would not have been forecast by many people twenty years earlier. He was born in 1871, and thus older than most of the people we have encountered, and for many of them he occupied the position of guru. His credentials were working class: born in a tenement house, he left his Christian Brothers education at twelve, was apprenticed to the printing trade, and thenceforth developed his powerful if rather narrow intellect through the National Library and reading-clubs. Already active in the little societies that sprang up during the mid-1880s, he joined the IRB – though by 1901, while his name was still on the books in the Bartholomew Teeling branch, he rarely attended meetings. Griffith was politicized by a spell in South Africa in the late 1890s; his passionate support of the Boers a few years later went with a ready suspicion of cosmopolitan financial interests and imperial conspiracies, which could shade into anti-Semitism as well as Anglophobia. But he emerged as the most rhetorically powerful Irish journalist of his time, and an original and creative political thinker.

In a series of periodicals from the turn of the century Griffith propagandized his own brand of separatist political culture, drawing highly coloured and partial lessons from Irish history: those evenings in the National Library instilled a reverence for Davis, Mitchel and the Young Irelanders that recurs throughout his journalism. His papers the *United Irishman* and its successor *Sinn Féin* embraced a wide range of contemporary causes, denouncing the genteel Irish establishment in scathing and iconoclastic prose. Griffith was passionately anti-Dreyfusard, partly from an admiration of French *étatisme*, partly from his own weakness for conspiracy theories featuring Jews and Freemasons, and partly because he instinctively distrusted any cause taken up by well-meaning liberals. His interest in French politics also reflected his readiness to employ imaginative parallels from abroad – most famously, the example of how Hungary had achieved dual-monarchy status under the Austrian Empire, published as the bestselling pamphlet *The Resurrection of Hungary* in 1904. Despite his IRB connections, Griffith kept recurring to this possibility for Ireland, suggesting a link to the crown, and pouring cold water on the feasibility of physical-force, which infuriated many on the fringes of Cumann na nGaedheal and later Sinn Féin – the umbrella-groupings of radical nationalists which he fostered and sustained. His economic priorities were strongly marketed, with batteries of statistics, in order to prove the value and potential of self-sufficiency and a vastly increased population. Griffith tended to write most of his articles himself, in a uniquely strident, scornful tone that conferred great authority; though in person he was more self-effacing, as people found when they sought him out.

Long afterwards, Richard Mulcahy tried to analyse Griffith's influence on young nationalists around 1908, as they slowly realized that

> ... the type of home rule you were likely to get was not going to be all that you would want. When I say myself I am talking of the community or the class or the companionship that I represented. We had absorbed all Griffith's teaching in that respect; we regarded him as our great mind and our great leader, so that we were being conditioned, not in a party political kind of a way, but we were conditioned in relation to Irish life and its development and its fostering.[24]

In an unpublished memoir Kevin O'Shiel described his first encounter with Griffith. As student enthusiasts, he and a friend decided that they must meet this legendary figure and went to the Ship Tavern on Middle Abbey Street, which they knew Griffith frequented. The barman obligingly pointed out 'a small, broad-shouldered, stockily-built man, with a large moustache, drinking stout with a couple of friends'. The two undergraduates expressed their admiration of his work, which was shyly received; Griffith stood them a drink and then drifted away.[25] Later, O'Shiel would become closely connected to him. But the encounter suggests the intimacy of Dublin's small world (reminiscent of how the youthful Joyce sought out AE and Yeats); it is also notable that before meeting Griffith, his student admirers had never seen a picture of him and had no idea what he looked like. The editor who did so much to create the cult-image of figures like Maud Gonne managed to remain relatively anonymous himself.

The content of the *United Irishman*, as its name implies, harked back to the inspiration of 1798 which meant so much to Milligan and others, but it operated much closer to the cutting edge. (It also appeared weekly, not monthly.) The upheavals within the Irish Parliamentary Party that brought about an uneasy reunion of Parnellites and anti-Parnellites at this time, the sectarian machinations of the Ancient Order of Hibernians, the local interest-groups mobilized by the United Irish League – all were mordantly exposed and satirized, along with the inadequacies and iniquities of British government. Ireland would 'lead the world against the bloody, rapacious and soul-shivering imperialism of England'.[26] Griffith maintained a lofty and boundless contempt for the necessary compromises in which Redmond's Irish Parliamentary Party was inevitably immersed; this analysis was an article of faith for the disparate nationalists who gathered under the resonant name of Sinn Féin. The *United Irishman* also acted as a kind of house newspaper for Gonne's political women's association, Inghinidhe na hÉireann. There was a noticeable input from female journalists, including Mary Butler, Jennie Wyse Power, Nora Hopper, Hanna Sheehy-Skeffington and especially Maud Gonne, whose money helped to bankroll the paper until the fallout from her separation from John MacBride in 1903–4. The police, who kept a close eye on the radical press, wondered how the *United Irishman* survived, given that the printer and publisher Bernard Doyle was 'only a struggling man'.[27] In fact, Gonne provided twenty-five shillings a week, which paid Griffith's salary as editor, copywriter and compositor, and she also contributed the proceeds of some lecture-tours. Her own columns stressed social issues, Gaelic revivalism and examples of mythic legend and stirring prophecy, the nobility of the South African Boers, the decadence of English culture, and international conspiracies of several kinds, not least Jewish.[28] Griffith's paper also printed Gonne's play *Dawn*, which reprises some of these themes, along with the iniquity of emigration as a desertion of the motherland, even at the point of starvation. The *United Irishman* also spread far and wide the much mythologized 'Patriotic Children's Treat', which Gonne masterminded as a counter-demonstration to the royal visit in 1900 (an occasion also marked by the paper reprinting Gonne's incendiary 1897 article about Queen Victoria, 'The Famine Queen': John Mitchel *redivivus*).

The great contrast between the *United Irishman* and the *Shan Van Vocht* was the style, quality and rebarbativeness of the writing, which was very largely Griffith's own. Where its predecessor was flowery and Victorian, the *United Irishman* was uncompromisingly modern. Its editor had lived and worked abroad, was familiar with the new journalism, and had a keen eye for what was going in Europe and the Empire; he knew that the style of political journalism must be pointed, personal, deflationary and, where necessary, spiteful. Good manners had nothing to do with it. The paper also provided, in its early days, a forum for the cultural avant-garde: Yeats, George Moore, Oliver St John Gogarty, John Eglinton and Edward Martyn all published there. As we have seen, Frank Fay, later a key figure in the Abbey Theatre, was the *United Irishman*'s drama critic, using his columns to argue for didactic cultural nationalism – a stance he later abandoned – and several experimental plays were printed in its pages. However, this inclusive tendency, and the *United Irishman*'s role as flag-bearer for the dramatic avant-garde, would be compromised by the political – or unpolitical – direction taken by the Abbey Theatre under its benefactor Annie Horniman, an enemy to all things nationalist. Sympathy for dramatic experimentalism was also undercut by Griffith's violent distaste for the plays of Synge, and above all by his firm belief that art must serve as propaganda.

Propaganda for what? One reason why readers devoured the *United Irishman*, and later its successor *Sinn Féin* (which was printing 8,000 copies a month by 1911[29]), was that there was always a frisson concerning how far the papers advocated actual subversion of the state. The papers clearly preached separatism in an abstract, psychological and cultural sense; at the outset Griffith was still in the IRB, along with his inspirational colleague, the charismatic but short-lived William Rooney. But when it came to sentimental Fenian praise of 'The Sword', Griffith could on occasion be as lacerating as his rival D. P. Moran, who consistently lampooned such attitudinizing in the *Leader*. Bulmer Hobson's paper the *Republic* was in fact founded in 1906 in order to preach unambiguous separatism, at a time when Griffith was seen to be taking dilution too far. Despite his tradition of excoriating Redmond and the parliamentarians, he was coming to be considered distinctly unsound on the question of the British monarch. Again, in marked contrast with the *Shan Van Vocht*, Griffith used his papers to work out for himself alternative routes to practical independence – visionary though the route might be. This was the process behind *The Resurrection of Hungary*: that Ireland could attain autonomy within the United Kingdom by the construction of a dual monarchy. Since this depended upon a particularly skewed and idealized version of Austro-Hungarian history (particularly where the Magyars were concerned), it was read in some quarters as a Swiftian parody.

It also infuriated old-style Fenians, to whom the idea of any connection with the British crown implied a Faustian, not to say satanic, pact. Griffith, however, would return to the idea, bolstered by his *idée fixe* about the 1783 Act of Renunciation, which, according to his (inaccurate) reading, made the subsequent Act of Union invalid under constitutional law. This was of a piece with the oddly academic and finger-wagging tone which could invade his columns of stirring invective: the mark of the autodidact, which never left him.

Sinn Féin was funded by sales of stock to better-off supporters; debentures were taken up by Casement, George Gavan Duffy, Michael O'Rahilly and several foreign subscribers. Its editor received two hundred pounds a year but the paper could not afford to pay its contributors. Nonetheless, they included James Stephens, Padraic Colum, Susan Mitchell, Pádraic Ó Conaire, Séumas O'Sullivan, Joseph Campbell and William Bulfin. These were distinguished commentators by any standard; most of them would become star contributors to the more highbrow *Irish Review* edited by Thomas MacDonagh and Joseph Plunkett a few years later.[30] Less impressively, the articles by Sydney Gifford sustained the tone that had made the *United Irishman* popular, presenting Dublin as a decadent centre of foreign influence, where 'the deadly Jew-made fever has crept over Grafton Street', an infection that must be extirpated by Gaelic purism. (The influential nationalist journalist William Bulfin, in his bestselling *Rambles in Eirinn*, was equally unwelcoming to the idea that Jews might be tolerated in Ireland.[31]) But the reason why Griffith's newspapers remained *sui generis* was that they presented the familiar conundrums of the British–Irish relationship from a new angle, in prose that was demotic, hard-edged and sometimes mercilessly funny. The same was true of James Connolly's Marxist productions, though he and Griffith were ideologically many poles apart: Griffith favouring the economics of autarky and self-sufficiency, as preached by Friedrich List, and viewing international socialism as something akin to Freemasonry, a star exhibit in his capacious menagerie of *bêtes noires*.

Griffith's politics were serpentine enough, but his rival D. P. Moran, who edited and wrote much of the *Leader*, was even more unpredictable. Excoriatingly anti-English, far more stridently Catholic than Griffith, equally contemptuous of the Irish Parliamentary Party as Anglicized parasites, but unprepared to endorse Sinn Féin's radical alternative, he directed his eloquent and often hilarious abuse at most corners of the Irish political world. Terence MacSwiney, writing in the minuscule Cork journal *Éire Óg*, denounced the *Leader* for not living up to its anti-British pretensions, and for its 'egotistical and dictatorial tone'; he felt it lowered the 'dignity' of the national cause. His friend de Róiste was similarly shocked at the 'bitter scornful attacks' on Sinn Féin in the *Leader*, correctly suspecting his colleague Daniel Corkery.[32] From a different angle, secular or Protestant feminists like Rosamond Jacob and Cesca Trench loathed the *Leader* – 'a hateful little paper', in Cesca's view, and 'the most unpleasant and lowest down paper in the country', according to Jacob[33] – but Moran's brilliant phrase-making and nicknames tended to stick. The *Leader* also had a special line in Irish self-castigation. For instance, it unexpectedly contradicted the stock-in-trade allegation, subscribed to by John Redmond as well as by the Fenian orthodoxy, that British policies had depopulated Ireland; Moran preferred to blame the Irish themselves for not patronizing native industry and culture, and selfishly emigrating in search of supposed betterment which would, he promised them, turn into Dead Sea fruit in their mouths. Moran's 'Philosophy of Irish Ireland' was projected through a campaign in his columns to make people wear Irish clothes, eat Irish food and endow their children with Irish names; he scornfully described so-called nationalists setting off to Sunday Mass with 'their recreant skins' cast in decadent English worsteds.[34] He violently attacked all manifestations of popular English culture, especially imported plays 'where religion is besmeared; idling is glorified; cadging and thievery are presented as "smart" arts; the heroes are cads; and the heroines are – well, the modern theatre has a name for them – "women with a past".'[35]

The scatter-gun abuse of the *Leader* was both a strength and a weakness. Events seemed to outdistance Moran, though his religious sectarianism and endorsement of *petite bourgeoise* values were in some ways prophetic of the post-revolutionary future. In the years up to 1916, however, it is hard to better Patrick Maume's summing-up: 'Moran was the fox to Griffith's hedgehog; he lost out to Griffith in historical reputation because, while he knew many things, Griffith centred his life on one thing Moran did not take into account: the extent of nationalist discontent with the British state, and the ability of a determined minority in times of crisis to channel these discontents into a nationalist project more radical than seemed possible in 1900.'[36]

A different strain of polemic was reflected in W. P. Ryan's *Peasant*, which was nationalist in a more sardonic and pluralist way – and also socialist, which differentiated it sharply from Griffith's output. The *Workers' Republic* (1898–1903) and the *Irish Worker* (1911–14) presented the ideology of the labour leaders and 'agitators' James Connolly and Jim Larkin to a receptive, and often surprisingly large, audience. And as the Gaelic League became more widespread and implicitly more political, its journalistic activities became more important, especially through *An Claidheamh Soluis* under the editorship of Patrick Pearse. The premises of the paper, originally managed by that 'struggling man' Bernard Doyle, moved around Dublin's North side, from Ormond Quay to Sackville Street to Rutland Square, conveniently close to Gaelic League meeting-rooms and Tom Clarke's shop. The advertising and editorials, as well as much of the copy, remained largely in English for several years, with Irish taking over as cultural and political issues became more prominent. This process was encouraged by a subsequent manager, Michael O'Rahilly, self-styled Gaelic aristocrat and increasingly violent separatist. His inclinations were more crudely political, and he took a dictatorial line in suggesting cartoon subjects to contributors such as Cesca Trench.

> Cartoon No. 4, Wait and see. *Fan go bfeicid tu*. Picture of Irish Ireland (*Gaidil na hÉireann*), a beautiful girl lying on the ground tied hand and foot, gagged by *Béarla* [English]. The sword of Anglicization is piercing her through and a pool of blood has flowed from the wound. She is just making an effort to rise.

'Cartoons like these,' O'Rahilly added, 'would I think be very effective but they should be very simple and easily understood. Crude rather than subtle, you understand. We of the Claidheamh have to deal with a nation of political *infants*.'[37]

At a different level from the weekly (and sometimes daily) polemical sheets were the literary journals, weekly or monthly, which were more closely connected to the world of high culture and experimental writing. These included the *Irish Homestead* under AE and Susan Mitchell, which, though the organ of the Co-operative Movement, carried pieces by James Joyce as well as others of AE's protégés; its office in Merrion Square was, for moderate nationalists, a kind of alternative drop-in centre to Tom Clarke's shop across the Liffey. It was staffed by AE, magnificently unworldly but sharp for his purposes, and the high-spirited Mitchell, whose caustic verse-parodies of well-known Dublin personalities were widely feared and treasured. The *All Ireland Review*, edited and largely written by the eccentric revivalist writer and prophet Standish O'Grady, similarly cast a wide cultural net, and to read it is to hear echoes of the pluralist Ireland that was central to the imagination of a certain segment of the revolutionary generation. O'Grady's political principles followed his own apocalyptic-unionist line, alternately abusing and cajoling the landlord classes, who – he believed – held the key to Ireland's salvation. But his literary evocation of a Carlylean world of ancient Irish heroes in books such as *History of Ireland: The Heroic Period* had entered the bloodstream of nationalist revivalism. The *All Ireland Review* preached spiritual epiphanies and denounced materialism, often through the medium of heroic serial stories, but it also afforded the editor space to reply brutally to bemused letter-writers and to address open manifestoes to those who had incurred his displeasure – notably Yeats. 'Frankly, and quite between ourselves, I don't like at all the way you have been going on now for a good many years. You can't help it, I suppose, having got down into the crowd.'[38]

O'Grady also used his paper to preach the virtues of paganism, which he rated very highly, and to deride Catholic pieties – which cannot have helped him win a large constituency. The *All Ireland Review* struggled along at the mercy of O'Grady's chaotic financial management, as he tried to treble the subscription charge while keeping the street price at threepence. 'I regard it as a connecting link between the classes and the masses,' he wrote, 'the gentry and the people, the educated and those who, without being what is called educated, are a reading, considering, thinking kind of people, and who, as such, exercise an influence over considerable numbers.'[39] This was a perceptive analysis of the position occupied by many young radicals; but they were not going to be persuaded by the *All Ireland Review*, and looked to more extreme publications.

There was also the short-lived *Dana* (immortalized by Joyce in *Ulysses*), featuring literary high culture, and the more directly political *Irish Review*, edited at various times by Thomas MacDonagh, Padraic Colum, Joseph Plunkett and Tom Kettle. It was founded 'to promote the application of Irish intellect to Irish life'; when Plunkett took over from Padraic Colum in the summer of 1913, it moved to 17 Marlborough Road in Donnybrook, the suburban house where he was living with his sister Geraldine. Their mother, Countess Plunkett (who was also their landlord), provided the £150 necessary to keep the magazine going under its new editor, after the first backer withdrew his financial support. Printed by Ernest Manico in Temple Bar, it published art plates by Jack and John B. Yeats, William Orpen and AE, as well as articles and stories by James Stephens, Patrick Pearse, Joseph Campbell, Arthur Griffith, Douglas Hyde and many others. Under Plunkett, the increasingly political direction of the journal was indicated by a series of pseudonymous articles such as 'Ireland, Germany and the Next War' (in July 1913), in fact written by the Plunkett family friend Roger Casement.

The *Irish Review* continued simultaneously to provide a useful out-let for Plunkett's and MacDonagh's play-scripts as well as more high-falutin literary journalism than was found elsewhere. This was also catered to by the self-consciously internationalist and modern-minded Thomas Kettle, who had learnt his trade as a student journalist editing *St Stephen's* at University College. Kettle, the star of his uni-versity generation, had also studied in Germany, and read widely in French and German; an early interest in Sinn Féin, and a brief fling with socialism, did not survive his reading of Nietzsche. His constitutional-nationalist political ambitions, as seen in an earlier chapter, were not harmed by his marriage to Mary Kate Ryan's enemy Mary Sheehy, more conventional than her sister Hanna Sheehy-Skeffington. This connected him to the Irish Parliamentary Party elite, whose ranks he would eventually join. He had already tried to rejuvenate the party through the Young Ireland branch of the United Irish League, founded in November 1904. People attracted to this ginger-group, however, often found the party impervious to their efforts, and drifted to more advanced sectors of the political spectrum. Kettle's strategy was different; like so many of his contemporaries, he started a journal, the *Nationist*, which lasted for six months from September 1905. 'Nationist' was coined in deliberate contradistinc-tion to 'nationalist', and Kettle derided what he saw as the woolliness and impracticality of Griffith's thought. The journal reflected his own interest in the growth of democracy and nationalism in Europe at large, which he applied to Ireland in a distinctly cosmopolitan way; this attracted contributors such as the feminist and pacifist Sheehy-Skeffington (whose influence soon predominated), Joyce's friend Constantine Curran, the clever young lawyer Hugh Kennedy and the poet–playwright Padraic Colum. Unlike many of his IPP colleagues, Kettle was a passionate advocate of women's suffrage. Arguing against Irish exceptionalism was a central theme; readers of the first issue were encouraged to accept the country as 'a great complex fact; an organism with all the complications of modern society'.[40] Like the *Peasant* or the *All Ireland Review*, it sustained a rhetoric of pluralism and scepticism. Its pages preserve an aspect of these years that would not survive the coming armageddon of revolution, civil war and the establishment of a conservative Catholic state.

The same was true of the *National Democrat*, published and largely written by Hanna and Francis Sheehy-Skeffington from 1907, and congratulated by one correspondent for being 'undismayed by episcopal hostility'.[41] Within Dublin, the *Democrat*'s initial subscribers seem to have been the middle classes of Rathmines and Rathgar, with an interest in labour and social questions;[42] but the editors were anxious to extend the sales to Britain as well, and distributed the magazine through Peter Murphy, a Liverpool agent who also handled *Sinn Féin*, the *Leader*, the *Republic* and provincial Irish newspapers. (Murphy's Irish Depot and Catholic Depository was the kind of commercial institution which enabled the Irish living overseas to sustain their national and religious identity; it advertised 'Prayer Books, Beads, Statues, Holy water Fonts, Scapulars, medallions, religious books, oleographs, Irish historical and other works, pictures, views, etc., jewellery, ornaments, Blackthorns, all the leading Irish papers and a large selection of Gaelic books, and Irish manufactured stationery.'[43])

To some Irish nationalists resident in England, however, the enlightening of Albion was a lost cause. One correspondent, asked by Skeffington to distribute the *National Democrat*, demurred on the grounds of its socialist leanings and belief in the international fellowship of the workers. 'If the "National Democrat" advocates the claims of Ireland's rights to "Nationhood", I shall be pleased to help it in every positive way, but I don't believe in appealing like a nation of beggars to the English Democracy for help or support of our clan, because they also are members of the Robber Band who plundered Ireland.'[44] But employment in the Robber Band's country was not incompatible with spreading the word. P. S. O'Hegarty, having passed his civil service examinations in 1902, used his comfortable desk job in London as a base for journalistic operations, dispatching his official work rapidly and then devoting himself to writing subversive articles.

> I would not like to say how much stuff for the mosquito press I wrote in the peaceful seclusion of St Martin's Le Grand, looking out on the inner courtyard, with sitting opposite me a Cockney, decent, cheerful, plodding and utterly devoid of imagination or alertness of mind, as

only a Cockney can be, who found it nearly impossible to do his day's work although he came in at 9 and stayed till 6.

Revisiting the office in the 1920s, O'Hegarty found his old colleague still at his desk, piled high with files. 'I nearly sat opposite him from force of habit.'[45]

Back across the Irish Sea, nationalist activists in Ireland kept an eye on British opinion. Down in Cork, Liam de Róiste was sending material on Irish-Irelander activities to the Davis Press Agency, started up by O'Hegarty in West London, which supplied, in de Róiste's words, 'a counterblast to the news supplied by the English press agencies' such as Reuters. 'Very many people,' de Róiste reflected, 'estimate your influence and standing by the notice given you in the daily papers, though one now thinks there is sufficient knowledge [now] of how false reports can be.'[46] The tireless de Róiste also acted as agent for *Banba* and other journals, as well as contributing notes, letters, articles and verses to W. P. Ryan's *Irish Peasant*. Finally, in 1906, after dreaming of it for years, he brought out his own little journal aimed at advanced nationalists in Cork – the *Shield*, an eight-page monthly. De Róiste used his contacts and expertise gained in the commercial department of his hated employers, Skerry's College, and found a sympathetic printer in Edward Mooney at the Shandon Printing Works – 'a quiet type of man, with unusual ideas of affairs – influenced by reading English socialistic publications'.[47] De Róiste's companions in the Celtic Literary Society were, as usual, infuriatingly sceptical about his latest fad, but the first issue appeared in August and sold a thousand copies, nearly breaking even. The paper lasted into 1907, racked by financial problems, while de Róiste oscillated between black despair and euphoric hope that it might become a weekly. When the *Irish Peasant* was closed down at the fiat of Cardinal Logue (it had made fun of clerical pretensions), de Róiste disloyally hoped that the *Shield* might take it over, but his own devoutness put paid to the idea, after the usual agonies of introspection.[48] He remained passionately determined to make his mark by publishing in other journals, and eventually managed to place his vast manifesto-poem, 'Ireland Calls', in Griffith's *Sinn Féin*, covering nearly two pages with invocations which owe as much to Walt Whitman and Herbert Spencer as to James Clarence Mangan.

Men of the Irish race: men of a nation noble
Sons of mighty sires, who climbed the mountains of fame –
Climbed it o'er rough rocks and sharp; in the noble endeavour
To breathe the pure air of freedom: in the clear, bright light of the sun –
Of the sun of Justice whose beams undimmed, unsullied, unbroken,
Shine on for ever and ever, above the fleeting clouds
Of men's ideas and opinions.

Hear ye – though weak the voice: that calls midst the noisy clamour
Of tongues that babble and babble; like the ancient builders confused.
They prate for the future glibly; and promise for men unborn
'For ever and ever' they promise – forgetting the nation's soul;
Forgetting the laws of growth;
Forgetting the laws of development; the principles of existence;
The never-ending progressions; the evolutions and changes;
The expanding and extending; that mark the living things.

The twenty-fourth and final stanza left de Róiste's readers in no doubt: 'Better to die for an Ideal, under the standard of Right/Than compromise with Wrong, and live the life of a Harlot.'[49]

III

These magazines and journals reached far fewer people than the mainstream nationalist dailies such as the *Freeman's Journal* and the *Independent*, but they helped to construct a radical alternative worldview. They also gave a voice to a wide range of talented individuals operating in spheres outside the establishment. Above all, the activities of the Sheehy-Skeffingtons highlight the importance of women journalists, and the opportunities given by periodical publishing to women denied a role elsewhere – or pressed by popular acclaim into a role which was confining as well as celebrated, as happened with Constance Markievicz and Maud Gonne. Maud Gonne's beauty, her fondness for dramatic platform appearances and the shadow of scandal that surrounded her private life obscured her commitment to the new politics of publicity. This involved a variety of demonstration-tactics as well as an impressive amount of hard journalistic work; she was also enabled by a large private income. The far less wealthy Markievicz, on her way to socialism and already heading the Fianna, her youthful militia, was rather unfairly seen as an upper-class eccentric out for kicks. A more serious commitment is implicit in her columns in *Bean na hÉireann* ('Woman of Ireland'), the journal of Gonne's organization Inghinidhe na hÉireann, edited by Helena Molony, which ran from 1908 to 1911. Molony, a combative and talented actress with a weakness for drink, pursued a radical existence on many fronts; she had learnt her trade on James Connolly's *Workers' Republic* a decade earlier.

Journalism was also the field where in these years the women's suffrage movement and the labour movement intersected with the politics of radical nationalism – sometimes antagonistically. Griffith remained anti-socialist, for one thing, and several nationalist agitators felt that the women's cause should be strictly subordinated to the national issue. But the journalism of people such as Delia Larkin reminds us that in 1911 an Irish Women Workers' Union was actually established, and that women were coming to the fore in socialist as well as in republican politics. There is a tendency to see the radical, or, more accurately, anti-establishment, press of these years as exclusively represented by Griffith and Moran, speaking through the *United Irishman* and the *Leader* – one of those binary oppositions beloved of Irish history. But the range of journals and interests, bringing in labour interests, feminism, and the socialist pluralism represented in the Sheehy-Skeffingtons' *National Democrat* and W. P. Ryan's *Peasant*, suggests a different and more complex picture.

The *Irish Peasant*, which began publication from Navan as a weekly in 1905, took a more sanguine and relaxed view of Irish possibilities than Moran's *Leader*, reflecting its editor's different personality. It was founded by James McCann, an imaginative local entrepreneur, and soon reached a far wider audience than local dissidents in County Meath. The *Irish Peasant* boasted two remarkable editors, first Pat Kenny and then (from December 1905) W. P. Ryan. Anti-grazier, anti-clerical and pro-industry, the journal's opinions had to be expressed in coded language: there was no public opinion worthy of the name in Ireland, it declared, but 'a triumphant dictation founded on political ignorance and lack of character and citizenship'.[50] Ryan's cheerful secularism in educational matters, the subversive and quizzical editorial tone, and his ridiculing of clerical opposition to mixed Gaelic League classes precipitated the paper's suppression, in its first incarnation, at the hands of Cardinal Logue. The paper continued as the *Peasant*, now published in Dublin; from February 1907 it merged with Cathal O'Shannon's *Irish Nation* and carried on under the dual name till December 1910. Bulmer Hobson was contributing feisty editorials by 1908, and the paper eventually absorbed Hobson's own short-lived but influential journal, the *Republic*.[51] Rosamond Jacob, on one of her forays into Dublin radical life from her Waterford base, visited the *Peasant* office in the summer of 1910 ('awful looking' on the outside) and was pleased to find Ryan 'very affable in a melancholy way: he looks like a Russian anarchist, with very straight thick black hair and an ugly straight black beard.'[52] By that date, Ryan had much to feel anarchical about. Other hard-line separatists saw him as more socialist than nationalist. The brisk young Ulster extremist Pat McCartan dismissed him as being 'of the Gaelic League literary type; right enough of a kind but not the kind we want'.[53]

By 1910 Griffith too looked less and less like 'the kind we want'. As Sinn Féin expanded and set the tone for political debate among radical nationalists from about 1905, advanced nationalists from IRB-dominated organizations began to try to make their own running. Accordingly, the awkwardly evolving relationship between Sinn Féin and the Dungannon clubs floated by Bulmer Hobson and Denis McCullough was reflected in the evolution of new journals. Griffith still retained kudos with young republican journalists as their 'prickly but acknowledged guru',[54] but he was being outpaced. From 1906, when Griffith's paper *Sinn Féin* succeeded the *United Irishman*, the tension between his idiosyncratic strategies of separation and classic Fenian verities became clearer. Bulmer Hobson, with his habitual optimism, cheerfully decided to enter the lists. In May 1906 Liam de Róiste heard that 'Bulmer Hobson, of Belfast, intends bringing out a journal, to be called "The Republic", to openly preach separation of Ireland from England, by Sinn Féin means'; the following December he recorded 'sending a subscription, which I can ill afford, to Bulmer Hobson for the "Republic", which is to be out this week'.[55] Aided by

Denis McCullough and McCullough's father, a compositor who had worked on the *Northern Weekly*, Hobson featured sparky articles by Robert Lynd and others, including Hobson himself and his patron F. J. Bigger. 'Think of me here in this respectable suburban residence,' Bigger wrote dramatically to Alice Stopford Green from Ardrigh in January 1907, 'writing such articles as that anti-militia one in last week's R[epublic], and the anti-police one in this week's and the anti-Belfast one in next week's, and forsaking '98 heroes – I must stop it or I am lost body and soul.'[56]

Hobson had raised £125 to start the paper, supplemented by 500 five-shilling shares.[57] But he could never handle money (a failing bemoaned by McCullough, who conspicuously could), and the *Republic* did not pay its way; it had to be run down the following May, by which time Hobson had insouciantly decamped to Dublin, leaving McCullough 'high and dry'. Hobson, unfazed, reprinted some of its key articles as pamphlets (including Lynd's thoughtful analysis of the Orange Order), and ignored criticism from people such as Alice Stopford Green, who felt that his aggressive style had frightened off potential supporters.[58] Griffith evidently decided to avoid this danger, while broadening his own readership. In August 1909 he started *Sinn Féin* as a daily paper, to appear along with the weekly version. In an attempt to reach an audience in provincial Ireland, the daily (four pages, costing a halfpenny) included literary criticism, fashion items and cartoons, as well as the standard fare of Gaelic columns and political character-assassinations. But it also meant taking a conciliatory line that would not frighten the rural *petite bourgeoisie*, as well as involving ingenious balancing-feats where funding was concerned.[59] The ubiquitous Seán T. O'Kelly, Gaelic Leaguer and hopeful admirer of Mary Kate Ryan, was Secretary and Manager; it achieved a circulation of just over 3,000, when the weekly was selling 3,500. O'Kelly judged later that it was 'doomed from birth', though contributors included James Stephens, Séumas O'Kelly, Michael O'Rahilly, and Sydney and Grace Gifford.[60] To true believers, Griffith's attempt at reaching a wider audience inevitably meant dilution, and possibly corruption. P. S. O'Hegarty complained to George Gavan Duffy in September 1909 that 'Griffith has watered down everything as low as he possibly can. In Thursday's issue he proposes an alliance with the Tories! And the only definite idea in the paper seems to be to conciliate the unionists at all hazards. I believe in conciliating them but not at the expense of lowering our own practice or profession of nationalism.'[61]

To the separatist mind, Griffith was appearing more and more like the outdated but energetic old agrarian radical and Home Ruler William O'Brien, attempting to put together a feel-good coalition of moderate nationalists across a broad front, and in the process selling the pass as far as any real degree of independence was concerned. Attracting defectors from the IPP to Sinn Féin was not O'Hegarty's idea of constructing a bridgehead into radical separatism. After six ambitious months the daily *Sinn Féin* ceased publication in January 1910. The response of Griffith's IRB opponents was to start a new paper, *Irish Freedom*, which would 'unambiguously reassert republican virtue' – Bulmer Hobson's *Republic* reborn.[62]

Controlled in succession (and partly financed) by McCartan, O'Hegarty, Hobson and – once more – MacDermott, *Irish Freedom* was the preserve of the Young Turks, and got off to a good start: 7,000 copies of the first issue were printed, and 6,000 of the second. By 1912 MacDermott could boast that its circulation was double that of *Sinn Féin* and *An Claidheamh* combined.[63] IRB members were levied a shilling a month towards its support, making it a more or less official organ of the movement. Regular contributors included Pearse, Ernest Blythe, MacSwiney and O'Hegarty, while the business end was handled by Éamonn Ceannt, O'Rahilly and Béaslaí, with Cathal Brugha and Liam Mellows also involved. All would play a prominent part in 1916, and, unsurprisingly, the journal advocated unequivocal separatism and republicanism. O'Hegarty, writing as 'Lucan', added in religious toleration, free education, universal adult suffrage and equality before the law, though MacDermott editorialized that nationalism required the sacrifice of individual freedoms.[64] The paper took an anti-Partitionist line early on, and by 1914 was effectively preaching armed insurrection. Cesca Trench was amused to hear the newsboys outside the Rotunda shouting, '*Irish Freedom, Daily Mail, Daily Mail, Irish Freedom.*' She at first found it 'frightfully rabid, it quotes bits from Indian papers about the English and urges all its young readers, "Fianna" it calls them, first to hate England, 2nd to love Ireland: a thoroughly bad principal [*sic*] I think!'[65] But by 1914 she had decided it was

> a really very striking paper sometimes ... What strikes me most is the extreme youth of everyone concerned with it. Seán MacDiarmuid can't be more than 25, with his cleanshaven boyish face and his dreamy blue eyes, and the others must be younger, from their looks. The way he writes, it's all so young and honest and certain of himself and extreme, and yet every now and then there's a suggestion that if England would do the decent thing an arrangement might be arrived at.[66]

This inference was a response to the fact that Home Rule had, finally, been passed into law, during tortuous negotiations at Westminster over the previous two years. Redmond had thus apparently regained the initiative, though the measure as passed was dismissed as inadequate by *Irish Freedom* and its readers, while Ulster's resistance continued to block its implementation. It was, nonetheless, a critical juncture for separatists. Internecine strife soon broke out in the *Irish Freedom* office, highlighting a struggle between the older IRB generation, who were making a last push to regain control, and the young extremists (supported by Tom Clarke, middle aged though he was). This too was a key moment of inter-generational conflict. The future was with the young people, though when MacDermott was hospitalized with polio in late 1911, his opponents mounted what Piaras Béaslaí called 'an amazing appalling rotten beastly filthy unheard-of disgusting inconceivable mysterious repulsive abominable' attempt to kill the paper off.[67] Béaslaí weighed in by delivering his own copy for the paper to Tom Clarke's shop, in order to prevent its being spiked by enemies in the *Irish Freedom* office, and MacDermott eventually regained control. By now he and his mentor Clarke (to whom he was introduced by Hobson in 1907) were closely allied within the IRB. Though he had seen off the older Fenian generation, MacDermott would soon become more and more suspicious of his contemporaries Bulmer Hobson and P. S. O'Hegarty, thinking them not sufficiently extreme. This would be of decisive importance later, when the exhortations of the separatist press suddenly came within the bounds of reality. But in the pre-war era the freedom of the radical press from government censorship is striking. When drastic interference was inflicted upon independent-minded journals in Edwardian Ireland, it was far more likely to come from outraged senior Catholic clerics, who felt that their authority had been breached, than from the offices of Dublin Castle.

IV

By the same token, much of the driving power of the radical press was directed at the pretensions of other authorities besides the British state and the Irish Parliamentary Party. The tocsin to radical action against the older generation was also sounded by feminist and socialist journalism in the pre-war era. *Bean na hÉireann*, the voice of Inghinidhe na hÉireann, which was produced from November 1908 to February 1911 under Helena Molony's editorship, advocated 'militancy, separatism and feminism'. James Connolly and Bulmer Hobson wrote for it, as well as Constance Markievicz and Sydney Gifford. Arthur Griffith also contributed under a pen-name, declaring that Ireland was ready for 'a gynocracy . . . I am weary living in a world ruled by men with mouse-hearts and monkey-brains and I want change.'[68] The paper made room for socialist as well as feminist manifestoes. Suffragism presented more problematic issues: though consciously feminist, the idea of appealing to the British parliament for anything at all was anathema to several of *Bean na hÉireann*'s moving spirits. The editors and many of the contributors felt that national independence was the priority, putting their faith in a future, untainted, Sinn Féin government giving women the vote.

But they did not expect such a government to emerge peacefully. What is striking in *Bean na hÉireann* from as early as 1909 is the militancy of its pronouncements. Articles addressed 'The Art of Street-Fighting', and Helena Molony's ruminations on 'Physical Force' in September–October 1909 can be read as a deliberate response to Griffith's arguments in *Sinn Féin* that the militarist option was irrelevant, as it would simply be crushed by the might of the British Empire. In other articles too the need for bloodshed is discussed equably and even impatiently, and warm support expressed for revolutionaries in Egypt and India. Markievicz, much involved in her militaristic boy-scouting movement, issued a call to arms in the November 1909 issue. Her article 'Women, Ideals and Nationalism', originally a lecture delivered to the Students' National Literary Society, left its audience in little doubt:

> Arm yourselves with weapons to fight your nation's cause. Arm your soul with noble and free ideas. Arm your minds with the histories and memories of your country and her martyrs, her language, and a knowledge of her arts and industries. And if in your day the call should come for your body to arm, do not shirk that either.[69]

While prioritizing the nationalist over the suffrage campaign, Markievicz's contributions also condemned 'the old idea that a woman can only serve her nation through her home', and her own activism on several fronts bore this out. (So did the shambolic condition of her own household, mordantly noted by the bourgeoise Rosamond Jacob.)

After *Bean na hÉireann* ceased publication, Markievicz contributed to the *Irish Citizen*, established in 1912 as the journal of the Irish Women's Franchise League – specifically feminist but also (especially under the guidance of Louie Bennett) a strong voice for trade-union rights. Socialist journalism was first represented by Connolly's *Workers' Republic* in 1898, published from the Abbey Street headquarters of his Irish Socialist Republican Party. Appearing irregularly, it was internationalist rather than nationalist, carrying syndicated articles from the left-wing press in Germany and Britain. The paper died around the time that Connolly left Ireland for a protracted sojourn in America. It would revive in 1915, with a different emphasis. A far more influential paper was the *Irish Worker*, edited by the controversial syndicalist Jim Larkin and contributed to by his sister Delia (founder of the Irish Women Workers' Union in 1911 and the Irish Workers' Dramatic Society a year later).[70] Larkin started it in June 1911; he had earlier enjoyed a brief fling editing the *Harp*, which featured revolutionary socialistic manifestoes and libellous editorials. The *Irish Worker* cast a wider net. A weekly costing one penny, it sold very widely – just under 95,000 copies were in circulation within three months of its foundation.

The paper came into its own when recording the seismic effects of the 1913 Lockout, when Larkin's Irish Transport and General Workers' Union tried to challenge the employment practices of William Martin Murphy's transport and commercial empire. The *Irish Worker* specialized in exposing the corruption and exploitation of bosses, preached a robust version of syndicalism, and implied separatist and republican politics, though both the Larkins would later be marginalized by the current of Irish nationalist politics, and their Irish political careers ended in disillusionment. Not long after its foundation, Rosamond Jacob decided that 'the *Irish Worker* has changed from a fairly good Nationalist paper to a scurrilous rag full of abuse & personalities, no longer bothering itself to be patriotic.'[71] But it attracted contributors such as AE, Standish O'Grady, James Stephens, W. P. Ryan and the playwright St John Ervine. In the years up to the Rising, the *Irish Worker* represented a forum for discussion of class, feminist and economic issues, often expressed with a Griffithite tone of withering irony; the Irish businesses specifically targeted (Jacob's Biscuits, Gouldings Fertilizer, Thompsons' Sweets, Pembroke Laundry, Keogh's Sack Factory) added an equally Griffithite frisson of local reference and knockabout personal invective. But Larkin and his paper remained suspicious of Sinn Féin, which he judged to be consistently opposed to the interests of labour.

The *Irish Citizen* also started out as a weekly costing a penny, but its tone was more sober, which may be why it sold far fewer copies (3,000 per issue, whereas at its lowest the *Irish Worker* managed 20,000). Male suffragists such as James Cousins and Francis Sheehy-Skeffington were closely involved, as well as Hanna Sheehy-Skeffington and Louie Bennett, with the women eventually taking over more or less full control. Its primary objective, when founded in May 1912, was 'to form a means of communication between Irish Suffrage Societies and their members' and to publicize suffrage activities 'untainted by party bias', but the heightened political tempo of the next few years meant that national politics on other levels inevitably entered its pages. The editors' determination to expose the misrepresentations offered by the mainline press also meant that it was bound to be combative and at times subversive.

This owed a good deal to the influence of Francis Sheehy-Skeffington, who exercised most of the control between 1913 and 1916. An

Ulsterman who had cut his teeth on student journalism, he was never a friend to pietistic nationalism, and may have been responsible for the *Citizen*'s tactless and rather condescending mockery of the nationalist women's organization Cumann na mBan ('Association of Women'), established to support the (male) Irish Volunteers. The *Irish Citizen* referred to them, unforgivably, as 'slave women'.[72] It also campaigned against 'the old idea of motherhood', perhaps reflecting Hanna Sheehy-Skeffington's impatience with domestic role-stereotyping. A superbly revisionist reviewer of the scandalous memoir by Katharine O'Shea, widow of Charles Stewart Parnell, analysed Parnell's fate as 'the Nemesis of the anti-feminist ... to fall victim to a woman of the highly-sexed, unintellectual type, developed by the restriction of women's activities to the sphere euphemistically styled "the Home"'.[73] This could have been written by either of the Sheehy-Skeffingtons, and accurately reflected their iconoclastic approach to domestic pieties.

The suffrage issue challenged other boundaries too. Much space was devoted to the debate between militant and peaceful suffrage tactics, some of the contributions suggesting a distinctly radical notion of the position of women in contemporary society, and a strong sense that the advanced position of the Pankhurst sisters could profitably be adopted in Ireland. There was a distinct aura of threat: 'What Will She Do with It?' asked one cartoon depicting a suffragette, armed with the vote, looking contemplatively at a hand grenade and a flask of paraffin. Though the relationship of suffragism to advanced nationalism is a tangled pattern, there is certainly evidence that the advocacy of rebelliousness, the desirability of imprisonment in a martyred cause, contempt for members of the Irish Parliamentary Party and the duty of assailing the representatives of British rule in public translated easily from the suffrage cause to the cause of Ireland. And this was not affected by the actual passing of a Home Rule Bill in 1912–14, complicated as it was by Ulster's resistance and the opposition of the House of Lords. The stance taken by the radical press, at all levels, had long presented the Home Rulers at Westminster as a rhetorical irrelevance, and the terms of the Bill as falling far short of meaningful independence (particular scorn was directed at the continuing presence of Irish MPs in the imperial parliament, and that body's retention of power over taxation and land-purchase arrangements). The militarization of Irish society, as will be seen in the next chapter, accentuated this reaction. For the readers of advanced papers, another political reality existed beyond the world of political negotiations in London, and the machinations of the Ancient Order of Hibernians at home.

With the outbreak of war in 1914, the stance of the *Citizen* implied a further degree of subversion. Many of those associated with it were pacifists. However, other elements, especially suffrage societies with large unionist memberships, threw their energies into the war effort. There was also the underlying argument – as in Britain – that enacting the role of full citizens would qualify them for the vote when hostilities were over, but several Irish radicals saw through this wishful thinking. The suffragist and trade-union organizer Louie Bennett wrote despairingly to Hanna Sheehy-Skeffington that their pro-war colleagues were 'like sheep astray and I suppose when the necessity of knitting socks is over – the order will be – bear sons. And those of us who can't will feel we had better get out of the way as quickly as we can.'[74] Depressingly for people who felt like that, the majority of suffragists probably supported the Allied cause. Nonetheless the debates in the columns of the *Irish Citizen* continued to question the war effort, and to argue the possibilities for female enfranchisement in the aftermath of the juggernaut.

The outbreak of war provided new opportunities for subversion, and heralded a new era, to be discussed in the next chapter. But its effect on the world of publishing and printing should be noted here. The publishing of anti-recruitment posters and pamphlets boomed, many of them printed on Constance Markievicz's private press. She told Cesca Trench that they were all the more effective when composed by one of her Fianna scouts: 'you see, to appeal to a certain class of people, the ones we want to prevent enlisting, you must get one of their own class to write for them, they *know*.'[75] Above all, those who had been practising radical journalism for the past fifteen years or so threw themselves into the so-called 'mosquito press', producing gadfly anti-war and pro-separatist propaganda sheets which danced around the censor.

Thus the coming of war projected the activities of subversive journalists into a whole new realm. But the radicals had already received an education in political organization and rhetorical invective through the explosion of journalism originating at the turn of the century. This phenomenon had also done lasting damage to the image of the constitutional nationalists of the Irish Parliamentary Party. The blizzard of news-sheets wrote the revolution into the hearts and minds of young radicals far more potently than the poems of Yeats or the fictions of George Moore. It also flourished in the conditions of repressive tolerance which characterized Edwardian Ireland, and ended with the coming of the world war.

And that war brought other implications too, grasped at once by some of the revolutionary generation. Long afterwards, in a vivid unpublished memoir, Gearóid O'Sullivan remembered a Dublin afternoon stroll in late June 1914 with a republican friend.

> That afternoon I was walking up past the Black Church with Seán Mac-Dermott when a newsboy shouted at the top of his voice, stop press!!! Stop press. I paid a penny for a copy of the 'Pink' as the *Evening Telegraph* was familiarly known. The ordinary price was a halfpenny.
>
> Having read the stop press news I was asked by Seán what it was all about. 'Nothing', said I, 'only some old Duke shot in the Balkans.' 'Give me that,' said Seán excitely. As he read the few lines his piercing eyes seemed to dart from their sockets. Holding the paper in his left hand, staring at me intently, he smacked the back of the paper with the back of his upturned right hand (this was a usual method of emphasis with him) and addressed me: 'Look it, Gearóid, this is no joke for us. We're in for it now. Austria will move against these fellows' (I didn't know who 'these fellows' were), 'Russia will back these fellows up, Germany and Italy will back Austria, France will take on Germany. You'll have a European war; England will join – and that will be our time to strike.
>
> 'I must go back. See you tonight', and he left me.[76]

Thus we come back, 'by a commodious vicus of recirculation', to James Joyce's windy breath of Aeolus. It seems only apposite that the revelation of the long-awaited apocalypse came, like so much else in the era, through the cry of a newsboy in a Dublin street.

WAR!!

ENGLAND, GERMANY AND IRELAND.

The mighty British Empire is on the verge of destruction. "The hand of the Lord hath touched her." The English live in daily terror of Germany. War between England and Germany is at hand. England's cowardly and degenerate population won't make soldiers: not so the Germans. They are trained and ready.

WHAT WILL ENGLAND DO?

She'll get Irish Fools to join her Army and Navy, send them to fight and die for her Empire. England has never fought her own battles. Irish traitors have ever been the backbone of her Army and Navy. How has she rewarded them? When they are no longer able to fight she flings them back to Ireland, reeking with foul filthy diseases to die in the workhouses.

WHY SHOULD YOU FIGHT FOR ENGLAND?

Is it in gratitude for the Priest-hunters and the rack of the Penal days! The Gibbet! The Pitch Cap! The Half-hangings and all the Horrors of '98?

Is it in gratitude for the Famine when One Million of our people were slowly starved to death, and Christian England thanking God that the Celts were going, going with a vengeance?

Is it in gratitude for the blazing homesteads and the people half-naked and starved to death by the roadside?

STAND ASIDE

and have your revenge. Without Ireland's help England will go down before Germany as she would have gone down before the Boers had not the Irish fought her battle in South Africa. The English know this and they have offered us a bribe and call it

HOME RULE.

It is not yet law, but believing us to be a nation of fools she wants payment in advance, and has sent her warships to our coasts to entrap young Irishmen.

THE VIGILANCE COMMITTEE

feels bound to issue this solemn warning to young Irishmen against joining the English Army or Navy—for your own sake, as well as for your country's sake. You denounce as traitors the men who sold their votes to pass the Union. You denounce Judas who sold Christ, but generations yet unborn will curse YOU who now join England's Army or Navy. Aye, will curse not alone the dupes who join, but also those who neglect to aid the VIGILANCE COMMITTEE in their crusade against the most Immoral Army and Navy in the world.

The political and historical reasons against Irishmen joining the Allied war effort, as spelt out in an anti-recruitment flyer, 1914.

6

Arming

Is it only half fun? Or children playing battle. Whole earnest.
How can people aim guns at each other. Sometimes they go
off. Poor kids.

            – James Joyce, Ulysses[1]

I

As he looks out over Dublin Bay on the evening of 16 June 1904,
Leopold Bloom is musing about children's lives, not contemporary
politics. But Joyce wrote the 'Nausicaa' section of his panoramic book
in the aftermath of the Easter Rising, and the reflections on violence
studded through Bloom's soliloquies must be read in this light. By
early 1914, 'aiming guns at each other' had become a way of life in
Ireland, with about 250,000 men (and quite a few women) in Ireland
enrolled in some kind of paramilitary organization. These forces,
which sprang up like dragons' teeth, drilled and armed openly, with
an extraordinary degree of connivance from the authorities. It was
only when hostilities broke out in Europe in August 1914 that some
selective efforts were made to control – and redirect – the militarization of Irish society. But it was also the outbreak of war – as Seán
MacDermott saw from that Dublin newsstand – that presented the
IRB with its traditional opportunity for an insurrection. Nonetheless
the IRB comprised a very small number of people; and 'outside the
IRB there were few Republicans, and Griffith knew it and so did we',
as Patrick McCartan recalled later.[2] It is unlikely that armed rebellion
would have come, at least in the form it did, without the spectacular

commitment to military posturing, and the cult of guns which characterized radical Irish circles from 1912.

Violence, so long part of the rhetoric of 'advanced nationalism',
became translated into reality. This built on many of the attitudes,
antagonisms and alliances already established among the revolutionary generation. But it was also projected into actuality through the
surge of paramilitary activity that began in Ulster during 1912, regis-
tering opposition to the prospect of the Home Rule Bill, and the
opposing movement which developed among nationalists. This readiness to take arms reflected the long-standing Irish exposure to the
reality of militarism, as well as to its rhetoric: the army was an established presence in barracks and 'garrison towns', and Irish soldiers
were prominently distributed through that army, at every level. The
implicitly intimidatory presence of barracks, and the high number of
Irish recruits into the British Army (notably from the urban working
class, but also from rural areas), provided a consistent target for Sinn
Féin rhetoric; the high profile given to this issue indicates the prominent role the army occupied in Irish life, as employer as well as symbol.
Anti-recruiting activities, from the Boer War onwards, provided an
important forum for displaying nationalist probity, and would become
a focus of subversive activity from August 1914. Liam de Róiste's
complex feelings about having two brothers as British soldiers were
confided to his diary: 'they have always been cut off from me.'[3] Liam
Mellows, and some other future revolutionaries, grew up in an army
family; some, including James Connolly, Michael Mallin and Tom
Barry, actually served in the army themselves. In Irish life, the position
occupied by the Royal Irish Constabulary was also prominent, similarly providing a target for nationalist opprobrium, since they were
armed and, to a certain extent, paramilitary, though in a ceremonial
rather than an activist way. 'The police were more military and the
military more police-like than in Britain';[4] the relationship between
them was correspondingly complex and uneasy.

The antagonism expressed by advanced nationalists towards the
militarist forces of law and order did not prevent separatists enthusiastically following their example. With the exception of rare pacifists
such as Francis and Hanna Sheehy-Skeffington, radical nationalists
warmly endorsed the idea of possessing guns, taking part in drilling

and other exercises, and theoretically preparing to 'strike a blow for freedom'. For many of the revolutionary generation, the idea of arming had become central to their self-image as Irish nationalists well before the acquisition of arms in 1913–14. The language of 'striking a blow for Ireland' was a well-worn trope. But some of them, like Liam de Róiste, had already begun uneasily considering the logical next step. In one of the frequent moments of self-doubt recorded in his diary during 1903, he wondered if all his efforts in little Cork societies, striving for political and cultural independence, were worth it. 'It is evident that as long as England is in the ascendant, we shall have to fight for freedom. How can we fight? It becomes more and more difficult with the complexity of life.' A few months later he was sanguine again:

> Perhaps our independence cannot be rescued without war. Well, we must only face the armed struggle as former generations of Irishmen faced it. If it can be attained without a physical conflict, it would be a blessing. The attainment of our independence will mean a revolution. Many people fear when they hear that word. They attach some terrible and sinister meaning to it. Revolutions are taking place frequently. They do not appear such desperate things as some imagine.[5]

By January 1906 he was reconsidering what fighting actually meant, in the wake of a violent affray at a Kerry election meeting. 'It makes me tremble. Blood! Heads battered in; oaths and curses; malignant hatred displayed; innocent and unoffending persons harmed and injured; passions let loose. And in the ultimate, all for what?' The uncomfortable thought occurred that this kind of thing was exactly what his political involvement might one day entail: 'Mayhap war itself, with sickening sights, and possible carnage; burnings and destruction? For Ireland? And what is Ireland? This sod of turf beneath my feet; these people around me? The sod is clay, as clay in any part of the world might be. The people around, as people in general anywhere, would shout one up today and howl one down tomorrow.' As usual, rhetorical questions enabled an evasion of awkward answers. But de Róiste also reflected that some of his companions believed that any 'freedom' not attained by physical force was invalid. 'To them "physical force" is a creed and an object in itself.'[6]

Nonetheless, before the crisis of 1912, how far a militarist organization actually implied violence was a moot point. As early as 1902 Bulmer Hobson tried to organize a nationalist boy-scouting movement, revived as Fianna Éireann in 1909, with Constance Markievicz on board; this echoed not only Baden-Powell's celebrated movement, but also religion-based youth-groups which employed military models and rhetoric. In September 1912, as the crisis over the Home Rule Bill escalated, a Young Citizen Volunteers movement was founded in Belfast, intended to develop patriotic values through 'modified military and political drill', and aimed at young men rather than at boys. While declaring itself non-sectarian and non-political, this initiative coincided with the signing of the Ulster Covenant and seems to have been the forerunner of the great wave of volunteering put in motion by the Ulster Unionist Council four months later, which founded the Ulster Volunteer Force, or UVF.

Building on widely diffused organizational initiatives centred on Orange Order halls across the province, the Ulster Volunteer Force came into being in January 1913, declaring its intention to prevent the implementation of the Home Rule Bill by force. Mobilizing a third of the male Protestant population of the province, it was rapidly backed by an influential array of prominent retired military men, and covertly supported by many serving officers within the army. Their leader was Edward Carson, a lantern-jawed Irish lawyer and Conservative politician with a fearsome legal reputation and a powerful platform presence; despite his Dublin background and metropolitan career, he rapidly became the symbol of Protestant Ulster's resistance to the perceived tyranny of the nationalist majority. The Ulster Volunteer Force drilled, created enormous public demonstrations and, most importantly of all, imported arms in large numbers. And no matter how extreme their declarations of intent to fight against the policy of the elected Liberal government, that government decided not to proceed against them in any way.

This supine acquiescence was not the least of the factors which encouraged nationalists to follow suit. The tiny Irish Citizen Army, organized by radical trade unionists during the Dublin lockout of 1913, invoked the example of the Ulstermen, as did a couple of autonomous militias attached to the Ancient Order of Hibernians.

The Citizen Army also reflected the increased tempo of labour unrest in Dublin at this time; between February and August 1913 there were thirty major labour disputes in Dublin. These mostly involved the ITGWU. Connolly's tiny Irish Socialist Republican Party, founded in 1903, amalgamated with the Socialist Labour Party as the Socialist Party of Ireland in 1904, but maintained a rather sketchy existence. It was effectively relaunched in 1909 at a meeting convened by the labour leader William O'Brien. This called for independent labour representation on elected bodies, support for the national language and the democratic advance of socialism within Ireland; a separatist agenda was not formally in evidence. The great labour crisis of 1913 mobilized many of the Dublin proletariat, as well as some middle-class supporters; though the Citizen Army never numbered more than a few hundred, and was founded as a civic defence organization, it employed aggressively militarist language. After a period of demoralization and inefficiency following the collapse of the lockout, and with James Larkin's departure to America on a fundraising tour in October 1914, the Citizen Army became James Connolly's organization, supported by Michael Mallin as Chief-of-Staff. Mallin was one of several ICA members with British Army training, and from 1915 the ICA would practise drilling, mock street-fighting and the taking of buildings. With the outbreak of war, Connolly decided it would act as a revolutionary vanguard force.

But the most influential reaction to Ulster's example came in November 1913 with the formation of Óglaigh na hÉireann, the Irish Volunteers. The original inspiration was declared in the journal of the Gaelic League, *An Claidheamh Soluis*, in an article by the academic historian Eoin MacNeill; the more militarist figure of Michael O'Rahilly was also involved in the initiative, as was their Gaelic League colleague Patrick Pearse. This was the military organization that so many of the revolutionary generation had been waiting for. And, though the Irish Volunteers' declared *raison d'être* was the defence of the Home Rule Bill now proceeding towards enactment, many of its moving spirits had a more proactive agenda in mind. This was borne out by the membership of the organizing committee of the new movement, which was rapidly commandeered by influential members of the IRB.

Thus subversion happened in public, through the formation of groups such as the Fianna, the Citizen Army, the Ulster Volunteer Force and the Irish Volunteers. It is nonetheless striking how many people in this era in Ireland put their faith in possessing arms, while not actually facing up to the consequences. In this, they reflected an emotion widely shared across contemporary Europe. In the military boy-scouts movement started by Bulmer Hobson and Constance Markievicz, the longing for guns figured large, though they often had to be replaced by hurley-sticks. Backed by the kind of militaristic drill afforded by Con Colbert at St Enda's, this training could be very effective; there was much concentration on 'scouting' and 'first-aid' techniques. More crudely, they could also practise street-fighting and vigilante activities, as in ambushing marches of the Protestant Boys' Brigade. And eventually, as one ex-Fianna scout recalled, there was the possession of 'a real gun . . . a great sensation'. Sometimes these came from surprising sources, as recalled by another old Fianna member. His branch got their much envied .22 rifles from Father Paddy Flanagan, the parish priest in Ringsend. 'He was not the ordinary type of popular curate,' this witness coyly added. 'Would it be indiscreet to mention that he was the inventor of the sawn-off shotgun?'[7] He was not, but the admiring assertion of such a claim is in itself significant.

Memoirs such as Seán Prendergast's, compiled for the Bureau of Miltary History, vividly illustrate the way in which membership of the Fianna acted as a conduit into the Volunteers movement and the Citizen Army, and actively prepared for militarism.[8] Prendergast, who joined up in 1911, found himself learning military drill, first-aid, signalling, scouting, map-reading and even shorthand (this last from a clerk working in the Land Commission). The boys' uniform, initially featuring Boer-inspired slouch hats and blouses, was redesigned to incorporate military tunics with epaulettes, thanks to a captain who worked as a clerk in Clery's drapery department, and a Mounties-style hat; the adults who trained them, like Liam Mellows, often appeared in kilts. Urban working-class boys found their weekends transformed by route marches and mock battles in the Dublin suburbs, or camp-outs at Countess Markievicz's cottage at Balally in the Dublin Mountains. Her Rathmines home, Surrey House on Leinster Road, was also open to them, representing an escape from the confines of home, where they could observe the radical *bon ton* at play (even though 'Madame's' easygoing habits and constant smoking shocked some). If they failed to turn up through illness, the Countess was liable to appear at their homes and carry them back to convalesce in the untrammelled surroundings of Surrey House, over the protests of their mothers.

Above all, young as they were, they had access to arms. Prendergast's company first obtained French bayonets in April 1913. 'Strange how the minds of young rebels work! Even at this stage many of us were thinking of becoming armed. Some did.' A few revolvers were subsequently legally obtained on hire purchase, and in late 1914 their captain, Seán Heuston, managed to procure .22 Springfield rifles from America. The Fianna were also closely involved in disseminating the IRB journal *Irish Freedom*, in which Pearse's articles declaring the necessity of bearing arms for Irish 'virility' were beginning to appear.

II

Up to 1912–13, however, Irish nationalists older than the Fianna membership were not drilled into any kind of armed formation. Nonetheless the felt need was there. In October 1912 a fellow member of the Waterford Gaelic League surprised Rosamond Jacob by his 'whole-heartedness'. 'He believes in physical force and says there should be rifle clubs and that another opportunity like the Boer War should not be let pass ... he says he knows a lot of men – married men some of them – up and down the country who take no interest in constitutional politics, but would be ready to come out with a gun.'[9]

After the foundation of the Irish Volunteers a year later, nationalist drilling and paramilitary organization happened with extraordinary speed, first by means of cover organizations, then in the open under the eyes of the authorities, who appeared either helpless or conniving or both. The movement got off to a flying start, with 4,000 volunteers joining up after a public meeting in November 1913, stewarded – inevitably – by the Fianna; it met a felt need for militant nationalism. One reason for this was the idea that the bearing of arms somehow qualified a people for nationhood: an armed citizenry. This was one more historical echo from the Late eighteenth century in Ireland, picking up resonances from the Dungannon clubs, the Wolfe Tone societies, the cult of Robert Emmet and all the rest. It was remembered that the freedoms wrested from the British government in 1782, leading to a more autonomous Irish parliament, had come after militias called 'Volunteers' had been set up all over Ireland, threatening contagion from the recent American revolution. When an Irish national volunteering movement emerged in 1913, ostensibly to protect the recently passed Home Rule Act from being stymied by Ulster resistance, much was made of the historical parallel – though the more recent inspiration was in the north-east. The account of a Volunteers drill party which Eimar O'Duffy put into his autobiographical novel *The Wasted Island* makes this historical connection clear.

> Shortly before nine Crowley got out his motor and they drove over to the meeting-place, the field of a friendly farmer some five miles away. About twenty men were already assembled when they arrived, and half a dozen more straggled in during the next quarter of an hour. Under the cold light of the moon Bernard drilled them: a weird and romantic experience. Upon how many such assemblies had that disc looked down through the long history of Ireland's passion? Fenians, Confederates, United Irishmen, all had drilled and marched in turn under her gentle light. She had watched the tide of hope and despair generation after generation, and was still watching – for what? The ghosts of Ninety-Eight and Forty-Eight and Sixty-Seven seemed to be abroad that night.
>
> In the shadow of a hedge a policeman stood taking notes.[10]

O'Duffy himself played a central role in the administration of the Volunteers. As well as contributing a good deal to the organization's strategic thinking, he wrote much of the journal *Irish Volunteer*. Like other Volunteer officers such as Terence MacSwiney and 'Ginger' O'Connell, he wore his uniform on every possible occasion. Tutored by their mentor Bulmer Hobson, O'Connell and O'Duffy spent much time theorizing about guerrilla warfare ('hedge-fighting'); some of their IRB colleagues within the Volunteers were more inclined to open insurrectionism, a rift which would become clear in 1916.

Formally, however, the declared object of the Irish Volunteers was to protect the recently passed Home Rule Bill for Ireland, with the eventual aim of becoming 'a prominent element in the national life under a National government'. In other words, the Volunteers were to be an independent Irish army in waiting. But this presupposed the safe achievement of undiluted Home Rule: and, despite the passing of the Bill, the removal of the powers of the House of Lords (which had thrown out a Bill passed in 1893) by the 1911 Parliament Act, and the apparent victory for John Redmond and constitutional Home Rule, this seemed an increasingly remote possibility after 1912. The Irish Parliamentary Party at Westminster had brought off a technical victory, placing the capstone on the edifice begun by Parnell when he forced Home Rule on to the Liberal Party's agenda with the unsuccessful Bill of 1886. But a heavy shadow lay across it. Ulster's resistance, and the enthusiastic support offered it by the Conservative Party, required complicated and dedicated negotiations behind the scenes by Redmond and his lieutenants; at first devoted to keeping the Liberal government firm on the issue, discussions soon revolved around the hardening inevitability of negotiating some kind of separate arrangement for Ulster, a concept edging into more general acceptance. The kind of compromise which in retrospect seems inevitable was, however, scornfully derided by advanced-nationalist opinion – though a majority of them would tacitly accept such an arrangement a few eventful years later. In 1914, what Redmond and the Irish Parliamentary Party had achieved seemed to radical imaginations in Ireland an inadequate structure, flimsily assembled and founded on sand.

This was not only a result of the Ulster crisis. The complex of generational attitudes and subversive activities fructifying since the turn of the century had helped to create a situation where Redmond's Irish Parliamentary Party seemed more and more old-hat, collaborationist and unexciting. It was found wanting on all the issues that inspired the revolutionary generation (Irish language, cultural renewal, economic autarky, separatist traditions, the eradication of 'foreign' influence). The formula of Home Rule within the Empire seemed insufficient to many of the younger generation, who were not enthused by the pragmatic argument that it was a vital first step towards a more full-scale detachment, to be achieved by a series of non-violent initiatives. Above all, the credibility of the Home Rule solution was seriously undermined by the scale of resistance among Ulster unionists, and by the British government's pusillanimous response to that challenge. As Liam Ó Briain pithily put it to Seán T. O'Kelly, 'our military movement only became feasible thanks to Edward Carson.'[11]

The same case is powerfully argued by the unpublished memoir of the Trinity student Kevin O'Shiel. As Asquith and his colleagues backed down before unconstitutional challenges from unionists, O'Shiel's belief that a Liberal government would keep faith with the democratic mandate for Home Rule crumbled. A crystallizing moment occurred in March 1914, when a group of British Army officers stationed at the Curragh declared they would resign rather than obey an order to put down Ulster's resistance to Home Rule; after some confused negotiations and a couple of resignations, the so-called mutineers were reinstated. The prospects for implementing Home Rule in an unpartitioned Ireland seemed increasingly doubtful. This may account for the lack of enthusiasm which greeted the passing of the Bill, much noted by police observers at the time.[12] Those with socialist and secularist leanings, like Francis Sheehy-Skeffington, had further worries, as Rosamond Jacob recorded in March 1913 when she called at Belgrave Road. She found him disillusioned with the Citizen Army, and the general drift to militarism. 'He expects rough times if Home Rule materializes, fighting clerical and capitalist influences; says we shall probably all be executed or banished and that if Home Rule doesn't materialize there will be a rebellion against the Party' – which he would incite himself if he had to. After suffrage was won, Sheehy-Skeffington concluded, the first battle must be against the priests – a prophecy which Jacob received with predictable pleasure.[13] But these issues faded further into the future, as older lines of antagonism were drawn up.

As Dublin radicals debated, voluntarist militias continued to mushroom in the north-east under the umbrella of the Ulster Volunteer Force, pledged (by covenant) to fight against the government in order to stay in the union. Under the charismatic leadership of Edward Carson, their movement increasingly displayed the trappings of threatened rebellion. In the South, IRB infiltration of the Irish Volunteers continued apace. Within the Citizen Army organized by James Connolly too a separatist element was conspiring; and it is striking how few old Citizen Army recruits, recalling their enlistment much later when testifying to the Bureau of Military History, ever mention being motivated by class solidarity. Nationalism trumped socialism, at least in their memories, and very probably at the time as well.

The career of Michael Mallin is enlightening. Born in 1874 in the Liberties of Dublin to a carpenter and his silk-worker wife, he followed a family tradition by joining the British Army in 1889 and served in the Royal Scots Fusiliers, spending six years in India. In 1894, home on leave, he met Agnes Hickey, from a Fenian family in Chapelizod; their correspondence indicates his increasing radicalization during his time in India, as well as a fervent Catholicism.[14] He returned to Ireland in 1902, and they married the next year. After trying many jobs, Mallin became a silk-weaver (the Irish poplin industry was undergoing a revival) and by 1908 was prominent in the trade union. He emerged as a strike leader during 1913 and subsequently started his own shop, which folded. There were stabs at other ways of making a living (chicken-farming in Finglas, a cinema venture in Capel Street, piece-work weaving at home), but he was also forced to consider emigration. Then, in October 1914, after Larkin's departure and Connolly's ascendancy, he became an important figure in the ITGWU. Despite rows with his own union, thanks to Connolly's patronage he succeeded his friend William Partridge as manager of the Emmet Hall, Inchicore. Labour and nationalist radicalization went together for Mallin. At first unwelcome in Fianna circles, he had started his own nationalist scouting group, and soon rose through the ranks of the Citizen Army; he also at this time began to acquire guns from hard-up soldiers at the nearby Richmond Barracks. He would follow Connolly into the paths of nationalist revolution a year or so later.

The mainstream nationalist militia followed a more chequered ideological course. The Gaelic Leaguers in the office of *An Claidheamh Soluis*, who originated the idea of the Irish Volunteers, soon found themselves in a complicated position. Though MacNeill's article 'The North Began' started the ball rolling, credit for inspiring the nationalist Volunteers was also claimed by Michael O'Rahilly. The rich son of a Kerry shopkeeping dynasty, he lived a dilettante life in Dublin and had (as seen in the last chapter) found his niche as business manager of the Gaelic League magazine *An Claidheamh Soluis*.[15] After travels in the USA, a large private income allowed him to develop strident and uncompromising ideas about the necessity for language revival and separatist activism, as well as a deep dislike of Britain and Britishness, loudly expressed. He built a holiday bungalow at Ventry, County Kerry, where he became close to Ernest Blythe and Desmond FitzGerald, who had temporarily settled in the area to perfect their Irish-language skills and mobilize the rather refractory local population. The Volunteering movement also gave full rein to O'Rahilly's obsession with heraldry, titles and coats of arms; his papers include much semi-mystical correspondence about the spiritual symbols of the Volunteers flag and the need to evoke occult Celtic harmonies.[16] More relevantly, he was also mesmerized by the ways in which new technologies such as motor-cars and aeroplanes could be used for warlike purposes. O'Rahilly, whose Anglophobia had been nurtured by a sojourn in America, represented an extreme and violent tendency within the movement. In his view the eventual destiny of the armed citizenry was to strike a blow for freedom against British government, and in this he was not alone.

Other early enthusiasts such as Roger Casement emphasized that the organization's proper name must be the 'Irish Volunteers', avoiding the words 'national' or 'nationalist': sectionalism must be guarded against, and patriotism seen to outweigh politics. This was often exposed as an unrealistic ideal, but the organization of the Volunteers was clearly influenced by the idea of a citizen militia. Officers were elected rather than appointed, brigade and battalion structures varied, and the leadership resembled a political committee rather than a military high command. As so often in Irish history, uncertainty of nomenclature indicated an amorphous and unstable nature. Separatists like O'Rahilly and Casement unwillingly realized that the movement also enthused loyal Home Rulers such as Tom Kettle; worse still, by the summer of 1914, John Redmond and the Irish Parliamentary Party involved themselves formally with the direction of the Volunteers, in what seemed to be an effective takeover of the public face of the movement. Local politicians began to dominate committees at ground level, and the influence of Joseph Devlin's confraternity, the

Ancient Order of Hibernians (deeply hated by Sinn Féin and the IRB for its conservatism and aggressively pious Catholicism), made itself felt. (Astutely using its status as a 'friendly society', the AOH had enormously strengthened its influence through monopolizing the organization of workers' insurance through the recent National Insurance Act of 1911.) In May the AOH branches were ordered to form their own Volunteer companies; there were already a large number of their members in the Volunteer ranks, along with those who had come in from the more radical breeding-grounds of the Gaelic League, Sinn Féin, the Citizen Army and the IRB. As they captured the national imagination, the Volunteers came to resemble a broad church.

One result was an explosion of numbers. Local studies show that the movement spread like wildfire, often endorsed by unlikely local notables, though these establishment figures tended to fall away as the Volunteers became more stridently nationalist.[17] From a force of about 20,000 in March 1914, the movement grew to 150,000 by the following July, and the profile of its membership became accordingly more moderate, including a fair number of Protestants with British Army backgrounds. Even more repellent to radical nationalists was the ramifying influence of the Hibernians, an organization whose root-system proliferated all over Ulster, and which was seen by many as a worse enemy than the Saxon oppressor. Connolly, for instance, thought that the bigotry and politicking of the Hibernians were what kept the Orange Order artificially alive: 'to Brother Devlin, not to Brother Carson, is mainly due the progress of the Covenanting movement in Ulster.'[18] Seán T. O'Kelly remembered the AOH as Sinn Féin's real adversary in the pre-Rising years: 'the bitterest enemies we of the independence movement had to fight', organizing thugs who threw lime and beat them 'black and blue' at election meetings.[19] Hobson and his Dungannon Club companions had long seen Devlin and his associates as a real threat to nationalist revival, referring to them as 'Ribbonmen', with all the attendant implications of archaism and confessionalism. Ironically, when Hobson and Denis McCullough had initially recruited Seán MacDermott, they had been worried by his AOH, or 'Mollie', tendencies, which they were determined to eradicate. 'He was an extremely religious man at the time,' McCullough later recalled, 'but we cured him of that.'[20]

The hatred of the radicals for the Hibernians helps to explain the fury of some of the IRB cabal within the Volunteers at seeing Redmondites apparently take over their movement from the summer of 1914: it betokened the importation of all the old clientilist and collaborationist values which they abhorred. Since the turn of the century it had been an article of faith for Sinn Féiners and other radical nationalists that Redmond and his party represented all that was ineffectual and corrupt about parliamentary nationalism, demonstrated time and again in their trimming approach to issues such as local government, compulsory Irish in the National University, and finally the dilution and postponement of Home Rule. The Volunteering movement had sprung up, it was felt, in manly opposition to the supine values and attitudes of Redmond and his followers. Yet, in June, Redmond succeeded in getting a guaranteed majority of his nominees on to the Provisional Committee. Accordingly, this unexpected turn of events produced a lasting and antagonistic split within the IRB. The agonies of those who accepted this are vividly expressed in a dramatic letter from Casement to McCartan, beginning 'Last night we committed *Hara Kiri*!' Casement nonetheless went on to defend the capitulation as 'an act of larger patriotism – not of small surrender', essential in order to preserve unity among the Volunteers, and to avoid the charge of deliberately wrecking Home Rule. 'But the real "principle" to stick to – is get rifles,' he added. 'If the Party are sincere & not public liars they will help us to get rifles.'

They were to do this by pressurizing the government to withdraw 'the insulting & outrageous arms proclamation aimed at a White race & designed to reduce our citizenship of this so-called United Kingdom to that of a servile coloured population. Don't say all this at your meeting but say it privately.' Casement, near the end of his tether, went on to plead his case, as someone who had given up 'a post of the highest honour & profit' and reduced himself to 'paupery' for the cause:

> I broke my career & surrendered everything – ease, comfort, wealth –
> when in broken and failing health too – in order to try & help Ireland
> to freedom. I mean to get guns into Ireland – & you can say so if you
> like . . . The young men with the rifles will make the new Ireland – once
> they get them they will not lay them down save with their lives.[21]

Others who endorsed the strategy of incorporating Redmondites into the Volunteers command included MacNeill, O'Hegarty and Hobson. As MacNeill admitted:

> A clear majority of the 25 [on the Committee], including the four clergymen, are A.O.H. men. Nevertheless the Volunteer idea & the Volunteer principles & programme will come out on top. There are a number of decent Irishmen among the 25, a number of unshaped men, & a number of wasters. The Volunteer idea will capture all but the last lot. As the men get armed by degrees, the whole situation & its possibilities will be transformed, and a new standard – or an old one – will be set up. As a friend of mine quotes, 'There was a young lady of Niger, Who went for a ride on a tiger, They returned from that ride with the lady inside, and a smile on the face of the tiger'.[22]

This suggests that, in MacNeill's view, the Volunteers were to be groomed for more aggressive purposes than defending Redmond's achievement. Hobson defended the decision all his life, taking credit for the responsibility and describing it later as 'one of the wisest & most misunderstood of my actions ... we never lost grip. I even appointed the office staff at headquarters while there was a Redmondite majority on the Committee.'[23]

But hardline IRB men were not convinced, and a lasting rift was created, separating MacNeill, Casement, Hobson and P. S. O'Hegarty (who thought this new access of membership could be used to advantage) from their more irreconcilable colleagues. Seán MacDermott was particularly irate, denouncing Casement and Hobson as sell-outs, and Tom Clarke wrote bitterly to Joseph McGarrity describing the betrayal of the Volunteers by Casement's 'master hand', with Hobson as his 'Man Friday'.[24] This enduring animosity, Redmond's apparent achievement of dominance and the eventual absorption of the moderate elements of the Volunteers into the war effort have tended to conceal the radical-separatist element there from the beginning. And, though MacNeill and even Casement appeared more moderate, their correspondence shows that a long-term militant strategy lay behind their actions. It might also be remembered that MacNeill's nominated liaison committee for the Irish Volunteers in December 1913 included, besides O'Rahilly, Éamonn Ceannt, Joseph Plunkett, Thomas MacDonagh,

Patrick Pearse and Seán MacDermott. All were future signatories of the 'Proclamation of the Irish Republic' at Easter 1916.[25]

III

The strategies of such people went underground after Redmond's takeover in the summer of 1914, while the social range and political variety of Volunteer members increased noticeably. The public rhetoric of Volunteering favoured protecting 'the rights and liberties common to all the people of Ireland'; as Matthew Kelly has demonstrated, the language among the National Volunteers stressed a defensive role, linking 'manliness' with 'arms-bearing' in a clear reference to the language of civic rather than revolutionary republicanism, which looked back to the rhetoric of the American War of Independence. MacNeill, himself a Northern Catholic, saw the movement as not only a response to the armed citizenry of Ulster, but also the possible beginnings of a rapprochement with the Northern brethren. From a later vantage, this seems puzzling; the logic of having one militia in the North, pledged to fight against Home Rule, and another in the South, pledged to fight on behalf of it, seems to be that they should end by fighting each other. This was what was in the mind of police inspectors when they repeatedly warned their political masters in 1914 that Ireland was on the brink of civil war.

For nationalist ideologues, however, it was more comforting to go back – yet again – to history, and specifically to the historical moment in 1798 when Catholics and Protestants allegedly came together in the interests of Irish independence. The use of this memory in Ulster was particularly complex, involving the traditions of Presbyterian radicalism, which had later mutated into hard-line unionism in the early nineteenth century. But for Protestant nationalists like Bulmer Hobson, Alice Milligan, F. J. Bigger and Roger Casement, Wolfe Tone's oath sworn on Cave Hill with his Ulster companions was a sacred memory, much invoked in the 1898 centenary and now revived in the militias of 1913–14. By the same token, Rosamond Jacob was obsessed by memorabilia of that golden moment: devoting much time to researching Tone's life, and sending away for relics of the martyrs of '98. (In 1912 she was pleased to receive a piece of bloodstained floorboard from the house where Lord Edward FitzGerald was apprehended; her derisive approach to Catholic 'superstitions' did not extend to the holy relics of nationalist martyrs.[26]) Bulmer Hobson was similarly preoccupied, and at this time Patrick Pearse's cult of Robert Emmet was reaching new heights – along with his belief that Dublin had been 'disgraced' by its somnolent reaction to Emmet's attempted putsch in 1803.

Up in Ulster, nationalists continued to cling to the idea of radical nationalism dissolving sectarian differences and overcoming the powerful network of the Ancient Order of Hibernians. Though by 1909 Hobson had privately become pessimistic about the non-sectarian prospects of the Dungannon clubs, this would not do for public consumption.[27] A few Ulster Protestants could find their way to nationalism by odd routes, such as Rory Haskin – a Belfast Protestant who spent six years in the British Army, then joined the Orange Order and the UVF, before undergoing a Damascene conversion to republicanism when he attended a Freedom Club (an IRB front organization whose members included Hobson, Ernest Blythe, Cathal O'Shannon and Joseph Connolly).[28] F. J. Bigger, as ever, remained *sui generis*: preaching the values of '98 to his acolytes, but remaining close to Joe Devlin, also a life-long bachelor and a frequent visitor at Ardrigh (which he would eventually buy from Bigger's estate). As politics in Ulster moved towards polarization, the boys' parties continued unabated at the house on the Antrim Road and in Shane's Castle; and, though Bigger was under police observation, the police sometimes joined in the partying too. After Bigger presented a stained-glass window to a local church in September 1913, his followers proceeded to Shane's Castle and plunged into rowdy celebrations, breathlessly described by Roger Casement, who referred to his host with a Gaelic approximation of a clan title:

> An Biggerac was in *great* form: not a chief merely but an emperor! Kilted; banners (6 or 7) pipers (7) pikemen (4) to precede him and clear the way wherever he went. I never saw anything like it. It makes me scream. He 'processes' now in walk . . . The Boys love it, and pipe go leor. He wound up with [an] R.I.C. constable's cap and baton, and

delivered a stump harangue thus garbed. Kilt etc. below, R.I.C. cap and baton above it, 2 a.m., in to Shane O'Neill's castle on . . . Empire! The speech began: 'Sons of the Empire! Children of the Blood! Will the sun never set on this great Empire of ours?' Which was greeted with a howl of 'Never! Never!' immediately followed by the chauffeur, decked out in Orange robes, declaring he would 'never, never surrender'! The fun is that the chauffeur is an Orange boy, a 'Scotch Protestant', so everyone took part, the three constables of Ardglass, poor souls, belts off, caps gone, and the pipes skirling like the devil, all singing 'God Save Ireland'![29]

This celebration of collaborationist 'Ulsterism', invoking the icons of both 'sides' in a spirit of camp homosociality, was the kind of culture where Bigger felt most at home; but for such romantics, the implications of the Covenant and the rise of the UVF held an ominous message. Two months after the occasion described by Casement, in more sober mode, Bigger made a visit to his ancestral territory around Templepatrick. Still hoping against hope that his traditionally minded unionist relatives could be converted to pluralist nationalism, he reported his impressions to Alice Stopford Green:

> Home Rule was lightly treated – no fear – some hopes, no truculence. I heard no disparaging word and saw no cold eye, all was kindness & friendship. Of course I know their every phase of life and thought, their every word and action but yet what a distance there is between the road I am on, the one I have travelled and am travelling and the one they are on – They know the Hearts of Steel [a Protestant agrarian radical movement in eighteenth-century Ulster] & '98 & dwell there and then the break comes – it must be the National schools [i.e. the effectively denominational system of education which developed from the 1830s]. How fine the next generation will be if we get an Irish Ireland atmosphere – they will lead any other crowd in Ireland in patriotism I am sure.[30]

But this was wishful thinking, and a few weeks later his description of New Year's Eve celebrations at Ardrigh carried an ominously militarist implication:

> all the boys present – some in kilts others in old Volunteer uniforms – all armed fully with rifles and pikes – pipes go leor & drums with standard.

I received them at the door (a lovely clear cold frosty star-lit night) at midnight – then we had heavy firing of shot from the balcony and 'A Nation Once Again' from the pipes – then a quick march in fully drilled ranks down the road and then up the road ½ mile in tense excitement. The local police on night duty and very interested but came in for refreshments after saluting the standard. And so we heralded in 1914.[31]

As the critical moment of resistance to Home Rule approached, it seemed less and less likely that Irish unity could be found under a Bigger-designed goose-wing helmet.

Even as romantic a nationalist as Bigger's friend Roger Casement had to wonder where the descendants of the 1798 republicans were now. Six days before the Covenant was signed on 28 September 1912, he watched the 'appalling grim Ulster Hall faces' marching past his Belfast window, and wrote to his cousin Gertrude, using family pet names:

I tremble for the piety of this realm, this Ulster so bathed in the tears of righteousness (self-righteousness), so washed in papish blood and cleansed in the furious sweat of riot. Pious, God-fearing, humble Ulster, only seeking the Christian path of self-denial, self-effacement, that leads to the narrow path of renunciation by which no papist may pass, to Harland and Wolfs [sic: Harland & Wolff, the Protestant ship-building firm], or any other means of employment ... Adios my Geelet, Thy Scodge goes off to Corny O Gallogher [a celebrated traditional musician] full of fury against the ineffaceable ugliness of Carson & co: how truly *awfully* ugly he is![32]

When the Covenant was signed a few days later, he wrote again: 'I *love* the Antrim Presbyterians ... they are good, kind warm-hearted souls, and to see them now *exploited* by that damned Church of Ireland, and that Orange Ascendancy gang who hate Presbyterians only less than papists, and to see them delirious before a Smith and a Carson (a cross between a badly reared bloodhound and an underfed hyena sniffing for Irish blood in the track) and whooping Rule Britannia through the streets is a wound to my soul.' They must be wooed from their 'perverted, abominable creed'; he added, prophetically, that he 'prayed for the Germans' and their coming to teach them a 'Protestant' lesson.[33]

Casement's mind was already running on conflict. In late November 1913 he declared that an open confrontation with the opponents of Home Rule would be 'far better than to go on lying and pretending – if only we could be left free to fight out our battle here ourselves'.[34] But this brutal logic seems to have evaded most nationalist ideologues, who preferred to declare, as Patrick Pearse did, that it was a glorious thing to see arms in the hands of Irishmen, no matter who they were or for what purpose they were intended. Casement also felt, inconsistently, that '[The UVF is] the only really healthy thing. It is fine; it is the act of men; and I like it, and love the thought of those English Liberal ministers squirming before it.'[35]

The language of hyper-masculinity might be noted: arms were closely connected with the definition of manhood, as elsewhere in contemporary Europe. Practical implications were another thing. When the thought occurred to Pearse that Redmond might actually want to gain control of the Irish Volunteers in order to pit them against the UVF, he became intensely worried.[36] More rational observers at this time also subscribed to the idea that the enmity felt for the British government among Northern unionists and Southern nationalists could bring them together in an unholy alliance: such a scenario was sketched in various unlikely quarters, including George Birmingham's satirical novel *The Red Hand of Ulster*, and a Press Association interview given by the widow of Charles Stewart Parnell. Asked what the dead Chief would have made of the current political situation, she speculated that 'Sir Edward Carson's little army would have appealed strongly to him – only he would have tipped the Ulster rebellion into the Home Rule cauldron and directed the resulting explosion at England.'[37]

More surprisingly, this fantasy was subscribed to by people actually from an Ulster background, who might have been supposed to know better. Eoin MacNeill, whose political antennae were admittedly not the sharpest, caused a near-riot when he called for three cheers for Carson's Volunteers at an Irish Volunteers meeting in Cork. In March 1914 he still saw the UVF as representing a development favourable to nationalism. 'It would be simply heavenly,' he wrote to Casement,

> if the Government undertook to suppress our Volunteers and Carson's together. Is there any way of getting them to do it? . . . We have them in

a cleft stick. The question of arms need not discourage us. We have to get
the young men to understand that now every one of them can get military training and can join in a permanent national militia to be ready for
arming at any time and to be ready to come out on command.[38]

And the seer from Lurgan, AE, put his faith in the admiration felt by
an advanced-nationalist friend on the day the Covenant was signed:

> I found him with his eyes shining as though they were swimming in
> whiskey – though they were not – and he said to me 'Isn't it splendid!
> Isn't it splendid. They won't have it!' and then he caught my psycho-
> logical eye fixed upon him and he said 'I know it is unreasonable. But
> there is something deeper than reason.' Yes there was something deeper
> than reason. It was the powerful Irish character calling to the powerful
> Irish character – deep calling to deep – and it is upon this fundamental
> unity of character that I base my belief in the success of self-government.[39]

By this demonstration of their 'powerful Irish character', he thought,
the Ulster unionists 'endeared themselves to their southern fellow
countrymen by this exhibition of their manhood, though its purpose
ran counter to the political desires of Nationalists'. But such wishful
thinking was doomed to disappointment, as was MacNeill's wish to
see both Volunteer forces suppressed by the government in 1914 – an
event which he innocently believed would unite them in a common
cause. Instead the events of 1912–14 destroyed many of the assumptions upon which idealistic Protestant nationalists believed an
independent Ireland could be based.

Moreover, the attitudes of the revolutionary generation towards
Ulster remained ambivalent. Piaras Béaslaí saw all Ulster people as
aggressively bad-mannered and tediously talkative: 'they are all the
same, Catholic and Protestant.' Rosamond Jacob's opinions clearly
prejudiced her receptiveness to Gaelic League history classes; after
one of these she confided to her diary, 'Strange what miserable worms
passed for heroes in ancient Ulster & what childish creatures the
whole nobility were.' When other hardline nationalists like Terence
MacSwiney reflected upon the North (which was not often), they
were in no doubt: Ulster could and must be made to see that its interests lay with Ireland, not Britain. Helena Molony dismissed the UVF

as merely an outburst of 'insolence and self-conceit'. Those who had actually lived in Ulster were more realistic; Margot Trench noted in October 1914 that the pro-German rhetoric of nationalism would mean 'goodbye to unity between north and south for two genera-tions'.[40] But few of her friends were as pessimistic.

Many advanced nationalists, in any case, saw no point in trying to appease Northern fears. Liam de Róiste was suspicious of Protestants in general. Attending a commercial course at the London School of Economics in 1914, he was disappointed to find that an Irish fellow student 'is a Protestant, so not as nice a type as one would like', though he amended his opinion when he found that his colleague went to Speakers' Corner on Sundays and harangued audiences about the ini-quity of British government in Ireland.[41] Northern Irish Protestants, however, were considered past redemption, and de Róiste dismissed them in his 1915 diary as 'Irishmen who do not believe in Irish nationality'.

> They are as aliens in Ireland. For a good while I was of the opinion that it was possible to win them, by argument or a show of good feeling, to Irish nationality. I have modified that opinion somewhat. It will be easier to mould them into the Irish Nation by standing up to them as men. Their traditions, so carefully fostered by the Big Brother, lead them to despise Irish nationalists. They will not be shaken in that by argument, or false tolerance. To make them respect Irish nationality they must be fought. 'Civil War' some will cry. Well, there are worse things than civil war – national slavery for instance.[42]

This echoed not only a famous utterance of Patrick Pearse, but the declarations of Ulster Protestant Covenanters, in the distant as well as in the recent past. The rise of an armed citizenry, North and South, suggested to idealistic nationalists the revival of that supposed polit-ical unity between Catholic and Protestant in 1798, so often invoked and so hard to recapture. But it also evoked more ominous historical associations, such as the Protestant Covenanters of the seventeenth century, and a longer memory still of implacable antagonism.

IV

Historical precedents were a shaky guide to the kind of confrontation now brewing. Another marked divergence from previous crises was that the armed citizenry now included women. The contribution of women to cultural organizations had already been established and was decisively influential; their input into political bodies was a thornier issue, given the fact that the suffrage cause loomed over so much (and mobilized so many different kinds of women). Maud Gonne's organization, Inghinidhe na hÉireann, was influential beyond its numbers, and served as a training-ground for a generation of political women. By 1909 the newspaper *Bean na hÉireann*, as mentioned in the last chapter, was taking a very militaristic line indeed. Volunteering suggested another route, and in April 1914 a new organization emerged, Cumann na mBan. Its role was 'to assist in arming and equipping a body of Irishmen for the defence of Ireland', which suggests a definitively auxiliary role in relation to the male Volunteers; but strong elements within the movement suggested an impetus towards playing a more independent part. The membership was generally republican, middle class and well educated. Cumann na mBan women were a much less amorphous group than the National Volunteers, whose swelling numbers brought in a wider and wider range of moderate and gentry elements, especially after the outbreak of international war. Above all the women no less than the men were preoccupied with bearing arms, as their emblem of a stylized rifle suggests.

As the Volunteering movement spread across the country, and became ostensibly taken over by 'respectable' elements, its relationship to other mass political movements, notably the Irish Parliamentary Party and the Ancient Order of Hibernians, remained complex and uncertain. The part played within the movement by IRB extremists was less ambiguous, but more secretive. The experience of Frank Drohan (born in 1879), a coachbuilder's son in Clonmel, was probably typical; by 1910 he was using the local Gaelic League branch as a cover for an IRB cell. In 1911 Seán MacDermott visited town and set up a Munster network. By 1913 three IRB circles existed in Clonmel, and these formed the basis of the local Volunteers; they were trained at night by an ex-British Army sergeant and bought guns under the guise of 'hardware' from Hearne's ironmongers in Waterford.[43] A Sligo schoolteacher, Alex McCabe, followed a similar path: he joined the IRB when studying in Dublin, and on his return to Sligo used the local Volunteers corps as a cover for setting up IRB circles dispersed around the county. The ubiquitous Seán MacDermott was involved here too, and probably the Sinn Féiner priest Father Michael O'Flanagan of Cliffoney.[44] In Dublin, another IRB member, Michael Stainer, shop assistant and treasurer of the Colmcille branch of the Gaelic League, was also Quartermaster of the Dublin brigade of the Volunteers; his job at Henshaw's ironmongers gave him access to firearms, and enabled him to reroute arms and ammunition from his employers to his comrades.

Less productively, Seán T. O'Kelly was detailed to fund an arms-buying trip to London by getting a large amount of gold from a sympathetic bank manager in College Green. (Significantly, the bank manager was not an IRB contact but provided help because 'as an ardent Home Ruler he believed the Volunteers had as much right to be armed as the Ulster Volunteers.') After staggering around London weighed down by bullion, O'Kelly returned to Dublin without guns; the gold, however, found its way to the tireless Seán MacDermott, who kept it for IRB purposes. By mid-1913 Piaras Béaslaí's diary records his attending regular IRB meetings, the purchase of detonators, and ambitious discussions about the use of aeroplanes and physical force. Around the same time Geraldine Plunkett remembered Liam Mellows arriving at 17 Marlborough Road with two Gladstone bags full of ammunition and gelignite, which were subsequently stored there. And the *Irish Volunteer* assured its readers in May 1914: 'The man who has once handled a rifle and is not smitten with the desire to own one is not an Irishman.'[45]

These activities and ambitions were helped by the lapse of the 1881 Peace Preservation Act in 1906; legal restrictions on arms importation were now distinctly sketchy, and police had to rely upon a rather open-ended Gun Licence Act to apprehend arms. Attempts to limit importation were laughed off. A scornful letter to the press from O'Rahilly in May 1914, calling for guns for the Irish Volunteers, added: 'The [Royal] Proclamation [of the previous December,

forbidding the importation of arms and ammunition into Ireland]
need worry nobody. The latest decision of the Government has proved
that the Proclamation only forbids the entry of small quantities of
sporting goods – Military Rifles in lots of 50,000 and cartridges by
the million are freely admissible without interference, prosecution or
punishment.'[46] What is striking overall is the importance placed on
the possession of guns, and the lengths gone to in acquiring them. 'WE
WANT RIFLES,' wrote Liam de Róiste to Roger Casement in June
1914, having apparently mastered his earlier doubts about violence.
'We are thirsting for rifles.' For his part, Casement was now preaching
that 'revolution' must replace 'resolutions'. 'If the people of Ireland
wanted [freedom] as much as the people of Ulster did not want it,
they must be prepared to fight for it.'[47]

Meanwhile, the public face of Volunteering remained outwardly
respectable, with recruits representing a fairly wide class spectrum. As
Redmondite influence became superficially predominant, ex-British
Army officers and local gentry climbed on board. The diaries of Diarmuid Coffey, who worked as a Volunteers organizer first in County
Clare and then at the Dublin HQ, provide vivid vignettes of this phase
of the movement. Coffey was an intellectual, subtle, slightly hesitant
figure, from a highly cultured family very much in the Dublin intellectual swim. His father George, Keeper of the Irish Antiquities in the
National Museum and a painter and writer as well as a noted archae-
ologist, came from an Ulster Catholic background. From the 1880s he
was a familiar figure in the intellectual nationalist world centred
on C. H. Oldham's Contemporary Club and John O'Leary's circle.
Diarmuid's mother, Jane L'Estrange, from an old Protestant family,
was involved in the Irish Literary Theatre, and the Coffey house in
Harcourt Terrace was a centre for cultural happenings, such as the
first performance of AE's play *Deirdre*. Diarmuid, an only child, went
to Trinity and became a barrister, but preferred a literary life. A language revivalist and Sinn Féin sympathizer, his nationalism was of a
fairly moderate kind, and his job as secretary to Colonel Maurice
Moore in the Volunteers headquarters from 1914 to 1916, while not
unduly demanding, gave him a detached vantage point from which to
view the build-up of tension in Ireland.

Coffey was in love with the more feisty, emotional and radically nationalist artist Cesca Trench, whose diaries, drawings and paintings are a valuable record of the life of the privileged young in this era. Coffey, though in some ways as anti-British as Cesca, remained a supporter of Home Rule in these years, and disagreed with her about many issues (not least women's suffrage); his diaries show his intense suspicion of 'The O'Rahilly' and more radical and separatist elements within the Volunteers. Yet he, along with so many, was preoccupied with putting guns in the hands of Irish people, and he was one of the party who sailed on the yachts belonging to his friends Erskine Childers and Conor O'Brien in July 1914 to collect guns from Germany and arm the Volunteers – an episode which he recorded in his diary, and wrote about publicly afterwards. The party included Childers's wife and Mary Spring-Rice, a radical nationalist from an impeccable Ascendancy background: the arrival of the main consignment of guns at Howth, just outside Dublin, was carefully choreographed as a major publicity coup for the Volunteers.

The Howth enterprise was – yet again – undertaken in response to a rival Northern initiative: the UVF had run in guns to Larne, County Antrim, on a large scale some weeks before, defying the government's attempt to impound arms en route to the North. (They had managed to seize 55,000 rounds of ammunition being shipped from Birmingham, but far more was getting through.[48]) This, as ever, enabled the UVF to present itself as a more efficient paramilitary force: its own publicity photographs indicate its possession of motor-cars, much emphasized at the time, and the financial resources and class position of many of its supporters. The plan for a rival project of nationalist defiance was first planned by Hobson, with finance arranged by Casement, who raised £1,500 from well-wishers.[49] Erskine and Molly Childers provided £400 as well as one of the yachts; after a series of missed encounters and communications gone astray, the arms were transferred from a German tugboat to the yacht, an event rhapsodically described by Childers's American wife.

I wish you could have seen the scene. Darkness, lamps, strange faces, the swell of the sea making the boat lurch, guns, straw everywhere, unpack[ed] on deck and . . . handed down and stowed in an endless stream; no supper, chocolate thrust into mouths of the crew and a mug

of water passed around when frail nature nearly spent – the Vaseline on
the guns smeared over everything . . . men sweating and panting under
the weight of the 29 ammunition boxes – heavy and hard to handle . . .
I nearly slept as I stood and handed down guns. It was all like a mad
dream, with a glow of joy and the feeling of accomplishing something
great at the back of it to keep the brain steady and the heart
unperturbed.[50]

The *Asgard* sailed openly into Howth Harbour on 26 July. By contrast with the heavily motorized UVF, the National Volunteers
transported many of their guns back from Howth by bicycle, each
weapon reverently laid across the handlebars. (Taxis had to be hired
to transport the ammunition.) Nor were the guns themselves at all up
to the standard of those purchased by the well-off and efficient Northerners. And they disappeared in various directions, not always
intended by their well-meaning couriers. It should be remembered
that the Childerses were still Redmondites at this stage, and thought
they were running guns in order to safeguard the Home Rule Act.
Molly Childers claimed that her husband subsequently 'hurried back
to London', where he 'received congratulations from members of the
Cabinet; the gunrunning was regarded as most helpful to the Government in their difficulty with Ulster.'[51]

They would shortly be disabused of this belief. Colonel Moore subsequently remarked to Coffey: 'The Sinn Féin are going to have a
celebration all over Ireland if they can and want to claim the gunrunning as their own whereas all they did was to steal the arms after it
was over.'[52] But, as ever, the vital thing was to see 'guns in the hands
of Irishmen': the fervent account in Cesca's diary is a good reflection.
Standing on the quay at Howth, 'we cheered and cheered and cheered,
and waved anything we had, and cheered again . . . To see and hear,
that was the best thing that ever happened to me in my life. We went
to some policemen who were standing there and said, "Isn't it grand?"
"It is," they said, "it's great", and broad smiles all over their faces.'[53]

The police were in fact notably acquiescent, declining to interrupt
the Volunteers on their triumphant passage into the city; the Under-
Secretary, Sir James Dougherty, similarly advised against attempting to
confront the gun-runners. But there was an unsuccessful attempt at

interception near Clontarf by a detachment of the Scottish Borderers, who subsequently fired on a hostile crowd at Bachelor's Walk and killed three people, with a fourth dying later in hospital. Yet again, the contrast with the authorities turning a blind eye to UVF importations of arms was bitterly noted, and another Rubicon passed. Liam de Róiste, studying in London, felt an impotent rage. His thoughts were already turning to dynamite, and the news of Bachelor's Walk confirmed it. 'I could have gone out in the streets, had there been anyone with me, and fought the English police or soldiers . . . I feel I could go to Dublin at once were I wanted there, or back to Cork.' Piaras Béaslaí, who heard the news when entertaining Killarney with his travelling players, shared in the general sense of outrage.[54] The huge public funerals were headed by the Volunteers, with their newly imported Mausers well to the fore. Mary Kate Ryan, whose opinions were becoming implacably anti-Redmond, wrote to her sister Min after attending the funeral of the fourth victim; she reported that the Citizen Army were much in evidence '& an immense crowd of Dublin working people. Not one respectable person else. They would not embarrass England by acknowledging such an atrocity!' For extremists, the desired crisis was one step nearer after Bachelor's Walk. 'Great news except for the people who were killed and their friends,' Rosamond Jacob recorded in her diary. 'You'd think it ought to have a very good effect.'[55]

V

The events of the fateful summer of 1914, and the government's inept and pusillanimous responses, had put Redmond's Home Rule strategy on the defensive; the *Irish Volunteer*'s reaction to the Curragh episode in March now seemed prescient. 'We sacrificed "unconstitutional" methods for constitutional, and if at the last minute England tells us that her constitution is a sham we must take her words and take back the arms we dropped.'[56] With underlying tensions within the Volunteers threatening his apparent dominance, deadlock over Ulster's resistance to Home Rule, and the escalating tempo of radical-nationalist emotion, the Irish Parliamentary Party leader needed the appearance of a *deus ex machina*. It came, as so often, from an utterly unexpected direction, when Austria's ultimatum to Serbia precipitated a European crisis, and Britain declared war on 4 August after Germany invaded Belgium.

The ensuing conflagration has, especially in recent years, come to be recognized as one of the defining points of modern Irish history. For one thing, an enormous number of Irishmen voluntarily enlisted, fought and died: the amnesia imposed on this phenomenon by the independent Irish state from the 1920s has been amply atoned for since. The motivations behind enlistment could be various. Tom Barry recalled that, as a seventeen-year-old, he 'went to the war for no other reason than that I wanted to see what war was like, to get a gun, to see new countries and to feel a grown man'.[57] When he returned to Ireland he became a legendary IRA combatant. Others followed a similar route, but the vast majority enlisted to fight Germans rather than to learn skills which could be later turned against the British. Above all, the language of militarism was now given shape. Kevin O'Shiel's memoir recalled that, before August 1914, people like him thought that physical force was a distant possibility; but the concept now emerged fully fledged, like a 'mad goddess'.[58]

And the war brought to a head the split already festering within the Volunteers. With Home Rule apparently stymied by Ulster resistance, Redmond's tactic was to throw the support of the Volunteers fully behind the war effort, reckoning that a short and victorious war would forge a feeling of unity between Volunteers North and South: that chimerical hope once shared by MacNeill, Bigger and others. In Redmond's calculation, the enthusiasm for the war effort expressed in unionist circles throughout the island would be turned to good effect, undercutting the opposition to Home Rule in the north-east – where the war effort was most fervently embraced. The UVF membership enlisted in hordes, effectively forming their own division within the army.

Recruitment to the British Army was less spectacular outside Ulster, but the numbers of the Irish Volunteers were hugely swelled by war fever. The membership of the movement peaked at about 190,000 in September 1914, an astounding proportion of the population of the country – which also suggests that the movement was very far from being composed principally of separatist republicans. While Rosamond Jacob saw Redmond's strategy as his 'crowning act of treason', and Mary Kate Ryan believed that he had now 'done his worst for the country', moderate nationalism at first fell in behind him.[59] The vast majority of the membership followed Redmond's pro-war line when the movement finally split in late September 1914. They included, very prominently, the charismatic nationalist politician and intellectual Tom Kettle, who committed himself whole-heartedly to the war effort and the Allied cause, and crusaded passionately for the cause of recruiting. For separatists, the support of the movement for Redmond was an appalling blow, as Desmond FitzGerald later remembered.

> The movement on which all our dreams had centred seemed merely to have canalized the martial spirit of the Irish people for the defence of England. Our dream castles toppled about us with a crash. It was brought home to us that the very fever that possessed us was due to a subconscious awareness that the final end of the Irish nation was at hand. For centuries, England had held Ireland materially. But now it seemed she held her in a new and utterly complete way.
>
> Our national identity was obliterated not only politically, but also in our own minds. The Irish people had recognized themselves as part of England.[60]

Working for Colonel Edmond Cotter, Edmond the uneasy Chief-of-Staff at Volunteers HQ in Dawson Street, Coffey had noted 'a stream of Unionists' coming in to join as soon as war was declared: most of them 'bounders' and 'incapable asses' who wanted to turn the Volunteers into a branch of the British Army.[61] Coffey found himself caught between such people and the IRB members of the Volunteers committee such as Bulmer Hobson and Michael Judge, and observed both sides with a certain contempt; he particularly despised O'Rahilly as 'a very useless type of person [who] swanks about in uniform and is just like a comic opera hero'.

Coffey's diary indicates that the split in the Volunteers, after Redmond publicly committed them to full-blown support of the war effort, had always been a mere matter of time. It came as the climax of a long campaign behind the scenes to drive out the subversive element. As early as 1 September, he and others were urging Redmond to 'execute a coup d'état' and to set up 'a strong central authority'; Eoin MacNeill, irresolute as ever, was at first in on the scheme but backed out. 'He does not stick to a settled course,' Coffey fulminated; 'I liken him to a man trying to swim to Tir na nÓg [the mythical Gaelic land of eternal youth] & thinking each point of the compass is it until he finally swims round in circles. Another man said he always conspires with each man against the man he conspired with last.'[62] Coffey remained with the moderates, doggedly believing that supporting the Volunteers might be a way of bringing pressure on the government to honour Home Rule; but, moving as he did through a wide social and political circle, he realized that this was not a view universally held. 'Dined with the Markieviczes to meet [James] Connolly the labour leader,' he recorded on 5 September 1914. 'I did not like him much. He is very red-hot anti-British which rather surprised me but I don't think I would trust him as far as I could throw him. He was very strong on how wrong it was to "give soldiers to the enemy". He may be right but I can't think of any way of making the I. V. [Irish Volunteers] any good unless we get help from the War Office & if the I. V. fail how can we insist on good terms in the amending bill [intended to arrive at an agreed version of Home Rule]?' Under the violently unionist General Kitchener, 'help for the Irish Volunteers' was never going to come from the War Office, but Coffey only realized this later.[63]

Nonetheless, in the early months of the war, the main Volunteering movement apparently resembled a Home Guard, continuing to follow British Army methods and models of military training, and staffed by people who believed in the war effort: not least as a strategy for advancing Ireland's claims to national autonomy in a post-war dispensation. The Gaelic scholar Eleanor Hull wrote excitedly to Coffey from London, rhapsodizing over 'the wonderful change that seems to be coming over public opinion in Ireland since the passing of the Home Rule Bill' and the potential for national unity: 'with Redmond recruiting for the British army and the Ulster covenanters going out to die for Catholic Belgium, what may not be accomplished!' Coffey poured cold water on her enthusiasm, telling her that encouraging recruitment 'will by raising opposition and counter movements do as much harm as good to the cause you have at heart'. But he defended Redmond's pro-war policy to his friend Kevin O'Shiel: the point was 'to educate the people into knowing clearly what they do want, what are the difficulties with which they are faced, what the present Home Rule Act really means, and how that Act should be altered to make it a base upon which a future Irish Constitution can be framed.'[64]

This showed a sophisticated understanding of the difficulties confronting Redmond, and his attempts to finesse them by negotiating with Ulster unionists behind the scenes. But Coffey's judicious detachment was hard to maintain after the split and secession following the Irish leader's speech at Woodenbridge, County Wicklow, on 20 September 1914, where he committed the Volunteers to supporting the war effort on the battlefront abroad as well as to the defence of the island of Ireland. This was a step which the radical element could be guaranteed to oppose, which may well have been Redmond's intention. The movement split at once, publicly and traumatically. The minority who seceded (taking with them the name 'Irish Volunteers') were the IRB-dominated element, whose feelings about the opportunities afforded by the war were very different. Some were frankly and even passionately pro-German, notably Roger Casement; for others, such as Terence MacSwiney, the years of rhetoric and polemic had at last produced a proto-nation in arms. MacSwiney's Volunteers uniform became a central part of his revolutionary identity, worn on all possible occasions, including at his marriage to Muriel Murphy a couple of years later. Thomas MacDonagh had also flung himself into the movement from the beginning, writing bloodthirsty marching songs instead of mystic poems;[65] after the split, his fervour knew no bounds. All of the secessionists, like Seán MacDermott, saw an international war as the classic opportunity for a Fenian insurrection against Britain.

Not for the first or last time in Irish history, in the case of a split the future was on the side of the dissident minority. Redmond's Volunteers would die in great numbers on the international war front, while the structure of the main Volunteering movement at home decayed and Hibernian-style politicking took over. By late 1915 the majority movement was a ghost of its former self, as Diarmuid Coffey sadly recognized. 'Had a talk with some of the officers. They all seem to think that the movement is petering out. They lay the blame chiefly on the committee & say that they the committee only want the Vols for

the purposes of ward politics. I am afraid there is a good deal in this.'
This is borne out by local studies which describe Volunteer companies
succumbing slowly to 'paralysis' as members left for the Front and the
remnant became immersed in political bickering.[66]

Meanwhile the rump of extremists laid plans for radical action, and
defined themselves decisively against the Home Rule enemy. By
1915 the dissident Irish Volunteers were engaging in pitched battles
against the AOH at political demonstrations. The split had clarified
and focused their mission: as one of them put it much later, 'we had
got rid of any ambiguous feeling which existed that we were only
bluffing.'[67] This was not apparent to the more cynical elements of
Irish opinion. One of the more extreme of the IRB military planners
was the poet, mystic, playwright and flamboyant revolutionary Joseph
Plunkett, who dedicated himself to distributing propaganda, planning
military manoeuvres and constructing wireless sets through which he
hoped to publicize the insurrection when it came. He was also
immersed in plans to contact subversive elements abroad, employing
his sisters on secret missions to extremist Irish-Americans. Though
severely ill once more with tuberculosis, he himself would make a
secret visit to Germany to arrange for German military aid in the
summer of 1915. To others he seemed an unlikely rebel leader: certainly in the view of his doctor, who was amused at the earnest
acolytes who trooped in to visit Plunkett in his nursing-home.

> I remember once finding a group of them seated around his bed with
> notebooks and pencils in their hands, while he was sitting up in bed,
> apparently giving them instructions. I, frankly, did not take this at all
> seriously and remarked: 'Napoleon dictating to his marshals' – a
> remark which was not well received. On another occasion I joked with
> him, saying, 'I suppose you sleep with a revolver under your pillow'
> and to my surprise he said, 'I do' and pulled one out.[68]

The years of agit-prop work in magazines and theatre, the mystical
nationalism absorbed from Pearse and MacDonagh, perhaps also the
implacable war forged against his parents along with his sisters and
brother, and now this world-historical opportunity: events had propelled Plunkett into the position of revolutionary hero. He was
engaged in a double race against time: an insurrection must happen

before the war ended, and before his own death. With his brother George and his sister Geraldine, he was largely living at the mill and farm complex at Larkfield in the Dublin suburbs, which had become more of an armed camp than ever. The settlement acted as a magnet for young men of Irish descent returning (or immigrating) from Britain; they had come to Ireland to avoid conscription and join another cause. At Larkfield they lived in semi-military conditions: drilled by George Plunkett, fed by the Plunkett sisters and employed in making ammunition – as recalled vividly in the absorbing autobiography of Joe Good. Séamus O'Connor visited Larkfield and found 'a motley collection of men' manufacturing makeshift pikes – 'simply sharp spikes fixed on ashen handles. It made me sad when I saw them.' Joe Good's account bears this out, adding details of how they also constructed shotgun cartridges, and crude hand-grenades out of sections of down-pipe, in expectation of a coming struggle. 'We had a good deal of fun, a lovely view of the Dublin mountains through the windowless frames [of the barn], and bragged that we were the first Irish garrison since that of Patrick Sarsfield.'[69] These refugees were known by the Plunketts as 'the lambs': possibly, as Joe Good sardonically pointed out, because they were to be led to the slaughter.

Thus the world war changed the fortunes of many of the people whose intersecting lives are considered in this book. Before August 1914, for instance, the position of Arthur Griffith was distinctly doubtful. He had alienated many of his old separatist colleagues by his continued insistence on the viability of a dual-monarchy route to independence, and Sinn Féin's essay into electoral politics was widely held to have misfired. The apparent return of Home Rule to the realm of practical politics had compromised his novel strategy of advocating a compromise route between republicanism and constitutionalism. The escalation of labour agitation and strikes from 1913 (in sleepy provincial towns like Sligo as well as in Dublin) tended to increase the marginalization of Griffith, never a friend to Irish labour; Larkin's feisty *Irish Worker* had stolen some of his thunder. He was still seen by many nationalists as a John the Baptist who had led the way to conversion a decade before; but now they looked for a new Messiah. No one visiting Griffith in his untidy editorial office in 1914 would have supposed that they were meeting the man who would less than ten years later be the first President of an autonomous Irish state.

But the war propelled him back into the front line of propaganda, saving him from irrelevance. It gave him an essential chance to recoup his 'advanced' credentials, and he seized it with both hands. His short, punchy news-sheets *Nationality* and *Scissors and Paste* enabled him to play the matador to John Bull with practised ease, as the censorship authorities tried to prevent the printing of *Sinn Féin*, the *Leader*, *Irish Freedom* and the *Irish Worker*. Madeleine ffrench-Mullen could tell Rosamond Jacob by the end of 1914 that Griffith's *Scissors and Paste* was on public sale, 'boys roaring it at every corner'. It only lasted three months but Griffith had regained some of his old power. Moreover, he was once again brought into the circles of the IRB, which paid for the production of *Éire*, *Scissors and Paste* and *Nationality*; MacDermott arranged for them to be printed by an Orangeman in Belfast 'who was prepared to take a chance, for a consideration of course, said MacDermott'.[70] Clarke and MacDermott disagreed over Griffith's political moderation, but they knew his value. And through his new papers, Griffith happily rediscovered the virtues of personal vituperation. Diarmuid Coffey recorded in his diary that 'George Russell ... is very indignant with Griffith for publishing an article about him in "Nationality" repeating things alleged to have been said in his (R's) house, but said he wd not reply as if he did G would probably say that his father was an informer and his grandfather a spy etc.'[71] He was back in business.

Even more effective was the *Spark*, edited by Seán Doyle under the sobriquet of Edward Dalton. Its four pages packed in a great deal of subversion per issue, emphasizing religion and nationalism, and violently attacking the immoral literatures of France and England. It also trumpeted the implacable pro-Germanism that from 1914 became part of the armoury of advanced-nationalist rhetoric. This was not only a tactical response to the hostilities of August 1914, adopting the cause of their enemy's enemy; for several years, Irish nationalists had approvingly noted German challenges to British imperial ambitions, and made much of Britain's hypocritical attitude towards the Reich's own expansionism. Roger Casement took this further, idealizing Germany as the deliverer of small nations, Ireland in particular. Doyle knew who the enemy was, and whose side he was on. The 'Redmondite Perverts' were denounced, and the gallant Germans praised. 'It is the war of the Irish Parliamentary Party and of the "Freeman's Journal". It is the war of William Martin Murphy, it is Carson's war. It is the war of the Castle hacks and the pensioners. It is the slum-owners' war, and the Music Hall artistes' war; but up to the present I do not see that it is the war of Ireland's priests.' Like *Sinn Féin* before it, the *Spark* attracted a wide range of contributors who wrote for no fee; they included Éamonn Ceannt, Arthur Griffith, Herbert Pim, Eoin MacNeill, Tom Kettle, Seán Etchingham, Eimar O'Duffy, Michael O'Rahilly, Bulmer Hobson, Father Michael O'Flanagan and Patrick Pearse. Rosamond Jacob found it incredible that the *Spark* printed what it did without getting shut down; suppression would come, but not before it had made a name for itself in the violently buzzing world of the mosquito journalism.[72]

The *Spark* reminds us that, with police reports detailing the interest of IRB cells in pro-German initiatives, the state could no longer engage in its hands-off attitude towards subversive activity. Ireland's spectacularly free press was no longer free. When Griffith's publications were censored, his radical credibility returned. Seán MacDermott too was just one of several IRB stalwarts who saw that war conditions potently revived the ancient Fenian mantra of 'England's Difficulty, Ireland's Opportunity'. Significantly it was in 1915 that IRB elements managed a more or less thorough takeover of the central body of the Gaelic League (whose membership began to decline, as it focused more on political organization and less on cultural jamborees). And Casement, whose opinions already approximated to pro-German imperialism, set to cutting his final ties with the British establishment, travelling first to the USA and then to Germany and trying ineffectually to set up a viable plan for German military involvement with an Irish revolutionary putsch. 'God save Ireland,' he informed Gertrude Parry, 'is now only another form of God save Germany.'[73]

The radicalization of less celebrated figures also proceeded apace. For Kevin O'Shiel and many others, any faith that a British government would honour its debt to constitutional nationalism was destroyed by the co-option into the war cabinet of the leaders of

Ulster unionist resistance, the Irish lawyer Edward Carson and the maverick Tory F. E. Smith. Both men had fomented treason in their UVF days before the war, yet both were now elevated to government roles. (Redmond, offered a much inferior part in the same administration, had no option but to turn it down.) The year 1915 also saw the rising profile of Patrick Pearse as orator-in-chief for the IRB extremists, most famously at the funeral of the Fenian survivor Jeremiah O'Donovan Rossa, where he preached the need for a blood sacrifice. O'Donovan Rossa had helped found the original Fenian movement in the 1860s, and his accounts of subsequent sufferings in British gaols had made potent nationalist propaganda; a career in America as a maverick journalist and energetic proponent of bombing campaigns in British cities had kept him prominent, though his latter years had seen a sad decline. A 'mild and genial old gentleman', he told one journalist that 'he had long ago lost all hatred against the British Government and was inclined rather to lament than to boast of the part he had taken in preaching the doctrine of assassination.'[74] But, as with other Fenian heroes, his return to Ireland in a coffin enabled a great republican demonstration. Pearse's fervent encomium on O'Donovan Rossa helped to make up for the fact that the old man had been a distinct embarrassment a couple of years before, when he temporarily repatriated himself to Cork and caused havoc among local extremists by innocently endorsing Redmond and Home Rule: 'comment is beyond me', de Róiste had confided to his journal.[75] But everything looked different now.

When de Róiste travelled up to Dublin for O'Donovan Rossa's funeral, he had no doubt that he was attending a great national event. The idea that the old Fenian might ever have supported Redmond 'or weakened in his hatred of English tyranny in Ireland' was now contemptuously rejected. Filing past the bier, de Róiste felt 'sorrow for the dead, hope for the future, strengthening of faith: the high principle of Irish Nationality, resolution in the great work for Caitlín Ní Uallacháin.' He marched in the funeral procession with the Cork Volunteers, carrying 'my beloved Mauser rifle'. In the huge procession he recognized Bulmer Hobson, Eoin MacNeill and many others, but was unable to gain entry to Glasnevin Cemetery to hear Pearse's historic oration (tickets for this were printed, and had to be obtained in advance). Nonetheless he was overwhelmed by the event: 'it was too stupendous, too vast'. He estimated that at least 10,000 Volunteers were in attendance, with spectators bringing the numbers up to 200,000. Though the *Freeman's Journal* loyally claimed the event as an Irish Parliamentary Party demonstration, de Róiste contemptuously noted that the Home Rulers had had nothing to do with it. This was, he observed, the separatist Irish nation in arms.[76]

And arms were by now securely in the hands of Irishmen, as Pearse decreed; the only question was how they would be used. At this time Francis Sheehy-Skeffington wrote an open letter to his friend Thomas MacDonagh, accusing him of double-think in speaking against war on the one hand, yet 'boasting of being one of the creators of a new militarism in Ireland' on the other. While accepting that MacDonagh was principled and idealistic, Sheehy-Skeffington pointed out that all militarisms started out that way, endorsing 'the old, bad tradition that war is a glorious thing'. What were instructions in bayonet-fighting for, he demanded, if not a preparation to kill one's fellow men?[77]

The same might be asked of many other preparations being carried out among radical circles in these years. In the light of the frank sedition of separatist rhetoric, the fervent support of Germany in extreme circles, and the more or less open stockpiling of weapons and ammunition, it is easy to wonder why the outbreak of insurrection on Easter Monday 1916 came as a surprise to anyone. But it should be remembered that the extremists were still a small number of people, noisy though they were; and that the level of separatist rhetoric had been inflated and reiterated to such a degree that it had become background noise. Both Seán MacDermott and James Connolly, when separately upbraided by worried colleagues for saying too much, too openly, rejoined by asking if their interlocutors had ever heard the story of 'Crying Wolf': they calculated that the government would become so used to their fulminations that they would stop taking them seriously.[78] In a sense this strategy worked, right up to the moment when the wolf appeared at the door. After the Rising, the Royal Commission into its origins concluded that the Irish administration had proceeded 'on the principle that it was safer and more expedient to leave law in abeyance if collision with any faction of the Irish people could thereby be avoided'.[79] Accordingly, they let the

UVF drill as threateningly as they liked, left Larkfield alone, and retreated from Countess Markievicz's house in Rathmines when a police visit found obvious evidence of subversive activity. This was the 'repressive tolerance' of the Castle dispensation, for which officials such as Matthew Nathan and Augustine Birrell (both supporters of Home Rule) paid with their jobs after the week of mayhem at Easter 1916. Volunteering pushed the logic of this policy to its limits.

The feelings of General John Maxwell, arriving in Dublin to put down the Rising, spoke for more than just the military mind. 'It is the Government as a whole that are to blame, ever since they winked at Ulster breaking the law they have been in difficulties & have hoped & hoped that something would turn up to get them out without their doing anything themselves – "Wait and see" well we have waited and now we see the result, viz. Rebellion and loss of life.'[80] There are arguments in favour of the government's policy; it may have avoided civil war in 1912–14, though who is to say that that outcome would not have arrived anyway, if a larger conflict had not intervened? It was that larger conflict that changed everything; Germany became the essential factor. The planning for the original Rising was contingent on a realistic level of German aid; those who tried to stop the plan at the last minute, such as Casement, MacNeill and Hobson, did so because they knew that this was not going to arrive. And that they were excluded from the original conspiracy reflected the lasting antagonism within the ranks of the separatists over letting the Redmondites on to the Volunteers Committee in June 1914. The cult of guns, and the extraordinary success of the Volunteering movement, decisively launched the drift to radicalism.

Paradoxically, the acceptance of violence and armed display followed hard upon the apparent constitutional success of 1912, and negated that success. Carson's initial defiance of the law and apparent endorsement of the gun were vital in radicalizing the opinions of many away from the possibilities of Home Rule: this was frequently observed at the time (by General Maxwell among others, as seen above). In MacNeill's words, Carson's almost single-handed responsibility for transforming and radicalizing Irish politics 'is not a paradox but the simple truth'.[81] But militarism also thrived on a long-term culture of violence and antagonism. The power of guns 'in the hands of Irishmen' could not be gainsaid. Seen from this angle, the creation of the Volunteers, officially intended to safeguard Home Rule, in fact became a key and deliberate element in its destruction.

But Redmond's Home Rulers were not the only actors in the mounting drama who were operating on the assumption of a future that would not happen. As the revolution approached reality, several of those who had prepared most enthusiastically for it would find themselves marginalized in turn. New faces emerged with the new militarism, while further changes would be enforced by the sheer attrition of violence and its consequences. The next two chapters will widen the focus to look at the sequence of events from the outbreak of insurrection in 1916 to the end of the civil war in 1923 before returning to a thematic treatment of the years that followed, from the perspective of those members of the revolutionary generation who survived.

An unconsciously prophetic cartoon by the St Enda's pupil Patrick Tuohy, responding to the school's acquisition of a rifle range in 1909; it mocks the alarmed reactions of the supposedly gentle and pacific figures of Patrick Pearse and Thomas MacDonagh ('Deadshot Tom and Pawnee Pearse'). Both would fight in the Rising seven years later (as would Tuohy himself) and be executed for it.

7

Fighting

I lived on a mountain top where there was no need for speech, even. I felt an understanding, a sharing of something bigger than ourselves, and a heightening of life. People could be more expressive, natural and affectionate. They were direct, and immediate contact was not difficult. Older people had no conscious out-thrust of age or experience; we all shared the adventure.

– Ernie O'Malley, On Another Man's Wound *(1936)[1]*

I

Many of the people whose lives run through this book had dreamt of an Irish revolution against British rule, and welcomed the advent of world war as both enabling and sanctioning such an eventuality. Several were involved in the frenetic planning of an insurrection originally tabled for Easter Sunday 1916 and instigated by the inner Military Council of the IRB: notably Joseph Plunkett, Seán MacDermott, Tom Clarke, Patrick Pearse and Thomas MacDonagh. Constance Markievicz's position in the Irish Citizen Army, and her closeness to James Connolly, brought her near the centre of intrigue; other ICA members, such as Helena Molony, were also fully informed.[2] A larger number were poised on the outer circles of conspiracy; Plunkett's sisters Geraldine and Mimi, and his brothers George and Jack, were not privy to the full plan until the last minute. Roger Casement was on his own revolutionary mission, though he knew a rising was imminent. Senior Volunteers in Dublin, including Éamon de Valera, were briefed by their IRB contacts. Prominent Irish Volunteers outside Dublin, such as Terence MacSwiney and Liam de Róiste in Cork, Denis McCullough in Belfast, and Pat McCartan working as a doctor in Tyrone, had been equally aware since January that plans were afoot. But they were not closely informed, especially if – like McCartan – they had earlier aired doubts to IRB colleagues about the wisdom of such a move. Richard Mulcahy, for instance, was more or less talked into it at the last minute. Specific details were given to McCartan and McCullough only on Good Friday.[3] Seán T. O'Kelly was closer to the Military Council, but even he was held at a certain distance.

Others who had been active in the preparation of a revolutionary mindset were openly sceptical about the feasibility of a rising without guaranteed German aid, and were therefore kept in the dark. A week before Easter, Min Ryan organized a fundraising concert for the Volunteers at the Foresters' Hall on Palm Sunday; here Bulmer Hobson made a speech implying that some rash action was in the air, and counselling caution, to the fury of several of his listeners. Eimar O'Duffy was of the same mind, as were Michael O'Rahilly and Arthur Griffith. And for many romantic adherents of the idea of rebelling against British rule, such as Rosamond Jacob, Cesca Trench and Maud Gonne, the Rising would come as a bolt from the blue. To some, it appeared as the inspirational annunciation of a long-promised epiphany. For others, the reality of violent revolution would awaken strong feelings of ambivalence, which were concealed at first but grew with time. The events of Easter Monday and following days would be recorded, preserved, mythologized and built into a narrative of liberation; the process would reaffirm the sense of being a special generation. The expectation of taking part in a great symbolic act had been imprinted on their consciousness through years of conditioning. The insurrection at once actualized that moment, and brought them up against reality, changing everything that had gone before. For this reason, the events of the Rising and its aftermath need to be rehearsed, as does the part played by several of the people whose lives and experiences have been traced thus far.

Despite the background of ostentatious subversion surveyed in the last chapter, the planning of the insurrection that burst into flame on 24 April 1916 remains oddly obscure. On some matters, at least, the revolutionaries managed to preserve a certain discretion – not least because they had to deceive so many of their colleagues as well as the authorities. By February 1915 those in touch with the extreme faction knew that a rising was planned.[4] Between then and May, the secretive inner group of IRB strategists called the Military Council was established; this included Patrick Pearse, Éamonn Ceannt and Joseph Plunkett; Tom Clarke joined in September, along with MacDermott (whose anti-recruiting activities had recently earned him a gaol term under the Defence of the Realm Act, which was increasingly restricting the movements of many would-be revolutionaries). In January 1916 James Connolly would be co-opted, after frantic negotiations following the discovery that his Citizen Army was planning its own putsch before the war ended. Plunkett's friend Thomas MacDonagh joined late, in April 1916. Those who had been key figures in the Volunteers, but who were now excluded from this inner circle, included Bulmer Hobson and Eoin MacNeill; an enduring schism had been created by the traumatic separation over accepting Redmond's nominees on to the Volunteer command in the summer of 1914, for which Hobson in particular would never be forgiven. MacNeill was about to incur even greater obloquy when he countermanded the insurrectionary order to Volunteer units during Holy Week 1916, leaving the inner circle to launch a desperate and essentially doomed venture on their own.

MacNeill had tried to restrain his insurrectionist colleagues at the Volunteers' headquarters in early 1916, and he was more closely informed about plans during the run-up to rebellion than he would later imply. McDermott had driven out to MacNeill's Rathfarnham house on Sunday, 16 April (taking Seán T. O'Kelly and two Ryan girls for 'cover'), and briefed him about plans for the following weekend.[5] During the following week MacNeill was kept irresolutely on side, persuaded by doctored documents threatening a draconian crackdown by Dublin Castle on the Volunteers, enterprisingly leaked on the Wednesday before Easter. This was one of the eventualities defined by the radicals as justification for an insurrection, along with the imposition of conscription or a German invasion. More bizarrely, further justification was provided by assurances from several members of the Plunkett family, well in with the Vatican, that the Pope approved the venture.[6] MacNeill then endorsed instructions to Volunteer battalions, telling them to be ready for defensive action and to resist disarmament by government troops; the step from there to an actual rebellion would be a very short one, as he must have realized, though he heard the details so late in the day.

Summonses were delivered to Volunteer brigades all over Ireland, often by women couriers, on Thursday, 20 April, and on Good Friday. O'Kelly's was issued by Patrick Pearse's brother Willie, summoning him to Beresford Place at 4 p.m. on Easter Sunday. 'You will provide yourself with a bicycle, a street map of Dublin City, a road map of Dublin District and a field message book. You will carry full arms and ammunition, full service equipment (including overcoat) and rations for eight hours.'[7]

But by Saturday everything had been thrown into confusion, precipitated by Roger Casement. German aid was the *sine qua non* for successful insurrection, and this had been intensively canvassed during 1915. Casement was unhappily resident in Berlin, after a disastrous period trying to raise German support in New York, where local Irish-Americans were nonplussed by his frenzied declarations and emotional manner. (The painter John Butler Yeats thought he was in the throes of a nervous breakdown, likening him to 'a very nice girl who is just hysterical enough to be charming and interesting among strangers and a trial to his [*sic*] own friends'.[8]) Moving to Germany exacerbated his highly strung manic state, not helped when Joseph Plunkett appeared in Berlin. Plunkett brought with him a beguiling and detailed plan for the German authorities, outlining a concerted effort underpinned by German arms and an invading force. The failure of the Germans to be convinced by this odd couple had far-ranging consequences. Casement plunged violently from hero-worshipping the Reich to denouncing German perfidy; his own failure to mobilize more than a few Irish prisoners-of-war into an 'Irish Brigade' compounded the disillusionment. Exhilarated by the brotherhood of Volunteering and by having shaken off the trammels of imperial service, he now became immersed in violent depression. 'Oh Ireland, why did I ever trust in such a government . . . they have no sense of honour, chivalry or generosity. They are cads. This is why they are hated by the world and why England will surely beat them.'[9] (As he would eventually realize, he was also being betrayed by his companion and lover, a shifty Norwegian sailor of fortune called Adler Christensen, who accompanied him back to Europe and embarked on a risky double game with the British diplomatic contacts.)

Casement, like his projected 'Irish Brigade' of fifty-six chancers, was by now a distinct embarrassment to the German high command, and out of touch with the conspirators at home; he heard of the insurrectionist plans, and the limited arms shipment offered by the Germans, only from a fellow Volunteer who had come to Germany to join the Irish Brigade, the shadowy Robert Monteith. With some relief the Germans agreed to transport Casement to Ireland by U-Boat, where he intended to put off any projected insurrection. With Monteith and another Irish Brigade member, he landed on a Kerry beach on Good Friday 1916 and was subsequently arrested, partly thanks to the inept organization of the local Volunteer battalion under the famously inefficient Austin Stack. Influential rumours at once raced off in several directions, compounded by the scuttling of an accompanying steamship with an arms cargo. The news persuaded the British authorities that an attempted rising, which they assumed was to have been led by Casement, had been short-circuited; warnings of the plans for an Easter insurrection had been relayed from intelligence sources in Washington and elsewhere, and reached the very highest sources in London, but were now cavalierly ignored.

To rebels in the know, the events in Kerry boded the end of any substantial German aid, but in the atmosphere of unsubstantiated rumour, the gullible could be persuaded to believe that it indicated hopes of a real invasion; Annie MacSwiney was told on the Wednesday of Easter Week by Tom Clarke, with 'joyous elation', that help was on the seas from Germany and that the Kaiser had recognized the Republic of Ireland.[10] MacDermott and MacDonagh had been broadcasting this probability to sceptical colleagues for weeks. Ruminating later on the part played by MacDermott, McCartan judged that his old Dungannon Club comrade 'was bright and energetic but mentally superficial; he had not an idea in his head when Hobson took him up & directed his "education"... he was cunning rather than clever, would do a crooked thing if it served his purpose.' Denis McCullough wondered if MacDermott was deluding himself as well as others, and McCartan felt the same was true of Plunkett. 'He deceived everyone about the great success he had in Germany re guns & support & probably deceived himself as well.'[11]

However, as the significance of Casement's lonely journey home and its fallout became clear, the Volunteers leadership were precipitated into frantic meetings. Following his Wednesday instruction to Volunteers to prepare for defensive warfare, MacNeill was informed by a delegation of 'moderates' (Hobson, 'Ginger' O'Connell and Eimar O'Duffy) the next day that this was a cover for an actual insurrection planned for Sunday. An angry confrontation with Pearse confirmed this. On Friday, MacNeill was swayed by the rumour of a German landing in Kerry, but by Saturday night he had shifted his ground again, realizing how far he had been misled. He produced a final decision on Saturday night and countermanded the mobilization orders. With unwonted decisiveness, MacNeill got this into the Sunday-morning papers, effectively blocking most of the planned Volunteer manoeuvres. Individual orders to a similar effect were frantically conveyed to provincial leaders, many of them delivered by Michael O'Rahilly, travelling expensively by taxi.

For the members of the Military Council, this was almost unbearably traumatic; rage, tears, lamentations and murderous intentions towards the 'moderates' were widely recalled by those who witnessed the frenetic gatherings on Sunday at Liberty Hall, Larkfield and other rebel conclaves. (Constance Markievicz offered to shoot Hobson and MacNeill herself.) The day that had been designated for the insurrection passed without public incident, though many Volunteers indeed assembled as originally instructed, only to disperse in an atmosphere of confusion and anti-climax. But by Sunday night, among the leaders at least, a different and more exalted mood had taken over. They would seize the moment nonetheless, attempt to countermand MacNeill's countermanding order, and mount an insurrection to preserve, on one level, the soul of the nation (a recurring phrase, significantly now adopted by the Marxist James Connolly) and, on another, their own revolutionary *amour propre*.[12]

The printing of their soon-to-be-historic 'Proclamation of the Irish Republic' went ahead, on the presses of the *Workers' Republic*. And their plan would follow Plunkett and Pearse's strategy of a spectacular uprising in the capital city, seizing central buildings and barricading streets, rather than the more pragmatic (and prophetic) outline of eventual guerrilla warfare across the country, originally advocated by Hobson. Connolly had also made a special study of urban risings in European cities, believing that in such circumstances 'civilian revolutionists' had the advantage over regular armies. But, above all, a rising in Dublin would raise the spectres of Lord Edward FitzGerald, Robert Emmet and the iconic figures of 1798, so omnipresent in the imaginations of the revolutionary generation – rather than the damp squibs of rural skirmishes in 1848 and 1867. Symbolic weight was already counting for more than practical methods.

II

Plunkett would later claim that 'everything was foreseen, everything was calculated, nothing was forgotten.'[13] But the precise, heavily theorized and rather classical stipulations which he liked to lay down ('Napoleon dictating to his marshals') were not a very accurate prognostication of the events of Easter 1916 in Dublin. The chaotic and last-minute nature of the leaders' deliberations was reflected in the way that the insurrection began. Seán MacDermott arrived at the revolution in a motor-car, with Tom Clarke; they were driven to the corner of the General Post Office on Sackville Street, where around midday they met a detachment from Larkfield, who had arrived by tram (their fares paid, as usual, by Plunkett money). The main body of Volunteers and ICA members marched more conventionally from Liberty Hall. Seán T. O'Kelly, who was with them, watched the windows of the GPO being broken by Diarmuid Lynch, at James Connolly's instruction, and realized the long-awaited rebellion 'was an accomplished fact'.[14] The occupation of the Post Office, a splendid neoclassical edifice recently restored, would become an iconic moment in Irish history, and the noble Grecian building provided an appropriate locale for the declaration of a republic.

Simultaneously, other buildings were seized. These were an odd choice in some ways, including Boland's Mill, Jacob's Biscuit Factory and the South Dublin Union (a complex of buildings dispensing poor relief, which amounted to a small village in themselves). The Shelbourne Hotel was left to the enemy, which made the occupation of Stephen's Green – the park in front of it – something of an own-goal. While a cursory attempt was made on Dublin Castle, the concentrated effort in the area was focused on the adjoining City Hall, from which the rebels were expelled within twenty-four hours. Other prominent buildings, which had been closely reconnoitred on marches and exercises the year before, were surprisingly ignored. Some of the most successful engagements, such as the killing rectangle set up by rebel snipers at Mount Street Bridge, which trapped waves of troops advancing down Northumberland Road, or the punishing engagement at Ashbourne Barracks stage-managed by Richard Mulcahy and Thomas Ashe, were no part of a pre-arranged 'clockwork' plan.

Hostilities were opened with an odd combination of chaos and effectiveness, and this approach dominated events throughout the week. Improvisation was the order of the day, along with the surreal effects of unexpected war in the centre of a large city: toy-shops exploding with fireworks, looters from the slums (adjacent to the fiercest fighting) prancing through the bullets arrayed in their finery, garrisons living off odd combinations of food sourced from commandeered premises, excited crowds thronging to spectator-points and keeping up a running commentary. But this was just the background to the reality of killing, in a savage episode of warfare that involved lethal hails of sniper-fire, machine-guns and field artillery, and eventually a gunboat on the Liffey blasting away at rebel strongholds. When it was all over, the area around Sackville Street resembled – as many observers remarked in awestruck tones – the shelled remains of Louvain, Amiens or Ypres. A favourite subject for souvenir photographers was the dramatically gaunt shell of the bombed-out DBC Café, where Mary Kate Ryan had held court in days gone by.

Within the rebel fortresses, the mood varied. In the GPO a certain elation was sustained, encouraged by Pearse's ecstatic but delusive communiqués about the country rising as one to the republican cause and German landings everywhere. Min Ryan cornered Tom Clarke in the GPO kitchens on the Tuesday night and extracted a more reasoned view. 'He . . . said that at all periods in the history of Ireland the shedding of blood had always succeeded in raising the spirit and morale of the people. He said that our only chance was to make ourselves felt by an armed rebellion. "Of course," he added, "we shall all be wiped out." He said this almost with gaiety. He had got into the one thing he had wanted to do during his whole lifetime.'[15] Clarke, a veteran of earlier struggles and imprisonment, spoke for a different generation; Min privately remembered, years later, her shock when she realized the inevitable end for most of the young rebels, including her sweetheart Seán MacDermott. By now unofficially engaged, they had last seen each other in the Red Bank restaurant on Good Friday. As it was a fast day, she had been surprised and rather disapproving to find him ordering a large steak. But he had left the rural pieties of his youth far behind him, and he knew he was going to need it.[16]

For others, the atmosphere of elation, and the conquest of fear, was sustained by an intensely religious atmosphere. Before going out to storm the city, whole battalions of Volunteers had taken Communion, in a spirit of solemn exaltation. During the occupation of the GPO the Rosary was said communally every night, and priests were on hand to hear confessions, despite the Church's extremely ambiguous view of the whole venture. (Some locations of worship were unconventional: in Boland's Mill a bread-van served as an impromptu confession-box.) Even anti-clerical Fenians like John MacBride, and people of unconventional or agnostic beliefs like Thomas MacDonagh and James Connolly, seem to have rapidly been affected. This confounding of Catholicism with the rebel cause would be of immense importance as the war gathered momentum in the ensuing months.

Another indication for the future might be seen in the attitudes towards women rebels. Some, notably Constance Markievicz, wielded guns, and Sheila Humphreys shocked her sister by her 'inhuman' delight in taking pot-shots at the enemy.[17] But, generally, women's roles were kept ancillary: cooking, nursing and carrying messages, often at immense personal risk. Phyllis Ryan's memory of her time in the GPO was dominated by endlessly carving sides of beef liberated from the neighbouring Metropole and Imperial hotels. Even members of the paramilitary Cumann na mBan, however much they argued for taking their place in the front line, were treated as helpmeets rather than as fellow soldiers.

Patriarchal attitudes were probably reinforced by the sheer

bloodiness of the carnage in areas of close engagement, the horrific mutilations wreaked by gunfire, shells and grenades exploding in confined spaces, and the terrible toll taken of civilian as well as of combatant lives. This was particularly the case around Sackville Street, and in the hinterland behind the Four Courts, where savage fighting took place in narrow commercial and residential streets. Here the 25-year-old Ned Daly, Kathleen Clarke's brother, emerged as one of the most competent insurgent leaders, wreaking considerable devastation on British forces, which culminated in a savage pitched battle over the barricades in North King Street. Daly's young age was representative: all the Volunteers (except one) occupying the hard-fought fortress of the Mendicity Institute on the quays, commanded by the 25-year-old Seán Heuston, were aged between eighteen and twenty-five. Observers constantly reiterate the extreme youth of the combatants; several Volunteer commanders tried to send their most enthusiastic teenaged followers back home, with varying success.

Among the rebels, inexperience was compounded by the nature of their weaponry: the 'Howth Mausers' dating from the great gun-running kicked like a mule, and the cocoa-tin bombs manufactured at Larkfield could be lethally unpredictable. Many of their military opponents, if better armed, were almost as inexperienced and disorientated; there is much evidence of traumatic reactions to the carnage, desertions of posts and loss of control among British Army units.[18] Among Volunteer battalion commanders, both MacDonagh and de Valera came near to cracking up completely. But other commanders – perhaps less intellectually sensitive – found their métier, emerging as dynamic and effective soldiers, and fully relishing the excitement, unpredictability and violence of the extraordinary situation which they had precipitated. Several, such as Ned Daly and Seán Heuston, would not survive the Rising and its aftermath. Others, such as Richard Mulcahy, Cathal Brugha and Oscar Traynor, would use these latent abilities in a longer war. A new ruthlessness would characterize the 'gunmen' in whose hands the prosecution of revolutionary action now rested.

The exhilaration experienced by some was intensified by the theatricality of the whole affair. The insurgents kept a close eye on opportunities to historicize the event in the making: above all the reading of the 'Proclamation of the Irish Republic' outside the GPO and the running up of a revolutionary tricolour above the building, accompanied by a green-and-gold banner bearing a harp, designed hastily by Constance Markievicz. The Citizen Army flag, depicting a worker's plough traced out in stars, was flown from the adjacent Metropole Hotel. This was the property of William Martin Murphy, perceived since the 1913 lockout as the arch-enemy of Dublin's proletariat – another poignant symbol of the world turned upside down. It has been suggested that the targeting of Jacob's Biscuit Factory and the South Dublin Union may also have been dictated by their symbolic value, as both had featured heavily in socialist campaigns against injustice and exploitation; but without solid evidence of the rebels' general plan, it is impossible to say.[19]

While witnesses of Pearse's reading of the 'Proclamation' after noon on Easter Monday more or less agree that the effect was perfunctory, the echoes resound still. The 'Proclamation' itself distilled Pearse's own idea of an apostolic succession of nationalist struggles into what has been memorably described as 'a kind of national poem: lucid, terse and strangely moving even to unbelievers'.[20] The promises of 'religious and civil liberty, equal rights and equal opportunities to all its citizens', cherishing 'all the children of the nation equally . . . oblivious of the differences carefully fostered by an alien government', suggested a radical tolerance which would remain a matter of aspiration for the future. It was also a rather airy rationalization of Ulster's resistance to Irish nationalism. More to the moment, the reference to Ireland's 'gallant allies in Europe' meant, as Cesca Trench at once noted, that charges of high treason would inevitably be levelled in the fullness of time.[21]

Pearse's emergence as supremo of the 'Army of the Irish Republic' (as the Volunteers and their insurrectionary allies were beginning to be called), and President of the Provisional government, was an unexpected development for this recent IRB recruit. Seen by many as erratic, unstable and (in Hobson's word) 'abnormal', his elevation infuriated Kathleen Clarke in particular, since she felt – not unreasonably – that her husband, Tom, was *ipso facto* President from his senior position within the IRB. But Pearse's identification with the 'Proclamation', his rhetorical power and the carefully constructed literary inheritance which he left combined to propel him to the forefront. His Old Testament-style fulminations against Redmond and the Home Rulers had reached apocalyptic levels just before the Rising: '[they] have done evil and they are bankrupt ... When they speak they speak only untruth and blasphemy. Their utterances are no longer the utterances of men. They are the mumblings and the gibberings of lost souls.'[22] This view of the desperate attempts of Redmond and his lieutenants to negotiate a Home Rule settlement around the Ulster impasse would soon become received wisdom. And the Rising became identified with Pearse's particular ideology of blood-sacrifice and mystical Catholicism. This not only dismissed the real issues of a divided island headed towards civil war or partition, but misrepresented or played down the several streams which had contributed to the revolutionary mentality.

III

The extraordinary and transfigured atmosphere of life within the rebel strongholds during the week that began on Easter Monday 1916 has been evoked in numerous sources. With the release of the Bureau of Military History witness statements, the volume of material has become overwhelming, and in recent years has been distilled into several classic accounts.[23] The individual experiences of many of the revolutionary generation during this apotheosis are enshrined for posterity, though some key figures did not leave their testaments, either because they disagreed with the whole enterprise (and refused to recognize the authority of the government trying to implement it), or because they did not survive to tell their tale. From the glimpses and memories recorded by others, the moods of Pearse, Connolly, MacDermott and Clarke within the GPO, and Markievicz at the College of Surgeons, were to varying degrees elated, punctuated by realistic episodes of recognition that they were, or would be, defeated.

For Joseph Plunkett and his siblings, the dreams of their rebellious youth had at last taken solid form. His own romance with Grace Gifford had developed apace with the blueprint for insurrection; they had planned a double wedding for Easter Sunday with his sister

Geraldine and Thomas Dillon (despite Geraldine's powerful aversion to Grace), but this can only have been a diversionary tactic. One of his last love-letters to Grace, two days before the Rising began, sums up the mood of the moment:

Holy Saturday 1916
My Darling Sweetheart,

I got your dear letter by luck as I was going out at 9 this morning and have not a minute to collect my thoughts since now 2.45 p.m. I am writing this at above address. Here is a little gun which should only be used to protect yourself. To fire it push up the small bar under the word 'Safe' and pull the trigger – but not unless you mean to shoot. Here is some money for you too and all my love forever.

Xxxxxxxxxxxx Joe xxx[24]

They would meet again the night before his execution, for their postponed marriage. Also active in Easter Week were the Plunkett brothers, George (who conducted the Larkfield 'lambs' by tram to the revolution) and Jack, while Geraldine rather frustratedly tried to play a part on the sidelines. Their sister Mimi had acted as courier to John Devoy and Clan na Gael in New York in the frantic weeks before the Rising, but she too stayed out of the action. After the Rising, their ineffective dilettante father Count Plunkett would briefly find himself catapulted into a symbolic leading role, and even their hated mother became an agitator for prisoners' relief and other republican causes.

Plunkett's friend and fellow poet Thomas MacDonagh, a late recruit to the Military Council (where his chief function was to lull his friend and university colleague MacNeill into a false security), was also a signatory of the 'Proclamation'. 'A man who is a mere author is nothing,' he had decided. 'I am going to live things that I have before imagined.'[25] He would become one of the canonized leaders of the rebellion, but his experience at Jacob's Biscuit Factory, which saw little military action, was less fulfilling. His own insecure, febrile and intermittently gloomy temperament had propelled him into an emotional state even before the upheavals of the Easter weekend (during Holy Week he had been notably indiscreet about the approaching event, as was recorded by a police spy whose evidence was breezily ignored by the Castle).[26] The British forces decided the Jacob's fortress did not merit a frontal assault, but they unnerved its occupants by buzzing it with occasional sniper-attacks and creating a diversionary racket outside the building at unexpected hours of the night. Sleep deprivation, isolation from other spheres of insurrectionary activity, and possibly the unrelieved diet of cake and biscuits made MacDonagh an erratic leader; much of the initiative passed to Major John MacBride, Maud Gonne's estranged husband, who had joined the rebellion by chance and was still wearing the smart blue suit in which he had set out on Monday to be best man at his brother's wedding. When the inevitable surrender came, MacDonagh's behaviour was irrational in the extreme, and the garrison began to dissolve into chaos. It was pulled back from the brink by MacBride's sensible advice to obey Pearse's order, to take the chance of liberty if they could, and to 'never allow yourselves to be cooped up inside the walls of a building again'.[27]

This and much else was recorded by the actress and activist Máire nic Shiubhlaigh, who had once created an unforgettable impression in *The Shuiler's Child* for the Theatre of Ireland, and was now acting as a cook in the kitchens of the occupied biscuit factory. Other veterans of agit-prop drama played a part on the stage of the Rising, including Constance Markievicz, Helena Molony, Máire's brother Frank and the glamorous actor Seán Connolly. Connolly was responsible for the first fatality (shooting a policeman outside Dublin Castle) and was later himself killed by sniper-fire on the roof of the City Hall. Markievicz was widely noted by the spectators, marching around Stephen's Green in a feathered hat and a characteristically *outré* uniform; she had apparently arrived there more or less by chance, and been appointed Second-in-Command by the rather irresolute Citizen Army Commandant Michael Mallin. Another thespian, Piaras Béaslaí, had taken a leading part in the Volunteers' split from Redmond and now emerged as Vice-Commandant of the 1st Dublin Battalion at the Four Courts, from where he saw a fair amount of action in Blackhall Street. Unrealistically averse to surrendering, 'he scoffed at the idea, pointing out that the position was "impregnable and could be held for a month".'[28] This reluctance may reflect the dreams he had confided long before to his diary when he was a discontented youth in bourgeois Liverpool, longing for nothing more than to make a mark in the world, fighting for Ireland.

The Ryan sisters and their circle were also centrally involved. Seán T. O'Kelly, as an influential IRB fixer, had been privy to the frenetic comings and goings in the days before, including several pivotal meetings when the conspirators were trying to keep MacNeill on board. Not a fighting man, O'Kelly's own experience of the military side of events was as aide-de-camp to Pearse. He had marched to the GPO from Liberty Hall with Pearse and Connolly on Easter Monday morning, supervised the running up of the flags bearing the tricolour and the harp, and posted 200 copies of the 'Proclamation', secured by flour paste, around the city centre. The more militant Richard Mulcahy found himself, with the charismatic but less practical Thomas Ashe, conducting effective guerrilla actions against police forces around the villages north of the city, where Volunteers and Fianna training in fieldcraft came into its own. The coolness and strategic brio which Mulcahy displayed marked him for a career as an army supremo that would stretch far into the post-revolutionary dispensation. Min and Phyllis Ryan were stationed, through their own determination, in the GPO, and undertook hair-raising courier missions through the gunfire. (These included taking a message from Pearse to his mother out in Ranelagh, which cannot have carried a high military priority.) Madeleine ffrench-Mullen played a similar role, while her partner Kathleen Lynn ran an effective field hospital; the Ryans' medical-student brother James also used his expertise to good effect, tending the injured James Connolly in the GPO and accompanying the insurgents in their terrible retreat to the warren of houses around Moore Street – the withdrawal in which Michael O'Rahilly, who had tried to stop the Rising but turned up to join in when it took place, met a brave death under fire.

Some, later to be celebrated as freedom fighters, took part on the spur of the moment: most famously the eighteen-year-old Ernie O'Malley, just beginning his studies in medicine, and ignorant up to then of much that was going on around him. Previously he had followed the tendency of his well-off family to jeer good-naturedly at the pretensions of the Volunteers; but in Easter week he became swiftly radicalized, borrowed a rifle and took part in some amateur sniping. O'Malley personified one portent for the future. Another was represented by Joe Plunkett's secretary from Larkfield, a handsome 26-year-old Corkman called Michael Collins, who ended up in the GPO, where he viewed the delusional bravado of his seniors with an impatience bordering on contempt. Clever, convivial and frighteningly single-minded, Collins had begun a successful career in London (Post Office, stock exchange clerk, Board of Trade); he was one of many rebel combatants who had returned to Ireland from Britain after the outbreak of war and thrown themselves into the radical-nationalist movement. Art Ó Briain, indefatigable organizer of radical Irish movements in London, later drew up an evocative list of 'London Gaels who lost their lives in Easter Rising 1916'. Patrick Shortes, born in 1893 in Ballybunion, studied as a scholarship boy at St Brendan's Seminary, Killarney, then All Hallows, Dublin, and a B.A. at UCD; he gave up his vocation and became a wireless operator until refused a licence in London due to political activities. Shortes had returned to Dublin in early 1916, as had Seán Hurley, originally of Clonakilty. Older London-Irish combatants included Michael Mulvihill, born in 1880 in Ballyduff, who, like Collins, did his civil service exams and entered the Post Office; he had joined the Gaelic League and Volunteers in London, returned to Dublin on Easter Sunday and met his death on the roof of the GPO. Patrick O'Connor, another Kerryman, born in 1882, had won the first place in the United Kingdom in the civil service exams and entered – inevitably – the Post Office service in 1900. He returned to Ireland twelve years later, and went to the GPO on Easter Monday night. Other Kerrymen who had worked in the postal services in London, joined the Gaelic League and GAA there, and returned to Dublin to fight included Tom O'Donoghue and Denis Daly, both originally from Cahirciveen; they both survived. Ó Briain also lists Donal Sheehan and Con Keating, two of the revolutionaries who were killed outside Killorglin on Easter Saturday, when their car took a wrong turning and plunged into the River Laune, on their way to commandeer the wireless station at Cahirciveen. They too had been radicalized through Gaelic League circles in London. Ó Briain's list sketches the kind of networks which stretched from the remote south-west of Ireland to the Irish-Irelander circles of Edwardian London, via the imperial structure of the Royal Mail, creating an unexpected but recognizable pattern of radicalization.[29]

IV

Outside the rebel redoubts ringing the city centre, several prominent figures of the revolutionary generation watched impotently, or tried to make their own contribution. Francis Sheehy-Skeffington had taken a leading part in opposing the war effort, campaigning against recruitment and arguing that Ireland should have remained neutral. His reasons were pacifist rather than nationalist, though the distinction was ignored by the authorities; he had made what were considered incendiary speeches, been arrested and gone on hunger-strike, and subsequently campaigned in America.[30] When the Rising broke out, he set himself to patrolling the streets, trying to stop looting; this led to his being apprehended by a homicidal British Army officer called Captain J. C. Bowen-Colthurst, who had him summarily executed, along with two other journalists, in Portobello Barracks.

The circumstances of the murder reflected the hysteria of the times (Bowen-Colthurst had already shot dead a defenceless youth called J. J. Coade along the way), but the authorities' attempts at a cover-up afterwards compounded what became seen as one of the most damaging episodes of British oppression in Ireland. The exposure and subsequent trial of Bowen-Colthurst only came about through the efforts of a fellow officer, Major Sir Francis Vane (who did not win much official approval for it). Moreover, by tricks of legal chicanery at the highest level, Bowen-Colthurst was tried by court martial rather than in the civil courts, the latter course having been relentlessly blocked. Judged 'guilty but insane', he served a few years' incarceration in Broadmoor and emigrated to Canada. The choice of victim could not have made worse publicity for the authorities. Sheehy-Skeffington's energy, charm, high principles, mild eccentricity and commitment to pacifism, egalitarianism and feminism had made him a central figure in Dublin's radical intelligentsia since his student days; his wife, Hanna, was not only an influential activist but a member of the powerfully connected Sheehy family (soon to be seen as part of the constitutional-nationalist *ancien régime* but still to be reckoned with). Her unremitting campaign against the British government, which included successful lecture-tours throughout the USA, was effective far outside Ireland.

Other vital figures from the pre-revolutionary dispensation sat on the sidelines, usually because they had opposed the whole affair – above all Eoin MacNeill, the deceived commander of the Volunteers. Early on Easter Monday afternoon, as he was cycling down Rathgar Road with Seán Fitzgibbon, they met their fellow Volunteer Liam Ó Briain; information was exchanged, and after a reconnoitre Fitzgibbon and Ó Briain confirmed that hostilities had begun. After raging at his betrayal by Pearse, MacNeill declared his intention to join the rebels, but in the event went home to Rathfarnham and stayed there. Arthur Griffith, who had done so much to influence so many of the rebels, was equally inactive, for reasons that remain obscure. The moderation of his nationalist strategy in the pre-war years was not forgotten, and he had not been in the confidence of the leaders. Nonetheless, observers would almost at once christen the Rising a 'Sinn Féin rebellion', and the aftermath would see yet another transformation in his position, and that of the uncertain political coalition which he had created.

Another figure, almost equally influential in the inspiration of a revolutionary generation, was sidelined for good. This was Bulmer Hobson, who on Good Friday was effectively kidnapped by the extremists and imprisoned in Martin Conlan's house in Cabra, before he could do any more damage (as they saw it). This came almost as a relief. 'I felt that I had done all I could to keep the Volunteers on the course which I believed essential for their success,' he later recalled, 'and that there was nothing further I could do . . . I had been working under great pressure for a long time and was very tired. Now events were out of my hands.'[31] He may have felt less philosophical at the time. On Easter Monday night, Seán T. O'Kelly was dispatched to release Hobson, finding him bad-temperedly reading a book under armed guard. As they walked back towards the city centre, with gunfire echoing in the background, O'Kelly later claimed he tried to persuade the reluctant Hobson to join the battle for which he had spent so much of his life preparing, and which he had done so much to bring about. Eventually Hobson said he would go home, fetch his rifle and find his Volunteers detachment, but this seems to have been simply a stratagem to get rid of the importunate O'Kelly. They shook hands by the canal and parted. Hobson walked home, and out of history. Like MacNeill, he stayed inside for the rest of the week, nursing a sense of betrayal. Unlike MacNeill, he would never return to the political stage.[32]

Hobson's friend and patron Roger Casement was equally opposed to mounting a rising in the way that it fell out, and had travelled to Ireland to try to put a stop to it; but this would not be remembered as part of the myth already gathering around him. For Casement himself, his extraordinary return by U-boat, eventually washing up on Banna Strand in a collapsible dinghy, marked a kind of epiphany. Ill, exhausted, deeply disillusioned with his idealized Germans, he later remembered lying in the sand dunes listening to birdsong and feeling calm and happy for the first time in years.

> Although I knew that this fate waited on me, I was for one brief spell happy and smiling once more. I cannot tell you what I felt. The sand-hills were full of skylarks, rising in the dawn, the first I had heard for years – the first sound I heard through the surf was their song as I waded in through the breakers, and they kept rising all the time up to the old rath at Currahane where I stayed and sent the others on, and all round were primroses and wild violets and the singing of skylarks in the air, and I was back in Ireland again.[33]

The adversity that had marked this stage of his life – his ineffectual negotiations in America and Germany, his plunge into depression, the betrayals and inept conspiracies which bedevilled him, and the pressures of his driven and contradictory private life – seemed to vanish. Like Pearse 200 miles away in the GPO, he was embarked on a Christological journey to martyrdom, and into the canon of Irish nationalist sainthood. Ardfert Police Station was the beginning of his road to Calvary.

Thanks to MacNeill's countermanding order, the confusion that bedevilled the Kerry Volunteers was reflected elsewhere in Ireland, leaving other revolutionaries marooned or inactive. Denis McCullough, titular President of the IRB Supreme Council, remained in Belfast. Here the anti-Redmond Volunteers were a rather sketchy presence, given the power of Joe Devlin's Hibernian network. Both McCullough, as Commander in Belfast, and his friend Pat McCartan, in charge of the Tyrone Volunteers, found their forces resistant to the orders that came from Dublin; this was unsurprising, since Pearse's idea was that they should march south-west towards Galway to 'hold the line of the Shannon', a manoeuvre that would take them through redoubtable unionist and Protestant heartlands, with the inevitable result of ambushes by the UVF. Discipline was already collapsing among the men gathered at Coalisland when the countermanding order arrived to undercut the commanders' plans completely. After chapters of accidents and confusions (McCullough at one point literally shot himself in the foot), the Volunteers returned by train to Belfast, McCullough paying their fares. There they disbanded, disconsolate.

The Galway forces were better prepared under Liam Mellows, but, though he managed a more decisive mobilization, the failure of arms to arrive and the early notification of the local authorities stymied an effective display of force. The same story was true all over Ireland.[34] The general confusion and inactivity in the provinces would have a potent effect on revolutionary mentality after the Rising; as the Dublin insurrection passed into myth, a powerful sense of guilt was exploited by provincial leaders, determined to expiate their record during Easter 1916. (Paradoxically, they would eventually do so by adopting the tactics of country-wide guerrilla disruption advocated by Bulmer Hobson, though nobody gave him credit at the time or afterwards.)

Nowhere was this sense of shame following a missed chance of martyrdom more potent than in Cork. Liam de Róiste, so indefatigable in organizing and consciousness-raising for so many years, had moved into the Volunteers headquarters at Sheares Street for Holy Week, awaiting orders. Instead, he and Tomás MacCurtain received on Saturday the shocking news of Casement's arrest, brought by a courier from Kerry. Nonetheless, on Sunday they prepared for significant action, distributing first-aid outfits along with weaponry, and putting a force of 154 Volunteers on the train from Cork to Crookstown, while others set off by bicycle. The plan was to meet other forces (to a total of about 1,200 men) at various points in the west of the county. At this point James Ryan arrived in the city with Mac-Neill's countermanding order, so MacCurtain and MacSwiney intercepted the force at Crookstown and cancelled their mobilization orders.[35] Confusion was compounded by Marie Perolz arriving with contradictory orders from Pearse (the first of a blizzard of dispatches to hit Cork).

Irresolution reigned among the leaders, who from Monday sat and waited in Sheares Street; a rumour that the Dublin disturbance was simply an uprising by the Citizen Army, which Mary MacSwiney dismissed as a 'rabble', acted as a further disincentive to action. To the annoyance of many rank-and-file Cork Volunteers (more numerous and better prepared, armed and drilled than in most provincial centres), the brigade commanders remained undecided. To angry emissaries from the beleaguered capital, such as Nora Daly, 'they both seemed to think Dublin was wrong and they were right. They said they had documents to prove they were right.'[36] At the end of the week, a bizarre and obscure deal was arranged via the Lord Mayor and local clerics whereby the Volunteers' guns were to be given up but not impounded by government forces; arrests and seizures of arms nonetheless followed, exacerbating the general ill-feeling.

Above all Terence MacSwiney was struck by an immediate and abiding sense of failure. Since his boyhood he had been confiding to his diary dreams of martial glory and bloodthirsty vows against the Saxon, but when the call came he spent the week dithering indoors and reading Thomas à Kempis's *Imitation of Christ*. As the epic nature of the Dublin insurrection became known, his and MacCurtain's private opinion that 'the Dublin crowd were daft'[37] changed to a determination to equal their sacrifice. Their friend and fellow Cork revolutionary, P. S. O'Hegarty, was out of Ireland during the Rising, having been transferred to Welshpool by his Post Office employers (they may have finally realized just how little work he did in office hours). Seán MacDermott visited him in May 1915, as an emissary of the IRB, and outlined the plans for a rising – much as they were to happen a year later.[38] Perhaps because of his distance from the scene of action, not to mention his distaste for religion, O'Hegarty retained a detached attitude towards sacrificial violence, an agnostic approach to the excesses of devotional martyrology, and a belief that the spectacular gesture of 1916 should pave the way for a political transformation, rather than sounding the trumpet for a campaign of war. He was not alone in this, but MacSwiney's priorities would carry the day.

Apart from Cork, the county that might have been expected to rise, given the weight of history attached to it, was Wexford. There was a well-established revolutionary nexus in the county: not only the Ryan siblings and their followers, but Robert Brennan, the journalists Seán Etchingham and Larry de Lacey, and a strong IRB circle. The *Enniscorthy Echo* was a notably nationalist paper, advancing Sinn Féin ideas from an early stage, and supporting the Volunteers, whose local journal was printed at their offices; the radical IRB man Seán O'Hegarty (brother of P. S.), who also worked for the *Echo*, was arrested for seditious pro-German propaganda. However, Wexford was also home to John Redmond, to the influential Esmonde family (Catholic gentry nationalists) and a solid Irish Parliamentary Party elite; in 1916 the county town remained quiescent and supportive of the authorities (to the contempt of the Ryan family). Neighbouring Enniscorthy saw more action than many places, involving the holy ground of Vinegar Hill, scene of a last rebel stand in 1798. When the rebels actually seized the town on the Thursday after Easter, some of them were even armed with pikes. They held out for four days, instituting a virtual republican administration, including a police force, and raising many new recruits. But the local barracks remained in RIC hands, and the constabulary regained control by the end of the weekend, leaving the memory of a symbolic victory. As in Dublin, the possibility of rebellion had become more than a chimera, and this would create a lasting impression.[39]

V

By the Friday after Easter Monday, the storm-centres of the Rising in Dublin were erupting into a spectacular *Götterdämmerung*. Whole buildings were ablaze, with the shop-windows of Sackville Street running as molten glass on to the pavements, and the shelling and gunfire were relentless. The doomed central garrison eventually fought its way through the little streets behind the GPO, loopholing their course from house to house. The ignition of an oil depot in Abbey Street completed the inferno, 'a solid sheet of blinding, death-white flame rushes hundreds of feet into the air with a thunderous explosion'.[40] One Volunteer enterprisingly telephoned the fire brigade from within the GPO, only to be crisply told that they were to be left to be burned out. Others reacted differently, glorying in the destruction; for many the circle of fire, while spelling the beginning of the end, also confirmed the impact of their insurrection.

This was evidenced in more than the million pounds' worth of damage to buildings on Sackville Street. When it was all over 450 people in total had been killed, 2,614 wounded, 9 missing; of those, 116 soldiers had been killed, 368 wounded and 9 missing, along with 16 policemen dead and 29 wounded. Out of 1,558 combatant insurgents, 64 rebels had died.[41] The toll of civilians was surprisingly and, to some, shockingly high. Throughout the battle-zones, the bodies of people and animals had lain rotting in the unseasonably warm weather, and subsequently been buried rapidly in odd places. The buildings went on smoking and collapsing for days.

The decision to surrender was taken by the leaders in a house in Moore Street around midday on the Saturday, and carried by Nurse Elizabeth O'Farrell (under constant threat of gunfire) to Brigadier-General W. H. M. Lowe. As the news spread to other outposts it was received in some quarters with disgruntlement and even anger. But the outcome was strongly defended by Seán MacDermott and others, stressing their status as prisoners-of-war and arguing that, though the leaders would no doubt be shot, the rank-and-file would eventually be released to continue the struggle: and that, above all, the inspirational and radicalizing effect of their revolutionary gesture would endure. In the circumstances of their defeat and capture, the rebels were determined to present themselves as soldiers who had fought a clean fight. Most indeed managed to do so, in a manner that impressed many of their opponents, and this too would contribute powerfully to the revolutionary myth. Numerous accounts of chivalrous and 'gentlemanly' behaviour were broadcast, sometimes from British Army personnel who had been captured or otherwise dealt directly with insurgents. After the surrender, though some thuggish and sadistic behaviour is recorded, relations between the soldiers and their captives often showed a marked degree of respect.[42] There had been some shooting of unarmed targets, and evidence that the rebels used soft-nosed bullets to terrible effect, but the overall impression created by the rebel army was that they had fought with discipline as well as valour.

This helped to obscure the chaotic, amateurish and contradictory manner in which the insurrection had begun; it would also, in time, weight opinion heavily on the side of those who had actively embraced it, rather than on their more cautious comrades. As it was, general opinion (especially in Dublin) seems initially to have condemned the Rising as an act of destructive madness; famously, the captured rebels were abused by Dublin crowds as they were led through the streets. But this was particularly true in Protestant working-class areas, and other sectors where men were away fighting at the Front. There is also much anecdotal evidence of isolated expressions of support, and more thoughtful observers noted a groundswell of fellow feeling among elements of the populace who claimed they would have supported the rebels, if they had had a chance. An underlying sympathy among many observers was noted by Major Henry de Courcy-Wheeler, the astute Anglo-Irish Army officer who witnessed Pearse's surrender. As Ceannt's and de Valera's forces left the South Dublin Union and Boland's Mill respectively, they were cheered by the local populace; and there is much anecdotal evidence of support from priests and nuns, whatever line their senior colleagues might have taken in public.

Those who were probably furthest from feeling sympathy were members and supporters of the Irish Parliamentary Party, since the conclusion rapidly reached by politically minded observers was that this extraordinary event would banish hopes of Home Rule – and certainly the already faint hope of a Home Rule Ireland which could include Ulster. The record of Redmond and his colleagues, so recently presented as the men who had brought Parnell's dream into reality, was rapidly effaced. One sharp-eyed English visitor, joining the spectators to watch Dublin go up in flames, realized that it was 'much more than the burning of a city – it means the ruin of a cause, the grave of a hope, the dissipation, perhaps for many years, of a great political dream'.[43]

By the time of the surrender, Dublin was under the military rule of General Sir John Maxwell, who had superseded Lowe on 28 April, having been sent expressly by Asquith. Maxwell saw his task as the repressive restoration of order, and the meting out of the ultimate penalty – after brief court martial trials – to the leaders of the insurrection. This was no more than the rebels expected. From Richmond Prison Seán T managed a brief note to Mary Kate, reporting a conversation with MacDermott on his way to trial. 'I am afraid his chances of escaping the final penalty are small. He was however in the best of spirits. He doubtless fully realises the peril of his position.'[44] This was true of all the leaders, who almost universally preserved a transfigured and defiant attitude, in the best traditions of national martyrs. A note of tragic romance was supplied by Joseph Plunkett's marriage to Grace Gifford the night before his execution, leaving her as an awkward bequest to his hostile family. The wedding, held late at night, was brief; later they were allowed a ten-minute meeting in a cell packed with observers, and she left dazed. 'We who had never had enough time to say what we wanted to each other found that in that last ten minutes we couldn't talk at all.'[45] The soldier attending them left his own version. 'I brought the priest and the girl into the prison and when I took her out she was quite cheerful like, and she looked around and said, "This isn't such a gloomy place as I thought it was." She was a cool one.' [46] Overall, a dignified and philosophical acceptance of their fate, 'carefully choreographed by their leaders, exerted a greater emotional charge than the six days of scrappy fighting that preceded it'.[47] The focus accordingly shifted to the manner in which the authorities had reacted; and they would play their pre-ordained part with militaristic obtuseness and heavy-handed coercion. Both sides colluded in the making of martyrs.

After being held, often in makeshift conditions that were appallingly basic and insanitary, a good many ex-combatants were released – especially teenaged boys and women, seen as particularly troublesome prisoners. Incarceration together at Richmond Barracks enabled the leaders to keep up their *esprit de corps*. Apart from the signatories of the 'Proclamation', who seem generally to have accepted that they were doomed to the penalty for treason, several hoped that internment would enable them to regroup and fight another day, as would indeed be the case. Political imprisonment had a long and respected history in Ireland, and traditionally formed the foundation of many political careers. Given the pressures attendant upon prosecution procedures, internment was often adopted as an easier option; the legal proceedings that did take place often followed an uncertain course and were ridiculed by those on trial. Behind the scenes, Redmond, Dillon and other Irish MPs argued desperately for leniency towards the rebels, anticipating the consequences of creating martyrs. While some death sentences were handed down to secondary leaders such as Harry Boland, they were often commuted to imprisonment. For Eoin MacNeill and Arthur Griffith, arrest, trial and imprisonment came as a serendipitous chance of reintegration into advanced-nationalist circles. But MacNeill, whose defence at his trial rested on his strong repudiation of armed insurrection, remained an object of hatred for many who had fought.[48]

For the signatories of the 'Proclamation' and other prominent leaders, the result of their trials for fomenting insurrection with foreign aid at a time of war was a foregone conclusion, and the sentences of death were not commuted. They were tried, rather questionably, under the wartime Defence of the Realm Regulations by field courts martial. The executions between 3 and 12 May of Patrick and Willie Pearse, James Connolly, Thomas MacDonagh, Joseph Plunkett, Éamonn Ceannt, Seán MacDermott, Tom Clarke, Ned Daly, John MacBride, Michael Mallin, Seán Heuston, Con Colbert, Michael O'Hanrahan and Thomas Kent were followed by the hanging of Roger Casement at Pentonville on 3 August. Most of the leaders, while they pleaded not guilty, did so because they denied that they owed allegiance to the government and were not, therefore, committing treason. A few argued against the evidence produced, and Mallin tried to claim that he was under Markievicz's command, rather than the other way round. Markievicz herself escaped execution, as did de Valera, Ashe and Mulcahy, despite their prominent combatant roles; by 9 May, according to Maxwell, the government was leaning heavily towards moderating death sentences.[49]

Over the summer, a powerful campaign had got under way arguing clemency for Casement and a commutation of the death sentence; this was opposed behind the scenes by circulation of extracts from his sexually explicit diaries, which had been seized from his London lodgings. Casement, like several other revolutionary leaders, used his trial to produce a stirring testament firmly rooted in the established convention of a nationalist conversion-narrative, and dismissing the claim that his activities in Germany should be considered treasonable. He returned to the question of the Ulster Volunteer Force, its defiance of the law, and the answering gesture of the Irish Volunteers. 'The difference between us was that the Unionist champions chose a path they felt would lead to the woolsack [F. E. Smith had become Lord Chancellor]; while I went a road I knew must lead to the dock. And the event proves we were both right.' As for his companions in the revolutionary movement, their actions showed the irrelevance of Home Rule compared with true independence. 'If we are to be indicted as criminals, to be shot as murderers, to be imprisoned as convicts because our offence is that we love Ireland more than we value our lives, then I know not what virtue resides in any offer of self-government held out to brave men on such terms.' Privately, he was less controlled, and a late letter to his sister conveys something of his state of mind:

> If I could only tell you the whole story, but that too is part of my punishment – of the strange inscrutable fate that has come to me – that I am not only being put to death in the body but that I am dead before I die – and have to be silent and silent just as if I were already dead – when a few words might save my life – and would certainly change men's view of my actions. Long ago, years ago, I wrote these lines of another – but they are my own – my epitaph on my own fate perhaps more than on that of the man I penned them of: 'In the mystery of transgression is a cloud that shadows Day, For the night to turn to Fire – showing Death's redeeming way.'[50]

Pearse's statement at his trial was unequivocally dramatic and effective.

> When I was a child of ten I went down on my bare knees by my bedside one night and promised God that I should devote my life to an effort to free my country. I have kept that promise. As a boy and man I have

worked for Irish freedom, first among all earthly things. I have helped to organise, to arm, to train and to discipline my fellow countrymen to the sole end that, when the time came, they might fight for Irish freedom. The time, as it seemed to me, did come, and we went into the fight. I am glad we did. We seem to have lost. We have not lost. To refuse to fight would have been to lose; to fight is to win. We have kept faith with the past, and handed on a tradition to the future.[51]

Others, such as MacDonagh, had equally high-flown speeches posthumously invented for them. Many testaments were left behind, ostensibly as letters to wife and family, but also aimed at a wider audience. Seán MacDermott's last letter to his siblings was characteristically insouciant ('just a wee note') but ended: 'I feel a happiness the like of which I never experienced in my life before, and a feeling that I could not describe. Surely when you know my state of mind none of you will worry or lament my fate . . . I die that the Irish nation may live.'[52]

These testaments reflect a genuine state of exaltation, but were also part of the revolutionary strategy, and would prove infinitely more potent weapons in the cause of separatist nationalism than Howth Mausers or Larkfield billy-can bombs. They tapped into the long tradition of speeches from the dock enshrining national martyrology, endorsed by Catholic traditions of holy dying and sacrificial blood. James Connolly received Communion before his death and enjoined his wife to adopt Catholicism. Roger Casement similarly converted, as did Constance Markievicz. The socialist activist Michael Mallin, in a passionate and harrowing last letter, asked his wife not to remarry and called for his children to become priests and nuns. Very rapidly, the language of mystical Catholicism fused with national purism in a new – or ancient – revolutionary rhetoric. The *Catholic Bulletin* quickly adopted the rebel cause, collecting evidence of such miraculous interventions as Cathal Brugha curing his gunshot wounds by the application of holy water from Lourdes. As early as 17 May, at a memorial Mass in San Francisco, the Reverend F. A. Barrett specifically identified Pearse, Clarke and the rest with the 'saints and martyrs' of the Catholic Church; in a 'brilliant triumph' they had redeemed Ireland from the stain of those 'thousands of Anglicized degenerates [who] have died for the heretical power that slew their fathers and persecuted their Faith; at the magic words "Faith and Fatherland" the chivalrous sword of truth leapt from her scabbard . . . The insurrection has safeguarded our Faith. Before the war we were daily approximating to England, our Catholic ideals were disappearing, the process of Anglicization went forward apace. That fatal process is arrested.'[53]

The implications for a Home Rule policy, now irredeemably associated with British imperialism, were all too clear. Though Redmond and his colleagues launched a desperate last effort to get Home Rule implemented, Partition was now an inevitable part of the deal. In any case, the revolutionary leaders' entry into Valhalla meant that negotiation – or 'give and take' – no longer stood much of a chance, as Yeats declared in one of the troubled poems inspired by the Rising, and released slowly to the public over the next months.

> You say that we should still the land
> Till Germany's overcome;
> But who is there to argue that
> Now Pearse is deaf and dumb?
> And is their logic to outweigh
> MacDonagh's bony thumb?
>
> How could you dream they'd listen
> That have an ear alone
> For those new comrades they have found,
> Lord Edward and Wolfe Tone,
> Or meddle with our give and take
> That converse bone to bone?

Home Rule, and an unpartitioned Ireland, were not the only futures now receding from the realms of possibility. As with the patriarchal attitudes demonstrated within the GPO and elsewhere, the promulgation of traditionalist attitudes to faith and fatherland shifted the emphasis from the broader forms of liberation variously hoped for by people such as the Sheehy-Skeffingtons, the MacDonaghs, Bulmer Hobson, Patrick McCartan, Kathleen Lynn, Louie Bennett, the Gifford sisters, P. S. O'Hegarty, Rosamond Jacob, Mabel FitzGerald, Kevin O'Shiel, Cesca and Margot Trench. Feminism, socialism, secularism and various forms of pluralism were now discounted.

Cesca Trench, so ecstatic at the time of the Howth gun-running, and given to much self-congratulatory Anglophobic ranting, found herself appalled at the carnage of the Rising. Just before the end of hostilities she wrote:

> This mad affair has done irreparable damage to the cause of Irish free-
> dom which it is meant to serve, as it can only succeed by a miracle
> which isn't likely to occur. God help us, I think it will break all our
> hearts . . . It was done against the leaders of the Irish Volunteers & all
> the sensible men among them, but there are many who will suffer inno-
> cently. Séumas [James] Connolly is a man whose chief merit is his desire
> to see his country free, but he has no other qualifications for an affair
> of this kind. Most of the others are high-minded but utterly lacking in
> judgement, poets, or they wouldn't have run us into such idiocy.[54]

In this she may have been influenced by her fiancé, Diarmuid Coffey, who had maintained his scathing analysis of the revolutionary elem-ent among the Volunteers and the threat they represented to Home Rule. But the executions swayed Cesca's opinions in favour of the rebels, and in this she reflected a much wider mood.

Another nationalist from a Protestant background, Rosamond Jacob, found herself deeply affected by the eerie atmosphere after the dust had settled. The news had filtered through to Waterford the day after the rebellion began, and as usual she found herself arguing with her friends, particularly Ben Farrington, who, though a Sinn Féin sup-porter, was 'just as I expected – what good would this do, and the country didn't sympathize with it etc., etc.' Jacob herself felt deeply disturbed and excited, and her sense of living on the margins was unbearably accentuated. She spent much time with her nationalist friends the Powers at the Metropole Hotel in the town, where many of the revolutionary leaders (including Pearse) had stayed in the past. The news of the executions struck a knell; Kitty Power said that she 'never would have thought she could hate England more than before'. They consoled each other by reading Pearse's writings in back num-bers of *Irish Freedom* and the *Irish Review*. Jacob, who had met Pearse in the past and been disappointed by his unattractively plump appearance and flabby handshake, now revised her opinion drasti-cally; as soon as she could get to Dublin she made a pilgrimage to

St Enda's, tried to buy copies of Pearse's last pamphlets, and eventually managed to pay her respects to his mother and sister, sitting reverently in their drawing-room and looking at relics of the dead brothers. Above all, she was 'all the time suffering from envy & jealous of the people I met who had been out in the Rising; it seems as if I was destined to be an outsider & a looker-on all my life; *never* to be in it.'[55]

Everywhere there were changes. Jacob visited the smoking ruins of the GPO, and learnt that her friend Madeleine ffrench-Mullen and her brother Douglas were in gaol, having served respectively in the College of Surgeons garrison, and with Ceannt in the South Dublin Union. Another radical friend, Elizabeth Somers, had been arrested and interned, while her mother and brother had lost their jobs. Jacob's friend Hanna Sheehy-Skeffington, steely despite her traumatic widowhood, was refusing to see her brother, who was in the British Army, and at daggers drawn with her father-in-law, who wanted to take his grandson Owen from her. (Nonetheless Jacob rather censoriously judged that 'she seems to see Owen somewhat as a burden – only for him she could easily have got herself killed at Easter, and she'd rather he was a girl anyway.') Hanna was in the process of becoming a powerful and influential voice for Irish republican claims and a witness to the horrors of British military rule; she would make a successful tour of America in 1917, to the irritation of conservative Irish-Americans, one of whom damningly described her as 'a suffragist, pacifist, vegetarian, prohibitionist, anti-tobaccoist and professional writer, and looks all these things'.[56]

Jacob found her liberal Quaker relations in Rathgar, the Webbs, surprisingly sympathetic towards the rebels, while regarding the enterprise as mad ('not knowing anything about their expectation of German help, or MacNeill's goings on').[57] She heard accounts of other survivors whom she had met in pre-revolutionary days, such as the Gifford sisters, Muriel MacDonagh and Grace Plunkett, both now the unhappy widows of two signatories. Muriel would drown while swimming the next year, while Grace had retreated to the Larkfield commune, where, as we have seen, she suffered the miscarriage or abortion allegedly witnessed by her new sister-in-law Geraldine. She subsequently spent much time trying to extract money from the unsympathetic Plunkett parents, and producing her trademark caustic cartoons for the republican cause.

For the Ryan sisters and their friends, who had been at the storm-centre, life after the Rising was also dramatically turned upside down. The eldest sister, Nell, who had been at home in Wexford throughout, was interned 'on the ground that she is of hostile associations and is reasonably suspected of having favoured, promoted or assisted an armed insurrection against His Majesty'.[58] Mary Kate was also arrested, probably because of the suspicious company she kept (the regular attendants at her Ranelagh Road flat, O'Kelly, MacDermott, Liam Ó Briain and Seán Forde had all taken a prominent part in the Rising). She was soon released but Nell was passed through several gaols – Kilmainham, Mountjoy, Lewes, and finally Aylesbury, along with Helena Molony, Marie Perolz and Constance Markievicz. She remained in exile until October, studying Russian and Persian in prison and receiving gifts from admiring local suffragettes, as well as eggs, butter, onions and honey from the bounty of Tomcoole.[59]

Min and Phyllis, though they had played an active part in the GPO and as couriers, were not arrested, but their brother James was imprisoned in Stafford, and later in the celebrated internment camp at Frongoch, where so many revolutionaries ended up. The comradely atmosphere there made it a memorable experience, and he later wrote to his imprisoned sister Nell, only half in jest: 'I always keep telling people that you don't mind in the least being away, and I know from experience that it is quite true. You would hardly believe how sorry I feel sometimes that the whole thing is over. Indeed if it were not for the pleasure it seems to give others I don't see any advantage at all in being out.'[60]

James returned, along with many others, in the summer of 1916, finding Dublin changed and lonely, with the searing loss of old friends. 'But new ones are ready to take their places, that's as far as opinions etc. go . . . The people are regenerated right enough, so there it ends.'[61] Richard Mulcahy, another friend (and future husband of Min Ryan), was imprisoned in Knutsford and Frongoch, retaining vivid memories of the initial privations of solitary confinement and constant hunger. However, thanks in part to pressure brought by Redmond and his colleagues in official quarters, the Irish prisoners were subsequently put under conditions of internment instead, an open-door policy which allowed them 'the run of the place and complete association with one another'.

> ... our minds were quite relaxed and unconcerned and waiting with a cheerful outlook for changes in the situation. There was nothing we could do about anything. We were all quite satisfied that something important had happened. We were all satisfied that there was a sufficient number of us in the position of prisoners to have a strength that could afford to feel quite peaceful, and there was a tremendous development of a feeling of satisfactory comradeship.[62]

Seán T. O'Kelly, faithful follower of the Ryan sisters, remained in prison (Wandsworth, Woking, Frongoch and Reading) until December. The following year he would be transferred under internment conditions to Oxford and Gloucestershire. Throughout, he kept in touch with the girls as they accustomed themselves to an altered world. Min was haunted by her last visit to MacDermott (who had become her 'matrimonial aspirant' by the end of 1915[63]), a poignant event she remembered vividly for the rest of her life.

> It was ridiculous in a way because there was no sign of mourning. We [her sister Phyllis and herself] had to hold up, of course, when he held up, and so we showed no sign of sorrow while we discussed things ... He had five good cigarettes and a few 'Wild Woodbines' that the soldiers had given him, and he was arranging to smoke them so that they would last him almost up to the end. When we left him at 3 o'clock he had two cigarettes still to smoke, and he was to be shot at a quarter to four. He spoke with much affection of several young men and women he used to meet with us, and the most pathetic scene was where he tried to produce keepsakes for different girlfriends of his we mentioned. He sat down at the table and tried to scratch his name and the date on the few coins he had left and on the buttons which he cut from his clothes with the penknife somewhat reluctantly provided by the young officer who stood by ... When the priest appeared at three o'clock ... we stood up promptly and felt a great jerk, I'm sure all three of us, to say good-bye. I was the last to say good-bye to him and he said, just said: 'We never thought that it would end like this, that this would be the

end.' Yes, that's all he said, although he knew himself, long before that, what the end would be for him.[64]

After her brief imprisonment Mary Kate continued with her UCD duties, enduring accusations from the President, Dr Coffey, that she preached subversive politics to her students.[65] The whole family frequently returned to the farmhouse at Tomcoole, and their letters to the imprisoned members of the family describe the routines of the farming year, the dairy, the turkeys and hens, the horses, the sale of stock, the flower-garden by the house coming into its own in the early summer, the state of the grass in the meadow, the saving of the hay. But they also measure the unmistakable shifting of attitudes, the increasing sympathy of neighbours towards a known republican family, the decline of the old Home Rule order in its heartland of Wexford town. In June a local priest had written to Mary Kate, still in Mountjoy Gaol, of the change of spirit in the county. 'Even facial expressions have changed for the better. Remorse has set in. And many are struggling to swallow their words and whitewash their works. But lime cannot be had for the asking nowadays.'[66]

That August saw a double wedding at Taghmon Church, of Chris Ryan to Michael O'Malley and Agnes to Denis McCullough, released from Frongoch only just in time. A large and reverent crowd assembled; the wedding car was driven by an ex-employee of White's Hotel, Wexford, of whom the Ryans approved because he had been dismissed for republican activities. With Nell in prison and so many friends recently dead, it was a subdued affair; several guests wore sombre clothes and as a mark of respect there was no dancing. The brides wore Irish poplin, and the service was in Irish.[67] O'Kelly wrote disconsolately to Mary Kate from prison of his wish to be there: 'I am drawing mental pictures of all garbed in fine new finery . . . You will I hope permit me to think of myself as being somewhere near you on that day in particular whispering a word or two in your ear as occasion offers and being treated now and then to a smile in return.'

After her own release from Mountjoy in June, Mary Kate had finally sent a letter to him declaring some form of commitment. 'I have been walking on air since the moment I read it,' he wrote from Wandsworth; 'it sent the blood coursing through my veins in a wild manner and the excitement is violently renewed each moment I get time to think the matter over to myself and to read that joyful message once again.'[68] Throughout his internment, his letters relived his long courtship of her, the happy days they had spent together, his jealousy of her other admirers, and the Whit Sunday at Tomcoole when he sensed she might love him. 'I think now I could make out for you a fairly accurate list of all the dresses or costumes you have worn since that day. What would you think of that – I would not guarantee to describe the hats though, that would be too much to expect wouldn't it. You will laugh at this now and think how silly I am, but even so I don't mind.'[69]

But he also admitted that 'I might be one hundred times worse off than I am now', which was no more than the truth. His incarceration was eased by the influence of clerical friends in Dublin and well-connected London acquaintances (including Casement's friend Ada MacNeill, and the Gavan Duffy family). His fellow inmate Douglas ffrench-Mullen was able to pull similar strings, since his Indian Army father turned out to have been the former commanding officer of the Governor of the prison. '"My God," cried the Governor, "my old commanding officer . . . Where are we? What's the world coming to?" he added, putting his elbows on the desk and holding his head in his hands.'[70] Ffrench-Mullen, famously loquacious, subsequently spent much of his time dining in the Governor's residence, lecturing him and his family on the iniquities of British rule in Ireland. (Earlier, in Richmond Prison, he had demonstrated similar sangfroid by demanding access to a piano so he could keep up his practice routine.) More practically, he arranged for Irish prisoners at Woking to be spared ordinary prison regulations, and the Governor promised O'Kelly (with whom he also enjoyed long conversations about the Irish situation) that 'anything within his power he would grant.'

Here and in other places of detainment, O'Kelly noted that the authorities were surprised to find so many of the rebels were cultured, middle-class people, and adjusted their behaviour accordingly. His internment at Oxford the following year, in a guest-house at St Aldate's with Darrell Figgis, Joseph MacBride and Pat McCartan, was even more comfortable. They obtained readers' tickets for the Bodleian Library, dined with the famous classicist Gilbert Murray, were shown round the city by Ossie Grattan Esmonde (an undergraduate from the celebrated Wexford family), and explored the surrounding villages and churches.[71] Transferral to rural Gloucestershire was less welcome, as Liam Ó Briain reported gleefully to Piaras Béaslaí:

> The Ryans . . . miss Seán T sadly since he was sent to study English rural life. It was really a sardonic joke of somebody in office at which I am laughing ever since – he and Sceilg [the *Catholic Bulletin* journalist J. J. O'Kelly] and Figgis and Micheál Ó Foghlú etc. were just settling down to absorb British kultur in the Bodleian and inhale the classic spirit from the air of Oxford, when a stroke of the pen transformed them to the back of nowhere – Fairford, Gloucestershire! – where, figurez-vous, Sceilg and Figgis talking to Miss Hodge across the half door about the hens and the pigs and paying rustic compliments to the betrousered wenches who plod their weary way home from the fields of their daily labours.[72]

However, the local Chief Constable was surprised to find that the Irish revolutionaries were not peasants; he had earmarked them for farm-work but 'admitted he had been under a wrong impression as to the type of people he was to deal with' and rapidly changed their lodgings from local cottage rooms to the 'great style' of Fairford's Bull Inn.[73] When O'Kelly decided to abscond, in order to take part in the Sinn Féin election campaign in Longford, he simply walked away and caught a train, detouring via Reading Gaol to ask for a refund of money due to him from his time there the previous year. This was readily supplied. 'The Governor, Major Morgan, was very pleasant, asked for Griffith, MacSwiney and a number of other former prisoners, and wished us bon voyage.' Evading the police, he crossed to Rosslare, and was warmly received at Tomcoole and eventually Ranelagh Road. The Sinn Féin candidate Joe McGuinness won Longford; an early augury of the coming landslide, further flagged by de Valera's victory at Clare. By then the prisoners had been released in a general amnesty.[74]

From 1918, there was a certain sense of coming into their kingdom. The returning rebels received extraordinary public welcomes, with Dublin *en fête*; figures like Constance Markievicz, once parodied derisively by Dublin opinion, had assumed iconic status. (However, visiting Waterford to lecture on her prison experiences, she infuriated Rosamond Jacob all over again by her condescension and carelessness.) The repressive regime sustained by Dublin Castle, the looming threat of conscription and the loss of credibility by the Irish Party had contributed to a sea-change in Irish opinion.

When Seán T (now General Secretary of the Gaelic League) was finally married to Mary Kate in Rathmines Church in April 1918, with her brother officiating, their intimates and friends clearly represented the coming order. Liam Ó Briain was best man, and Min bridesmaid; she herself would be married the following June to another revolutionary hero, Richard Mulcahy. At Ranelagh Road, after Mary Kate's wedding, the guests included Father Pádraig de Brún, Arthur Griffith, the Cathal Brughas, J. J. O'Kelly, William Cosgrave, the Gavan Duffys, Lord Mayor Larry O'Neill, Arthur Clery and Jennie Wyse Power. Most of them were now leading figures in the Sinn Féin movement, which had been radically reconstructed in 1917 into a republican political party. Significantly, O'Kelly was recalled from his honeymoon in Kenmare by a telegram from de Valera, who had emerged as the leader of the revolutionary movement and needed his organizational powers for a coming by-election. With almost incredible ineptness, the government was now going to proceed with conscription, and Sinn Féin saw the opportunity to put a broad front together on the issue. It was on the point of succeeding the old Irish Parliamentary Party as the hegemonic power in Irish national politics, a development that would be sealed by its landslide victory in the post-war election of December.

The process of things 'changing utterly', discerned with poetic prescience by Yeats in the aftermath of the Rising, was clearly and irrevocably under way; but whether the changes would be those envisaged by the revolutionary generation remained to be seen. The gesture of sacrificial insurrection had transformed reality, in line with the heady expectations of the coming generation so often apostrophized by Pearse. The sanctification of violence, inaugurated with the spectacular seizure of the GPO that Easter Monday, was now established. But it was unclear how far it would bring about the kind of transfiguration which had been dreamt of by the young and impatient, in place of the compromises and negotiations for which they had spent so long deriding the soon-to-be-vanquished Parliamentary Party.

Yesterday
The R.I.C.
were
Irishmen
Who TOOK

To-day
Free State Soldiers
are
Irishmen
Who TAKE

Guns and Orders from England

in order to

Shoot down Republican Soldiers
Destroy Republican Printing Presses
Raid the homes of Irish Republicans
Fire on Irish Prisoners in the Jails
Fill the Jails with Irish Volunteers
Wage Economic War on the Dependants
of the Irish Republicans.

You did not Join the Irish Volunteers for this.

Don't be any longer Blind.

The Men against you are Fighting Without
Pay for the Old Cause which
will NEVER DIE.

A republican poster makes the case that the Free State represents a restoration of the *ancien régime*.

8

Reckoning

The hide was being flayed off the still living body of the Revolution so that a new age could slip into it; as for the red, bloody meat, the steaming innards – they were being thrown on to the scrapheap. The new age needed only the hide of the revolution – and this was being flayed off people who were still alive. Those who then slipped into it spoke the language of the Revolution and mimicked its gestures, but their brains, lungs, livers and eyes were utterly different.

– Vasily Grossman, Life and Fate *(2006)*[1]

I

Between the Easter Rising and the end of the world war, the face of Irish politics had changed, and the surviving revolutionaries had taken charge; but they did not present a united front. Nor was the future fixed. In the aftermath of the Rising, Seán T. O'Kelly was outraged at the efforts made by the Plunketts to emerge as a kind of First Family of republican politics, with the elderly Count pushed hard as a leader of a 'Liberty League' intended to take over the reconstructed Sinn Féin movement. O'Kelly believed that he was being manipulated by the influential Sinn Féin cleric Father Michael O'Flanagan, who wanted to become 'boss and political dictator' of Ireland, using Plunkett as his instrument and exploiting the martyred Joseph Plunkett's reputation. Though O'Flanagan was reconstructing himself as quickly as anybody else in these bewildering times, his unsupportive attitude in 1916 was held against him (he had allegedly referred to the GPO

259

garrison as 'murderers' who should be allowed to burn to death). 'And whoever heard tell of Countess Plunkett as a political leader?'[2] The one thing that united the revolutionaries was the need, as O'Kelly put it, to 'rid the country of the Party incubus'. Mary MacSwiney similarly feared the revival of a Home Rule agenda, on the basis of agreeing to Partition, and dreaded the thought of Redmond emerging at a post-war peace conference as Prime Minister of Ireland. 'Better martial law and General Maxwell.'[3] As ever, the one thing that the comrades could agree upon was that the real enemy was the Irish Parliamentary Party.

To their relief the Redmondites' fate was sealed by the failure of the British government (now headed by Lloyd George) to impose a form of Home Rule after the Rising. This abortive effort was compounded by the looming prospect of introducing conscription for Ireland, and the inept coercion measures introduced from Dublin Castle at the behest of the bone-headed military commander, Field Marshal Lord French (who would be appointed Lord Lieutenant in May 1918), enthusiastically rounding up respectable supporters of the Irish Parliamentary Party along with supposed radicals. As early as June 1916, the change in the public mood was noted by no less an authority than General Maxwell himself:

> There is a growing feeling that out of rebellion more has been got than by constitutional methods, hence Mr Redmond's power is on the wane, therefore this desire to curry favour with the people on the part of M.P.s by agitating for the release of Sinn Féiners.
>
> It is becoming increasingly difficult to differentiate between a Nationalist and a Sinn Féiner.
>
> Mourning badges, Sinn Féin flags, demonstrations at requiem masses, the resolutions of public bodies are all signs of the growth of Sinn Féin.
>
> Recruiting in Ireland has practically ceased . . .
>
> If there was a General election very few, if any, of existing nationalist M.P.s would be re-elected so there is a danger that Mr Redmond's party would be replaced by others perhaps less amenable to reason.[4]

From a different perspective, others also sensed that the wind was changing. Down in Cork, Liam de Róiste, attuned as ever to the *zeitgeist*, noted excitedly: 'We live in a new era.'[5]

For the revolutionaries, the post-Rising fallout, and the large-scale imprisonment and deportation of leaders, initially led to a certain vacuum of power, with efforts made to fill the gap by short-lived organizations such as Kevin O'Shiel's Irish Nation League. Nationalist journalism, despite censorship restrictions, was as effective as ever; even in internment and gaol, the revolutionaries kept their hands in by publishing free-sheet periodicals with titles like *Barbed Wire*, unhampered by the prison authorities. Outside prison walls, the *Catholic Bulletin*, edited by J. J. O'Kelly, continued to be the repository for the celebration of the cult of nationalist martyrs. Significantly two newspapers supporting the doomed Irish Parliamentary Party, the *Evening Telegraph* and the *Freeman's Journal*, went into liquidation in September 1919, and when the *Freeman* revived under a new owner it took a line far more tolerant of Sinn Féin. This was yet another sign that the party, now reconstructed as a republican movement, was claiming the future.

Backed by the groundswell of prisoners' aid societies, dispersing lavish funds raised from Irish communities worldwide, organized by local clubs, adhering to a new ideology and energized by the revolutionary indoctrination and *esprit de corps* infused through prison and internment experiences, the revolutionaries took over Sinn Féin and swept the country. One surprising result was the re-emergence of Arthur Griffith as a key player, rehabilitated by imprisonment, and benefiting from the fact that what was essentially a new organization still retained the old name of Sinn Féin. From gaol he had issued influential memoranda, blueprints for action and manifestoes to the faithful.[6] Released, he revived his influential paper *Nationality*, preaching the need to 'scotch the old snake' of the Irish Parliamentary Party and to make Ireland's claims felt at the Versailles Peace Conference. As with Father O'Flanagan, some did not forget his chequered past history; Michael Collins privately referred to him as 'pretty rotten' on the separatist issue, and reassured Thomas Ashe (in Lewes Gaol) that 'Master A. G. is not going to turn us all into eighty-two-ites.'[7] In other words, any arrangement under the British crown resembling Grattan's Parliament of 1782 was out of the question. Griffith accordingly had the political nous to concede the presidency of Sinn Féin to a new-minted hero of the Rising, Éamon de Valera.

Though he rapidly became the acknowledged leader of the revolutionary movement and would dominate Irish political life for much of the century, de Valera had come to prominence suddenly, and from a position of some obscurity. Thirty-three years old at the time of the Rising, to observers like Rosamond Jacob he was an unknown quantity: the subject of rumour and speculation, and sometimes described as a mysterious 'Spaniard'. In fact, though born in America to an Irish immigrant mother and her short-lived Basque husband, he had grown up in rural County Limerick among his mother's family. His career as a teacher had not brought him into the circles of Mary Kate Ryan's Ranelagh salon, or Griffith's watering-holes, or the newspaper offices of the radical press. He himself was conscious that he was at an angle to this universe, remarking to Mary MacSwiney in 1922, 'every instinct of mine would indicate that I was meant to be a dyed-in-the-wool Tory, or even a bishop, rather than the leader of a revolution.'[8] It is significant that he saw his destiny as bishop rather than simply priest. He had elevated himself from an impoverished background through brains and hard work, attending one elite boarding-school and teaching mathematics and physics at another. Radicalism had played little part in his life until he took up the Irish language around 1908, and his politics seem to have been Home Ruler rather than republican until he joined the Volunteers in 1913. Even then, though he went with the dissidents in 1914, he was not in the inner circles of the IRB, and left the movement after 1916. But through membership of the 3rd Battalion of the Irish Volunteers he had become closely associated with the charismatic Thomas MacDonagh, and this was the first step on the road to his command at Boland's Mill.

De Valera was narrowly spared execution, not so much because of his American birth as because Maxwell was assured that he was an unimportant figure. His rapid prominence owed much to his status as a surviving commander of a 1916 garrison, as well as his age, his imposing presence (he was extremely tall), his schoolmasterly authority and his self-belief; he also had a gift for inspiring admiration and affection in many of his comrades, though this was a far from universal reaction. His taste for power was helped by his ability to project a kind of aloof charisma, though, on a 1919 fundraising tour in America, Patrick McCartan also noted his colleague's growing distaste for contradiction and even discussion. These tendencies were accentuated by his long experiences of religious institutions; he told his election supporters in 1917 that he had been associated with priests all his life, 'and the priests know me and are behind me.' In October 1917 he became President both of Sinn Féin and of the Irish Volunteers. But to many of the people who had been immersed in revolutionary organizations before the insurrection, he was a new and slightly surprising figure, whose unexpected dominance was not entirely welcome.

From 1917, especially after the serendipitously timed release of the prisoners, the movement entrenched itself in Irish political life. The process was accompanied by a flow of post-Rising propaganda which, though crisply described as 'bilious, turgid and maudlin' by a later historian of the organization, caught the mood.[9] Less pietistically, local elements began to make threatening moves towards an aggressive land agitation policy. 'Cattle drives' carried out by landless men against the bitterly resented grazier farmers in the West had already flared up in 1907–8, and were revived in the winter of 1917/18, encouraged by elements of Sinn Féin. Even de Valera briefly lent his support to the vague concept of 'even land division', and fields were occupied 'in the name of the Irish Republic', to the alarm of more conservative leaders. Acute social conflict was only narrowly averted in some instances.[10] The remnants of the Citizen Army, as well as representatives of the trade unions movement, were also swept up into Sinn Féin. Their belief that a new Ireland could be socialist as well as republican was uncomfortably received by their more cautious colleagues, though for the moment the cause of Sinn Féin and freedom from British rule could be invoked as a unifying mantra. Griffithites, nonetheless, stressed more easily negotiable themes such as over-taxation, and the need for representation in settlement negotiations after the world war ended. More military-minded radicals (including, rather ambivalently, de Valera) talked of guns, drilling, reviving the spirit of Volunteering and fighting for the republic. 'Soldiers' and 'politicians' were already regarding each other suspiciously, and the implicit tension between moderate and extremist elements stretched to other issues besides that of separation from British rule. Radicals like Máire Comerford would later come to see the division as prophetic.

But, as 1918 dawned, the British government yet again offered unintended succour to the revolutionaries, by moving towards compulsory conscription of Irishmen into the British Army. Even before Irish opinion had turned conclusively against the war effort, compulsory drafting of Irish civilians had been deemed unacceptable; to introduce the idea at this stage was incomprehensibly obtuse. A general sense of outrage enabled a powerful opposing coalition across Irish life, allowing senior clerics to appear on platforms with Sinn Féin ex-prisoners, while British policies of ineffective coercion and random internment on trumped-up charges (notably an outlandishly conceived 'German Plot' in May 1918) played even more generously into the nationalists' hands. W. B. Yeats, observing Irish politics as closely as ever, wrote imploringly to the Liberal politician Lord Haldane after a visit to Dublin:

> I have met nobody in close contact with the people who believes that conscription can be imposed without the killing of men, and perhaps of women ... there is in this country an extravagance of emotion which few Englishmen, accustomed to more objective habits of thought, can understand. There is something oriental in the people, and it is impossible to say how great a tragedy may lie before us. The British Government, it seems to me, is rushing into this business in a strangely trivial frame of mind. I hear of all manner of opinions being taken except the opinion of those who have some knowledge of the popular psychology ... it seems to me a strangely wanton thing that England, for the sake of fifty thousand Irish soldiers, is prepared to hollow another trench between the countries and fill it with blood. If that is done England will only suffer in reputation, but Ireland will suffer in her character, and all the work of my life-time and that of my fellow-workers, all our effort to clarify and sweeten the popular mind, will be destroyed and Ireland, for another hundred years, will live in the sterility of her bitterness.[11]

But his words fell on deaf ears; and Yeats's own opinions were, by now, moving towards support of the Sinn Féin programme, precipitated by despair at the destructiveness of British policy.

This process was facilitated, for him and for others, by the fact that Sinn Féin remained an apparently broad church. To the fury of many members, even Eoin MacNeill – of all people – now reappeared as a prominent figure, astutely defended by de Valera and others. Those 'out' in 1916, even if not very notable as combatants, were nonetheless in the ascendant. Seán T. O'Kelly, returned from his comfortable internment, emerged as Sinn Féin's Director of Organization. But the reins of power increasingly were assumed by new people, notably Michael Collins and his dashing friend Harry Boland, who exerted a decisive influence in nominating Sinn Féin candidates at elections (only three candidates at the post-war general election had not been gaoled or interned). Their efforts culminated in a dramatic landslide success at the polls in December 1918, effectively eradicating the Irish Parliamentary Party. The 69 Sinn Féin victors, representing 73 seats (since some were elected twice over), included Liam de Róiste, James Ryan, Desmond FitzGerald, Robert Barton, Richard Mulcahy, Terence MacSwiney, Piaras Béaslaí, Patrick McCartan, Seán Etchingham and several other familiar names from the pre-revolutionary era. Constance Markievicz was also returned: one of only two women candidates, despite the new franchise, and the prominence of women in the revolutionary movement before 1916. The anomaly was angrily noted by Rosamond Jacob and other activists, who despaired of making headway against entrenched male attitudes 'outside Dublin'.[12]

II

The elected members constituted a legislative assembly which, following the original Griffithite line, boycotted Westminster and withdrew to Dublin to set up their own parliament, Dáil Éireann ('Assembly of Ireland'). Twenty-eight Sinn Féin deputies assembled in Dublin's Mansion House on 21 January 1919 (the remainder being in gaol or otherwise engaged), accompanied by enthusiastic supporters, and found themselves almost incredulously faced with the opportunity to make their dreams and theories come true. Máire Comerford remembered it long afterwards:

> No day that ever dawned in Ireland had been waited for, worked for, suffered for like that January Tuesday.

People waiting asked one another, 'Did you ever think you and I would live to see this day?'

I was with a Wexford contingent.

Never was the past so near, or the present so brave, or the future so full of hope.

We filed into the Round Room and pressed round till every inch of standing room was full.

I don't believe I even saw the seating arrangements that first day, the crowd was so great.

We did see Cathal Brugha presiding and we repeated the words of the Declaration after him, and felt we had burnt our boats now. There was no going back.[13]

Comerford was there as a Sinn Féin member, not as an elected representative (*Teachta Dála*, or 'TD', meaning member of the assembly). However, women were more prominent in the national organization of Sinn Féin, where Kathleen Lynn was Vice-President, Hanna Sheehy-Skeffington Director of Organization and Áine Ceannt (widow of the 1916 signatory Éamonn) Director of Communications. After the election, the party had been defined as 'a large legislative assembly, a small executive and an intermediary body which helped bridge the gap between them . . . democratic almost to excess'; the mass membership may have reached about 130,000.[14] A complex party structure was created, from local clubs up to the *ard-comhairle* (governing body). It boasted an ambitious agenda, which included not only alternative governmental institutions at home but the development of consular representation abroad. (This created social opportunities much relished by upwardly mobile sophisticates such as Art Ó Briain and the O'Kellys.) The Dáil's publicity department under Robert Brennan produced an efficient and influential news-sheet, the *Irish Bulletin*, edited by Desmond FitzGerald and contributed to by Erskine Childers and Frank Gallagher; the staff moved its production process around various safe locations, including the Irish Farm and Produce shop in Baggot Street (where it had moved when its Henry Street premises were destroyed in 1916), Robert Brennan's basement in Belgrave Square and Diarmuid Coffey's mother's drawing-room. Much power was vested in the Dáil's Standing Committee, and in its President, de

Valera. The Dáil laid down the blueprint for a shadowy secessionist government, republican in form. Its relationship to, and authority over, the remnants of the paramilitary Volunteers was declared, but remained questionable. Nonetheless the revived Volunteering movement, now openly organized by the IRB, was increasingly called the Army of the Irish Republic, or the IRA.

In early 1919, the drift to guerrilla war against government authorities was not yet inevitable. Many Sinn Féiners saw their new-found position as public representatives primarily as enabling them to present their case at the Versailles Peace Conference, where Seán T. O'Kelly and Mary Kate found themselves in February. They settled into the Grand Hotel, headquarters of the Sinn Féin delegation; letters to the other Ryan sisters were grandly headed 'Gouvernement provisoire de la République irlandaise'.[15] Seán would remain in Paris and later Rome for much of the next two violent years – a fortunate circumstance for himself, later bitterly noted by his enemies. Ill for some weeks, he was nursed in the Irish College at Rome, and cemented an important relationship with several influential Vatican figures. The experience reinforced his already devout Catholicism, which would characterize his later political career. Through the efforts of envoys like O'Kelly, a large amount of the money raised by the Dáil was earmarked for the purpose of pressing the Sinn Féin case on generally uninterested foreign representatives.[16]

Hopes of official American support for the Dáil's initiative remained high, but were unfulfilled. Trying another tack, Patrick McCartan made enterprising overtures to the new Russian government. Early contact had been established with Bolshevik envoys in New York, sending imaginative blandishments ('the Republic of Ireland is, as you know, working directly and consciously towards an economic basis of government: that is, towards an application of the Soviet principle').[17] The irrepressible McCartan travelled to Russia in early 1921, confident that he could persuade Foreign Minister Litvinov to recognize the nascent Republic of Ireland. Unfortunately the diplomatic weather had turned, and the Russians were now hoping for an agreement affording formal recognition from Britain (which would indeed be signed, ironically, the following St Patrick's Day). McCartan's carefully constructed arguments that perfidious Albion was an implacable enemy both to the Russian and to the Irish revolutionary regimes fell on barren ground. He tried to persuade his sceptical Bolshevik acquaintances that the Irish were essentially pro-communist, while also suggesting under the heads of a draft Irish–Soviet Treaty that the Republic of Ireland would protect the interests of the Catholic Church in Russia.[18] But his hopes were finally dashed when his chief contact was suddenly spirited away to a 'sanatorium' for a 'rest'; unsurprisingly, McCartan never heard from him again. All that was left for him was to compile a long and perceptive report on conditions in Russia, and to make his difficult way home. He had discovered, as Casement had in Washington and Berlin and O'Kelly at Versailles, that the international diplomatic influence wielded by Irish revolutionaries was necessarily limited.[19]

Simultaneously, and more to the point, raids were beginning to be carried out on police barracks in rural Ireland by the IRA, and the Anglo-Irish War was sputtering into life. Assassinations of policemen, though denounced by several influential clerics, were becoming the real currency of revolt. This escalation of violence had much more to do with local initiatives than Dáil policies; the soldier–civilian divide was now openly evident.[20] The reconstituted Volunteer newspaper *An tÓglách*, now edited by Piaras Béaslaí, printed injunctions to revolutionary violence which echoed the language of paramilitarism elsewhere in Europe. An article called 'Ruthless Warfare', anonymously contributed by Ernest Blythe, declared that anyone supporting conscription 'merits no more consideration than a wild beast and should be killed without mercy or hesitation as opportunity affords'.[21]

The 'glory days' of democratic Sinn Féin were over, and the locus of decision-making was shifting elsewhere. Irish 'experts' in London, such as the acute British civil servant Lionel Curtis, judged that at this point control passed 'from the intellectuals to leaders of a different type':

With such forces at their disposal, the leaders would probably have ventured on open rebellion if matters had come to an issue before the war. But in 1919, realizing the terrific power of modern artillery against troops in the open field, they resorted to the weapons with which centuries of agrarian oppression had familiarized Ireland. As formerly the landlords and their agents, so now officers of Government became marks for the bullets of assassins.[22]

The Dáil continued to sit secretly, and to represent a cross-section of the revolutionary movement. Early on, a 'Democratic Programme' had been articulated, drawn up largely by the labour leader Tom Johnston, aided by the ubiquitous O'Kelly and Mary Kate, and read aloud to the assembly by their friend and brother-in-law Richard Mulcahy.[23] In a formulation lifted bodily from Pearse's pamphlet *The Sovereign People*, the 'Democratic Programme' vested national sovereignty in the whole nation, along with 'the soil and its resources and all the wealth producing processes'; private property rights were to be subordinate to 'the public welfare' and guarantees of comfortable subsistence and free education issued to all the nation's children. Radicals like Máire Comerford would remember its promises sadly in the distant future.[24]

The 'Democratic Programme' may have been drawn up with an eye to the contemporaneous International Socialist Congress in Switzerland, where Irish labour was claiming the right of representation. This was yet another initiative of Griffith's, his belief in the value of international publicity outweighing his dislike of socialism. The language of social – even socialist – egalitarianism continued to be yoked to that of nationalist struggle, notably in a speech of de Róiste's at the 1920 Trade Union Congress in Cork.

> The workingmen of Ireland during the past five or six years had shown that they were the only democracy in Europe that understood thoroughly what democracy was ... They were animated by the three greatest forces on earth – the spirit of democracy, the spirit of nationality, and the spirit of true religion ... these three forces were combined in Ireland, and they were invincible and unconquerable ... If democratic forces did not win the alternative was the old system of militarism and capitalism, crushing the workers in all countries.[25]

But the language of workers' democracy faded fast, while the third element of de Róiste's triumvirate came into stronger and stronger relief; observers were already noting the 'sombre bodyguard of priests' surrounding de Valera as he ascended political platforms, and

Rosamond Jacob was characteristically alert to the growing identification of Catholicism with nationalist identity. The transformation of the Anglo-Irish Tory grandee Lord Midleton's sister, the Hon. Albinia Brodrick, who rechristened herself Gobnait ní Bruadair and became a dedicated Sinn Féiner, should have pleased Jacob. But ní Bruadair's declaration of love for 'her beloved people and their religion' was a step too far. 'I'm in a fright now for fear she may turn Catholic herself, like Casement and Madame de Markievicz. I do dislike to have things look as if no one could be a Sinn Féiner without being a Catholic.'[26]

III

With the failure of the Versailles initiative, the Irish revolution continued to lurch into a more militaristic mode. The IRA was organized into an elaborate structure of brigades, battalions and commands, though it proceeded 'by instinct rather than theory'; pre-war training and drilling in the Volunteers could only count for so much.[27] As Chief-of-Staff, Richard Mulcahy threw himself into its organization, maintaining a huge correspondence with comrades in the provinces and responding to an enormous variety of inquiries, preserved meticulously in carbon copy. Despite his military success in 1916, he would henceforth fight his battles from behind an administrative desk, which may have better suited his austere and shy character. The threat of anarchy loomed in certain parts of the country where the police authority was compromised or routed by the increasingly daring and effective ventures of IRA flying columns. The Royal Irish Constabulary's pleas to be released from its paramilitary role fell on deaf official ears. Its possession of weapons attracted more and more expropriatory raids from the IRA, and its relationship to local communities, always equivocal, became impossible to sustain. In the year from January 1920 to January 1921, the number of police stations in County Mayo was exactly halved – a pattern repeated in other areas where guerrilla activity was rife.

Simultaneously the 'virtual' government of the Dáil asserted its own authority over aspects of local government, police and litigation – scoring a considerable propaganda victory with the last, since the

Sinn Féin courts actually worked effectively and were sometimes patronized by the most unlikely clients. This success owed much to the conservative nature of many of the judgments passed down, and to the involvement of priests; Sinn Féin ideologues such as Darrell Figgis argued strongly against the nascent revolution falling into 'the snare of class war'. The much mythologized 'Limerick Soviet', which ran the city for twelve days in April 1919, in defiance of crown authorities, did not contradict this. (Far from a Soviet-style takeover, it was a general strike against the government's security policy; though thirteen creameries were also claimed to be under workers' control, this was a rhetorical rather than an ideological gesture.) Other arms of the state, such as the Post Office, were exploited as networks of communication, heavily infiltrated by republican sympathizers. As with the rebel occupation of Dublin in 1916, the longer Sinn Féin's rudimentary alternative state lasted, the more credibility it accrued.

But the survival of this ostensibly pacific strategy, as with the Land War boycott forty years before, depended upon the sanction of violence as well as on the support of the community; the scorched ruins of country barracks stood behind the decorously convened Sinn Féin courts. So did the money raised by local levies, and the enterprising loan schemes pioneered and administered by Michael Collins. Above all, terror and counter-terror marked the course of events in certain areas of the country where support for the IRA was shored up by its growing powers of intimidation.[28] With the opening of the bloody year of 1920, as authority leached away from the forces of the crown, Lloyd George's coalition government embarked on the draconian and disastrous policy of drafting in hastily recruited military police, soon to be dubbed 'the Black and Tans'. Their record of undisciplined operations against the civilian population, and their random 'reprisals', gave the revolutionaries both an identifiable enemy in the classic mould of the vicious oppressor and another invaluable propaganda victory.

By May 1920 a government report written by Warren Fisher provided a devastating picture of British rule in Ireland: 'woodenly stupid', completely out of touch with any opinion outside Ascendancy circles, and incapable of realizing that 'two-thirds of the Irish people and over 70 of their MPs are Sinn Féin and that the murder etc. gang are a few hundreds'. This exasperation was echoed in a significant Cabinet report a couple of months later, recognizing that the majority of the Irish population outside Ulster, including unionists, 'were embracing, however reluctantly, the new ideas, and were not unwilling to make use of the Sinn Féin courts; in the circumstances, it was necessary that the Government should review its policy, and the length it could go to in offering concessions.'[29]

The same Cabinet minute recognized that, with the passing of the Government of Ireland Act earlier that year, 'Ireland' as traditionally conceived was no more. The island was now formally partitioned. The separation of the north-east had long been inevitable – a policy floated behind the scenes in government circles since the stand-off of 1911–12, and implicitly but silently acquiesced in by more nationalists than liked to admit it. Southern unionists had long forecast their eventual abandonment (as they saw it) with considerable foreboding. The unionist lawyer James Campbell had presciently told the government in May 1916 that partitioning Ireland would be 'a desperate and dangerous gamble', which, even if successful, would 'permanently divide the Irish nation into two hostile sections, each bearing the statutory brand of a distinctive religious sentiment'. As to the promises made to nationalists and unionists alike by British politicians, 'one side or the other is going to be deceived in this matter with the inevitable consequences of bitter recrimination and renewed agitation.'[30]

Sinn Féin revolutionaries felt no differently, but since the facing down of the government by the UVF in 1912, Partition was always on the cards. Friends of Ulster unionism, entrenched at the centre of Lloyd George's government, saw to it that the revived Home Rule Bill – which came into being as the Government of Ireland Act (1920) – would underwrite the new six-county statelet in the North, whereas the Act's stipulations for the remaining twenty-six counties were a dead letter from the start. The all-Ireland dreams, fantasies and wishful thinking of Ulster nationalists such as Bulmer Hobson, Alice Milligan, Patrick McCartan, Denis McCullough, Roger Casement and F. J. Bigger were equally moribund. Bigger would retreat into regretful antiquarian seclusion at Ardrigh, removing himself from the vanguard of cultural nationalism, while Hobson, McCartan and

McCullough made their lives in Dublin. Alice Milligan would eventually and unhappily return to the North, and a very different world from the revived Gaelicist order which she had so enthusiastically evangelized before the revolution.

The creation and maintenance of Northern Ireland, however, claimed little of the revolutionaries' attention, as the war prosecuted by the IRA in the rest of the island proceeded to escalate. The derring-do and bravado of IRA flying-column actions in the mountains of the south-west was counterpointed with gangland-style assassinations by Parabellum automatic pistols. The bloody month of November 1920 saw an ambush at Ballinalee, County Longford, led by the legendary IRA leader Seán MacEoin, in which as many as twenty crown forces died; the killing of fourteen British officers in their Dublin hotel bedrooms; the shootings of two republican prisoners in crown custody for 'trying to escape'; the firing into a Dublin football crowd by Black and Tans with thirteen fatalities; and the savage Kilmichael ambush by Tom Barry's flying column in west Cork which killed eighteen Auxiliary policemen, in circumstances that are still controversial. Martial law was subsequently declared in Munster, though assassinations and 'executions' continued unabated on both sides. But the greatest republican victory of the year was Terence MacSwiney's death by hunger-strike in Brixton Gaol on 25 October 1920.

MacSwiney had agonized since Easter 1916 about his need to expiate the failure of Cork to rise in a sacrificial rebellion alongside Dublin, and his own irresolution in subsequently handing over Volunteers weaponry to the authorities; guilt and self-recrimination were expressed to friends and poured out in introspective poetry.[31] Internment in Frongoch after the Rising had helped to rehabilitate him, as so many others inactive at Easter. He subsequently threw himself into Sinn Féin organization, was elected TD for Cork while still in gaol and entered local politics along with his companions Liam de Róiste and Tomás MacCurtain. When the latter was murdered by police in disguise, MacSwiney succeeded him as Lord Mayor of Cork, proposed by de Róiste. He was simultaneously Commandant of the IRA's Cork No. 1 Brigade, in which capacity he horrified P. S. O'Hegarty by outlining 'fiendish and indefensible' assassination projects.[32] Constantly cautioned and arrested, MacSwiney was heavily involved in raising finance through a Dáil loan organized by Collins; here and elsewhere his punctilio and pomposity annoyed many colleagues, including de Róiste (Collins was particularly irritated by MacSwiney's insistence on translating every document laboriously into Irish[33]). Finally, the troublesome Lord Mayor was arrested in August 1920 for possession of a police cipher, refused to recognize the court and commenced a hunger-strike.

He had embraced this tactic during a previous incarceration, a tactic which was not supported by his colleagues and was strongly opposed by his wife, Muriel Murphy, whom he had married in June 1917. The wedding was the culmination of a long campaign on her part, beginning when she arranged a meeting through friends in 1915, overcoming his reluctance 'because of the horrible imperialist family I was born into'; she pursued their relationship through her indefatigable prison-visiting.[34] 'Remember your department belongs in the next world,' she had written prophetically to him during a manic period of sleeplessness in their early marriage; 'I have charge of this.'[35] Twelve years younger, attractive, independently well-off, strong-minded and erratic, Muriel, as well as their baby, would feature strongly in the publicity campaign which gathered momentum as MacSwiney's hunger-strike in Brixton Gaol inexorably continued for weeks on end. But her feelings were against it, and she recorded later that she always knew it would end with his death.

All told it lasted an astonishing seventy-four days and attracted worldwide attention. MacSwiney's status as elected Lord Mayor and member of the Dáil was emphasized for propaganda purposes, rather than his role as IRA Commandant; so were his ostentatious devoutness and commitment to self-sacrifice. He was attended throughout by priests, Sinn Féin comrades, his sisters Mary and Annie, and his wife. A parade of visitors came across the Irish Sea, including his old friend Liam de Róiste, who, in late August, was surprised to find Mac-Swiney still looking strong and Muriel 'exceptionally bright and cheerful', though 'kept up by excitement; I think the others are a bit nervous of her. No wonder.' De Róiste himself felt that 'her apparent unconcern is only her way of keeping up before people; there is not the least sign of her recent "illness".' But he, and everyone else, was aware that MacSwiney was on a course set for death.

Meetings were held every day in Art Ó Briain's London office, to deal with the avalanche of inquiries and the extraordinary international interest. In the intervals between giving interviews to the Dutch and Greek press and dealing with an appeal from Brazilian Catholics to the Pope, de Róiste became weary of 'half-cracked' people turning up to express support, expecting 'the people in the office to be as "cracked" as themselves'.[36] Colleagues such as Collins and Béaslaí privately disapproved of MacSwiney's strategy; his sisters violently endorsed it; his wife found it difficult to support. But in this heroic martyrdom, MacSwiney found the role he had been seeking since his ambitious and frustrated youth. His laborious writings found a new audience, at an undreamt-of level; even his five-act play *The Revolutionist* was rapidly (and cannily) mounted by the Abbey Theatre in Dublin. 'I think the last pages would greatly move the audience,' Yeats judged, 'who will see the Mayor in the [play's] hero.'[37]

The martyr's sisters would guard the sacred flame of his memory all their lives; the restive Muriel would eventually follow a more rebellious and iconoclastic path. But in the autumn of 1920 an enormous public followed his slow road to a terrible death. The Church expressed a surprisingly unequivocal degree of support, with Mac-Swiney receiving daily Communion and declaring that his strength was being sustained by divine intercession. He clearly saw the eleven republican hunger-strikers simultaneously engaged in Cork as his disciples, and, in a prayer which he composed on the fifty-seventh day of his strike, he offered his suffering and death to God 'for Ireland's resurrection'. Pleas for intervention from all sides (including the King's private secretary) met a stony government response – possibly because Arthur Balfour, with a long record of obduracy towards Ireland, was deputizing for his coalition colleague Lloyd George. When the end came, on 25 October, the public reaction was immense: 30,000 people filed past the bier in St George's, the Catholic cathedral in Southwark, and – for all the government's efforts – the vast funeral in Cork claimed worldwide attention. As for MacSwiney, he was seen – like the rebels executed at Easter – to have been at last assumed into Valhalla. Father Dominic O'Connor, the priest who had attended him in Brixton Prison throughout, remarked that a new martyr had gone to join 'Tomás [MacCurtain], Eoghan Roe [O'Sullivan], and Joan of

Arc'.[38] Rosamond Jacob, who had visited the MacSwiney household in Cork long before and found the siblings unsympathetic, felt torn when she listened to Min Ryan's account of the funeral. 'It was plainer still how she had enjoyed that. Hanna and I agreed that such things are a kind of emotional orgy. I know I am capable of such enjoyment myself and it is revolting to think of.'[39]

IV

Mary MacSwiney later declared that one of her brother's last remarks to her was 'Thank God, there will be no more compromises now.'[40] By the end of 1920 the initiative seemed to have left what Collins contemptuously called 'the forces of moderation'. Gunmen like Ernie O'Malley remembered long afterwards that, bivouacked out on the hillsides, they thought they were witnessing a new Ireland coming into being.

> Gone was the country of the soft brogue or blarney, the foxhunting days and the pleasant parties or tennis tournaments. Instead was a hard, steady Ireland, cool, assertive. It had pitted its strength against the Empire and the latter was beginning to waver. The mentality of the island seemed to have changed; the political type with his flow of eloquence and his mouthings, his bland assurances, his ability to 'pull wires', and his gymnastic feats of conscience seemed to have disappeared. There was no room for oratory. The nation was at war ... Simple country boys, simple in that they were not sophisticated, had found they possessed organizing and administrative ability. They had made themselves respected by their own people and, more difficult still, by those of their own class.[41]

But this was an idealized retrospection, written much later with knowledge of what was to come. The elections for the second Dáil in May 1921, tightly controlled by Collins and Boland, were significant. Out of 125 candidates, 47 were in gaol and 52 'on the run'. Several knew nothing of their candidacy till elected. The tiny remnant of the Irish Parliamentary Party abstained, as did Labour; all constituencies in the new twenty-six-county Ireland were uncontested. By contrast, every seat in the new unit of Northern Ireland was fought, returning 40 unionists, 6 nationalists and 6 Sinn Féiners (all of the last living in the South). The new Dáil represented the IRA rather than the Sinn Féin movement at large. Some sitting deputies who were not representative of O'Malley's hard new Ireland, and felt the time had come for peace, found themselves the objects of hostility from the leadership. They included that seasoned armchair revolutionary Liam de Róiste, now less inclined towards the whole-hearted blood sacrifice which he had theoretically endorsed back in 1914. His long experience in the Cork Young Ireland Society, the Celtic Literary Society, the Cork Dramatic Society, Cumann na nGaedheal and all the rest had paved the way for a political career in the new dispensation. Re-elected as a Dáil TD, he was now an experienced Chairman and member of economic committees, as well as an Alderman of Cork Corporation, chairing its Law and Finance Committee, and a member of the Cork Harbour Board. A well-disposed English writer on a fact-finding tour in April 1921 thought him 'a typical Republican of the Cork school . . . He too is an "intellectual" but a humorous glint behind spectacles and an occasional droop at the corners of the mouth seem to betray less sternness and a warmer humanity [than his colleague Barry Egan].' De Róiste defended the idea of a republic to his visitor, but 'preferred not to dogmatize about it while the matter is under consideration by the parties concerned . . . all our economic interests, all our future in fact, is bound up with you.'[42] Behind the scenes, elements of the IRB leadership were similarly recognizing that the time was coming to make terms, and the British government, with Ulster removed from the equation, were already extending feelers in that direction. The 'simple country boys' conjured up by O'Malley, however, would be less inclined to negotiation.

With the calling of a truce in July 1921, various lines of communication were established with British politicians and civil servants. Official opinion, both in Dublin Castle and in Whitehall, had long accepted that Dominion Home Rule was the least that could be offered to nationalist Ireland – a far more viable option now that the aggressively unionist element of Ulster had been mollified. But the irredentists among the revolutionaries wanted much more, and there were already ominous signs of impending dissension. In fact, the antagonisms that would flare up into civil war six months later had long been evident. In Father O'Flanagan's bitter words, Sinn Féin after 1917 had been built upon an uneasy compromise between hard-line republicans and moderates, 'and the so-called Treaty [in 1921] was the wedge that burst the sections asunder.'[43] The patterns of division were not always clear; de Valera's and Collins's respective attitudes to ending hostilities, for instance, exactly contradicted the line that each would subsequently take. While negotiations proceeded in London, back in Dublin de Valera was clearly swayed by Brugha, an extremist Anglophobe even by IRA standards, and Stack, whose administrative incompetence made him frankly long for the simplicities of open warfare. By the same token, those who eventually went to London to negotiate the Treaty with the British government were not representative of the more irreconcilable wing of the revolutionary movement.

Whether this was a deliberate decision on de Valera's part is impossible to ascertain. But the pivotal role was played by Arthur Griffith, whose dual-monarchy ideas on Anglo-Irish relations had – a decade or so before – been so heavily criticized by radical nationalists. Since 1916 he had apparently reconstructed himself into a republican, and by 1919 his newspaper *Nationality* was declaring that 'nothing short of an Independent Irish republic will satisfy the aspirations of the people of Ireland.'[44] But this may have been aimed at Versailles rather than at Whitehall, and he travelled to London in late 1921 on the understanding that the time had come to treat with the enemy, and therefore compromises would have to be made. This may have been a general (if implicit) view, but Griffith took it further than many expected. By privately committing himself to Lloyd George's seductive proposals for an oath of fidelity to the crown, and agreeing to leave the fate of Northern Ireland to a boundary commission to be assembled at some future date, he brought the rest of the Irish delegation to agree to the Treaty – which was very far from establishing 'the republic'. The Platonic shape of that revolutionary ideal had been conjured up over the last two years by revolutionary zealots in the meeting-rooms of the Dáil and on the hillsides of Munster. In an earlier era it had been debated in student societies, over meals at the Vegetarian Restaurant, on long nights in Gaelic League summer-schools, and in the clusters of radical households at Ranelagh or on the South Circular Road. But it would remain a chimera.

Hard-headed people like Collins, anxious to get their hands on the levers of power and realistic about the limited long-term prospects of guerrilla war, felt that the dominion status offered by the Treaty would enable the eventual achievement of republican 'freedom'. For them, in Ernest Blythe's words, republicanism was 'not a national principle but a political preference . . . a means to an end, not an end in itself'.[45] De Valera suddenly and unpredictably repudiated this approach – though, according to General Jan Smuts, who brought his own experience as an ex-freedom-fighter to bear on the negotiations, the Sinn Féin leader had privately endorsed a dominion-style settlement the previous July. Patrick McCartan similarly recalled a conversation with de Valera just before the negotiations, when he explained he was ramping up the 'republic' campaign in order to make Lloyd George realize he had to take this into account. 'In plain English he virtually said that if we talked too much republic we might not get dominion status accepted. He was in a sort of confidential mood and said that the voting would be rather interesting as the real men would be for peace and those of the Dáil who did nothing would be immutable. He believed association with the British Empire would be best for Ireland.' As for McCartan himself, 'I voted for the damned Treaty because I thought it was in danger – and it was, until Burgess [Cathal Brugha] made his silly attack on Collins and Griffith took advice and did not overstate his case. The longer I listened to our leaders the more I became convinced that we got much more than we deserved and that if we did not accept it England could afford to leave the rest of the fight to ourselves.'[46] Internecine warfare was indeed the outcome. Almost at once the revolutionary movement began to split, and long-simmering antagonisms and resentments boiled to the surface.

The Dáil ratified the Treaty establishing the Irish Free State by seven votes in January 1922, but a large rump followed de Valera in rejecting the decision and abiding by the allegedly superior authority of the rapidly mythologized 'second Dáil'. Power shifted from the ministers of the Dáil to the Provisional government headed by Collins and Griffith pending an election, but the constitutional position remained murky.[47] An attempt was made to evade open hostilities by rigging the election under Treaty conditions, with guaranteed proportions for the two opposing sides, but Collins – who had rapidly emerged as the supremo of the new order – eventually reneged on it. Public opinion in any case was overwhelmingly in favour of the Treaty, as even its opponents gloomily admitted. This did not stop them taking up arms against it. The IRA split into two factions, and the new army of the Irish Free State under Mulcahy found itself at war with old comrades, who kept the name of 'IRA' and declared that their objective was 'to guard the honour and maintain the independence of the Irish Republic'. Kevin O'Higgins, one of the most uncompromising members of the new government, referred to the dissidents more crisply as 'a combination of degenerate Apaches' and to de Valera as 'a crooked Spanish bastard'. His Free State colleagues did not escape his tongue either (Collins was branded 'a pasty-faced blasphemous fucker from Cork').[48] Mutual recrimination became the order of the day.

From the other side, young republicans such as Todd Andrews were shattered by the Treaty Debates. 'For years I had lived on a plane of emotional idealism, believing that we were being led by great men into a new Ireland. Now I had seen these "great men" in action to find that they were mostly very average in stature, some below average, some malevolent and vicious.'[49] What Mulcahy called the 'wonderful brotherhood' of the revolutionary Volunteers was painfully fractured. As a prominent defender of the Treaty, he himself was the target for painful attacks. 'No matter what good things are in the Treaty, are they worth all this unhappiness, Dick?' wrote Mary MacSwiney in a savage letter. 'Do you not realize that we hold the Republic as a living faith – a spiritual reality stronger than any material benefits you can offer – cannot give it up. It is not *we* who have changed it is you.'[50]

When hostilities broke out between the ex-comrades in Dublin that July, with the Free State forces shelling rebel strongholds on Sackville Street while their opponents loopholed their way out of the surrounding buildings, the conditions of 1916 were re-created with a brutal irony. In another gruesome echo, assassinations on one side were met by summary executions on the other: Mulcahy deliberately used the term 'reprisals' in an official announcement. The violence, trauma and body-count of the Civil War, which ended in the dissidents dumping their arms in the summer of 1923, took over from the preceding hostilities against the forces of the crown. Between 1919 and 1921 about 1,500 were killed, besides the 220 fatalities of communal violence in the North; 1922–3 brought the total to more than 4,000, while the Northern toll reached 500. Arguably it burnt a deeper mark into Irish historical memory: certainly a more painful one. 'I knew that it was the actions of the Irregular-republicans which killed idealism in my own soul; idealism that is, in connection with this country and its people,' de Róiste recorded in his diary a year later. 'And I *know* they killed it in many others as well.'[51]

The nature of the violence also laid bare latent divisions among the revolutionaries, and unpalatable truths about the nature of revolution, already spelt out in the intimidation, score-settling and sectarian episodes which had characterized some IRA actions during the previous campaign. Threats were made, *inter alia*, to exterminate 'every male member' of certain family connections, arousing ancient echoes of communal conflict. There was a marked exodus of frightened Protestants from some areas of the new Free State, especially during and after the Civil War. The roots of that conflict lay, on one level, in the powers claimed by people who had experienced a certain liberation from authority, while remaining conditioned by authoritarian backgrounds; their life as guerrilla comrades had given them a taste for power as well as a cavalier attitude towards democratic decisions. Less obviously, the impetus to civil war owed much to the purist hopes and dreams nurtured by Pearsean arguments for separatism. However, high-souled patriotism was not much evident in the violent and demoralizing recriminations that broke out.[52] The official journal of the new Free State referred to the republican irreconcilables as 'conscienceless, rotten and petty tyrants' who deserved no mercy.[53] The spectres of untrammelled warlordism and communal conflict were kept at a distance, especially when the contemporary upheavals in Central and Eastern Europe are borne in mind, but sometimes hovered disconcertingly near.

The more abstract issues that divided the two sides were not to do with the reality of sundered republican brethren in the north-east (whom Collins was covertly arming, before his own untimely death in an ambush by anti-Treaty forces in August 1920 – ten days after Griffith's sudden death from a cerebral haemorrhage). Forms of words, flags and emblems, and ancient hatreds seemed to mean more, as did the idea of fealty to the crown, even in the diluted and formalized way prescribed by the Treaty. It should be remembered that the republican schoolteacher Thomas Ashe, now a canonized martyr since his death on hunger-strike, used to encourage his classes to walk over the Union Jack, and declared his own wish to urinate on it.[54] For a generation pre-occupied with the materialism, decadence and impurity of Englishness, salvation could be ensured only by separation. Muriel MacSwiney, appalled by the Treaty, could not bring herself to blame anyone Irish for it. She wrote, some time later (from the Pension International, Wiesbaden), to Richard Mulcahy, who had been best man at her wedding to Terence in 1917. Mulcahy, one of the Treaty's most fervent supporters, was by now a hate-figure for irredentist republicans, but Muriel wanted to make clear that she did not blame him personally. 'I don't feel anything against anybody but England for what has happened ... Although I think this treaty is by a long way the greatest infamy that the enemy has ever perpetrated on us & I will always oppose it or anything like it I feel nothing against any Irishman; the whole weight of my venom is directed against the English people ... I shall spend my life not, as up to this, working for the complete independence of Ireland's Republic but also working for the destruction & downfall of England & of every single English person I come across. The English people are to me now a plague of moral lepers.'[55]

Others, such as Máire Comerford, decided early on that those who supported the Treaty were engaged in a deliberate project of counter-revolution against the social radicalism of the 'real' revolution. For Liam Mellows, the Irish future was necessarily anti-materialist – echoing Pearse, who had preached in 1913 that it would be better that 'Dublin should be laid in ruins' than that the existing condition of contentment within the British Empire should continue. 'We do not seek to make this country a materially great country at the expense of its honour,' declared Mellows; 'we would rather have this country poor and indigent, we would rather have the people of Ireland eking out a poor existence on the soil, as long as they possessed their souls, their minds, their honour.'[56] This represented Gaelic League values in ruthlessly concrete form, and 'the Irish people' may be forgiven for not finding them universally attractive. From the other side, the ex-revolutionaries who founded the new state saw their role as necessarily ruthless in a different cause, and sometimes gloried in it. Richard Mulcahy, who had found his métier as a military organizer and would hold a number of ministerial posts in the new regime, emerged as a noted pragmatist, accepting full responsibility for the execution of ex-comrades (including Rory O'Connor and Liam Mellows) who had taken the Irregular side. More than three times as many executions were carried out by the Free State government as by the British during the previous war. Long afterwards, Mulcahy was clear in his own mind about this traumatic time. 'The fundamental and traditional character of the people stood fast and constructive in spite of the drama, the indiscipline that drama makes up, and the chancers who are nurtured in its atmosphere, and whose operations disintegrate the natural solid foundations of a people.'[57] The Free Staters represented the true values of Irishness, guarding the revolution from 'chancers'.

Less tangible issues than life and death, still hotly debated, concerned the relationship between 'republicanism' and 'democracy'; and the pursuit of the ideal by a diminishing band of idealists (or fanatics) against the overwhelming endorsement by their countrymen of a compromise Treaty that might – and did – lead to more. In some ways, the lines along which the revolution divided had been clearly anticipated by contemporary observers, and the fissure pointed up separations and tensions that had always been there. In some of the confrontations one can discern the forces of Catholic piety and social conservatism asserting themselves against the more anarchic brio of certain members of the revolutionary generation (including several women). From one angle, the Civil War pitted the 'new men' of the IRA, often the younger sons of farmers and those without 'a stake in the country', against an elite in the making who saw their time had come. Statements from Kevin O'Higgins and others in the latter camp suggest a distinct class bias; O'Higgins, like W. T. Cosgrave, represented a new, managerial and potentially conservative element within the movement. But the activities of the Irregulars were not purely grounded in disagreements over the interpretation of the Treaty. Operations also reflected the paying off of old scores, the settling of long-standing resentments, and antipathy towards people perceived as aliens, outsiders or sympathetic to British rule.[58] The war was traumatic in many ways. And in several instances the separation cut through family lines and sundered old comrades and brothers-in-arms, most famously Michael Collins and Harry Boland.

Married couples were also split. Mabel and Desmond FitzGerald came near separation over his endorsement of the Treaty, she – as ever – taking a more radical line. Several women who had been married or closely related to key revolutionary leaders repudiated the Treaty in the name of the dead; they included Áine Ceannt, Mary MacSwiney, Kathleen Clarke, Margaret Pearse and Maud Gonne MacBride (as she was now generally known). For the Ryan girls, the Treaty was intensely and intimately traumatic. Min, who had married Richard Mulcahy in 1919, became with him a linchpin of the new regime – though it is a fair bet that her first love, Seán MacDermott, would not have endorsed the Treaty, had he lived to see it. Agnes and Denis McCullough also supported the Treaty and the political party – Cumann na nGaedheal, later Fine Gael – that grew out of it. But their sisters Phyllis, Chris and Nell, their brother James and above all the dominating and charismatic figure of Mary Kate set themselves firmly against it. Mary Kate and Seán T. O'Kelly would – like James – be consistent supporters of de Valera and founder members of Fianna Fáil, the 'slightly constitutional' party which he founded in 1926 on the basis of opposing the Treaty, and which propelled him to supreme political power in Ireland for decades from the early 1930s. The rift between Seán T and Denis McCullough, his closest friend as well as his brother-in-law, was particularly searing.[59] Phyllis at one point instructed Min – unsuccessfully – to leave her husband over his support of the Free State. The Ryan family and their spouses tried to preserve some vestiges of that powerful bond, forged in the heady days of student radicalism before the war, and during the astonishing years of the revolution; there were gatherings at the farm at Tomcoole in the summer, where the children holidayed with their cousins and politics were not spoken of. But the wounds went deep, and Phyllis did not speak to her pro-Treaty siblings for some years. Many of those brought together in the fervour of their youth must have silently echoed the words of the anti-Treaty IRA leader Liam Lynch, dying after a shootout with Free State forces in the Knockmealdown Mountains on 10 April 1923: 'It should never have happened.'[60]

As the dust settled and the new Free State came into being, with it came an inheritance of antagonism and the creation of a new political class. From his vantage as a recently appointed Senator, W. B. Yeats observed the ministers of the new government:

> They had destroyed a system of election and established another, made terrible decisions, the ablest had signed the death-warrant of his dearest friend. They seemed men of skill and mother-wit, men who had survived hatred. But their minds knew no play that my mind could play at; I felt that I could never know them. One of the most notable said he had long wanted to meet me. We met, but my conversation shocked and embarrassed him ... Yet their descendants, if they grow rich enough for the travel and leisure that make a finished man, will constitute our ruling class, and date their origin from the Post Office as American families date theirs from the *Mayflower*.[61]

Even among these victors, there were powerful dislikes and ancient feuds. After the sudden deaths of Collins and Griffith in 1922, the successor strong-men of the regime were W. T. Cosgrave and Kevin O'Higgins, who were not representative figures from the pre-revolutionary era; O'Higgins himself admitted to his fiancée that he 'had no pre-'16 record – the little good that's in [me] dates from that'. In fact his family background was that of the old Parliamentary elite, since, being a nephew of T. M. Healy, he was closely related to the powerful O'Sullivan nexus from Cork. He was also the son of a local JP, had been educated at Clongowes, and had spent a frivolous UCD career as a lackadaisical law student. Cosgrave also came from the solid and moneyed Catholic middle class, and emerged into politics through the Volunteers and the reconstructed Sinn Féin of 1917. Such men represented a new wave of activists, detached from the visionary republicanism and cultural excitements of the pre-revolutionary era. Michael Hayes, who had been formed in that older tradition, noted that O'Higgins 'didn't understand to the same extent what [the revolution] was all about ... he reduced it to the notion of the Irish people getting a parliament.'[62] To some, this looked uncomfortably close to Home Rule.

When this is taken with the fact that by the time of his death by assassination in 1927 O'Higgins was privately preoccupied by the project of a reunited Ireland coming back under a dual-monarchy, it can be seen why some of the disgruntled revolutionaries saw the ghosts of the Irish Parliamentary Party all around them. Hayes's friend Mulcahy, though serving (rather uncomfortably) in office alongside O'Higgins and Cosgrave, looked back to that pre-revolutionary era too, and retained a fidelity to the old IRB. (The punctilious Mulcahy was equally uncomfortable with the freewheeling approach of Collins's ex-*squadristi*, still influential in the upper echelons of the Free State Army, and his suspicions would be vindicated when they threatened a mutiny in 1924.) But the more influential figures in the new Free State were sceptical about much that had gone before, in the carefree days before 1916. Their priority was to build a new regime that would be stable, conservative and fiscally solvent. Given the challenge of the Civil War, with the Irregulars ordering the assassination of pro-Treaty ministers, TDs and even newspaper editors on sight, a ruthless pragmatism was understandable. But it also announced an end to the dreams of a new Ireland nurtured by many of their older colleagues.

SOME WORK BEFORE US.

The priorities of the new Free State as seen by the *Leader*, 7 January 1922.

9

Remembering

I cannot and will not write about the people and times when we were young for reasons that are long and complicated. Briefly the phoenix of our youth has fluttered to earth such a miserable old hen I have no heart for it . . .
— *Bulmer Hobson to Denis McCullough,*
30 April 1956[1]

I

For years afterwards, the revolutionary generation lived on their memories. In many ways, the same was true of the new state which they had helped to bring about. Commemoration, public remembrance and the manipulation of historic recollection had long been inseparable from Irish public life, creating a framework of activity which asserted national identity and underpinned the state. In recent years this phenomenon has generated a historiography all of its own, including some deeply absorbing explorations of the traumatic spaces which the Civil War rendered unavailable to communal memory.[2] Many of the revolutionaries had been brought up on commemorations of the Manchester Martyrs of 1867, and were powerfully influenced by the great memory-fest of the 1798 Rising Centenary in 1898, which cultural entrepreneurs such as Alice Milligan had done so much to market. They were equally familiar with the uses of memorial marches to Wolfe Tone's grave at Bodenstown, and the celebration and decoration of 'rebel' graves and monuments all over the country. The founding of the Free State suggested a whole new agenda of iconic dates and events to be celebrated; but this activity had to be approached in a gingerly, embarrassed and competitive fashion. If the function of public commemoration was to create the bonding cement of social memory, this implied the creation of an agreed version of history. And one inheritance of the traumatic split over the Treaty and the subsequent Civil War was a wide, if often unspoken, chasm between different interpretations of what the revolution had actually been about.

This disagreement revolved around events from the Truce to the Treaty and thereafter, which is one reason why the commemoration of the 1916 Rising was seen as a safer option. The religious implications of Easter Monday added to the potency, and a tradition of celebrations began from 1917, heavily freighted with sacred symbolism. There was a brief attempt to commemorate 6 December, the ratification of the Treaty, as 'Independence Day', but it was rapidly abandoned. The Free State preferred to take over the memory of the 1916 Rising, along with occasional cautious obeisances towards broader forms of commemoration. However, any attempt to mark the deaths of the 50,000 Irishmen who had fought for the Allies in the world war were furiously derided by irreconcilable republicans such as the MacSwiney sisters. 'How the poppies fly in Ireland since the Free State came into existence – Union Jackery of every description foisted on the country by Collins and Mulcahy and the rest.'[3]

But allowing the British Legion a presence on the streets once a year on Armistice Day was not the main issue. The manipulation of public memory could not accommodate the more savage reality of the assassinations and executions perpetrated upon each other by Civil War and Irregular forces in the demoralizing fallout of the revolution. Nor could it incorporate the underside of antagonisms, feuds, score-settling and the 'drumbeat of retaliation' to which so much military activity had marched in the latter stages of the upheaval.[4] These silent spaces have been resoundingly filled by historians in recent decades, when much attention has been devoted to the seamier and more atavistic side of revolutionary activity. But in the years following 1922, as the revolutionary generation grew into middle age, remembering in public was an exercise demanding very careful negotiation.

By contrast, private responses to the gathering momentum of

commemorative record could be both scathing and despairing. To later historians, the achievements of the Free State set up under the Treaty appear resoundingly impressive; against threats of anarchy, instability and economic insecurity, the new government constructed a democratic polity with stable finances, an impressively impartial and principled civil service, an unarmed police force and a political system which would eventually absorb the malcontents who had fought against the Treaty. But none of these achievements counted for much with the people who had fought for the new Jerusalem of a visionary republic. And even for some of those who accepted the Treaty and made it work, post-revolutionary reality was a long and bitter disillusionment.

II

Public memory of the events of 1916–21 necessarily stressed the language of bloodshed, redemption and glory, borrowing the familiar conventions of hagiography – a literary mode which rapidly transferred into the biographies of dead heroes (Louis Le Roux on Pearse, Béaslaí on Collins). The dead were everywhere, elevated into ceremonial niches; their public celebration often masked an ill-concealed contest for possession. That the martyrs of 1916 had not lived to see the War of Independence and the Civil War theoretically meant that they could be enlisted for either side – though, by and large, their widows, siblings and parents tended to claim them for the side of purist republicanism. Medals were struck, slide-shows and films presented, and relics paraded, in a manner actually anticipated by the martyrs themselves; as when Seán MacDermott spent some of his last hours cutting buttons off his clothes, to be distributed as keepsakes among his followers, or Pearse told his mother that she would occupy a blessed position as the mother of a saviour. Le Roux's 1932 biography closed with a plea for Pearse's official canonization and Margaret Pearse herself had prophesied in the Treaty Debates that the day would come when the bones of her dead sons 'shall be lifted as if they were the bones of saints'.[5] Redemption, epiphany and resurrection provided recurring tropes for the Rising and its aftermath. In the manner of religious cults, public statuary and commemorative sites were tentatively developed, accompanied by an angry undercurrent of argument regarding inclusions and exclusions. And the same disagreements bedevilled and complicated the reception of the written history of the revolution.

This appeared early, in semi-official works such as Piaras Béaslaí's immense biography of Michael Collins (1926). Originally commissioned by the government, it was written with an overpowering agenda, and rapidly seen as such.[6] Béaslaí had come a long way since his ambitious and frustrated youth in Bootle; a powerful figure in the Gaelic League and an influential Volunteer, he had had a good war and his candidature was approved by the Collins family, though opposed by several colleagues. In the course of writing it, Béaslaí fell out with the army and resigned his rank. But he had always been one of nature's hero-worshippers; he was determined to let nothing stand in the way of his heroic story; and he knew he was right. Always possessive, he excluded all mention of Collins's fiancée Kitty Kiernan, for reasons oddly reminiscent of the youthful tirades in his diaries against his friends' girlfriends. ('Again and again I wonder how she attracted Michael. I can discern in her no brains, no beauty, no charm of manner. Enough of this painful subject.'[7]) He threatened others who wrote on Collins with law-suits for plagiarism, and he settled scores all around him. As one reviewer put it, 'he goes out of his way to minimize the importance . . . and to question the motives of certain persons from whom he and his associates parted later.'[8]

The book began a venerable and often mawkish tradition of celebrating Collins's glamorous image and early death, but it was often inaccurate as well as pietistic. Impartially offensive, Béaslaí infuriated Arthur Griffith's widow, Maud (among many others), by his treatment of her husband. P. S. O'Hegarty, though pro-Treaty, maintained a long campaign in the columns of the *Irish Statesman* against Béaslaí's unreliability and elisions, pointing out that he presented a history of the military side of the revolution that placed all authority with Collins and his 'squad', cavalierly ignoring the structure of the IRA, the role of GHQ under Richard Mulcahy and the history of the Volunteers. Though Mulcahy himself revered Collins, this travesty was unbearable to him, and after his resignation from the Free State government in 1924 he devoted himself to annotating Béaslaí's work at enormous length, in a commentary that eventually stretched to over 400 pages. Unlike O'Hegarty, Mulcahy kept his reaction private, observing loyalty to the Free State side. The development of anti-Treaty historiography demonstrated less circumspection, notably where Dorothy Macardle's *The Irish Republic* (1937) was concerned. This frankly pro-de Valera version of the revolution, highly readable and widely praised, incensed Mabel FitzGerald, who described it as '1,000 pages of untruths'. Mabel also deeply resented the way that Robert Brennan and Frank Gallagher had written out the part played by her husband Desmond from the story of republican journalism and the now-legendary *Irish Bulletin*. 'I had been on their side because of the principle of the Republic,' she wrote later, 'though all the men I admired were on the other side, but I was gradually sickened with lying propaganda against better men.'[9] Patrick McCartan was equally critical of Macardle, though he took an indulgent line towards death-or-glory memoirs by republicans such as Dan Breen, whose self-inflationary *My Fight for Irish Freedom* was published with McCartan's aid in 1924. 'Dan is one of the best and in need of money; he is one of the wrecks of our glorious and inglorious movement.'[10] The enterprise succeeded, and Breen's adventure-story sold 20,000 copies. McCartan's contacts with well-off Irish-Americans were also pressed into service for a number of publications claiming to put the revolutionary record straight, climaxing with W. P. Maloney's *Forged Casement Diaries* in 1936, for which Bulmer Hobson and McCartan raised £150 and arranged a publisher.[11]

As memoirs, biographies and general histories of the revolutionary period began to mount up, the version of history reflected a shift in the political balance of the Free State. From 1926 de Valera and his followers were negotiating themselves back into constitutional politics, under the party umbrella of 'Fianna Fáil' – a stratagem which involved taking the oath, over whose unacceptability they had fought a civil war. This might be seen either as a sign of sophisticated political maturity, or as a piece of bare-faced cheek which betrayed that they had been worsted in the argument. Mulcahy, who naturally subscribed to the latter view, felt that de Valera was disliked by pro-Treatyites even more after he entered the Dáil (and came to power constitutionally in 1932): he was now seen to be having it both ways. 'We could have made the status [of the Free State] what we wished had we not been cursed by the most fatal friends Ireland ever had as leaders,' McCartan lamented to his American friend William Maloney in 1924. 'They have made our state a partitioned nation in factions, with the interest of the nation subordinated to those of the faction-ists.' Above all, the fault lay with the Machiavellian de Valera, to whom he had once been close: 'the most honestly dishonest man I ever met. He kids himself and poses. Give me a bloody crook if this be honesty.'[12]

III

By the 1930s the ex-revolutionaries had long been accustomed to abusing each other in private; and it was now possible to suggest pub-licly that the revolution had brought in its wake certain elements of disillusionment. In fact, this subversive current had begun early on. Before the Rising the iconoclastic young Eimar O'Duffy had embraced various radical beliefs, including socialism and atheism, and had been periodically evicted from his respectable parents' house in Harcourt Street. A star of the pre-war UCD generation, he became influential both as an officer and as an administrator in the early Volunteering movement, and was, as already mentioned, a lively member of the Plunkett–MacDonagh circle around the Hardwicke Street Theatre in pre-war days. In 1919, now discontentedly working as a dentist (like his father before him), O'Duffy published a sprawling *Bildungsroman* called *The Wasted Island*, which was one of the first novels to build the great set-pieces of recent history, such as the Howth gun-running and the occupation of the GPO, into a fictionalized form. Since O'Duffy was present at both events, the presentation also carries some credence as an historical account.

The Wasted Island eviscerates the 'Castle Catholic' world of O'Duffy's youth with a scalpel, but also reflects his own odyssey towards disillusionment with the pieties, certainties and pretensions of the revolutionary generation. O'Duffy's novel reconstructs the arguments of young revolutionaries from middle-class backgrounds, and the action of the novel in some ways endorses them; Home Rule is treated throughout as a corrupt and exhausted compromise. But the revolutionaries do not get off lightly either. There is, for one thing, an unmistakable and particularly savage portrait (as 'Austin Mallow') of the 1916 hero Joseph Plunkett. O'Duffy knew the Plunketts well (he had stayed at Larkfield when thrown out of home) and Joe Plunkett's household with his sister Geraldine at 17 Marlborough Road, where weapons were stockpiled and journals published, is identifiably lampooned. O'Duffy added hookahs of hashish into the mix, and parodied Plunkett's mystic poetry with heartless gusto. Suggestively, one of the heroes of the novel, Stephen Ward, is based on Bulmer Hobson, and the protagonists of the novel take the Hobsonite line about the futility of 1916, advocating instead a considered guerrilla war. At the end, the growing resort to violence is seen to lead towards a bitter disillusionment, and the novel's only real victor is a trimming solicitor with a Redmondite background.

The Wasted Island was angrily received by contemporaries, but later evaluations suggest that O'Duffy, even thus early, spoke for several of them.[13] He subsequently became a journalist working on several republican enterprises (including editing the army newspaper *An tÓglách*); he also endured a spell teaching at Mount St Benedict, always hospitable to nationalist intellectuals at odds with the world. Further satirical novels followed (as well as a play, *Bricriu's Feast*, which energetically returned to jeering at the Plunketts, and precipitated a crisis in the Hardwicke Street Theatre, still struggling along on Plunkett money). O'Duffy's subsequent job with the Free State Propaganda Department was, unsurprisingly, terminated. and he lived peripatetically in Paris and London until his unexpectedly early death in 1935.

O'Duffy, while an original spirit, was not alone in his opinions; the outcome of the Anglo-Irish War and the disintegration of the revolutionary movement into internecine war were inevitably reflected in a literature of disillusionment. This can be sharply discerned in the journalism of O'Duffy's admirer P. S. O'Hegarty, notably his short-lived pro-Treaty periodical called the *Separatist* in 1922.[14] Here O'Hegarty argued that the very fact of agreeing to a truce and to negotiations with the British presupposed some sort of continuing association with the Empire, which could be amended into a more separatist form if 'both of the war parties' in the Dáil stood aside and made room for a new generation. Given the extreme youth of so many of the revolutionary generation, this demand was unlikely to be met, but close observation of the Treaty Debates concentrated O'Hegarty's mind; and in 1924 he published a slashing commentary on the War of Independence called *The Victory of Sinn Féin*. O'Hegarty's admiration for the sacrificial gesture of 1916, and the sweeping victory of 1918, was more or less unabated, though he had felt some ambivalence at the time; he fully endorsed the policy of withdrawal from the institutions of the British state and applauded the discipline, imagination and radicalism of the reborn Sinn Féin movement from 1917. But, in his opinion, the 'bloodshed, treachery and sickening hypocrisy of the last two years [1922–4]' had corrupted this magnificent challenge.

Much more controversially, he declared that the 'moral collapse' had been instigated by the preceding Anglo-Irish War. His account was markedly at variance with the 'four glorious years' theme already well entrenched in contemporary commentary.

> The first shootings stirred and shocked the public conscience tremendously; but as they became more common, as the British failed completely to bring anybody to book for them, and as the shooting evolved until it became a guerrilla war, the public conscience grew to accept it as the natural order of things ... The eventual result of that was a complete moral collapse here. When it was open to any Volunteer Commandant to order the shooting of any civilian, and to cover himself with the laconic legend 'Spy' on the dead man's breast, personal security vanished and no man's life was safe. And when it was possible for the same Commandant to steal goods and legalize it by calling it 'commandeering', and to burn and destroy goods and legalize that by saying they were Belfast or English goods, social security vanished. With the vanishing of reason and principle and morality we became a mob, and a mob we remained.[15]

In line with the ideas floated in the *Separatist*, O'Hegarty's preferred alternative would have been a strict adherence to pacific principles, after the sacrificial violence of 1916 – which he believed, not very convincingly, would have won the day in the end. More interesting – and, in its way, just as subversive – was his declared belief that both the first and second Dáils were 'a collection of mediocrities in the grip of a machine', voting as instructed by de Valera, Griffith and Collins, and appointing meaningless yes-men as ministers. 'The same principles have since been followed, with the result that the average level of ability and intelligence in the present Dáil is appallingly low, much lower than it was in the Irish Parliamentary Party.'[16] *Lèse-majesté* could hardly have been taken further.

O'Hegarty began to write his polemic in June 1923 (though it incorporated material lifted directly from the *Separatist* some time before). It is unsurprising that much of his venom is directed at de Valera, for precipitating a civil war in the interests of his own overweening ambition and self-regard. Many felt the same. 'He [O'Hegarty] overshoots the mark towards the end,' McCartan thought, 'but I agree with AE [in the *Irish Statesman*]. It is the kind of stuff we need at present.'[17] More controversial was the savage misogyny whereby O'Hegarty blamed the women members of the Dáil ('The Furies') for a bitter destructiveness and endorsement of violence, which he located squarely in the 'hysteria' of feminine nature. This lends his polemic a reactionary tinge, and a hysteria of its own, which undercuts the general critique and has been much commented upon. O'Hegarty blamed women for many things: he thought Erskine Childers had been literally driven mad by his wife, and that Ascendancy converts to nationalism such as Childers and Barton were afflicted with 'feminine' personalities – 'anarchistical and selfish'.[18] These unreconstructed views sit oddly with his own history of religious agnosticism, intellectual sophistication (he was already building up one of the great libraries of modern Irish literature) and socially advanced beliefs. The personal tone of his self-flagellating peroration is nonetheless striking:

> We devised certain 'bloody instructions' to use against the British. We adopted political assassination as a principle; we devised the ambush; we encouraged women to forget their sex and play at gunmen; we turned the whole thoughts and passions of a generation upon blood and revenge and death; we placed gunmen, mostly half-educated and

totally inexperienced, as dictators with powers of life and death over large areas. We derided the Moral Law and said there was no law but the law of force. And the Moral Law answered us. Every devilish thing we did against the British went its full circle and then boomeranged and smote us ten-fold; and the cumulative effect of the whole of it was a general moral weakening and a general degradation and a general cynicism and disbelief in either virtue or decency, in goodness or uprightness or honesty ... And the shock of that plunge from the heights to the depths staggered the whole nation. The 'Island of Saints and Scholars' is burst, like Humpty Dumpty, and we do not quite know yet what we are going to get in its place.[19]

This cannot have been welcome reading for many of O'Hegarty's comrades, but with some at least it struck a chord. His critique also expresses the frustration of a generation who had worked for an intellectual revolution and seen themselves supplanted by the values of the 'gunmen'. Their resentment may or may not have been logical – much of their rhetoric had, after all, preached the cleansing necessity of violence – but it was, in a sense, inevitable.

There are further indications that others were reassessing recent history, and reconsidering the outcome, notably in the pages of the *Irish Statesman* between 1923 and 1930. Too easily dismissed as the last redoubt of suspect Anglo-Irish liberalism, the paper financed by Horace Plunkett and edited by AE was nothing if not pluralist. The novelist Liam O'Flaherty fulminated in 1925 that 'in art, in literature, in architecture, in general culture we are submerged beneath the rotting mound of British traditions, traditions which have their spiders' legs in the columns of the *Irish Statesman*',[20] but – true to Russell's spirit of inclusive tolerance – this sulphurous view appeared in the pages of the journal itself. The leitmotif of the *Irish Statesman* was rigorous self-criticism, which met the national mood; more gloomily, for its short-lived Cork rival the *Irish Tribune*, 'the signal tone was disillusion',[21] though this may have reflected the view of its literary editor, the inevitable Daniel Corkery.

Until the *Statesman* folded in 1930 Russell attempted a more optimistic world-view, trying to believe that the violence which had traumatized Ireland was a passing illness contracted from abroad, rather than a native malady. 'What took place here was an infection from the high fever which in Europe existed ... our militarism was as definitely of epidemic character as that black influenza which a couple of years before swept over the world.'[22] But Russell's own reactions to the revolution were bewilderingly inconsistent, ranging from romantically endorsing rebel sacrifice to viewing the outcome with deep scepticism. His symposium-novel *The Interpreters* (1922), which attempted to analyse the varying strands constituting the revolutionary mentality, did not leave readers much the wiser, and nor did his habit of telling correspondents what they presumably wanted to hear.[23] His spate of poetic effusions and invocations after 1916 was checked by the traumas of the Civil War, and the articles he contributed to the *Irish Statesman* suggest a more considered analysis. This would change to deep disillusionment in the early 1930s, punctuated by denouncement of Catholic thought-control ('smug Catholic self-satisfaction with its own sanctity') and the 'half-crazy Gaeldom' endorsed by de Valera.[24]

IV

Not all Catholic journals were self-satisfied: the Jesuit periodical *Studies* was prone to carrying *Statesman*-like articles offering prognoses about the state of the new nation, such as a thoughtful piece from Russell in 1923 comparing recent revolutionary failures in Russia and Ireland. Lenin and Bukharin had to realize that 'intellect, science, administrative ability could not be improvised, being evolutionary products'; in the same way, the recent Irish revolution had happened too quickly to create true infrastructural change.

> Our spiritual, cultural and intellectual life has not changed for the better. If anything, it has retrograded. Nothing beautiful in the mind has found freer development. In so far as anything is done efficiently, it is done by administrators, educationists, officials and guiders of industry, who maintain, so far as permitted by circumstances, the habits engendered before the war for independence.[25]

As the Free State settled into conservative and introspective mode, and de Valera divested himself of his irreconcilable republican companions (who retained rights on the hallowed names of 'Sinn Féin' and 'the IRA'), an increasing number of old revolutionaries began to reassess the glorious years. Reflections of this appeared in another little journal, *Ireland Today*. Edited by an old republican cabal in the early 1930s, it was mordantly critical of both constitutional parties, as well as of the failed promises of the revolution. Contributors included Sean O'Faolain, Frank O'Connor, Bulmer Hobson and Peadar O'Donnell.[26] Desmond Ryan, son of the anarchically minded W. P. Ryan who had edited the *Irish Peasant* and fallen foul of the episcopacy many years before, had been sent by his father to St Enda's and subsequently taught there. Spellbound by Patrick Pearse, he had acted as one of his aides in the GPO, and published in the slipstream of 1916 several works breathlessly celebrating his inspirational hero, as well as romantic socialism. But emigration to England and a nervous breakdown changed Desmond's world-view and, like many others, his opinions hardened in the 1930s. In 1932 he published *The Invisible Army*, a lightly fictionalized treatment about the recent upheavals which has more in common with *The Wasted Island* than with Béaslaí's *Collins*. At the end of the book the hero looks on the ruins of Dublin, after years of pointless and mishandled violence on both sides:

> A thousand similar tragedies had been compressed into five years which history books would never mention or, at best, dismiss in a line: men taken from their beds and shot, struck down on hillsides or murdered in fields; women killed by stray or nonchalant bullets; children maddened or smothered in the womb; civilians mangled in the city ambushes; seeds of insanity or consumption sown in the internment camps – epics never to be told, of humble martyrdom already half-forgotten in the lengthening Truce.[27]

Ryan's copious writings about the revolution, which continued for decades, revolve around the figures of Pearse and Connolly. But his impressionist memoir *Remembering Sion: A Chronicle of Storm and Quiet* (1934) suddenly complicates his heroic view, and Pearse appears as someone with a Napoleon complex, glorifying war for its own sake, but hampered by the inexperience of 'a very respectable Dubliner who has never left his city or his family circle for very long'. The portrait, while still positive, admits that Pearse's character was in some ways fanatical, absurd and humourless, with 'a strain of goody-goodyness'.[28] The roll-call of writers whose disillusionment echoes Ryan's, brilliantly analysed by Frances Flanagan, is impressive: they might be extended to include Robert Lynd, Brinsley MacNamara, Michael Farrell, Darrell Figgis, Francis Stuart, Stephen McKenna, Seán O'Casey, Liam O'Flaherty, Sean O'Faolain and Frank O'Connor.[29]

The list incorporates people who had supported the Treaty, as well as those who had been disillusioned by it; and those who, like Eimar O'Duffy, felt and said that dominion status with partition was effectively on offer before the Anglo-Irish War had started, and might have been settled for then. Many of them had an awkward or hostile relationship with Catholicism – notably O'Casey, O'Faolain, Figgis, O'Duffy, O'Hegarty, O'Flaherty and Ryan. Such people were also passionate admirers of Joyce and particularly of *Ulysses*, whose appearance coincided with the inauguration of the Free State. Perhaps Joyce's achievement was an emblem of the kind of cultural innovation which they had hoped would follow their revolution, but which seemed singularly lacking in the new Ireland.

The acceptability of admitting disillusionment, and the disappearance of the social agendas subscribed to by many of the revolutionary generation before 1916, was first highlighted by the controversy over Seán O'Casey's plays of the early 1920s interrogating the events of the revolution – *The Shadow of a Gunman*, *Juno and the Paycock* and, above all, *The Plough and the Stars*, which convulsed Dublin in 1926. This dealt specifically and critically with the rhetoric of 1916, counterpointing self-deluding blood-sacrifice values with the actuality of impoverished lives, random violence and everyday hypocrisies. The Free State was increasingly puritanical: censorship of 'obscene' literature was already on the cards, and would be officially introduced in 1929. Thus the introduction of a prostitute on the Abbey stage was sure to attract protest, but the real shock-value of the play lay in the treatment of the Rising. Though Yeats made sure that the first performance was attended by politicians such as Ernest Blythe, Kevin O'Higgins and the Lord Chief Justice Hugh Kennedy (referred to loudly as 'bloody murderers' by one playgoer), this did not defuse the gathering explosion.

Those who protested violently included the widows and survivors of 1916, featuring Hanna Sheehy-Skeffington, Tom Clarke's widow Kathleen, Patrick Pearse's mother, Kevin Barry's sister and Dan Breen; several actors in the initial production also found it strong medicine (though Arthur Shields, who had actually fought in the Rising, played Lieutenant Langon with aplomb). The play was seen in part as traducing the ideals of 1916, and therefore as a reflection of the moral bankruptcy of the Free State, especially since the Abbey had been officially subsidized by the state from the preceding year: 'Up the Republic!' was one of the slogans shouted by the protesters. But the controversy also gave O'Casey the opportunity not only to hit at those who had – in his opinion – diverted the Citizen Army from social radicalism in 1913 to solipsistic nationalism in 1916, but also to attack the post-revolutionary dispensation that perpetuated an agreed lie about what had actually happened, creating a sterile cultural environment. In a public letter, he specifically targeted the cult of official commemoration. 'The people that go to football matches are just as much a part of Ireland as those who go to Bodenstown [the site of an annual pilgrimage to Wolfe Tone's grave], and it would be wise for the Republican party to recognize this fact, unless they are determined to make of Ireland the terrible place of a land fit only for heroes to live in.'[30]

V

Despite O'Casey's warning, as the revolution receded into history, its commemoration became part of the political landscape. Some survivors, however, were still capable of creating an awkward presence, and introducing unwelcome ghosts to the feast. That so many of them (or their relicts) deeply disapproved of the Cumann na nGaedheal government headed by William Cosgrave, and later (though to a lesser extent) that of de Valera's Fianna Fáil, made for difficulties from the beginning. Memorial sculptures and sepulchral monuments raised thorny questions of precedence and allegiance. Arthur Griffith's widow Maud was particularly hard to please, feeling – reasonably enough – that she had been left ill-provided for and unappreciated after her husband's sudden death in 1922. Though a state pension was eventually awarded her, she continued to fulminate about the misrepresentation of her husband until the end of her life. Other relicts felt similarly aggrieved. In 1924 all the relatives of the 1916 martyrs, except for the family of Michael Mallin, boycotted the government's 1916 celebration (and one of them complained later that he had not been invited). However, prominent irreconcilables such as Oscar Traynor and Mary Mac-Swiney were always ready to organize rival events. Fianna Fáil's political ascendancy from the early 1930s created a new situation, when – to the fury of Mulcahy and others – they cavalierly dropped hundreds of people from the established invitation lists for the commemoration ceremonies. Mulcahy excluded himself from the commemoration of the most successful military engagement of 1916, the attack on the RIC at Ashbourne, even though he had been its main architect – the difficulty here being the presence of his much-disliked brother-in-law and political opponent, Seán T. O'Kelly.[31]

Other official ceremonies of remembering (notably the installation of Oliver Sheppard's *Death of Cuchulain* statue at the GPO in 1935) faced criticism and boycotting by purist republicans such as Maud Gonne MacBride, as well as by their opponents on the pro-Treaty side. By the same token, veterans' organizations such as the Old IRA Men's Association were always ready to claim that the government was not awarding appropriate recognition to the makers of modern Ireland. In 1941 the twenty-fifth anniversary of the Rising was marked by the striking of medals, a large military parade and other symbols of patriotic confidence; but there was also a current of self-criticism, discernible in publications such as the *Bell*, founded in 1940 and edited by Sean O'Faolain.

A product of Cork's intellectual republican circles, where he had been much influenced by the nationalist views of the playwright–critic Daniel Corkery, O'Faolain – after a rebellious youth making bombs for the Irregulars – had kicked over the traces. International travel and a cosmopolitan education in the 1920s, along with a series of successful collections of short stories and banned novels, had placed him at a definite angle to the Irish universe, and invited the fury of republican ex-comrades. He exploited this vantage creatively for the rest of his life, in idiosyncratic biographies of national heroes (Hugh O'Neill,

Daniel O'Connell, Éamon de Valera, Constance Markievicz) as well as in fiction and criticism. He had been involved in the republican journal *Ireland Today* in the 1930s, but left in 1936 when its editor, Jim O'Donovan, accepted a story implicitly endorsing murders such as that of Admiral Boyle Somerville recently carried out by the IRA. O'Faolain sent O'Donovan – himself a consistent IRA supporter – a long letter which is a kind of testament to disillusionment, citing what he and his generation had wanted from the revolution: 'freedom from cant, freedom from lies, freedom from hypocrisy, freedom from fear, love of beauty, and a desire, above all, for a fullness of being in every man'. Instead of this *Ireland Today* was pandering to

> the old, sloppy, cant-ridden, sentimental, good-hearted, kindly, easy-going, formalist Irish mind . . . making a kind of hero out of the type of Irishman who has no norm, no position, is meandering around in his own yearning, sloppy heart . . . Don't you see the fellows who shot Somerville and [John] Egan are the mush who are reducing Irish life to imbecility? You know these chaps. I know them. We worked and fought with them. They'd plug you or me in two seconds in a moment of hysteria.[32]

Like Yeats and AE before him, O'Faolain set himself to examining and exposing the inheritance of violence, the limitations of intellectual life and the power of the Church in contemporary Ireland. But even O'Faolain trod gently where the question of the inheritance of 1916 was concerned, conscious that 'here, we know better than most how much a man's emotional bloodstream is made up of memories.'[33] Memory continued to be an awkward area of negotiation in the Free State, and subsequently in the Republic of Ireland – as the 26-county unit was designated in a unilateral declaration by a coalition government in 1948. Matters were, as usual, negotiated differently in Northern Ireland, where commemorations of 1916 were simply banned by the government, though there was some relaxation at the end of the 1940s.

Time did not heal everything, and memories were long. As the received history of the revolution calcified, some of those who had been most influential in the years up to 1916 found themselves progressively written out of history. Bulmer Hobson, encountered earlier in this book as an enthusiastic and charismatic young Quaker convert to republicanism, energetic IRB leader, founder of the Dungannon clubs, organizer of the Fianna, editor of *Irish Freedom* and author of *Defensive Warfare*, was not invited to the fortieth anniversary of the 1916 Rising in 1956, because 'he didn't take part in the fighting'.[34] Ten years later he was similarly absent from the half-centenary in 1966. Hobson's post-revolutionary life was spent first as a publisher with the Three Candles Press, and then as a civil servant – Deputy Director of Stamping in the Revenue Office. He also edited the beautifully printed official *Handbook* of the Free State ('the so-called Free State', as he referred to it in private), to the fury of the *Catholic Bulletin*, which violently asserted that Hobson was disqualified for such a task by his Protestant background.

These were not the only slings and arrows he suffered. He was never forgiven by former comrades for, back in his revolutionary days, allowing Redmond's nominees on to the Volunteers Provisional Committee, and above all for arguing against the Rising. Malicious rumours continued to circulate about his having been court-martialled by the IRB. In self-defence he tried to set the record straight by publishing a *Short History of the Irish Volunteers* in 1919, and depositing lengthy statements with the Bureau of Military History, but most of his energy in the 1930s went into writing a stream of intelligent but disregarded pamphlets and articles about national economic policy. In the same era he helped to set up the avant-garde Gate Theatre, a central institution of Dublin's modest counter-culture, recalling his efforts to bring radical drama to Ulster three eventful decades earlier. An unforgettable vignette recalls him standing outside the triumphalist window display of Rising memorabilia adorning Hodges Figgis Bookshop in 1966, nearly blind, his face pressed up close against the glass.[35] Exclusion (yet again) from the half-centenary commemorations helped to galvanize him into a final statement, and he published an autobiography in 1968, bringing together much of the memoir and commentary he had written in the wilderness years; but he remained the forgotten man of the revolution.

By then there was a distinct sense of predictability about celebrations of the past, and a sense too that modern life allowed little time for these rituals. 'The citizens of Dublin have become so used to seeing handfuls of old men marching behind the national flag,' complained an association of IRA veterans in 1962, 'that they no longer turn their heads to look at them, while the drivers of buses and cars can hoot them out of the way and break their ranks with indifference, if not contempt.'[36] By that date, many of the revolutionary generation were dead, and those that remained, very old. This did not stop some of them from having their say. 'I know more about the events both before and after the Rising than anyone now alive,' Kathleen Clarke told the Taoiseach, Seán Lemass, in 1965 (Lemass himself had been 'out' in 1916 but rarely made a major issue of it). Her particular point was that she was not only 'the only widow alive of the signatories of the 1916 Proclamation', but that her husband, Tom, should have been acknowledged as the President of the Platonic Republic thus declared. 'Sean MacDermot [sic] was always complaining to Tom that Pearse wanted everything. He was not satisfied with getting honours he may have earned but wanted to grab what was due to others ... Surely Pearse should have been satisfied with the honour of Commander-in-Chief when he knew as much about commanding as my dog ... I have remained silent in public for fifty years but the circumstances which first forced me to remain silent no longer exist and the matter is now one of history.'[37]

VI

By now the government had put in place official projects to record the memories of the revolutionary era. In 1947 the Bureau of Military History had been set up, with the object of collecting 'witness statements' from those involved in the events of 1913 to 1921, which they defined as 'the revolutionary period'. These testimonies were to be collated and stored, along with relevant 'contemporary documents', which were also canvassed.[38] The plan had originated in 1933, in Fianna Fáil's second year of office, and was initially suggested by the Minister for Education, Thomas Derrig. The project languished for a decade before being revived by a committee of professional historians. The idea appealed to Seán T. O'Kelly, now President of Ireland; cautious as ever, he stressed that the commission collecting the testaments would have to be chosen carefully to avoid 'the refusal of vital witnesses to collaborate with it'.[39] As it happened, several did. But the idea of accumulating records of supposedly straightforward personal experience, innocent of an interpretive gloss, took hold. This, it was held, would create a reliable narrative of what had really happened. The increasingly reactionary P. S. O'Hegarty was particularly scathing about 'our own social ideologists' constantly interpreting the Rising in the light of 'this or that post-insurrection ideology, and trying to prove that it was really about land nationalization or "a workers' republic" – that term being used in its current unsavoury, bloodstained and post-Lenin sense'.[40] O'Hegarty's opinions had returned to a more traditionalist nationalism than his splenetic analysis of the revolution in 1924, and his bestselling *History of Ireland under the Union* (1952) was a fairly straightforward account of national liberation, with some important personal testimony incorporated. From another angle, his old Cork comrade Liam de Róiste (still involved in Cork politics and a leading light in the Irish International Trading Corporation) shared some worries about what the Bureau might bring to the surface; he knew 'some seventy men' in Cork who had been involved in Easter Week 'and are not at all agreed as to the story that should be told'.[41]

Though several prominent historians served on the committee, including Robert Dudley Edwards, G. A. Hayes-McCoy, Denis Gwynn and T. W. Moody, the administration devolved to the Department of Defence rather than to the groves of academe. Investigators, usually army officers, contributed a good deal to the way oral evidence was recorded and shaped into 'witness statements'. Significantly, the cut-off date of July 1921 was firmly adhered to. Anything after the Truce was deemed too controversial. Neutrality remained an issue throughout, though the department insisted that no governmental influence was exercised on the nature of the evidence collected, and that 'nothing would be released to historians or to the public during the lifetime of any person who took part in the events.' (They were as good as their word, the records remaining inaccessible until 2003.)

The material accrued like a coral reef, despite the refusal of several prominent actors to co-operate. After a long cat-and-mouse game de Valera channelled his own version of events through his strict control of an elephantine official biography reverently written by Lord Long-ford and T. P. O'Neill; from his first years in public life he had shown an almost neurotic obsession with controlling the official version of events in which he had played a part. Others declined to co-operate on principle. Elizabeth Farrell, who had served in the GPO in 1916, turned down the opportunity because 'all governments since 1921 have betrayed the Republic.' Con Kearney, active in an IRA unit in Limerick, refused for more personal reasons. 'I remember those times with a feeling of aversion and self-disgust which increases as the years go by.'[42] From the other side, this feeling was echoed by Alfred Cope, a Dublin Castle official who had played an important though shad-owy part in peace negotiations back in 1921. He remembered it as 'the most discreditable [period] of your country's history', and any attempt to recapture it through memory could only be 'a travesty . . . it will simply perpetuate the long-standing hatred of England and continue the miserable work of self-seeking politicians who, for their own aggrandizement, have not permitted the Christian virtues of for-giveness and brotherhood to take its place. Ireland has too many histories; she deserves a rest.'[43]

Richard Mulcahy and Piaras Béaslaí also kept aloof, preferring to construct their own records. Nonetheless a hoard of material accumu-lated over the decade of the Bureau's activity (1,773 statements, adding up to about 36,000 pages of evidence, and 150,000 pages of associated documents), and vanished into the government's safekeep-ing. This indeterminate sequestration infuriated some historians (and some of those who would have liked their version of events made publicly available), but Richard Hayes, the Chairman of the Advisory Committee, took the firmly Olympian opinion that the public should be kept out. 'If every Seán and Séamus from Ballythis and Ballythat, who took major or minor or no part at all in the national movement from 1916 to 1921, has free access to the material it may result in local civil warfare in every second town and village in the country.'[44] When the statements became available no local civil wars broke out, though a certain amount of score-settling was clearly discernible. Above all, the evidence of everyday involvement in the revolution was richly enhanced. Some accounts were marred by overexacting detail and an implausible degree of total recall, but aspects of local history, family connections, female involvement, the position (and infiltration) of the police, and the potency of anti-British feeling were vividly illuminated, as were the actual events of the 1916 Rising, and the activity (or inactivity) of the provinces. Notably lengthy statements and associated document collections were contributed by Seán T. O'Kelly, Kevin O'Shiel, Seán MacEntee, Ernest Blythe, Helena Molony, Robert Barton and George Gavan Duffy; they clearly suggest that their donors wanted to leave a decisive autobiographical statement behind, but not to go public with it.[45]

A similar, but even more tactfully concealed, repository of memory concerned the Military Service Pensions Collection, which recorded claims of military activity (first up to the key date of July 1921, later extended to 1923). Starting in 1934, 280,000 files were accumulated, in conditions of strict confidence; the applications, buttressed by references from colleagues, suggest much about the straitened circumstances under which citizens of the Free State laboured, as well as presenting details about the history of military violence. Those who had fought in the Volunteers, and then the IRA, during the epic years continued to rail against the new state for not delivering what they had fought for, and for treating them with less than appropriate respect. This feeling lay behind the abortive army mutiny of 1924, as well as the short-lived but briefly potent Blueshirt movement of the early 1930s. Old IRA organizations continued to express disillusionment and frustration, and their national conventions consistently denounced governments for victimizing them, truckling to 'foreign imperialism', allowing 'aliens' to control the industries of the country and perpetrating the continuing Anglicization of Irish society.[46]

Besides the world of public anniversaries and officially recorded memory, however, history continued to be debated by those who had made it, and memories continued to circle and conflict. The legendary IRA leader Ernie O'Malley, obsessed by recapturing the past, determined on his own equivalent of the Bureau of Military History. O'Malley had endured a traumatic career as an Irregular leader in the Civil War, near-fatal injuries after a murderous shoot-out in the Humphreys' house in Ailesbury Road in 1922, lengthy imprisonment and a punishing hunger-strike; travel on the Continent and a return to his medical studies at UCD did nothing to reconcile him to the new

Ireland. He instead went to the USA in 1928 as a fundraiser for de Valera's new newspaper, the *Irish Press*, and subsequently embarked on a restless life in intellectual and Bohemian American circles, marrying a rich sculptress and spending much time in New Mexico and the writers' retreat Yaddo in New York State. The results were two distinguished volumes of memoir, *On Another Man's Wound* (1936) and *The Singing Flame* (posthumously published in 1978), which stand with Desmond Ryan's *Remembering Sion* and the fictions of O'Malley's friends Liam O'Flaherty, Frank O'Connor and Sean O'Faolain as the most distinguished writing to come out of the revolution. (The content and style of O'Malley's work in fact owe much to these fictions, which inform and influence it.[47])

For O'Malley, reared in a prosperous middle-class family with British Army and mildly imperial affiliations, the Rising had come as a thunderclap, making him – in his biographer's words – 'a rebel as much against this family world as against British rule in Ireland'.[48] His vehement, questioning, intellectual temperament sustained him through a restless existence of pain and disillusionment; it also made him awkward and uncompromising. His return to Ireland in 1935 with the prospect of a military service pension was shortly followed by the publication, to considerable acclaim, of *On Another Man's Wound*. But by 1948 O'Malley's life of art-collecting, writing and farming in County Mayo had begun to pall, his marriage was in trouble, and he set out to reclaim history. For the next six years he criss-crossed Ireland in his old Ford, driving up boreens and searching out old companions in order to record, and in a sense to relive, the glory days of the revolution. Estranged from his wife, in constant pain from badly healed wounds, O'Malley spent the late 1940s and early 1950s transcribing his old comrades' memories of the revolution into a huge series of notebooks.[49] The 500-odd interviews, intended to construct a military history of the revolution, survive, largely unedited: the memories recorded therein suggest a less sanitized and more embittered memory of revolutionary violence than those in the Bureau of Military History. Violence, expropriation, intimidation, random killings and enduring resentment can be inferred through many of the recollections he recorded.('Sandy Nagle should never have been shot; he was a harmless ould devil.'[50])

O'Malley also tried to leave his imprint on the historical interpretation of his times by recording a series of talks for Irish radio – as did
Seán T. O'Kelly and several other contemporaries determined to enter
their mark on the historical record. (O'Malley also left his imprint on
the construction of a received idea of Ireland in another and more
exotic way – by acting as adviser to the film director John Ford during
the shooting on location of *The Quiet Man*.) Before his death in 1957,
aged only fifty-nine, O'Malley was a familiar figure in Dublin's
National Library, wearing an ancient duffel coat, ragged jersey and
tweed trousers, filling copious notebooks with material about the
events of 1916–1923 compiled from newspaper files.[51] But his contribution to his generation's history lies in his exalted, if unreliable,
memoirs, and in his attempts to record the voices of his comrades in
order to re-create the epic days of a simpler time. 'How does one reconstruct a spiritual state of mind?' O'Malley asks himself at the outset of
On Another Man's Wound. The process of reconstruction reflected the
fact that the spiritual state of mind had evaporated; recaptured neither
in the intellectual circles he frequented around the *Bell* and Jack Yeats's
studio, nor in the crude and naive memoirs by contemporaries like
Dan Breen, Tom Barry or Liam Deasy. O'Malley's own books reflect a
life which he himself described as 'broken', and an inability to fit into
the world the ex-revolutionaries had made. Facing death, he first left
instructions to be buried upright, facing eastwards towards his enemies
the British, but added a coda: 'in fact they are no longer my enemies.
Each man finds his enemy within himself.'[52]

VII

O'Malley haunted de Valera's Ireland like a living ghost. Some of
those who had actually died continued an oddly active afterlife –
notably Roger Casement, whose life generated far more comment
than that of any other 1916 martyr. In part this was because of Casement's high-profile career as a campaigner for human rights in the
Congo and Amazon basins, and the drama of his conversion from
imperialism to nationalism; his good looks, charisma and title all
added to the glamour. (Rather than a consular official from an

insecure and dysfunctional middle-class Ulster background, he was generally portrayed as an aristocratic knight-errant.) The circumstances of his return to Ireland and capture, the campaign for a reprieve and the bravery with which he met his terrible death by the hangman's noose all added to the mystique. But, above all, the enduring obsession with Casement's life was related to his sexual reputation. The diaries recording his homosexual adventures, and the unprincipled use made of them by the British government, ensured an extraordinary afterlife, the subject of countless books, articles, plays and novels, which continue to appear. And from the moment of his execution, those who knew Casement and had loved or been dazzled by him set themselves to guarding – or rehabilitating – his memory.

Most of his old revolutionary comrades, such as Bulmer Hobson, could not credit that the sexual diaries were genuine; outraged by the suggestion that Casement might have been homosexual, Hobson determined to write a book about him, but never did. Instead he supported the enterprise of William Maloney, a Scot of Irish descent who, after a traumatic record in the First World War, had emigrated to America, married money and become a prominent figure in Irish-American republican circles.[53] *The Forged Casement Diaries* was published in 1936 and presented the case that the 'Black Diaries' were actually constructed by interpolations from diaries kept by one of Casement's immoral antagonists in Peru, Armando Normand, known for his depraved exploitation of natives. (Besides the fact that Normand's depredations were heterosexual, this ingenious theory hardly squares with the actual nature of Casement's diary entries – yearning, sentimental, affectionate, full of regretful accounts of unsuccessful cruising as well as consummated encounters.) Others who knew Casement were unconvinced by this theory. John Devoy, who disliked him (and thought Maloney was a British spy), had been in little doubt that Casement was 'an Oscar Wilde',[54] and Patrick McCartan reported that the dead hero's devoted cousin Gertrude Parry had implied to him that the diaries might be genuine. McCartan himself thought it hardly mattered: 'If I were her I'd let them do their worst even though I knew the diary stuff were true. We know all about Oscar Wilde but who thinks now of his sins?'[55]

Opinion in the Free State took a less breezy view, though one of the

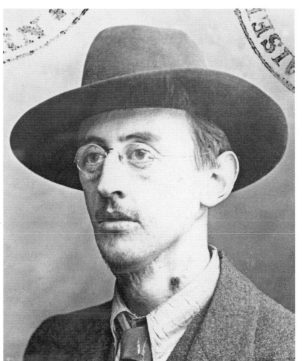

18. Joseph Mary Plunkett, showing signs of a recent operation on the tubercular glands in his neck.

19. A snapshot of Tom Clarke outside his celebrated shop, with the proprietor's name in Irish, and a hoarding announcing that he stocks *Irish Freedom* (as well as *Tit-Bits*).

20. Patrick Pearse (*on the far right, back row, in hat*) at a Gaelic League event in Omeath, County Louth. Beside him (*left to right*) are Mary Hayden, Dora Sheridan and Ned Sheridan; (*front row*) Willie Pearse, Eibhlín Nicholls, Harry Clifton, and a Mr and Mrs Geohegan.

21. St Enda's boys being drilled, probably by Con Colbert, dressed in kilts.

22. Volunteers transport their German rifles back from Howth by bicycle, July 1914.

23. Thomas MacDonagh.

24. Piaras Béaslaí.

25. Roger Casement (*second from left*), looking old and weary, on the German submarine that took him back to Ireland in April 1916. His companions are (*left to right*) Captain Robert Monteith, Lieutenant Walter, Julian Beverly (also known as Bailey) and Captain Raimund Weisbach.

26. The ruins of Mary Kate Ryan's old haunt, the DBC café in Sackville Street, after Easter 1916.

27. Dáil Éireann meets
in the Mansion House,
Dublin, in 1921.

28. Richard Mulcahy in
the uniform of the Irish
Republican Army,
painted in 1921 by his
fellow revolutionary
Patrick Tuohy.

29. Four of the Ryan siblings in 1916: (*left to right*) Min (later Mulcahy), Mary Kate (later O'Kelly), James and Phyllis (later O'Kelly).

30. At the double wedding of Agnes Ryan to Denis McCullough and Chris Ryan to Michael O'Malley, Tomcoole, August 1916. The chauffeur had just been dismissed from White's Hotel, Wexford, for republican activities, so was much approved of by the brides' family.

31. The body of Terence MacSwiney lies in state in Southwark Cathedral,
attended by the Carmelite Father Dominic O'Connor.

32. Muriel MacSwiney
on an American
publicity tour, 1922.

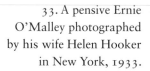

33. A pensive Ernie
O'Malley photographed
by his wife Helen Hooker
in New York, 1933.

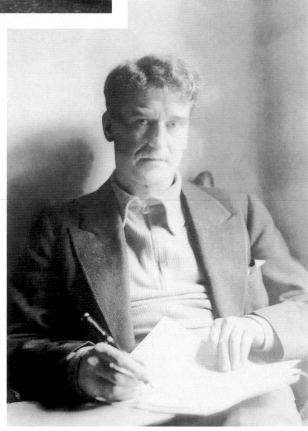

more intriguing statements locked away in the Bureau of Military History recorded Casement's writing an apology 'for any scandal he had given' before his last-minute reception into the Catholic Church – and then tearing it up. Another witness statement, from his unsuccessful defence lawyer, asserted that Casement himself had brought up the issue of his diaries, claiming their subject-matter 'was inseparable from the manifestation of distinguished genius'.[56] But when a nephew of Casement's friend F. J. Bigger suggested that his uncle had found and destroyed evidence that fully corroborated Casement's secret life, the outraged reaction of McCartan, Maloney and their friends was to consider threatening his life by setting some old IRA comrades on to him. The overwhelming consensus among Irish nationalists was that the legend of the Black Diaries represented the British establishment's perfidious attempt to traduce the memory of a great hero; W. B. Yeats, while privately believing 'if Casement were homo-sexual, what matter?', fixed the forgery theory in a popular ballad-poem after Maloney's publication, and the die was cast for decades. Casement's death was seen as a double martyrdom. When his bones were returned for solemn reinterment at Glasnevin in 1965, a rumour circulated that his body was miraculously undecayed.[57] It would take the slow release of transcripts and facsimiles of the immensely copious diaries, detailed analysis by graphologists, a series of thoughtful biographies and, above all, the dawning of a more liberal and balanced attitude in Ireland to sexual orientation before Casement in all his complexity could be welcomed into the pantheon of Irish history.

Those who died during the Troubles, or shortly afterwards, came nearest to retaining their illusions, as well as a legendary aura. In July 1927 another charismatic revolutionary had died, aged fifty-nine and worn out by campaigning, in the public ward of Sir Patrick Dun's Hospital. Constance Markievicz had graduated from the well-known Dublin 'character' of pre-revolution days to iconic status; imprisoned for her militaristic part in the Rising, she had returned to a royal welcome in Dublin and been elected as one of the very few women in the Dáil, serving briefly as Minister for Labour. Violently opposed to the Treaty, she had become marginalized from the post-revolutionary dispensation, though her theatrical style and imperious manner kept her a familiar figure on platform politics. She played a prominent part on the Rathmines and Rathgar Urban District Council, and shortly before her death was elected a TD for the new Fianna Fáil Party. The astonishing trajectory of her life remained radical, feminist and socialist to the end. She spent many of her last years in an attempt to reconcile Connollyite socialism with Catholic doctrine, and also returned to writing plays for the Republican Players Dramatic Society – another echo of earlier times. It seemed to Mary Colum, who had known her in her prime, that 'her former violent self was reduced to something burnt out ... haggard and old, dressed in ancient demoded clothes.'[58] The last play she wrote was about the revolution; it was called *Broken Dreams*.

The vast attendance at Markievicz's funeral provided one of the great public spectacles of Dublin life in the era. Her death also provoked her old friend and enemy W. B. Yeats to a powerfully affecting elegy, recalling Constance and her sister Eva, who had died a year before, after an equally radical career in feminist and socialist causes. The essentially reactionary message of the poem – that both women sacrificed their beauty to sterile opinions and political conspiracy 'among the ignorant' – would not have pleased its subjects. But the final invocation of their ghosts, with its mysterious closing image of an inferno devouring history, suggests the regret inseparable from lives lived at full revolutionary tilt and ending too soon.

> Dear shadows, now you know it all,
> All the folly of a fight
> With a common wrong or right.
> The innocent and the beautiful
> Have no enemy but time;
> Arise and bid me strike a match
> And strike another till time catch;
> Should the conflagration climb,
> Run till all the sages know.
> We the great gazebo built,
> They convicted us of guilt;
> Bid me strike a match and blow.

Other living ghosts continued to flit around post-revolutionary Dublin. Grace Gifford Plunkett lived an impoverished life, supporting herself by contributing cartoons to republican publications in the 1920s and working for advertising agencies. She rented a series of small flats around O'Connell Street, ate her meals in cinema restaurants, and socialized with actors and writers. Her finances were eased by a state pension in 1932, and the outcome of her threatened litigation against her unwelcoming in-laws. She occasionally appeared on a commemorative political platform, but generally withdrew from public activity, dying in 1955. Her sister Muriel, the widow of Thomas MacDonagh, had met a mysterious death by drowning long before; another Gifford girl, Sydney, sustained a journalistic life as 'John Brennan', and eventually wrote her own lively memoir of a revolutionary youth.

Hanna Sheehy-Skeffington, another radical woman marked by a tragic death in 1916, remained a central figure in Dublin's left-wing circles through the post-revolutionary decades. She lived conveniently close to companions such as Kathleen Lynn and Madeleine ffrench-Mullen in Belgrave Road, Rathmines, home to so many middle-class revolutionaries, where her landlady was, inevitably, Countess Plunkett. Thanks to the proximity of other old comrades such as Robert Brennan and his wife, the area was known as 'Rebel Road'. Hanna retained her feminist and egalitarian beliefs, and still expressed them with the acid humour characteristic of the *Irish Citizen*, which she kept going into the 1920s. Like many of her friends she opposed the Treaty but was disillusioned by Sinn Féin's failure to advance women in politics, reducing them once more to camp followers. With Jennie Wyse Power, Kathleen Clarke and other survivors, she played a prominent part in local politics, as a member of Dublin Corporation; Clarke would become Dublin's first woman Lord Mayor. Hanna's campaigning against the Treaty in the USA, and her activity as an envoy to the League of Nations, kept her in the public eye, but as the Free State gained credence she was marginalized more and more. Along with other irreconcilables, such as Maud Gonne, Dorothy Macardle and Grace Plunkett, she formed an informal group who met to commune about the iniquities of the new order. They called themselves, with a heavy irony, 'The Optimists'.[59]

Increasingly disillusioned with nationalist politics after de Valera entered the Dáil, Hanna remained absorbed in labour and feminist causes; Ireland, she told the Women's International League for Peace and Freedom in 1926, was 'the worst example in the world today of a victim of imperialistic capitalism or of economic imperialism'. 'What a time we live in!' she lamented to a feminist friend a few years later.

> Here we are rapidly becoming a Catholic statelet under Rome's grip – censorship and the like, with a very narrow provincial outlook, plus a self-satisfied smugness. Result of a failure in revolution really. I have no belief in de Valera. Well meaning, of course, better than Cosgrave, but really essentially conservative and church-bound, anti-feminist, bourgeois and the rest. A sort of professor-type like Wilson and enamoured of phrases and abstractions.[60]

She continued to teach, to write for the republican paper *An Phoblacht* and to look for enlightenment from Soviet Russia, which she visited with high hopes in 1930. She adhered to her principles and her radicalism, standing out against the governing consensus by presenting her son Owen and his new wife with a copy of Marie Stopes's book on contraception, and dying 'an unrepentant pagan' in 1946. But she spoke a language of radicalism which had died away around her, and would not be rediscovered for some decades.

Hanna's friend Rosamond Jacob, with whom she had smoked cigarettes and discussed sex in long-ago Edwardian Dublin, remained equally uncompromising. In 1919, with her mother's death, she finally succeeded in moving from a genteel life on the sidelines in Waterford to the sisterhood of Dublin's Bohemia, living in a series of central flats with women friends before usually falling out with them, and embarking on an unhappy love-affair with the radical republican Frank Ryan, recorded in her copious diaries. Arrest and imprisonment in 1923 fulfilled her taste for drama, as did her secret and rather tortured sexual affair with Ryan, compounded of guilt on his part and frustration on hers. Twelve years younger than her, he refused to acknowledge their liaison in public, preferring to turn up drunk at her flat late at night or meet her for an uncomfortable tryst in the garage below. Eventually Ryan, often on the run from government forces, went off to fight on the republican side in Spain, and went from there – inconsistently – to Nazi Germany, where he died in 1944.

Like Hanna, Rosamond turned to internationalist and feminist causes, and despaired of Irish radicalism. Though her nationalism remained more sentimental and backward-looking than Hanna's, she continued to be plain-spoken, abrupt, introspective, and prone to blurting out unwelcome truths to unreceptive people. After adhering closely to Sinn Féin in the 1920s, and initially supporting Fianna Fáil, she became disillusioned with de Valera; his devotee Dorothy Mac-ardle pleased her by confiding that though 'he had the finest character she knew, she always felt half its capabilities were smothered & kept from functioning by being a Catholic.' The constitution he intro-duced in 1937 did not surprise Rosamond, enshrining what she saw as 'the Catholic dislike of liberty for anyone'.[61] From the 1930s her political energies were directed towards the Irish Friends of Soviet Russia, the Republican Congress, internationalist and pacifist organi-zations, the White Cross and private acts of philanthropy for the forgotten relicts of long-dead revolutionary comrades. Unsurprisingly, she went through a period of Freudian analysis; this was replaced by a later fling with psychic experiences and séances, though her natural scepticism tended to reassert itself. Her struggles to publish intro-spective and didactic fiction continued all her life, as did her preoccupation with 1798; she saw her novel about Matilda Tone, *The Rebel's Wife*, in print before she died, but had to pay for it herself. A lonely and uncompromising old age was ended when she was knocked down crossing a road in 1960.

Rosamond, unlike most of her Republican Congress friends (such as Ryan, Seán Russell and Jim O'Donovan, editor of *Ireland Today*), did not support Hitler as Britain's enemy. Nor did she embrace com-munism and repudiate nationalism as energetically as Muriel MacSwiney, whose erratic life took her from Ireland to Weimar Berlin and then Paris. There was a brief period immediately after her hus-band's death as poster-girl for the republican cause; Muriel was described on her first American tour as a docile, waif-like widow, but came into her own on a second visit. 'Agnostic, foe of Catholicism, pacifist,' in the nervous view of the *Washington Post*, 'though she mentions the deaths of Arthur Griffith and Michael Collins in the calm way one would speak of two pawns of an opposing chess-player swept from the board, and withal a devout believer in Irish autonomy at whatever cost – such is the Muriel MacSwiney of 1922.'[62]

In that year, she officially renounced the Catholic Church, which was 'always on the side of British imperialism'.[63] This was part of a comprehensive rejection of the Irish pieties so fervently treasured by her late husband, though she always revered his memory. Muriel accordingly became alienated from many old comrades, above all from her sisters-in-law Mary and Annie MacSwiney, who had never approved of her. In 1937 Mary explicitly forbade one of her brother's prospective biographers to correspond with Muriel. 'She is not normal and her views on all that concerns Ireland are warped and distorted.'[64] Máire, her daughter by Terence, was taken from Germany by her aunts to live with them in Ireland, an event which Muriel saw as a 'kidnap', and to which she never reconciled herself – though Máire later testified that she had arranged the escape on her own initiative, longing for a stable life.[65] They never spoke again, though Máire once glimpsed her mother reading in the National Library, and on another occasion heard her speaking in her 'beautiful' Oxford-accented English at a neighbouring table in Bewley's Café. They did not acknowledge each other. Muriel lived in Paris and London, continuing to pursue radical causes, firing off long and often manic salvoes against Irish conservatism and the 'Holy Roman Capitalist Church' all her life. Máire, by contrast, grew up happily, by her own account, in the bosom of devout republican nationalism, and married the son of another republican hero, Cathal Brugha.

The post-revolutionary lives of several other women who had played a powerful part in the Irish radical world before 1916 were equally frustrated. Alice Milligan, pioneer journalist and dramatic impresario, suffered through her Northern connections in the War of Independence; she and her brother (an alcoholic ex-British Army officer) were driven out of their Dublin flat under threats from the IRA in 1921, and she lived out the rest of her long life unhappily in Northern Ireland, caring for relatives, and always in need of money. During the revolutionary period she continued to write poems, in a florid Victorian mode which looked increasingly archaic; publication proved more and more difficult, and she took refuge in various forms of psychic activity, convinced that her gift for divination would help Ireland to evade Partition. But Milligan remained marooned across the new Border in an unsympathetic family environment, making odd forays to friends in Dublin, and more or less forgotten by the inheritors of the Irish revolution – with the exception of the award of an honorary degree from the National University of Ireland in 1941. She died in 1953, aged eighty-seven.

Other old revolutionaries, at odds with the new state, were equally restless. In 1925 Pat McCartan found himself between two stools: 'to the Free Staters I am a republican and to the "Republicans" I am a Free Stater. But to myself I am neither.' Two years later he assured Maloney: 'you'll soon hear a demand for the English to come back. Hundreds are wishing it & saying so privately.'[66] McCartan tried emigration to the USA and a medical practice there, but returned to a career in Ireland and the fulfilment of a late marriage. His life as a revolutionary had left him with a permanent sense of rootlessness. 'I was quite happy in the mountains of Tyrone,' he reflected in 1926, 'and would probably have married some publican's daughter who had been a few years in a convent and could scream Songs of Araby or some atrocity but the lights of the Great White Way or the things which they stand for separated me from the life of a flourishing vegetable.' His secret mission to America in 1917 had changed him for life, 'though I did not realize it until after my return in 1921. The houses and streets in the local town looked very cold and deserted on Christmas Eve and those in the village worse. My mind was made up. It was Dublin or New York.'[67] Like many, his horizons had been broadened, though his extraordinary youth of republican conspiracy in the Dungannon clubs, and his negotiations with Russian Bolsheviks in 1921, receded into the past. McCartan relived it by writing a memoir of his time in the USA with de Valera and keeping up his contacts with old friends through a lively and disputatious correspondence. He was also influential in extracting money from rich Irish-American sympathizers for W. B. Yeats's Irish Academy of Letters (partly intended as a refuge for writers unfriendly to the regime), and helped to raise a subscription for the poet's old age in 1938.[68] McCartan ran for President of Ireland as an independent republican candidate in 1945, losing to the ubiquitous Seán T. O'Kelly; a few years later he was a founding member of the new party Clann na Poblachta.[69] Up to his death in 1963, in any discussion of 1916, McCartan stoutly defended his old Dungannon Club associates Bulmer Hobson and Denis McCullough, and others whose revolutionary careers had faded out from the public version of the national past. In some cases their own memories were locked up in the Bureau of Military History; for others, notably that of McCullough's brother-in-law and close friend Richard Mulcahy, memory would be preserved in less official forms.

From the early 1920s Mulcahy, now General Mulcahy, was living with his wife, Min, and their growing family in Lissenfield, a rambling eighteenth-century house which they rented from the new government; preserved within its fields, it remained something of a time-capsule on the suburban Rathmines Road. Mulcahy's political career as Minister for Defence lurched off-track after the attempted army mutiny of 1924, which enabled O'Higgins to force his resignation, along with that of the entire Army Council. McCartan characteristically thought his friend 'should have made himself Dictator instead of obeying the little clique of West Britons in his Cabinet', but this was never Mulcahy's style.[70] For opponents of the Treaty, Mulcahy would always carry the opprobrium of the executions of seventy-seven republicans in the Civil War. During the 1920s his attitude to commemorative events was notably ambivalent, for reasons that were personal as much as political, and he was uncomfortable with more sophisticated colleagues (when Mulcahy said that O'Higgins 'suffers from manners', he did not mean it as a compliment).[71] He returned briefly to office as Minister for Local Government in 1927, but was soon relegated (though he re-emerged as Minister for Education in the coalition governments in the late 1940s). During de Valera's long ascendancy from 1932, Mulcahy devoted himself to building up the opposition party, Fine Gael, of which he was a chief architect.

As the Mulcahys' star fell, that of their anti-Treaty relatives rose. Seán T. O'Kelly, always close to de Valera, emerged as an *éminence grise* in Fianna Fáil and an inevitable member of its governments. Preoccupied by matters such as the need for public prayers in the Dáil, he contributed decisively to the pietistic nature of public life, and would eventually succeed Douglas Hyde as President of Ireland. From 1919 he had spent most of his time representing the revolutionary government on the Continent; his avoidance of the actual fighting was noted sarcastically by the Mulcahys and McCulloughs, who believed that O'Kelly had persuaded Mary Kate, Phyllis and James

Ryan to oppose the Treaty after their initial support. The terrible rupture of the Split was not easily healed; Phyllis's high-handed command that Min leave her husband was not forgotten, and nor was Mary Kate's severance from her Treatyite sisters. Phyllis shared the O'Kelly home on Stephen's Green, and there was not much coming and going from there to her Mulcahy and McCullough sisters in Rathmines. But their formidable sister Jo, 'Sister Stan' at Loreto Convent, kept the peace between them, and the home farm of Tomcoole continued to be a focus of family life, even though their Wexford sister Nell remained the most implacably anti-Treaty sister of all. (During the Civil War she had been interned and gone on hunger-strike; despite family pleas, her brother-in-law Mulcahy had refused to accede to her demands.) Notwithstanding Nell's adulation of de Valera and passionate commitment to Fianna Fáil, political discussion was suspended on summer holidays in the square white farmhouse with the Gothic porch and monkey-puzzle tree, and the next generation grew up in an enduringly close cousinhood.

In the 1920s Mary Kate continued her academic career at UCD, and Seán T his peripatetic work for the nascent Fianna Fáil Party; they necessarily spent much time apart. In 1934 she died after a lengthy and lonely illness in a German nursing-home. Seán T subsequently married Phyllis, and as President and consort they would eventually live in the old Viceregal Lodge in Phoenix Park, rechristened Áras an Uachtaráin. By contrast, in Lissenfield, the Mulcahy family subsisted through the 1920s and 1930s without much money; Min maintained a kind of Tomcoole life by running an effective small farm there, with cows, pigs, dozens of domestic fowl and an orchard. Her husband was deeply committed to his work for Cumann na nGaedheal and subsequently Fine Gael; his children noted that he refused to talk of past politics, preferring to look to the present. ('Haven't we enough to do with the country in the state it is, without worrying about what happened in the past.'[72]) Nor did Min's and Agnes's children ever realize just how politically radicalized their mothers had been in their youth.

But, as time went on, provoked by what he saw as Fianna Fáil's deliberate attempt to take over the official memory of the revolution, Richard Mulcahy determined to build up his own archive of memory.

After retirement in 1961 he not only gave interviews to radio and television journalists, but also began to accumulate a large collection of tape-recorded and transcribed memories of the revolutionary era. Old friends and relations, such as Denis and Agnes McCullough and Michael Hayes, were summoned to Lissenfield for lengthy sessions of recollection and discussion, circling around recurrent questions. How did it all happen? When did the tipping-point come? How had their generation replaced the Home Rule compromise with a new, radical alternative? What had really happened in 1916? Why did the movement split? Others were less prepared for this interrogation of the past; it was in answer to such a summons that Bulmer Hobson declared that 'the phoenix of our youth has fluttered to earth such a miserable old hen I have no heart for it.' P. S. O'Hegarty similarly refused to associate himself with the false claims paraded by the pious and the opportunistic after the event. 'I have watched history being made in Ireland in the last twenty years,' O'Hegarty had written in 1922, 'and in the last six years I have seen things set down about the Insurrection of 1916 and its genesis, which I know to be untrue. But nobody will ever be able to overtake them, and they will go down as history. What we call history is largely man's imagination.'[73]

Others of the Irish revolutionary generation (unlike their Russian contemporaries) continued to enjoy the old-age luxury of sharing their disillusionment with each other. In this, like so much else, the generation of 1916 resembled the generation of 1914 elsewhere in Europe, profiled by Robert Wohl.[74] Seán T. O'Kelly compiled long accounts of his revolutionary experiences, incorporating many judgements on his comrades and ex-comrades, and broadcast them on Irish radio in the 1950s. After hearing a later talk of O'Kelly's in April 1965, Liam Ó Briain, who had been best man at Seán T's marriage to Mary Kate in 1919 and subsequently a pro-Treaty opponent, wrote in friendly remonstrance defending Arthur Griffith's record: 'I want to take out of your mind the fixed idea you have that A. G. degenerated, that he fell to pieces in that last year of his life and was unworthy of his own past and his own teaching; and try to get into your mind that he was the same A. G. he had always been.' But they agreed to argue about it over lunch in Jammet's celebrated restaurant.[75] By this stage Seán T had taken to making emollient public speeches hinting that the

Civil War could have been avoided.[76] In a similarly reflective and conciliatory mode, Liam de Róiste set to editing his youthful diaries in 1943, and was struck by how puritanical he had been when a young revolutionary in pre-1916 Cork. 'I have grown tolerant,' he reflected; 'the inconsistencies of men no longer trouble me, only stimulate a sense of humour.'[77]

A year later, in 1944, Mabel FitzGerald wrote once again to her old employer and admirer, George Bernard Shaw. Like the Mulcahys and McCulloughs, Desmond and Mabel FitzGerald had opted for the Treaty – in Mabel's case against her will. Desmond's ministerial career in Cumann na nGaedheal had not been a conspicuous success, and colleagues like Mulcahy considered him over-intellectual, precious and out of touch. In the 1930s he turned back to his first love, philosophy and the teachings of St Thomas Aquinas. Mabel remained more sceptical. 'I have, unfortunately, little conscious need of religion,' she wrote briskly to her husband's friend the Catholic philosopher Jacques Maritain. 'I have to make it a matter of a series of efforts.'[78] She had also left her revolutionary youth behind her, though her opinions remained as decisive as ever. 'The Mabel who tried to live like a peasant in Brittany and Kerry,' remarked a younger relative, 'as an older woman terrorized her daughters-in-law with inflexible standards re china and bone-handled knives.'[79] Mabel herself admitted to Shaw:

> I have changed my own views greatly since youth. About adult suffrage, for instance. I find the masses always wrong, they seem to stand for the worst in man. Certainly not for integrity, which I put first as the essential virtue in private and public life. Also I am convinced that education is necessary to the forming of views that are worthwhile at all, and I don't believe that the majority of people can take education. If poverty and dirt and disease could be abolished, and I hope they may be, the multitude would want more dog racing, more drink, more pictures, more tabloid views from the cheap press . . . Adult suffrage seems to have led only to the supremacy of the people without standards and values and of the half-baked educationally. Government and all control will soon be in the hands of the uneducated or the semi-educated . . . They already dominate everything here and you seem to be heading for the same situation in

England. And aren't they complacent! I don't believe that things are any
better in Russia either; the complacency is there all right.[80]

Shaw, receiving this late letter, must have vividly remembered the
'spoiled beauty' whom he had mocked, thirty eventful years before, as
an educated woman trying to be a peasant.

Mabel, like Bulmer Hobson, Denis McCullough, Alice Milligan
and many others, had come from Ulster in her idealistic youth,
inspired to cast in her lot with nationalist revolution, and to remind
the North of its republican heritage. But by now a unionist hegemony
in the north-east had been cemented by Partition, effectively accomplished in 1920 and tacitly acquiesced in both by the Free State and
by de Valera's successor regime. When the Boundary Commission in
1925 tamely accepted the status quo, Liam de Róiste recorded that
'"public opinion", in Cork at least, is not very perturbed one way or
the other . . . the bulk of the people have no strong convictions or feelings over this Boundary settlement. It does not enter into our lives in
the South.'[81] Even Patrick McCartan admitted to a persistent sense of
separateness: noting in 1925 that Denis McCullough still retained a
grádh, or affection, for people like Joseph Campbell, who had taken a
different side over the Treaty, he added that they all shared a sense of
being Northerners. 'We are a different race. We are nearer to Craig &
the Orangemen than to Cosgrave & his tame shoneens. We say what
we mean & mean what we say.'[82] What had actually become of the
sundered north-eastern counties remained one of the largely unspoken
failures of the revolutionary past, preserved in unsatisfactory stasis by
the fallout of the revolution in the 'South' and the evasions of memory. This was clearly seen by a young Irish historian in 1955:

> As long as our recent history is presented as a one-sided justification of
> the roles played by our leaders in 1922, so long will it be impossible to
> make it palatable to the children. When will all the survivors of the civil
> war – on both sides – be big enough to admit their failure of judgment?
> As long as they keep silent their followers are committed to justifying
> Fianna Fáil and Fine Gael in terms of mutual hate. Until it is clear to
> the meanest intelligence that one can be a good Irishman and disagree
> with Fianna Fáil or Fine Gael or even with the Rising of 1916, Irish
> unity will continue to be a vain hope.[83]

The mechanisms of public memory and amnesia continued to operate by keeping the two Irelands in mutual isolation, preserved by mutually exclusive views of history. The first steps towards breaking this down were to be taken, ten years later, by a 1916 veteran, the Taoiseach Seán Lemass, when he travelled to Belfast to meet Northern Ireland's premier, Terence O'Neill, in 1965. That process of rapprochement between unionist and nationalist traditions had been cherished, with varying degrees of realism, by many of the revolutionary generation. But it would be overtaken and swamped by the more atavistic forces unleashed on both sides, invoking the exclusivities of received history, and the sanctions of inherited violence.

Conclusion: Freedoms

At the twenty-fifth anniversary of the Easter Rising, the 81-year-old President of Ireland, Douglas Hyde, delivered an address to the nation – largely scripted by the Taoiseach, de Valera, and Michael McDunphy, soon to become Director of the Bureau of Military History. It began by invoking the idea of freedom. 'Up to twenty-five years ago we were a people without power in our own land. Twenty-five years ago, in Easter Week the chains that bound us began to be broken at last, and gradually they were thrown off, so that we here today are a free people.'[1] Hyde, de Valera and McDunphy would not have been aware of how closely the words echoed Redmond's long-ago speech at Wexford in 1915, proclaiming that 'we today of our generation are a free people', and tracing the incremental steps taken in that achievement; yet, even if they had recognized the echo, it would not have mattered to them. The revolutionaries and their inheritors had long ago repudiated the Home Rule definition of 'freedom' and the kind of national future envisaged by Redmond and his cohorts; their achievement had been to make it apparently irrelevant. The world had changed, and much had been forgotten or revised: the idea that the past contained alternative futures was not to be entertained.

Nonetheless, when witnessing or recalling the Irish revolution, the diaries and recollections of people such as Geraldine Plunkett, Rosamond Jacob, Mabel FitzGerald, Hanna Sheehy-Skeffington, Kevin O'Shiel and Muriel MacSwiney suggest a striking anomaly. These young people came from backgrounds of privilege but recalled living under a sense of national oppression – which hardly fitted the objective conditions of their lives. 'Freedom', however, has many meanings; and, as Madame Roland remarked on her way to the guillotine, many crimes are

committed in its name. It was axiomatic for the revolutionary generation that they were not 'free'. Many who fought in, for instance, James
Connolly's Citizen Army could have made the case that they were
enslaved in terms of economic power – but very few actually articulated this. It is extremely striking how seldom a sense of economic or
class grievance comes through the recollections recorded by the Bureau
of Military History. Far more frequent are the traditional nostrums of
Catholicism, historical victimhood, glorification of past struggles and
resentment of English dominance. These were also the building-blocks
of much constitutional-nationalist rhetoric. But what happened in the
twenty-five years before 1916 was that the IPP seemed to lose credibility, in terms of this rhetoric, as Home Rule within the Empire advanced
nearer, and a new generation appropriated the old battle-cries in the
name of new concepts of 'freedom': though freedom is exactly what
many of them seemed spectacularly to enjoy in their separate spheres
of existence.

For people obsessed with history, and reclaiming it, this could conveniently be ignored; and the preoccupation with history is what
united many of the disparate people whose lives and minds have been
surveyed in this book. From their very different backgrounds, Rosamond Jacob and Michael Hayes made pilgrimages to the Dublin scenes
of Edward FitzGerald's arrest or Emmet's execution; the profuse ver-
biage of serial romances in the *Shan Van Vocht* or pageant-scripts for
Inghinidhe na hÉireann went back to hallowed historical themes in the
national story; history lessons played a vital part in packing people
into Gaelic League summer-schools and night classes; the powerfully
mobilizing effect of the 1798 Centenary celebrations in 1898 recurs
constantly. Individual revolutionaries pictured themselves as doing
what their forefathers had done. The power of historical memory and
historical reiteration in nationalist rhetoric has a special significance in
this era. From the turn of the century, the Irish national struggle against
English oppression in the past had to be stressed, re-enacted, resorted
to more and more fervently – simply because the present was so different. By the turn of the twentieth century, English oppression manifested
itself in ways that were historical and cultural rather than economic or
political. Reforms in land tenure, taxation and local government had
transformed Irish society, and a solid rural bourgeoisie was firmly in

place. At least one ex-revolutionary, John Marcus O'Sullivan, admitted with relief in 1923 that this meant social revolution was never on the cards. 'It is well for us that the two revolutions, through which we have passed in the last half-century, were separate in time; that, in fact, the agrarian revolution was largely at an end before the struggle for national independence became fully acute. Had the two coincided, the outlook would indeed be menacing.'[2]

But the short-circuiting of agrarian agitation did not mean that other revolutionary tendencies were similarly muffled. By the turn of the century the policies put in place by the British government, and apparently to be continued by its Home Rule spin-off, would – in the minds of young idealists – impose a materialistic, Anglophone, unspiritual, provincial identity on the island as a whole: 'Anglicised, slavish and spineless', as Liam de Róiste bemoaned in his 1905 diary.[3] Later he reflected that he didn't care whether a free Ireland was a republic, a monarchy or a socialist state, 'so long as it is free from British rule'.[4] When Patrick McCartan was making his overtures to Bolshevik fellow revolutionaries in 1917, he received a letter from his comrade Séamus O'Doherty which more elaborately spelled out the same message.

> We cannot possibly, before the world, be put in the category of socialists as a nation but the socialist ideal is an ideal that makes for liberty for the individual and for the state and they are (the socialists) a force in every land that must and will be reasoned with . . . You go as a deputy from the nation and as you would and must speak for and defend the Orangemen of the North so you must speak for the socialists. The *elements* of the Nation don't weigh internationally. It is the *Nationalist* (the true nationalist voice) and that only must be heard . . . No matter what issue it raises, the demand of the people is for Freedom, that is why I crossed out the paragraph in your letter where you say that if a majority of the People decided against us we would submit. I don't of course believe that they would so decide but our convictions are not *conditional*. They are absolute.[5]

In one of his thoughtful essays on the recent upheavals written in the early 1920s, AE had surmised that the 'fundamental cause of trouble between Great Britain and Ireland', which had exploded into revolution, was not the historical record of exploitation and misgovernment so often instanced; it was 'the psychological factor . . . which made the Irish regard the State which inflicted such things upon them as a tyranny by aliens'.[6] This was no less the case when a more constructive style of government was embraced by the Liberal ethos of the early 1900s. Thus the revolutionary generation were, paradoxically, both empowered and alienated by their British rulers. One young revolutionary, telling the Bureau of Military History why he joined the Volunteers in 1914, expressed the feelings of many. 'The whole Irish people seemed to have become English and nationality seemed to have become a mere thread that was ready to break and plunge Ireland into an abyss of slavery.'[7]

This is close to the concept of 'actual slavery' invoked by Geraldine Plunkett, though it would not have meant the same thing to her family's army of domestic servants and urban tenants. But the dynamic power of nationalism trumped – as so often – a socio-economic analysis. In its pietistic aspects, it also trumped the secular, sceptical, pluralist instincts of the agnostics among the revolutionaries – as Rosamond Jacob continued to bewail in her diaries for decades, and as P. S. O'Hegarty and Bulmer Hobson found out in their subsequent lives as civil servants in de Valera's Ireland. Above all, the independent-minded women who had claimed autonomy and glimpsed new horizons in organizations such as Inghinidhe na hÉireann, various suffrage societies and, eventually, Cumann na mBan found their futures severely limited when the revolutionary wheel had turned. Some, like Louie Bennett, Rosamond Jacob, Kathleen Lynn and Mary MacSwiney, would continue their work in labour organizations or medicine or education, while never fully recognizing the state that had emerged from the Treaty and the Civil War. Others, like the Ryan sisters, would become central figures of a new Irish establishment. A very few, such as Muriel MacSwiney, would go on looking for revolutions elsewhere, all their lives.

Muriel's statement to the American Commission in 1920, quoted earlier, began 'My parents are not quite like myself.' The generation of 1916 can be seen as a self-conscious group of people, shaped by the circumstances of their time: Edwardian Ireland, with its odd mixture of social reforms, repressive tolerance, new ideas and an obsessive rediscovery of the past. Perhaps by 1912 the sense of a coming revolution, and a generation who conceived of themselves as bent on transformation, was established – even before the seismic events in Ulster and Europe that gave them their chance. For people like AE, the golden period of the revolutionary era was the decade from 1903 to 1913, when cultural enterprise and national revival went hand in hand – a period ended by the Ulster crisis and the wave of Volunteering. The actual fighting, particularly in the latter stages of the Anglo-Irish War and the Civil War, was often undertaken by people from a somewhat different background, owing allegiance to more straightforwardly Fenian and rural-agitation traditions. But the quiet revolution in the hearts and minds of young middle-class Irish people from the 1890s onwards had given them their chance. It is impossible not to speculate how different the new Free State would have been if it had enshrined more of the ideals, objectives, attitudes and eccentricities of the revolutionary generation – the educational ideas of Pearse, the organizational genius of MacDermott and Collins, the social egalitarianism of Connolly and Mellows, the cultural imagination of MacDonagh and Plunkett, the secularism of the Sheehy-Skeffingtons. Some of the survivors, as we have seen, were sharply conscious that the secular, anti-sectarian aspects of republicanism had given way to bigotry after 1916.

This kind of disillusionment commonly comes with age, but is perhaps inseparable from a post-revolutionary cast of mind. Writing a life of Constance Markievicz in 1934, Sean O'Faolain asked himself 'if revolutionary movements ever move towards defined ends, whether all such movements are not in the main movements of emotion rather than thought, movements arising out of a dissatisfaction with things as they are but without any clear or detailed notion as to what will produce satisfaction in the end'.[8] Writing about revolutionary idealism, Alexander Herzen remarked that 'the submission of the individual to society – to the people – to humanity – to the idea – is a continuation of human sacrifice … What the purpose of the sacrifice was, was never so much as asked.'[9] This thought is repeated in the closing stanzas of Yeats's poem on Easter 1916:

> Too long a sacrifice
> Can make a stone of the heart.
> O when may it suffice?
> That is Heaven's part, our part
> To murmur name upon name,

As a mother names her child
When sleep at last has come
On limbs that had run wild.
What is it but nightfall?
No, no, not night but death;
Was it needless death after all?
For England may keep faith
For all that is done and said.
We know their dream; enough
To know they dreamed and are dead;
And what if excess of love
Bewildered them till they died?
I write it out in a verse –
MacDonagh and MacBride
And Connolly and Pearse
Now and in time to be,
Wherever Green is worn,
Are changed, changed utterly:
A terrible beauty is born.

Maud Gonne, sharp for her purposes, spotted this note of doubt, and smartly attacked her old friend for expressing it. She argued that the poem was unworthy of its subject, since 'sacrifice has never yet turned a heart to stone', adding that revolutionaries such as Pearse and MacDonagh were not 'sterile fixed minds, each served Ireland, which was their share of the world . . . with varied faculties & vivid energy', creating spiritual beauty through material failure.[10] The argument has gone on from that day to this. But to 'know the dream' of the revolutionaries, it may help to strip back the layers of martyrology and posthumous rationalization, to get back before hindsight into that enclosed, self-referencing, hectic world where people lived before 1916, and to see how a generation developed, interacted and decided to make a revolution – which for many of them may not have been the revolution that they intended, or wanted.

Abbreviations

BMH	Bureau of Military History
CCA	Cork City and County Archives
MAI, BMH CD	Military Archives of Ireland, Bureau of Military History Contemporary Documents
NAI	National Archives of Ireland
NLI	National Library of Ireland
NYPL	New York Public Library
TCDA	Trinity College, Dublin, Archives
UCCA	University College, Cork, Archives
UCDA	UCD Archives

Notes

INTRODUCTION

1. F. S. L. Lyons, *Culture and Anarchy in Ireland 1890–1939* (Oxford, 1982), p. 177.
2. Some key works include Patrick Maume, *The Long Gestation: Irish Nationalist Life 1891–1918* (Dublin, 1999); Matthew Kelly, *The Fenian Ideal and Irish Nationalism 1882–1916* (Woodbridge, 2006); Paul Bew, *Ideology and the Irish Question: Ulster Unionism and Irish Nationalism 1912–1916* (Oxford, 1994); Michael Wheatley, *Nationalism and the Irish Party: Provincial Ireland 1910–1916* (Oxford, 2005); Fergus Campbell, *Land and Revolution: Nationalist Politics in the West of Ireland 1891–1921* (Oxford, 2005). The study of Irish feminism in the period has been brilliantly explored by Senia Pašeta, *Irish Nationalist Women 1900–1918* (Cambridge, 2013).
3. See, e.g., Krishan Kumar, 'Twentieth-Century Revolutions in Historical Perspective', in his *The Rise of Modern Society: Aspects of the Social and Political Development of the West* (Oxford, 1988), pp. 177–83. For more general discussion, Crane Brinton, *The Anatomy of Revolution* (London, 1953); Theda Skocpol, *States and Social Revolutions* (Cambridge, 1979). Also see J. Dunn, *Modern Revolutions: An Introduction to the Analysis of a Political Phenomenon* (Cambridge, 1972; revised edition 1989); and A. J. Groth (ed.), *Revolution and Revolutionary Change* (Aldershot, 1996).
4. Robert Gerwarth and Martin Conway, 'Revolution and Counter-revolution', in Donald Bloxham and Robert Gerwarth (eds.), *Political Violence in Twentieth-Century Europe* (Cambridge, 2011), pp. 140–75.
5. Lenin certainly reacted at once to the 1916 Rising, denying that it was an unrepresentative putsch and forecasting its importance as an early, if premature, threat to imperial power; he decided it had 'a hundred times more political significance than a blow of equal weight would have in

Asia or Africa'. V. I. Lenin, *British Labour and British Imperialism: A Compilation of Writings by Lenin on Britain* (London, 1969), pp. 164–8.

6. Lyons, *Culture and Anarchy*; and Tom Garvin, *Nationalist Revolutionaries in Ireland 1858–1928* (Oxford, 1987), a work of pioneering brilliance; and Pašeta, *Irish Nationalist Women*. This study is indebted to all three.

7. As the principals themselves sometimes implied: Belinsky accused Bakunin of being 'like a German, born mystical, idealist, romantic and will die like that, because you don't change your nature by throwing over philosophy'. Franco Venturi, *Roots of Revolution: A History of the Populist and Socialist Movements in Nineteenth-Century Russia*, translated from the Italian by Francis Haskell (London, 1960), p. 50. For the reflection on Chernyshevsky, below, see ibid., p. 145.

8. *Heralds of Revolution: Russian Students and the Mythologies of Radicalism* (Oxford, 1998).

9. The latest, and most authoritative, general treatment is Charles Townshend's magisterial *The Republic: The Fight for Irish Independence 1918–1923* (London, 2013).

10. See Fearghal McGarry, *Rebels: Voices from the Easter Rising* (Dublin, 2011), Chapter 1 and below, pp. 306–9, for the need for care with these life-stories.

11. Cf. *United Irishman*, 6 Jan. 1900, for a long letter from 'Clovis' invoking Mitchel, a coming war, and the need for 'a chosen one' and a guiding spirit.

12. Colin Reid, *The Lost Ireland of Stephen Gwynn: Irish Constitutional Nationalism and Cultural Politics 1864–1950* (Manchester, 2011), p. 9.

I FATHERS AND CHILDREN

1. Introduction to Clarke's *Glimpses of an Irish Felon's Prison Life*, quoted in Kieron Curtis, *P. S. O'Hegarty 1879–1955: Sinn Féin Fenian* (London, 2010), p. 21.

2. *Weekly Freeman's Journal*, 10 Oct. 1914, as quoted in Paul Bew, *Ideology and the Irish Question: Ulster Unionism and Irish Nationalism 1912–1916* (Oxford, 1994), p. 123.

3. The bicameral Irish parliament was not to have power over matters affecting the crown, peace and war, the army and navy, etc., though they would control the police after six years, and could also claim control over matters such as old-age pensions and insurance. There would still be a Lord-Lieutenant, with veto powers, and the imperial parliament retained amendment powers. Revenue, apart from the Post Office, was to be initially managed through the imperial Exchequer.

4. Clearly illustrated in Fearghal McGarry, *Rebels: Voices from the Easter Rising* (Dublin, 2011), Chapter 1.

5. Terence MacSwiney, 1902 diary, TS transcript, MacSwiney Papers, UCDA P48c/326r.

6. Ibid., 15 Feb. 1904, UCDA P48c/296.

7. *United Irishman*, 9 Nov. 1901, reprinted in John P. Frayne and Colton Johnson (eds.), *Uncollected Prose: Vol. II* (London, 1975), p. 260.

8. See R. F. Foster, *W. B. Yeats: A Life. Vol. II: The Arch-Poet 1915–1939* (Oxford, 2003), p. 46.

9. R. F. Foster, *W. B. Yeats: A Life. Vol. I: The Apprentice Mage 1865–1914* (Oxford, 1997), p. 513.

10. 9 June 1905, de Róiste diary, CCA 271/A/7.

11. See Karl Mannheim, 'The Problem of Generations', in *Essays on the Sociology of Knowledge*, Paul Kecskemeti (ed.) (London, 1952), pp. 276–322. Much is drawn together in Robert Wohl, *The Generation of 1914* (London, 1980), particularly Chapter 4 on Ortega y Gasset, who began marshalling his ideas in 'The Theme of Our Times' (1922–3). For a later reflection see June Edmunds and Bryan S. Turner, *Generations, Culture and Society* (Buckingham, 2002); and for a recent application of 'generations' to Italian history (with interesting Irish parallels), Arianna Arisi Rota and Roberto Balzani, 'Discovering Politics: Action and Recollection in the First Mazzinian Generation', in Silvana Patriarca and Lucy Riall (eds.), *The Risorgimento Revisited: Nationalism and Culture in Nineteenth-Century Italy* (London, 2012), pp. 77–96.

12. Ernie O'Malley, *On Another Man's Wound* (Dublin, 1979), p. 126.

13. J. W. Good, *Ulster and Ireland* (Dublin, 1919), p. 289. Good went on to instance the obvious exception: 'In the North, indeed, there has been no hint of a division of opinion; young Ulster talks exactly as old Ulster did, except that the note of its war-cries is even fiercer and more uncompromising.'

14. Wohl, *Generation of 1914*, pp. 3, 5.

15. Rosamond Jacob Papers, diary for 19, 25, 28 Jan. 1911, NLI MS 32,582/21 [i.e., Vol. 21 in NLI numbering; confusingly, this differs from Jacob's own numbering of these volumes].

16. Ibid., diary for 31 July, 1 Aug. 1911.

17. See his BMH statement, No. 1770, File 2, pp. 195ff. Also a scorching attack on Rathmines, pp. 209ff.

18. L. Paul-Dubois, *Contemporary Ireland* (Dublin, 1911), p. 122. Rosamond Jacob's Gaelic League friend Seán Ó Fhloinn gave her a copy on 28 Nov. 1908 (in French).

19. Mulcahy Papers, UCDA P7c/1; a pencilled note on top reads 'A Collins note'.
20. 12 Dec. 1904; Béaslaí Papers, NLI MS 33,957/6, No. 8.
21. MacSwiney diary, Feb. 1906, TS transcript, UCDA P48c/102, p. 43c.
22. De Róiste Papers, CCA 271/A/7.
23. 'Printed on Irish Paper with Irish Ink', Shandon Printing Works. Included with diary for 21 Jan. 1906, CCA 271/A/9. De Róiste optimistically recorded it as 'a success beyond all expectation', but the Cork Celtic Literary Society proceeded on a very uneven course.
24. 21 May 1911, NLI MS 32,582/21. He also annoyed her by his contempt for his native Kerry, and his admiration of Ulster.
25. See especially Tom Garvin, *Nationalist Revolutionaries in Ireland 1858–1928* (Oxford, 1987), Peter Hart, *The IRA at War 1916–1923* (Oxford, 2003), and David Fitzpatrick, *Politics and Irish Life: Provincial Experience of War and Revolution 1913–1921* (Dublin, 1977).
26. Given to him by a priest when he was in gaol; see MacSwiney Papers, UCDA P48b/327, for a poem inspired by this encounter. For reflections on spirituality and nationalism, his correspondence with Bulmer Hobson in ibid., P48b/318, 319.
27. A process commented upon in the novels of Canon Sheehan; also see MacSwiney diary, 10 May 1907, MacSwiney Papers, UCDA P48c/104, where a young Gaelic Leaguer priest from Ballyvourney confirms this.
28. See Bulmer Hobson's statement on the IRB in UCDA P120/24(1), and many other places.
29. Geraldine Plunkett Dillon, *All in the Blood: A Memoir of the Plunkett Family, the 1916 Rising and the War of Independence*, Honor Ó Brolcháin (ed.) (Dublin, 2006), p. 105.
30. FitzGerald Papers, UCDA P80/1398(2), p. 30.
31. This judgement on Waterford was Casimir Markievicz's, when the local theatre refused his play *The Memory of the Dead*, but Rosamond concurred in it frequently. See NLI MS 32,582/24, entry for 16 Mar. 1913.
32. 19 Aug. 1910, 19 May 1912, NLI MS 32,582/19, 23.
33. UCDA P48c/105, memoir by Pat Higgins, and 1905 diary, P48c/102, p. 34.
34. This was printed as a pamphlet, and is also reproduced as Appendix 6 to Joanne Mooney Eichacker, *Irish Republican Women in America: Lecture Tours 1916–1925* (Dublin, 2003), pp. 236–61.
35. 11 Dec. 1913, NLI MS 32,582/25.
36. 8 June 1914, Coffey/Trench Papers, NLI MS 46,305/1.

37. 28 Nov. (Mabel) and 1 Dec. (GBS) 1914, FitzGerald Papers, UCDA P80/1552; most of this marvellous correspondence is reproduced as an appendix to *Memoirs of Desmond FitzGerald* (Dublin, 1968).

38. See Ortega's 1914 lecture 'The Old and the New Politics', quoted in Wohl, *Generation of 1914*, p. 133. 'We are going to flood with our curiosity and our enthusiasm the most remote corners of Spain; we are going to get to know Spain and to sow it with our love and indignation. We are going to travel the fields like crusading apostles, to live in the villages . . .' etc., etc.

39. 'To an Old Comrade', quoted in Isaiah Berlin, *Russian Thinkers* (London, 1979), p. 101.

40. 16 June 1907, NLI MS 32,582/11.

41. The question of Casimir's nobility is exhaustively discussed in Patrick Quigley, *The Polish Irishman: The Life and Times of Count Casimir Markievicz* (Dublin, 2012), but left hanging.

42. 9 Mar. 1913, NLI MS 32,582/24. When this conversation took place the Countess was wearing a purple velvet costume as 'Peter Pan', being en route to a fancy-dress party.

43. Conor Morrissey, 'Albinia Brodrick: Munster's Anglo-Irish Republican', *Journal of the Cork Archaeological and Historical Society*, Vol. 117 (2011).

44. 11 Apr. 1911, NLI MS 32,582/21.

45. *The Collected Works of Pádraic H. Pearse* (Dublin [1916]), p. 223.

46. Foster, *The Apprentice Mage*, p. 286.

47. Four formidable Ryan sisters of Tomcoole, County Wexford, all married leaders of the revolution – Denis McCullough, Richard Mulcahy and Seán T. O'Kelly – who married two of them in succession. Of the twelve Ryan children born to a 150-acre farm, nine (several of them women) got university degrees.

48. Geraldine Plunkett Dillon, 'The Battle is Over 1913–1916', TS in MAI, BMH CD 5/6/1, p. 7.

49. Geraldine Plunkett Dillon, 'The Ireland I Lived In', MS in MAI, BMH CD 5/6/5, p. 90.

50. 'The Battle is Over', p. 50.

51. Edmunds and Turner, *Generations, Culture and Society*, p. 22.

52. Dáil Éireann, *Díosbóireachtaí Pairliminte: Tuairisg Oifigiúil (Parliamentary Debates: Official Reports)* (Dublin, 1922–), Vol. II, 1909 (1 March 1923).

53. But cf. Fergus Campbell, *The Irish Establishment 1879–1914* (Oxford, 2009), for a countering view.

54. Published as *Les Jeunes Gens d'aujourd'hui* by 'Agathon': see Wohl, *Generation of 1914*, pp. 7ff.
55. Rosamond Jacob's diary for 2 Mar. 1921, NLI MS 32,582/39: the runaway couple were Mrs Frank Stephens and Captain Jack White.
56. Diary, 10 Nov. 1919, 13 Nov. 1920 and 20 Mar. 1921, NLI MS 32,582/36, 37, 39.
57. Quoted in Garvin, *Nationalist Revolutionaries*, p. xi.
58. Mannheim, 'The Problem of Generations', p. 303.
59. Sean O'Faolain, *Vive Moi!* (second edition, London, 1993), p. 143.

2 LEARNING

1. (London, second edition, 1993), p. 46.
2. L. Paul-Dubois, *Contemporary Ireland* (Dublin, 1911), pp. 370–71.
3. Máire Comerford, when working for Alice Stopford Green; see her TS memoir in UCDA LA18/5.
4. The Intermediate Education Act of 1878 set up a Board of Commissioners who acted as an examining body and assigned money (around £32,500 p.a.) to schools, of both religious denominations, on the basis of the results of their examinations. The utilitarian approach made for rigidity and curricular conformity, but the arrangement did increase opportunities for secondary education among sectors previously underfunded. It also marked a break from previous policy, in accepting the denominational principle and funding Catholic schools. Further powers of inspecting schools were, after some wrangling, granted in 1908.
5. See Ciarán O'Neill, *Catholics of Consequence: Transnational Education, Social Mobility and the Irish Catholic Elite 1850–1900* (Oxford, 2014). For the Victorian commercial code see Donald Akenson, *A Mirror to Kathleen's Face: Education in Independent Ireland 1922–1960* (London, 1975), p. 12. See Senia Pašeta, *Before the Revolution: Nationalism, Social Change and Ireland's Catholic Elite 1879–1922* (Cork, 1999), pp. 29ff., for the increasing numbers of Catholics educated to secondary level; Tom Garvin, *Nationalist Revolutionaries in Ireland 1858–1928* (Oxford, 1987), p. 45, for an interesting table showing that numbers of Catholics reaching secondary and third-level education trebled between 1861 and 1911, at a time when the general population was declining. On the Christian Brothers, Barry Coldrey, *Faith and Fatherland: The Christian Brothers and the Development of Irish Nationalism 1838–1921* (Dublin, 1988).
6. Statements by Mahaffy and Christopher Palles respectively, quoted in Senia Pašeta, *Before the Revolution*, pp. 14–15.

7. For education in Cork see Patrick Maume, *Life that is Exile: Daniel Corkery and the Search for Irish Ireland* (Belfast, 1993), pp. 45ff. This discusses the implicit tension between Corkery's generation's wish to broaden out the curriculum into progressive areas – and the need to devote much time to learning Irish. This would be decisively resolved in the latter direction during the 1920s.

8. Leslie to Bigger, F. J. Bigger Papers, NLI MS 35,456/3, 8 Feb. 1910 and [n.d.].

9. For an attempt to apply such ideas to Irish national revival among emigrants, see John Hutchinson and Alan O'Day, 'The Gaelic Revival in London 1900–1922: Limits of Ethnic Identity', in Roger Swift and Sheridan Gilley (eds.), *The Irish in Victorian Britain* (Dublin, 1999), pp. 259ff.

10. Michael Hayes autobiography, UCDA P53/322(2), p. 10.

11. See below, p. 191.

12. Garvin, *Nationalist Revolutionaries*, p. 25. For the position of women teachers, Pašeta, *Before the Revolution*, pp. 89ff.

13. John Cunningham, *Unlikely Radicals: Irish Post-Primary Teachers and the ASTI 1909–2009* (Cork, 2009), p. 21.

14. Fearghal McGarry, *Rebels: Voices from the Easter Rising* (Dublin, 2011), pp. 5–6.

15. George A. Birmingham, *An Irishman Looks at His World* (London, 1921), pp. 135–6.

16. Garvin, *Nationalist Revolutionaries*, pp. 27, 53.

17. They included Thomas Ashe, P. J. Kennedy, who kept St Colman's College, Fermoy, 'Gaelic to the spine', Michael Hayes, Frank Fahy, Tomás Ó Deirg, Margaret Browne, and Annie McHugh. See Cunningham, *Unlikely Radicals*, p. 54; for the 'Gaelic to the spine' judgement (according to MacDonagh), p. 26. MacDonagh taught at St Kieran's College, Kilkenny, succeeding Francis Skeffington in 1901 (the College clearly had no objection to freethinkers), and then at St Colman's College, Fermoy, from 1903, until he joined Pearse in establishing St Enda's in 1908.

18. These included the Dominican College, Eccles Street, Loreto College, St Stephen's Green, Holy Cross, Clonliffe, the Catholic University and the new National University.

19. C. S. Andrews, *Dublin Made Me* (this edition Dublin, 2001), pp. 74–5.

20. Coldrey, *Faith and Fatherland*, pp. 75ff.; also Elaine Sisson, *Pearse's Patriots: St Enda's and the Cult of Boyhood* (Cork, 2004), p. 204, n. 50. The other revolutionaries educated at Blackrock were Fionan Lynch, Mort O'Connell, W. C. Corrigan, Michael Tubridy and Arthur Gaynor,

while Belvedere produced Joseph and George Plunkett, Domhnall Ua Buachalla and Cathal Brugha.

21. *Leader*, 1 Sept. 1900, quoted in Pašeta, *Before the Revolution*, p. 39.

22. MacSwiney diary, MacSwiney Papers, UCDA P48c/101 (4ff.).

23. Dick Humphreys, Rory O'Connor and Kevin O'Higgins went there, though O'Higgins began with the Brothers at Portlaoise.

24. Dick Humphreys to his mother, 2 Sept. 1912, Sighle Humphreys Papers, UCDA P106/527. See Ciarán O'Neill, *Catholics of Consequence*, p. 52, on Clongowes's late adoption of Gaelic games (in 1922).

25. Francis Hackett, *The Green Lion* (New York, 1936), p. 231.

26. See Geraldine Plunkett Dillon, *All in the Blood: A Memoir of the Plunkett Family, the 1916 Rising and the War of Independence*, Honor Ó Brolcháin (ed.) (Dublin, 2006), p. 221 and *passim*.

27. Colin Reid, *The Lost Ireland of Stephen Gwynn: Irish Constitutional Nationalism and Cultural Politics 1864–1950* (Manchester, 2011), p. 86.

28. See Dominic Aidan Bellenger, 'An Irish Benedictine Adventure', in W. J. Sheils and Diana Wood (eds.), *The Churches, Ireland and the Irish* (Oxford, 1989), pp. 401–15.

29. Quoted in Sisson, *Pearse's Patriots*, p. 68.

30. Ibid., p. 81. Casement also wrote about this in a 1909 essay on chivalry for the Fianna handbook.

31. Reid, *Lost Ireland of Stephen Gwynn*, p. 86.

32. *Muriel MacSwiney: Letters to Angela Clifford*, Angela Clifford (ed.) (Belfast 1996), p. 13.

33. 'The Ireland I Lived In', MS in MAI, BMH CD 5/6/5, p. 79.

34. Autobiographical TS in Louise Gavan Duffy Papers, NLI MS 46,271.

35. Rosamond Jacob diary, 17 July 1903, NLI MS 32,582/6.

36. Catherine Morris, *Alice Milligan and the Irish Cultural Revival* (Dublin, 2012), pp. 2–5.

37. Hilary Pyle, *Red-Headed Rebel: Susan L. Mitchell, Poet and Mystic of the Irish Cultural Renaissance* (Dublin, 1998), p. 60; also see pp. 12, 25.

38. A Gaelic League Pamphlet No. 6, by Mary E. L. Butler, dealt with 'Irishwomen and the Home Language', making this point forcibly. (Copy in MAI, BMH CD 277/1.)

39. Gaelic League Pamphlet No. 23, 'Ireland's Defence – Her Language'. (Copy in MAI, BMH CD 227/1.)

40. 'Is the Gaelic League a Progressive Force?', *Dana*, Vol. 1, No. 7 (Nov. 1904), pp. 216–20.

41. Radio broadcast 'In the Gaelic League', 17 Dec. 1952, quoted in Kevin Girvin, *Seán O'Hegarty* (Cork, 1907), p. 193; my thanks to Frances Flanagan.

42. Mulcahy Papers, UCDA P53/322(2), p. 8.
43. Mulcahy Papers, UCDA P7b/37(18), a speech delivered in Drogheda, 8 Feb. 1944.
44. Joost Augusteijn, *Patrick Pearse: The Making of a Revolutionary* (Basingstoke, 2010), pp. 207–8. For coverage of these Irish colleges see articles in *Sinn Féin*, 13 Sept. 1913, and the *National Student*, Vol. 2, No. 8, June 1912 (a rhapsodic article on Ring).
45. Diary for 6 Feb. 1906, CCA 271/A/10.
46. Ibid., 13 Aug. 1908, CCA 271/A/15.
47. *Vive Moi!* (second edition, London, 1993), p. 110; for Béaslaí see Béaslaí Papers, NLI MS 33,957/10.
48. Hayes autobiography, UCDA P53/322(4).
49. See diary for Aug. 1907, NLI MS 32,582/11. She thought that Waterpark was unsupportive of the League and nationalism generally (21 Mar. 1907).
50. Morris, *Alice Milligan*, p. 146.
51. Letters of 11 June 1912 and 24 Mar. 1914, Seán T. O'Kelly/Ryan Papers, NLI MS 46,305/1.
52. 'A Gaelic League Catechism', [n.d.], signed 'F. A. F.' – probably Frank Fahy, President of the Gaelic League of London, in MAI, BMH CD 227/1.
53. As Béaslaí reflected in his diary. See also MacColuim Papers, NLI MS 24,396 and *Inis Fáil*, Sept. 1905, announcing the impending return of MacColuim to give a talk. 'The story of Fionan's work in the building up of the London Gaelic League is one of the most interesting and suggestive in the whole Irish language movement. When he threw his energy into the work of laying its foundations, and became its first secretary, he had but few helpers, but he laboured with unceasing zeal, with rare grit, with ever-fresh persuasiveness, and gradually his efforts told. In his personality, too, he typified indescribably hearty and racy traits of the Gael', etc., etc.
54. See MAI, BMH CD 227/1, for Annual Report 1901 and e.g. *Inis Fáil*, Aug. 1905, describing at length N. F. Nic Eoghain's 'swiftly moving and fresh account of the spread of the national spirit in Dublin in the days that led up to Ninety-Eight', bringing new material on the United Irishmen to 'all, or very nearly all her hearers' and demonstrating 'what a splendid spirit animated true men and what a determined spirit must animate ourselves if Ireland is ever to be gladdened with the spirit of intellectual and spiritual liberty'.
55. Ó Briain Papers, NLI MS 8,417/1, lecture of 1911. Also see an address to a Forest Gate local school, 30 Nov. 1910. The Gaelic League of London

minute-books (NLI MS 9777) record everyone's names in Irish but the records are kept in English.

56. Ó Briain Papers, NLI MS 8,435/9, contain a handwritten list of 'London Gaels Who Lost Their Lives in the Easter Rising 1916', with details. They include Patrick Shortes, Seán Hurley, Michael Mulvihill, Patrick O'Connor, Donal Sheehan, Con Keating. Sheehan's life is typical: he was born in 1886 in Ballintubrid, County Limerick, educated at the Courtenay School in Newcastlewest, moved to London and became a bookkeeper at the Savoy Hotel. He joined the Gaelic League of London, returned to Ireland in 1914, and was drowned accidentally when his car went off Ballykissane Pier in County Kerry, en route to taking over the wireless station at Cahirciveen at the outbreak of the Rising. Ó Briain's list also gives details of those who fought and survived, such as Con Collins, Tom O'Donoghue and Denis Daly. Mulvihill, O'Connor, Collins and Daly were all Post Office employees. See also 'Events of Easter Week', *Catholic Bulletin*, Vol. 6, No. 9 (Sept. 1916): a useful biographical overview of many 1916 casualties, which shows a high proportion were returned emigrants from Britain.

57. To Stephen Gwynn, 16 Oct. 1929, NLI MS 8,600/13.

58. See 'Gaelic Mission to Protestants', *Irish Peasant*, 15 June 1907; a group of Irish Protestant Gaelic League members are rather nervously planning to work towards Church of Ireland services in Irish, Irish lectures in parish halls and teaching Irish in Protestant schools; they have asked the Ard-Chraobh if they have any objection to using the Ard-Chraobh rooms for meetings 'and they had not the slightest objection'. The tone is notably tentative.

59. 28 May 1910.

60. Kennedy Papers, UCDA P4/128.

61. For details see Timothy G. McMahon, *Grand Opportunity: The Gaelic Revival and Irish Society 1893–1910* (Syracuse, 2008), pp. 47ff.

62. Ibid., p. 68; also ibid, p. 53, for an interesting *Claidheamh* editorial of 1 Sept. 1900, and pp. 61ff. for 'The Battle of Portarlington'.

63. 'Priests and Irish Ireland', *Inis Fáil*, Dec. 1905.

64. *Irish Nation*, 4 Sept. 1909, quoted in McMahon, *Grand Opportunity*, p. 69.

65. See Lucy McDiarmid's chapter of this name in her *The Irish Art of Controversy* (Dublin, 2005).

66. Quoted in McDiarmid, *Irish Art of Controversy*, p. 61.

67. See 6 Feb. 1909, 20 Feb. 1909.

68. Peter Hart, 'The Geography of Revolution in Ireland 1917–1923', *Past & Present*, No. 155 (May 1997), p. 170. For *Sinn Féin* coverage see issues of 6 Feb. and 20 Feb. 1909.

69. *National Student*, Vol. 2, No. 3 (Jan. 1911).

70. Andrews, *Dublin Made Me*, pp. 132–3.

71. Eimar O'Duffy, *The Wasted Island* (New York, 1920), p. 144.

72. *National Student*, Vol. 2, No. 6 (Dec. 1911).

73. See account in *Irish Peasant*, 23 Nov. 1907.

74. Quoted in *Sinn Féin*, 5 May 1906.

75. See 'The New Spirit in Ulster', *Republic*, 16 May 1907, for an encomium on national feeling in QUB, the foundation of a flourishing Gaelic Society, the student preoccupation with 'the heroic figures and the unsolved problems of their own land', etc.

76. To McGarrity, 27 May 1910, Joseph McGarrity Papers, NLI MS 17,457(7). The previous quotation from *Irish Student* is from Vol. II, No. 2 (21 May 1910), preserved in McCullough Papers, UCDA P120/44.

77. See *National Student*, Vol. 2, No. 7 (Mar. 1912), for rebuttals.

78. Ibid., Vol. 1, No. 1 (May 1910).

79. Frederick W. Ryan, *A Plea for Irish Studies* (Dublin, 1908), p. 25.

80. Vol. 4, No. 2 (Dec. 1913).

81. Vol. 4, No. 4 (June 1914), preserved in McCullough Papers, UCDA P120/46.

82. Hayes autobiography, UCDA P53(322) (7).

83. 'The Battle is Over 1913–1916', TS in MAI, BMH CD 5–6/1, pp. 69, 71.

84. To Min, [n.d. but 1905], O'Kelly/Ryan Papers, NLI MS 48,443/2.

85. Kate to Min, 2 Nov. 1907, O'Kelly/Ryan Papers, NLI MS 48,444/2.

86. Same to same, 'Sat evg' [1908], O'Kelly/Ryan Papers, NLI MS 48,445/1.

87. Seán T. O'Kelly to Nell Ryan, 19 Oct. 1910, O'Kelly/Ryan Papers, NLI MS 48,445/3.

88. Mulcahy Papers, UCDA P53/322(7).

89. McCartan to Joseph McGarrity, 20 Dec. 1905 and 13 Jan. 1906, NLI MS 17,457; Hobson to Joseph McGarrity, July 1907, McGarrity Papers, NLI MS 17,612.

90. To McGarrity, 26 Feb. 1906 and 13 Jan. 1906, NLI MS 17,457(2); also to McGarrity, [n.d.], 17,457(19). 'It is in full swing now and gaining in prestige and in new members every day.'

91. To McGarrity, Apr. 1908, NLI MS 17,457 (5). For speculation about the Archbishop, 6 Sept. 1910, NLI MS 17,457 (5).

92. Susan K. Morrissey, *Heralds of Revolution: Russian Students and the Mythologies of Radicalism* (Oxford, 1998), p. 19.

93. Andrews, *Dublin Made Me*, p. 171.

94. O'Kelly/Ryan Papers, NLI MS 48,044/3.

95. Mulcahy Papers, UCDA P53/322(12): interview at Lissenfield.

96. Una to Min, 6 Mar. 1911, O'Kelly/Ryan Papers, NLI MS 48,445/5.
97. See Kevin O'Shiel's immense BMH Witness Statement No. 1,770, pp. 67ff.
98. Matthew Kelly, 'The Irish Volunteers: A Machiavellian Moment?', in D. George Boyce and Alan O'Day (eds.), *The Ulster Crisis 1885–1921* (London, 2005), pp. 64–85.
99. Mulcahy Papers, UCDA P7b/2(56).
100. Comerford Papers, UCDA LA 18/1, p. 25.

3 PLAYING

1. Written as a response to Terence MacSwiney's 'The Propagandist Playwright' (which was reprinted as Chapter 10 of MacSwiney's *Principles of Freedom* (Dublin, 1921)). See Ben Levitas, *The Theatre of Nation: Irish Drama and Cultural Nationalism 1890–1916* (Oxford, 2002), p. 198.
2. 'The Drama as a Nationalizing Force', *Sinn Féin*, 10 Nov. 1906.
3. See F. X. Martin, '1916 – Myth, Fact and History', *Studia Hibernica*, Vol. 7 (1967); Johann Norstedt, *Thomas MacDonagh: A Critical Biography* (Charlottesville, Va., 1980), pp. 5–6; Mary Trotter, *Modern Irish Theatre* (London, 2008), p. 70. For Esslin, Eugene McNulty, *The Ulster Literary Theatre and the Northern Revival* (Cork, 2008), p. 134. Yeats's constant invocation of the 'mob becoming a people' (in 'The Acting at St Teresa's Hall' and many other places) is a slightly garbled version of a statement in Victor Hugo's essay on Shakespeare (1864).
4. See R. F. Foster, *W. B. Yeats: A Life. Vol. I: The Apprentice Mage 1865–1914* (Oxford, 1997), pp. 261ff.
5. Lennox Robinson, *Curtain Up: An Autobiography* (London, 1942), p. 17. Later his own play *Patriots* would have a similarly galvanic effect on the young Sean O'Faolain: *Vive Moi!* (second edition, London, 1993), pp. 85ff.
6. *Freeman's Journal*, 7 Apr. 1902.
7. Nicholas Grene, *The Politics of Irish Drama: Plays in Context from Boucicault to Friel* (Cambridge, 1999), Chapter 1. In 1893, *The Shaughraun* and *The Colleen Bawn* ranked among the six top-grossing plays in British theatres.
8. Christopher Fitz-Simon, *'Buffoonery and Easy Sentiment': Popular Irish Plays in the Decade Prior to the Opening of the Abbey Theatre* (Dublin, 2011), pp. 23, 40–41. Also Cheryl Herr (ed.), *For the Land They Loved: Irish Political Melodramas 1890–1925* (Syracuse, 1991).

9. Ibid., p. 116; see Robert Hogan and James Kilroy, *The Modern Irish Drama: A Documentary History. Vol. II: Laying the Foundations 1902–1904* (Dublin, 1976), p. 35, for Frank Fay's cynical reaction. Fitz-Simon's Chapter 6 deals with Whitbread's 1798 hero-plays, which ran from 1894 to 1904; *Theobald Wolfe Tone* in 1898 was the high point, a conventional patriotic melodrama. Frank Fay reviewed it but implied that an Englishman could not do justice to the subject.

10. They included William Fay, May Craig, Barry Fitzgerald and F. J. McCormick.

11. *Samhain: An Occasional Review, Edited by W. B. Yeats* (Dublin, 1908), p. 5. This passage does not appear in the extracts from *Samhain 1908* in *Explorations* (London, 1962).

12. Sydney Gifford Czira Papers, NLI MS 18,815(2).

13. Ibid., NLI MS 18,817(6).

14. 'An Irish National Theatre', reprinted in *Explorations*, p. 115. See also 'First Principles', in *Samhain 1904* (*Explorations*, especially p. 146); and Adrian Frazier, *Behind the Scenes: Yeats, Horniman and the Struggle for the Abbey Theatre* (London, 1990), Chapter 2.

15. Foster, *Apprentice Mage*, pp. 294–300.

16. Kennedy Papers, UCDA D4/131.

17. *Explorations*, pp. 200–201.

18. 18 Apr. 1903; Frazier, *Behind the Scenes*, p. 89.

19. Kennedy Papers, UCDA D4/131.

20. Diary for 5 Feb. 1909, NLI MS 32,582/18.

21. See quote in McNulty, *Ulster Literary Theatre*, p. 58.

22. Frazier, *Behind the Scenes*, p. 91.

23. For text see Karen Steele (ed.), *Maud Gonne's Irish Nationalist Writings 1895–1946* (Dublin, 2004), pp. 204–12; also ibid., pp. 201–3, for Gonne's 'A National Theatre', *United Irishman*, 24 Oct. 1903.

24. Frazier, *Behind the Scenes*, pp. 114–15.

25. Levitas, *Theatre of Nation*, p. 16.

26. *Sinn Féin*, 31 Dec. 1906; Robert Hogan and James Kilroy, *The Modern Irish Drama. Vol. III: The Abbey Theatre – The Years of Synge 1905–1909* (Dublin, 1978), p. 120.

27. 'It would require a large and brutal book,' wrote Geraldine Plunkett Dillon sourly, 'to explain the mentality of the Abbey directorate' ('The Battle is Over 1913–1916', TS in MAI, BMH CD 5/6/1, p. 50).

28. See Catherine Morris, *Alice Milligan and the Irish Cultural Revival* (Dublin, 2012), pp. 37ff. and Chapter 5 for details.

29. Ibid., especially pp. 226ff.

30. *Samhain: An Occasional Review, Edited by W. B. Yeats* (Dublin, 1908), pp. 4–5. 'I have a right to speak, for I asked our own company to give up two of our Saturday performances that we might give the Independent Theatre and the Theatre of Ireland the most popular days.'

31. Diary for 26 July 1911, NLI MS 32,582/22.

32. Diary for 23 Feb. 1912, NLI MS 32,582/22.

33. *Irish Independent*, 4 Dec. 1908; my thanks to Lauren Arrington.

34. Robert Hogan, Richard Burnham and Daniel P. Poteet, *The Modern Irish Drama. Vol. IV: The Abbey Theatre – The Rise of the Realists 1910–1915* (Dublin, 1979), pp. 80–82; a TS of the play is in MAI, BMH CD 62/14.

35. Delia Cahill in *Bean na hÉireann*, Aug. 1910; my thanks to Lauren Arrington.

36. Hogan et al., *Rise of the Realists*, pp. 200ff., for a particularly violent attack by Lawrence on the Abbey's morality, and ibid., pp. 298ff., for the split. They produced George Birmingham's *Eleanor's Enterprise* with Constance Markievicz, Helena Molony and Seán Connolly, in the Gaiety, in 1914.

37. 15 Dec. 1906.

38. Hogan, et al., *Rise of the Realists*, p. 157.

39. 'All Ireland', leader in *United Irishman*, 24 Oct. 1903; also see Hogan and Kilroy, *Laying the Foundations*, pp. 83–5, 120–21.

40. Hogan and Kilroy, *The Years of Synge*, p. 107.

41. Ibid., pp. 102ff. See Levitas, *Theatre of Nation*, p. 102, for their connections to the now-defunct *Nationist*: Tom Kettle was chair of their committee, and Maurice Joy and Padraic Colum secretaries. Other some-time members included Stephen Gwynn, Patrick Pearse, Constance Markievicz, Thomas Koehler, the Walkers, George Roberts, Séamus Starkey, James Cousins, Edward Martyn and George Russell. One element in the bonding process was clearly having quarrelled with Yeats.

42. See 'The Freedom of the Theatre', *United Irishman*, 1 Nov. 1902.

43. Hogan and Kilroy, *The Years of Synge*, p. 229.

44. Norstedt, *Thomas MacDonagh*, p. 57.

45. W. J. Feeney, *Drama in Hardwicke Street: A History of the Irish Theatre Company* (London, 1984), pp. 49ff.

46. Ibid., p. 172.

47. Geraldine Plunkett Dillon, *All in the Blood: A Memoir of the Plunkett Family, the 1916 Rising and the War of Independence*, Honor Ó Brolcháin (ed.) (Dublin, 2006), p. 175.

48. Diary for 27 Dec. 1915, Coffey/Trench Papers, NLI MS 46,308/4.

49. O'Faolain, *Vive Moi!*, p. 9.

50. Ibid., pp. 85ff. Cesca Trench excitedly recounted to her sister Margot the effect of *Patriots* when it was played in Dublin. 'There was great applause from the gallery at some of the remarks. "Are they still going on with the old parliamentary methods – haven't they seen yet the utter futility of constitutional agitation?" *Great Applause.* "Arms – arms is what we want, arms and then freedom." *Immense applause.* "Think, think of Ireland, Ireland, the English banished from the country – (*subdued but determined applause*) & Ireland a free nation again!"' Cesca to Margot, [n.d.], Coffey/Trench Papers, NLI MS 46,330/1.

51. The record of their initial meeting on 1 Nov. 1908 is in UCCA, Corkery Papers, DC A/I/i/1. It involved Liam de Róiste as President, Corkery as Secretary, and in attendance D. Harrington, P. Higgins, J. Higgins, S. Meade, P. Harrington, R. Linehan, D. Breen, J. Jennings, T. O'Gorman, E. Lynam, J. P. Conlon and T. MacSwiney.

52. UCCA, Corkery Papers, DC A/I/i/1; record of first meeting of CDS, 1 Nov. 1908. For Corkery's ideas on staging see his article 'A Critic at the Munster Feis', *Leader*, 12 Sept. 1903, and 'The Irish Literary Theatre in Cork', *Leader*, 31 Dec. 1904.

53. Diary, 13 Oct. 1908, de Róiste Papers, CCA 271/A/15, records de Róiste's publication plans and later thoughts. Terence MacSwiney contributed a poem to *Fodhla*.

54. See Corkery to de Róiste, [n.d.], TCDA 10,539/480. Also UCCA, Corkery Papers, DC A/I/i/9: MS of Corkery's introduction to an edition of MacSwiney's plays.

55. From text in UCCA, Corkery Papers, DC G/I/i/164.

56. Hogan and Kilroy, *The Years of Synge*, p. 323. For texts of plays and lukewarm reviews see UCCA, Corkery Papers, DC G/VI/i/175.

57. TS diary transcript, 4 Dec. 1910, MacSwiney Papers, UCDA P489c/104, p. 40.

58. See the long article 'The *Leader* and Its Policy', intended for *Éire Óg*, TS in MacSwiney Papers, UCDA P486/341(4).

59. Corkery thought this his best; the *Cork Tatler* reviewed it respectfully on 22 May 1911. The text of 'The Eternal Longing' is in UCCA, Corkery Papers, DC A/VI/vi/47.

60. 'Terence MacSwiney: Lord Mayor of Cork', *Studies*, Dec. 1920 (reprinted in Móirín Chevasse, *Terence MacSwiney* (Cork, 1961)).

61. *The Revolutionist: A Play in Five Acts* (Dublin and London, 1914), pp. 59–60.

62. As St John Ervine remembered: see McNulty, *Ulster Literary Theatre*, p. 4.

63. Marnie Hay, *Bulmer Hobson and the Nationalist Movement in Twentieth-Century Ireland* (Manchester, 2009), p. 25. This was in Dec. 1900.
64. See, e.g., *Sinn Féin*, 16 June 1906, for a meeting of the Belfast Dungannon Club on 5 June, addressed by McCullough, Hobson and Seán MacDermott, and ibid., 18 Oct. 1906, for a lengthy description of a meeting in Carrickmore (where McCartan came from); McCartan and McCullough made vehement speeches denouncing British rule, while Hobson 'said that since the coming of the English to Ireland they had carried out a war of extermination, which was still going actually on. Either the English government or the Irish people had got to go.'
65. McNulty, *Ulster Literary Theatre*, pp. 35, 25.
66. Confusingly Milligan also produced a play of this name, in 1904, but the *United Irishman* unequivocally gives Hobson as the author of this version.
67. *Uladh*, No. 1 (Nov. 1904), editorial by J. W. Good.
68. Ibid., 'The Ulster Literary Theatre' by William Donn (not Good, as McNulty states).
69. Their repertoire was also taken up by Dungannon clubs in Britain; in Jan. 1906 the Dungannon Club played Purcell's *The Enthusiast* at the South Hampstead Club, Fleet Road, reviewed at length in *Inis Fáil* that month.
70. See a favourable report in *Sinn Féin*, 25 Apr. 1908, praising their 'sincerity, force and directness'. The 1908 programme at the Abbey included Mayne's *The Drone* and Robert Harding's *The Leaders of the People*, 'which deals with the thorny question of parties and politics in the North'. The plays they took to the Abbey in Mar. 1907 were Purcell's *The Pagan* and Rutherford Mayne's *The Turn of the Road*. Fred and Jack Morrow later decamped to the Theatre of Ireland.
71. *Uladh*, No. 2 (Feb. 1905).
72. F. J. Bigger was more optimistic in 'Ulster and Irish Ideals', *Irish Peasant*, 9 Feb. 1907, where he praised the ULT, and drew attention to the fledgeling Armagh Dramatic Society:

> Let no fear possess them if they as patriotic Irishmen step out and do what they know and feel to be the right and only course for Gaels to adopt at this juncture of their country's history, and that is to present on stage and in the concert hall the best of their country's art in music, song and dance, and in stage representation, *and none other*. This is no time for Irishmen to be sitting on the fence dilly-dallying with cosmopolitanism in the vague hope of pleasing everyone by avoiding their own. If we are not Irish, distinctly and definitely Irish, in our every phase of life, we are nothing, and doing nothing to build up the national life and character – self-relying, self-respecting, self-advancing.

73. *Uladh*, No. 2 (Feb. 1905).

74. 3 Aug. 1907, Henderson Papers, NLI MS 1730, quoted in Horgan and Kilroy, *The Years of Synge*, p. 186.

75. Quoted in Frazier, *Behind the Scenes*, p. 67, n. 8.

76. 'Plays with Meanings', *Leader*, 17 Oct. 1903.

77. See Alderman Thomas Kelly to Liam de Róiste, [n.d.], TCDA 10,539/485. Joseph Holloway was to design the theatre, originally the brainchild of William Rooney. The Building Fund was to be organized by Seán Doyle.

78. Robert Brustein, *The Theatre of Revolt: An Approach to Modern Drama* (London, 1965).

79. Stanislaus Joyce, *My Brother's Keeper* (London, 1958), p. 87. The English-language version of *Heimat* was called *Magda*.

80. Reprinted as Chapter 10 of *Principles of Freedom*.

81. Quoted in Hogan and Kilroy, *The Years of Synge*, pp. 142–3.

82. 9 Feb. 1907; quoted in ibid., p. 158.

83. 10 Sept. 1910; Levitas, *Theatre of Nation*, pp. 174–5, considers this aspect.

84. Grene, *Politics of Irish Drama*, p. 86; also pp. 86ff., 92–3, for background to Synge's inspiration.

85. See Timothy G. McMahon, *Grand Opportunity: The Gaelic Revival and Irish Society 1893–1910* (Syracuse, 2008), p. 174.

86. *Inis Fáil*, Nov. 1904. The review also admitted 'never was it so difficult to gather an audience for an Irish night.' The plays, at Kensington School, Forest Gate, were *Cuaird na Bainrioghna* and *An Dochtúir*. For Belfast, see, e.g., *Irish Peasant*, 6 Jan. 1906, for a hopeful bulletin by Seagan O'Cathain.

> By far the most important event in every respect was the Irish play at St Mary's Training College immediately before Christmas. The college students acted Dr Hyde's 'An Pósadh' in a manner highly creditable to themselves, to their Irish professor (Father Nolan), and to the institution to which they have the good fortune to belong. They gave the impression of being all native speakers, and yet, I learn that, with one or two exceptions, they were simply students of Irish. A delightful phase of the business was that the chief characters came from places as far apart as Kerry, Galway and Donegal, and undoubtedly the play gained a great deal and lost nothing by this arrangement.

This clearly skirts around the sensitive question of which regional dialect and pronunciation was the most 'authentic'. Also see Seán Athair, 'Gaelic Drama in Belfast', *Irish Nation*, 16 Apr. 1910.

87. McMahon, *Grand Opportunity*, p. 200.

88. See copy in O'Rahilly Papers, UCDA P102/277(10).

89. 8 June 1907.

90. Béaslaí Papers, NLI MS 33,938(6) [1913].

91. They included Fionan Lynch, Gearóid O'Sullivan, Diarmuid Hegarty, Con Collins, Muiris Ó Catháin, Tadhg Ó Scanaill and Colm Ó Murchadha; women's parts were taken by Máire ni Chonaill, Máire and Brighid Dixon, and Caitlin Wolfe. Béaslaí Papers, NLI MS 33,936 (8), contains an informative article detailing what became of them.

92. Béaslaí Papers, NLI MS 33,968(8). Interest was shown by the Gaelic Dramatic Club in University College, Galway (33,933/2), but nothing came of it.

93. Béaslaí Papers, NLI MS 33,953(8).

94. 24 Feb. 1914, FitzGerald Papers, UCDA P102/540(22).

95. Elaine Sisson, *Pearse's Patriots* (Cork, 2004), p. 91. For texts see Róisín ní Ghairbhí and Eugene McNulty (eds.), *Patrick Pearse: Collected Plays/ Drámaí an Phiarsaigh* (Sallins, County Kildare, 2013).

96. Yeats remembered this on his deathbed in 1939; see R. F. Foster, *W. B. Yeats: A Life. Vol. II: The Arch-Poet 1915–1939* (Oxford, 2003), p. 648. The St Enda's production 'The Coming of Fionn' was adapted from Standish O'Grady's *Finn and His Companions* (1891).

97. Trotter, *Modern Irish Theatre*, p. 70.

98. 6 Mar. 1909, George Roberts MSS, NLI MS 8320.

99. Lauren Arrington, *W. B. Yeats, the Abbey Theatre, Censorship and the Irish State: Adding the Halfpence to the Pence* (Oxford, 2010).

4 LOVING

1. (Berkeley, 1993), p. xv.

2. C. S. Andrews to Sean O'Faolain, 5 May 1965, quoted in Diarmaid Ferriter, *Occasions of Sin: Sex and Society in Modern Ireland* (London, 2009), p. 96.

3. Hunt, *Family Romance*, p. xiv.

4. Alan Hayes (ed.), *The Years Flew By: Recollections of Madame Sydney Gifford Czira* (Galway, 2000), pp. 5–6. Kevin O'Shiel's BMH Witness Statement No. 1,770 is equally scathing about Rathmines: see pp. 208ff.

5. To Min, 18 Jan. 1908, 27 Oct. 1908, O'Kelly/Ryan Papers, NLI MS 48,445/1.

6. Ibid., 9 Mar. 1909, NLI MS 48,445/2.

7. Seán T. O'Kelly to Nell, 19 Oct. 1910, NLI MS 48,445/3.

8. Kate to Min, 16 Feb. 1911, NLI MS 48,445/5.

9. Ferriter, *Occasions of Sin*, p. 37. See Ó Briain Papers, NLI MS 8,436/7, for passionate controversies about inauthentic practices in Irish dancing. See also *Weekly Freeman*, 13 Dec. 1902, for a huge, sentimental and self-congratulatory article on the subject.

10. Diary, 14 Feb. 1912, NLI MS 32,582/23. Also see entry for 17 Mar.

11. Hilary Pyle, *Cesca's Diary 1913–1916: Where Art and Nationalism Meet* (Dublin, 2005).

12. Diary, 11 Nov. 1911, Béaslaí Papers, NLI MS 33,957/12.

13. Diary, 1913. He stayed in touch with Bridie, as there are letters from him to her in NLI MS 33,974(7) and 33,970(1).

14. Plunkett Dillon Papers, NLI MS 33,731/1, Notebook No. 3.

15. FitzGerald Papers, UCDA P80/1504(1).

16. The fullest treatment of their relationship is Jennifer FitzGerald's article 'Desmond and Mabel FitzGerald', *Sentences: The Unofficial Journal for the Guides of Kilmainham Gaol*, Vol. 4, No. 1 (2005). Also see their correspondence in UCDA P80/1498–9.

17. To G. B. S., 15 Apr. 1949, FitzGerald Papers, UCDA P80/1677/1.

18. P. S. O'Hegarty to Stephen Gwynn, 16 Oct. 1929, NLI MS 8,600; similar opinions were expressed in *The Victory of Sinn Féin* (Dublin, 1924).

19. Maud Gonne, *A Servant of the Queen* (London, 1938), pp. 48–9.

20. For a detailed consideration see Caoimhe Nic Dháibhéid, ' "This is a case in which Irish national considerations must be taken into account": The Breakdown of the Gonne–MacBride Marriage 1904–1908', *Irish Historical Studies*, Vol. 37, No. 146 (Nov. 2010).

21. To A. Gregory, 27 Feb. 1905, in J. S. Kelly and R. Schuchard (eds.), *The Collected Letters of W. B. Yeats. Vol. IV: 1905–1907* (Oxford, 2005), p. 47; Gonne's letter to O'Leary is quoted in Nic Dháibhéid, 'Breakdown', p. 253.

22. As in Anthony J. Jordan's defensive works, *Willie Yeats and the Gonne–MacBrides* (Westport, Conn., 1997) and *The Yeats–Gonne–MacBride Triangle* (Dublin, 2000). Nic Dháibhéid remarks: 'Far from a proof of fabrication, this reluctance is more accurately interpreted as the maternal impulse to preserve Iseult's reputation – which would have been utterly ruined had she testified to MacBride's alleged molestation of her – from a charge which until recently carried an equal stigma for victims' ('Breakdown', p. 258).

23. Nic Dháibhéid, 'Breakdown', p. 257.

24. As Hanna Sheehy-Skeffington told Rosamond Jacob: R. J.'s diary, 29 Oct. 1918, NLI MS 32,582/23.

25. Diary entries for 20 Jan. 1903, CCA 271/A/1, and 9 Nov. 1905, 271/A/8.

26. BMH Witness Statement No. 805, p. 2; Marie Perolz's testimony is quoted in Fearghal McGarry, *Rebels: Voices from the Easter Rising* (Dublin, 2011), p. 66.

27. BMH Witness Statement No. 1,770, p. 170.

28. Annotation in de Róiste Papers, CCA 271/A/1 [1903].

29. Ibid., 5 Feb. 1906, CCA 271/A/10.

30. Ibid., 8 Feb. and 8 Jan. 1907, CCA 271/A/13.

31. Ibid.

32. 1909; see Richard Ellmann (ed.), *Selected Letters of James Joyce* (London, 1975), pp. 179–96.

33. Mulcahy Papers, UCDA P7/D/30, transcript of 1966 TV interview.

34. See countless rhapsodies in a special volume of her diary devoted to her sexual feelings, NLI MS 32,582/171; these quotes come from 7 July 1915, 8 July 1915, 3 Sept. 1917.

35. NLI MS 32,582/33, entry for 24 Mar. 1918; for Tony and Ben, 20 Nov. 1919.

36. Diary, 10 Feb. 1914, NLI MS 32,582/26.

37. Ibid., 29 Feb. 1923, NLI MS 32,582/171.

38. Ibid., 11 Sept. 1919, NLI MS 32,582/171.

39. Quoted in Leeann Lane, *Rosamond Jacob: Third Person Singular* (Dublin, 2010), p. 184.

40. Diary, 15 Aug. 1915, NLI MS 32,582/171.

41. Ibid., 6 Nov. 1919, NLI MS 32,582/36.

42. Ibid., 10 Nov. 1919, NLI MS 32,582/36.

43. Ibid., 2 Jan. 1918, NLI MS 32,582/33.

44. Ibid., 17 Sept. 1920, NLI MS 32,582/37. 'I couldn't make out much rules to go on [from Freud], or much evidence as to why one thing means another. Almost everything seems to mean sex organs.'

45. Ibid., 13 Nov. 1920, NLI MS 32,582/37.

46. Ibid., 31 Dec. 1913, NLI MS 32,582/36; also see Margaret Ó hÓgartaigh, *Kathleen Lynn: Irishwoman, Patriot, Doctor* (Dublin, 2006), pp. 37ff.

47. Ibid., 26 Mar. 1917, NLI MS 32,582/31.

48. Ibid., 13 Nov. 1919, NLI MS 32,582/33.

49. Ferriter, *Occasions of Sin*, pp. 89ff.

50. Quoted in Tim Pat Coogan, *De Valera: Long Fellow, Long Shadow* (London, 1993), p. 42.

51. Diary, 22 Oct. 1919, NLI MS 32,582/36. For Macardle's attire, see 24 May 1921, NLI MS 32,582/39. In another conversation (10 Nov. 1919) Hanna put her own coldness down to a prudish upbringing. See

also Margaret Ward, *Hanna Sheehy-Skeffington: A Life* (Cork, 1997), pp. 31–2.

52. Withers's love-letters to her are in the Coffey/Trench Papers, NLI MS 46,331/22, as is her correspondence with Ella Young (46,331/1).

53. Diary, 21 Sept. 1920, NLI MS 32,582/37.

54. Ibid., 25 Dec. 1917, NLI MS 32,582/24.

55. Diary, 1903, Béaslaí Papers, NLI MS 33,957. This is from a recollection of his love for his friend Billy McMullen, who became a Jesuit priest.

56. Letter to Muriel, quoted in Francis J. Costello, *Enduring the Most: The Life and Death of Terence MacSwiney* (Dingle, 1995), p. 87.

57. Quoted in ibid., p. 88.

58. As she recorded in a taped account in Béaslaí Papers, NLI MS 33, 914(11).

59. See Ruth Dudley Edwards, *Patrick Pearse: The Triumph of Failure* (London, 1979), p. 123, quoting *An Macaomh*, June 1909.

60. See Guy Beiner, 'Revisiting F. J. Bigger: A Fin-de-Siècle Flourish of Antiquarian-Folklore Scholarship in Ulster', *Béaloideas*, Vol. 80 (2012), pp. 142–62.

61. Jeffrey Dudgeon, *Roger Casement: The Black Diaries, with a Study of His Background, Sexuality, and Irish Political Life* (Belfast, 2002), p. 194.

62. Ibid., p. 190.

63. NLI MS 13,158. Denis McCullough later recalled that Hobson 'became very intimate with Casement and actually acted as his agent here [Dublin] in the matter of purchase of clothes and that kind of thing'. Mulcahy Papers, UCDA P120/34.

64. 7 Sept. 1909, Hobson Papers, NLI MS 13,158.

65. See particularly the Appendix to Séamus Ó Siocháin, *Roger Casement: Imperialist, Rebel, Revolutionary* (Dublin, 2008), and Dudgeon, *passim*.

66. Dudgeon, *Roger Casement*, p. 111.

67. Ibid., p. 123, suggests this argument might be 'a test run for arguments he was beginning to adopt for private use in discussion, or for his own psychoanalytic purposes'.

68. Intensively researched by Dudgeon, *Roger Casement*, Chapter 13.

69. Ibid., p. 215.

70. Ibid., p. 537 [Jan. 1913].

71. 19 Apr. 1911, Hobson Papers, NLI MS 13,158/7.

72. These are the works cited above by Dudgeon and Ó Siocháin.

73. By contrast, Grace's mother's reaction suggests something of the relationship between the rebel daughters and their background: in a newspaper interview just after Plunkett's execution, Mrs Gifford testified that she

had heard of the marriage only after the event, and had not even known definitely of the engagement; she went on to blame Constance Markievicz for setting up the whole thing. Grace, said her mother, 'was always a very headstrong and self-willed girl, and latterly had lived a more or less independent life.' *Lloyds Weekly News*, 7 May 1916, in Grace Plunkett Papers, NLI MS 21,593.

74. Diary, 18 June 1916, NLI MS 32,582/30.

75. Eric Hobsbawm, 'Revolution and Sex', in *Revolutionaries* (London, 1977), p. 218.

76. See Jérôme aan de Wiel, *The Catholic Church in Ireland 1914–1918* (Dublin, 2003).

77. Discussed in diaries for 27 Jan. 1921 and 14 Dec. 1921, NLI MS 32,582/39–40.

5 WRITING

1. Maloney Papers, NYPL, Box 6.

2. (Dublin, 1922), p. 18.

3. Moore's *Confessions of a Young Man* (London, 1888) profoundly influenced Joyce's *Portrait of the Artist*.

4. John Wilson Foster, *Irish Novels 1890–1940: New Bearings in Culture and Fiction* (Oxford, 2008).

5. To Stephen Gwynn, 16 Oct. 1929, NLI MS 8,600/13. Keats and Wordsworth are striking exceptions, but clearly he felt no pressure to include any Irish name but Yeats's.

6. 'Passion and Cunning: An Essay on the Politics of W. B. Yeats', in Conor Cruise O'Brien, *'Passion and Cunning' and Other Essays* (London, 1988), p. 8.

7. Michael Ryan's BMH Witness Statement No. 1,709, p. 7, itemizes such outlets after 1914.

8. Alan Hayes (ed.), *The Years Flew By: Recollections of Madame Sydney Gifford Czira* (Galway, 2000), p. 11.

9. Mulcahy Papers, UCDA P7/D/29, interview with Brian Farrell.

10. Hobson to Bigger, 5 Sept. 1911, NLI MS 35,456/1; Czira, *The Years Flew By*, pp. 64–5.

11. *Ulysses* (London, 2002 edition), p. 257.

12. Yug Mohit Chaudhry, *Yeats, the Irish Literary Revival and the Politics of Print* (Cork, 2001).

13. Matthew Kelly, *The Fenian Ideal and Irish Nationalism 1882–1916* (Woodbridge, 2006), p. 143.

14. See Marie-Louise Legg, *Newspapers and Nationalism: The Irish Provincial Press 1850–1892* (Dublin, 1998), Karen Steele, *Women, Press and Politics during the Irish Revival* (Syracuse, 2007), and Kelly, *Fenian Ideal*, p. 138.

15. Quoted in Steele, *Women, Press and Politics*, p. 20.

16. 'Memoirs', O'Kelly/Ryan Papers, NLI MS 48,044/3. Daly worked in Dollard's. The Clo-Cumann Gaelic printing company in Great Strand Street was set up by a group of Gaelic League members. The Bartholomew Teeling branch of the IRB, which O'Kelly joined, also included Richard Hayes (later film censor), Arthur Griffith, Dr Elwood of Roscommon, Dr Stephen Barry Walsh and Dr Dan Sheehan from Kerry. For Griffith's campaign against Browne & Nolan, *United Irishman*, 10 Nov. 1903.

17. As advertised in the *United Irishman*, 6 Jan. 1900. Ben Novick, 'Advanced Nationalist Propaganda and Moralistic Revolution', in Joost Augusteijn (ed.), *The Irish Revolution 1913–1923* (Basingstoke, 2002), p. 35, has useful details of presses and who they printed.

18. 'Ode for 6 October', in Henry Mangan (ed.), *Poems by Alice Milligan* (Dublin, 1954). Her best-known poem, 'When I was a Little Girl' (see Steele, *Women, Press and Politics*, pp. 56–7), while rhetorically effective, is undercut with a sentimentality and cuteness.

19. For a discussion of this see Eugene McNulty, 'The Place of Memory: Alice Milligan, Ardrigh and the 1898 Centenary', *Irish University Review*, Vol. 38, No. 2 (2008), pp. 203–21.

20. 'The Northern Men', *Northern Patriot*, Apr. 1896, quoted in McNulty, 'The Place of Memory', p. 214.

21. Karen Steele makes a good case for Milligan's consistent presentation of the importance of feminine agency in political action: *Women, Press and Politics*, pp. 57ff.

22. *Shan Van Vocht*, Sept. 1896.

23. 'Notes for the Gaelic Athletes', *Shan Van Vocht*, Mar. 1896.

24. Mulcahy Papers, UCDA P7/D/29, interview with Brian Farrell. Mulcahy also emphasized the inclusiveness of Griffith's message at this time; as a student at Bolton Street in 1908–9 he noticed that those who subscribed to *Sinn Féin* also took AE's *Irish Homestead*, politically much less radical. (But this is a recollection after the Treaty split, and Mulcahy was keen to claim this kind of pluralism and moderation as part of the agenda of the 'true' revolution.)

25. O'Shiel's BMH Witness Statement [actually a lengthy autobiography] No. 1,770, p. 510.

26. Quoted in Virginia Glandon, *Arthur Griffith and the Advanced-Nationalist Press in Ireland 1900–1922* (New York, 1985), p. 14.

27. NAI Police Reports, CBS 18921/5.

28. Steele, *Women, Press and Politics*, pp. 86ff., for examples.

29. Ibid., p. 142.

30. Czira, *The Years Flew By*, pp. 26–7, for *Sinn Féin*, also a portrait of Griffith off-duty.

31. William Bulfin, *Rambles in Eirinn* (Dublin, 1907; London, 1981 edition), Vol. III, pp. 213–15, for a rant against letting Jews into Ireland. For the Gifford quote, Czira, *The Years Flew By*, p. 107.

32. MacSwiney, 'The Leader and Its Policy', TS in MacSwiney Papers, UCDA P486/341; also de Róiste diary, 1 Feb. 1906, CCA 271/A/9.

33. Diary, 17 Mar. 1910, NLI MS 32,582/16, and Hilary Pyle, *Cesca's Diary 1913–1916: Where Art and Nationalism Meet* (Dublin, 2005), p. 160.

34. 'The Clothes We Wear', *Leader*, 20 Oct. 1900; for emigration see 19 Feb. 1901.

35. 1 Sept. 1900.

36. Patrick Maume, *The Long Gestation: Irish Nationalist Life 1891–1918* (Dublin, 1999), p. 63.

37. Printed circular with handwritten insertions in Coffey/Trench Papers, NLI MS 46,307/2. By 1914 his suggested subjects included the Irish language, English bribery and corruption, and the need to arm '100,000 men to change the course of Ireland's history'.

38. See R. F. Foster, *The Irish Story: Telling Tales and Making It Up in Ireland* (London, 2001), p. 17.

39. Printed circular with handwritten additions, Coffey/Trench Papers, NLI MS 46,307/2.

40. Quoted in Senia Pašeta, *Thomas Kettle* (Dublin, 2008), p. 43, the most incisive and analytical study of this underestimated figure.

41. W. Sears to Francis Sheehy-Skeffington, 18 Jan. 1907, Sheehy-Skeffington Papers, NLI MS 21,618/ii. He added that this was easier to bring off in Dublin than in the provinces, where 'we are all timid.'

42. See Henry Barber to Francis Sheehy-Skeffington, 26 Jan. 1907, Sheehy-Skeffington Papers, NLI MS 21,618/ii.

43. Eightpence per dozen, sale or return; see letter from Peter Murphy, 23 Jan. 1907, Sheehy-Skeffington Papers, NLI MS 21,618/i. There is also a similar letter from J. Sheehan of Sheehan's Irish Industrial Agency, Ludgate Hill, 14 Jan. 1907.

44. Séamus Bairéad to Francis Sheehy-Skeffington, Sheehy-Skeffington Papers, 14 Jan. 1907, NLI MS 21,618/i; he took two dozen copies and some handbills all the same.

45. To Stephen Gwynn, 16 Oct. 1929, NLI MS 8,600/13.

46. Diary entries 10 Nov. 1905, 30 Dec. 1905, CCA 271/A/8, and 27 Mar. 1906, 271/A/10. The Davis Press Agency was managed by Michael MacWhite, later an influential diplomat in the Irish Free State.

47. Diary entries for 22 July 1906, 21 Aug. 1906, CCA 271/A/12. Another example of the radical opinions common in the printing trade was the compositor on the *Irish Nation*, Adolphus Shields – Griffith's mentor, organizer of the first All-Ireland Labour Conference, and father of the actors Arthur Shields and Barry Fitzgerald.

48. Ibid., entries for 18 Dec. 1906, 1 and 8 Jan. 1907.

49. *Sinn Féin*, 1 Feb. 1913.

50. Quoted in Glandon, *Arthur Griffith and the Advanced-Nationalist Press*, p. 20.

51. These processes are indicated in MAI, BMH CD 8, which records Hobson's notes about the articles he contributed – including leaders of 9 May 1908 and 4 July 1908, 'Irish Politicians in English' and 'The Essence of Sinn Féin'.

52. Diary, 11 Aug. 1910, NLI MS 32,582/20.

53. To Joseph McGarrity, 4 Sept. 1910, quoted in Kelly, *Fenian Ideal*, p. 187.

54. Richard Davis, *Arthur Griffith and Non-Violent Sinn Féin* (Dublin, 1974), pp. 67ff.

55. De Róiste diary, 26 May 1906, CCA 271/A/11, and 11 Dec. 1906, 271/A/13.

56. 9 Jan. 1907, NLI MS 15,072.

57. Undated circular in de Róiste Papers, TCDA 10,539/307h.

58. See Casement to Hobson, 30 May 1907, NLI MS 13,158, and Hobson to McGarrity, 21 July 1907, NLI MS 17,612. McCullough's memories of the episode are in Mulcahy Papers, UCDA P120/36, transcript of a radio interview of 21 Apr. 1966.

59. Davis, *Arthur Griffith*, pp. 60–61, for details.

60. O'Kelly/Ryan Papers, NLI MS 48,044/4.

61. Quoted in Kelly, *Fenian Ideal*, p. 185.

62. Ibid., p. 187.

63. To de Róiste, 12 June 1912, TCDA 10,539/328.

64. Glandon, *Arthur Griffith and the Advanced-Nationalist Press*, p. 76.

65. To Margot, [n.d. but probably 1911], Coffey/Trench Papers, NLI 46,350/1.

66. 7 Oct. 1914; Pyle, *Cesca's Diary*, p. 156.

67. Diary, 1 Dec. 1911, Béaslaí Papers, NLI MS 33,957 (12).
68. Quoted in Glandon, *Arthur Griffith and the Advanced-Nationalist Press*, p. 139.
69. Quoted in Steele, *Women, Press and Politics*, p. 112.
70. On Delia Larkin, see ibid., pp. 139ff.
71. Diary, [the date is unclear], NLI MS 32,582/22, pp. 281–2.
72. Steele, *Women, Press and Politics*, p. 175.
73. 6 June 1914.
74. Steele, *Women, Press and Politics*, p. 190.
75. Pyle, *Cesca's Diary*, p. 179.
76. MAI, BMH CD 90 [O'Sullivan], pp. 1–4.

6 ARMING

1. (Penguin edition, London, 2000), p. 495.
2. Patrick McCartan, BMH Witness Statement No. 99, p. 7 (of handwritten comments on a typescript by Bulmer Hobson).
3. 23 May 1906, de Róiste diary, CCA 271/A/10.
4. See David Fitzpatrick, 'Militarism in Ireland 1900–1922', in Thomas Bartlett and Keith Jeffery (eds.), *A Military History of Ireland* (Cambridge, 1997), Chapter 17, p. 382.
5. De Róiste diary, 28 Jan. and 3 July 1903, CCA 271/A/1.
6. Ibid., 8 Jan. and 20 Mar. 1906, CCA 271/A/9 and 10.
7. Fearghal McGarry, *The Rising: Ireland, Easter 1916* (Oxford, 2010), pp. 32, 56.
8. BMH Witness Statement No. 755.
9. Diary, 18 Oct. 1912, NLI MS 32,582/24. Her interlocutor was Séamus de Búrca.
10. (New York, 1920), p. 420.
11. Liam Ó Briain's notes on O'Kelly's memoir, O'Kelly/Ryan Papers, NLI MS 48,044/1.
12. Matthew Kelly, 'The Irish Volunteers: A Machiavellian Moment?', in D. George Boyce and Alan O'Day (eds.), *The Ulster Crisis 1885–1921* (London, 2005), p. 67.
13. Diary, 19 Mar. 1913, NLI MS 32,582/24.
14. Brian Hughes, *16 Lives: Michael Mallin* (Dublin, 2012), pp. 36–7.
15. Some of the most sulphurous items in his archives are the letters from his son Aodhagán in the 1960s, claiming the founding role for his father instead of MacNeill and denouncing F. X. Martin for claiming otherwise, but it seems unlikely.

16. Its sunburst apparently symbolized Lugh the Sun god and the rescue of Ireland from the grip of the Fomorians. See O'Rahilly Papers, UCDA P102/223, correspondence with Móirín ní Sionnaigh.

17. Oliver Coogan, *Politics and War in Meath 1913–23* (Maynooth, 1988), pp. 2ff., gives a vivid illustration.

18. A. C. Hepburn, *Catholic Belfast and Nationalist Ireland in the Era of Joe Devlin 1871–1934* (Oxford, 2008), p. 4.

19. O'Kelly's draft memoirs, O'Kelly/Ryan Papers, NLI MS 48,044/2, 4.

20. TV interview transcript, 21 Apr. 1966, McCullough Papers, UCDA P120/36. Hobson's letters to McGarrity frequently denounce the opposition offered to the Dungannon clubs by the Hibernians and their clerical friends.

21. Casement to 'A cara dilis' [McCartan], 16 June 1914, Maloney Papers, NYPL, Box 6. Describing this agonized letter later to Maloney, McCartan wrote: 'part of his soul was in it' (5 Nov. 1923).

22. To McCartan, 10 July 1914, Maloney Papers, NYPL, Box 7, Folder 71.

23. Ibid., Box 6.

24. 17 July 1914, Maloney Papers, NYPL, Box 7, Folder 75.

25. See 4 Dec. 1913, Casement Additional Papers, NLI MS 36,203; Casement had commented to Alice Stopford Green some weeks earlier that he had had an idea for an Irish Volunteers force.

26. Diary, 26 Mar. 1912, NLI MS 32,582/22.

27. See Marnie Hay, *Bulmer Hobson and the Nationalist Movement in Twentieth-Century Ireland* (Manchester, 2009), p. 60.

28. BMH Witness Statement No. 223.

29. Casement to Gertrude Parry, 23 Sept. 1913, Casement Additional Papers, NLI MS 36,202/3. This event is also described in Clara Cullen (ed.), *The World Upturning: Elsie Henry's Wartime Diaries 1913–1919* (Dublin, 2013), pp. 11–12.

30. 24 Nov. 1913, Alice Stopford Green Papers, NLI MS 15,072.

31. To Alice Stopford Green, ibid., 7 Jan. 1914.

32. Casement to Gertrude Parry, 22 Sept. 1912, Casement Additional Papers, NLI MS 36,202, 22.

33. [n.d. but late Sept. 1912], Casement Additional Papers, NLI MS 36,202/3.

34. To Alice Stopford Green, 11 Nov. 1913, Alice Stopford Green Papers, NLI MS 15,072.

35. Ibid. Also see Casement Additional Papers, NLI MS 36,202/3, for similar letters to Gertrude Parry.

36. Seán Cronin (ed.), *The McGarrity Papers: Revelations of the Irish Revolutionary Movement in Ireland and America 1900–1940* (Tralee, 1972), pp. 44–5.

37. A Press Association interview carried in many newspapers on 18 May 1914; see R. F. Foster, *Paddy and Mr Punch: Connections in Irish and English History* (London, 1993), p. 128.

38. 13 Mar. 1914, Casement Additional Papers, NLI MS 36,203. Shortly after the foundation of the Irish Volunteers he told Elsie Henry that he hoped the ICA would amalgamate with them, 'and possibly the army of the North, Carson's, after Home Rule comes in'. Cullen, *World Upturning*, p. 17.

39. TS 'Conclusion of AE's speech' [at Irish Convention of 1917], Coffey/Trench Papers, NLI MS 46,302/3.

40. Béaslaí diary for 1912, NLI MS 33,957; Rosamond Jacob diary, 9 Feb. 1917, NLI MS 32,582/31; MacSwiney TS article *c*. 1905, MacSwiney Papers, UCDA P48b/344; Helena Molony to Gertrude Parry, late Sept. 1912, Casement Additional Papers, NLI MS 36,202/3; Margot to Cesca Trench, 2 Oct. [1914], Coffey/Trench Papers, NLI MS 46,330/3.

41. De Róiste to his wife, 15 and 20 July 1914, NLI MS 44,687(1).

42. 9 July 1915, de Róiste Papers, CCA 271/A/18.

43. See centenary issue of the Clonmel *Nationalist*, 1990, in O'Mahony Papers, NLI MS 44,304/3; also McGarry, *The Rising*, pp. 45–7, for the IRB's part in setting up Volunteering companies.

44. Michael Farry, *Sligo: The Irish Revolution 1912–1923* (Dublin, 2012), p. 19.

45. *Irish Volunteer*, 2 May 1914, quoted in Kelly, 'Machiavellian Moment?', p. 75. Previous references come from Seán T. O'Kelly's draft memoirs, O'Kelly/Ryan Papers, NLI MS 48,044/5; Béaslaí's diary, 12 Apr. and 6 May 1913, NLI MS 33,957/13; and Geraldine Plunkett Dillon's 'The Battle is Over 1913–1916', TS in MAI, BMH CD 5/6/1.

46. 4 May 1914; copy in O'Rahilly Papers, UCDA P102/337.

47. Mar. 1914, quoted in Kelly, 'Machiavellian Moment', p. 71; de Róiste to Casement, 22 June 1914, NLI MS 36,203.

48. Padraig Yeates, *A City in Wartime: Dublin 1914–1918* (Dublin, 2011), p. 3.

49. McCartan told Maloney it was Hobson's initiative, 5 Nov. 1923, Maloney Papers, Box 6. Hobson to McCartan, 13 Feb. 1924, ibid., lists the backers: Mrs Green £700, Erskine Childers £200, Mrs Childers £200, and further donations from Mary Spring-Rice, Berkeley and Casement himself. See Hay, *Bulmer Hobson*, pp. 159ff., for Hobson's part.

50. To Alice Stopford Green, [n.d.], quoted in Bruce Nelson, *Irish Nationalists and the Making of the Irish Race* (Princeton, 2012), p. 161.

51. Quoted in Nelson, *Irish Nationalists*, p. 163. Childers's views around this time are preserved in a letter to Casement of 6 June 1914. 'My opinion remains as before – it is in my book & that pamphlet – that everything we want can be obtained & much more easily – all essentials for a self-reliant national Ireland – without any question of revolutionary "independence" from the "master", just as his dominions have obtained it & can do as they will with it – & declare independence tomorrow if they choose.' This is in MAI, BMH CD 45/1/A2, a collection of papers from George Gavan Duffy. P. S. O'Hegarty's jaundiced view of the Childerses might be remembered here. He thought Childers's later irreconcilable republicanism came from his 'unreasonable and dangerous' wife, 'full of family pride and swank'; she and her husband 'had failed to make a noise in England'. Childers, a 'nervous wreck', was believed by O'Hegarty to have been 'drugging'. Letter to Stephen Gwynn, 16 Oct. 1929, NLI MS 8,600/13.

52. 28 July 1914, Coffey/Trench Papers, NLI MS 46,309/1.

53. Hilary Pyle, *Cesca's Diary 1913–1916: Where Art and Nationalism Meet* (Dublin, 2005), pp. 115ff.

54. De Róiste to his wife, 23 and 27 July 1914, de Róiste Papers, NLI MS 44,687/1; Béaslaí Papers, NLI MS 33,936/8.

55. Diary, 27 July 1914, NLI MS 32,582/27, and Mary Kate to Min, 'Sunday 27th' [Sept. 1914], O'Kelly/Ryan Papers, NLI MS 48,445/8.

56. *Irish Volunteer*, 4 Apr. 1914, quoted in Kelly, 'Machiavellian Moment?', p. 71.

57. Quoted in Keith Jeffrey, *Ireland and the Great War* (Cambridge, 2000), p. 21.

58. O'Shiel memoir, BMH Witness Statement No. 1,770, File 2, p. 155; File 3, pp. 399–400.

59. Diary, 4 Aug. 1914, NLI MS 32,582/27; Mary Kate to Min, 16 Oct. 1914, NLI MS 48,445/8.

60. Quoted in John Horne and Edward Madigan (eds.), *Towards Commemoration: Ireland in War and Revolution 1912–1923* (Dublin, 2013), p. 27.

61. Diary, *c.* 5 Sept. 1914, Coffey/Trench Papers, NLI MS 46,308/3.

62. Ibid., 1 and 5 Sept. 1914, NLI MS 46,308/3.

63. Later he realized that Kitchener would never have allowed this: see his BMH Witness Statement, duplicated in NLI MS 46,309/2.

64. 22 Aug. 1914, Coffey/Trench Papers, NLI MS 46,307/10; for correspondence with Hull, 21 Oct. 1914, see Coffey/Trench Papers, NLI MS 46,307/7.

65. See *Volunteer Gazette*, No. 1, Dec. 1913, MAI, BMH CD 107/2.

66. Coogan, *Meath*, p. 28; Charles Townshend, *Easter 1916: The Irish Rebellion* (London, 2005), pp. 70ff.; Kelly, 'Machiavellian Moment?', p. 84. The Coffey reflections are in his diary for 25 June 1915, Coffey/Trench Papers, NLI MS 46,308/4; Alice Stopford Green had warned him of this likelihood several months before.

67. Gary Holohan, quoted in McGarry, *The Rising*, p. 86; Kevin O'Shiel's BMH Witness Statement No. 1,770, pp. 506ff.

68. Quoted in McGarry, *The Rising*, p. 104.

69. Joe Good, *Enchanted by Dreams: The Journal of a Revolutionary*, Maurice Good (ed.) (Dingle, 1996), pp. 17–18. Also see Ann Matthews, *The Kimmage Garrison 1916: Making Billy-Can Bombs at Larkfield* (Dublin, 2010). Séamus O'Connor's account is in MAI, BMH CD 107/4/1, pp. 21–2.

70. Seán T. O'Kelly's account is in NLI MS 48,044/5; also Rosamond Jacob's diary, 25 Dec. 1914, NLI MS 32,582/27, and Pyle, *Cesca's Diary*, p. 178, for the censorship of *Nationality*.

71. 8 Feb. 1916, Coffey/Trench Papers, NLI MS 46,308/5.

72. Diary, 28 Oct. 1915, NLI MS 32,582/29. MAI, BMH CD 107/2/3 has a useful file of cuttings and letters as well as two issues of the journal; the list of contributors is as given by 'Roddy the Rover' (Aodh de Blácam) in *Irish Press*, 16 Apr. 1947. The quotation about the war is in the issue of 20 May 1915 (copy in MAI, BMH CD 327/11/3).

73. 12 Oct. 1914, Casement Additional Papers, NLI MS 36,202.

74. Quoted in Dermot Meleady, *John Redmond: The National Leader* (Dublin, 2013), p. 339.

75. De Róiste diary, 3 Nov. 1904, CCA 271/A/4, for rumours that O'Donovan Rossa drew an English pension; 271/A/5, Nov. 1904, for his failing powers and constant need of money; 271/A/6 for the revelation that he had attended Redmondite fundraisers in New York.

76. 29 July and 30 Aug. 1915, CCA 271/A/18.

77. 'An Open Letter to Thomas MacDonagh', *Irish Citizen*, 22 May 1915 (copy in MAI, BMH CD 62/10/1).

78. See the discussion of this deliberate technique of 'open' extremism by Desmond Ryan in Mulcahy Papers, UCDA P7/D/30.

79. Quoted in McGarry, *The Rising*, p. 115.

80. To his wife, 14 May 1916, Maxwell Papers, Princeton University, Box 6, Folder 9.

81. MacNeill says so very strongly in his memoir preserved in MAI, BMH CD 7.

7 FIGHTING

1. (London, 1936, reprinted Dublin, 1979), pp. 60–61.
2. See Molony's BMH Witness Statement No. 391.
3. Nora Connolly O'Brien's BMH Witness Statement No. 286 gives a full account of their involvement.
4. See Mabel to Desmond, 7 Feb. 1915, FitzGerald Papers, UCDA P80/1398. IRB Supreme Council meetings were relaying the message to American contacts in early Jan.: Charles Townshend, *Easter 1916: The Irish Rebellion* (London, 2005), p. 122. According to P. S. O'Hegarty, in May 1915 MacDermott outlined to him the plans for a Dublin rising, much as it was to happen, and said they would go ahead with or without German aid: *The Victory of Sinn Féin* (Dublin, 1924; reprinted Dublin, 1998), p. 2.
5. O'Kelly/Ryan Papers, NLI MS 48,044/1: a radio talk, the substance of which is repeated several times in O'Kelly's other autobiographical MSS.
6. Townshend, *Easter 1916*, p. 123.
7. O'Kelly/Ryan Papers, NLI MS 48,461/1.
8. Quoted in Séamus Ó Siocháin, *Roger Casement: Imperialist, Rebel, Revolutionary* (Dublin, 2008), p. 386.
9. Quoted in Michael Foy and Brian Barton, *The Easter Rising* (Stroud, 1999), p. 41.
10. Ibid., p. 113.
11. For McCartan's opinions, his letter to Maloney, 18 Jan. 1924, NYPL, Maloney Papers; for Denis McCullough, Fearghal McGarry, *The Rising: Ireland, Easter 1916* (Oxford, 2010), p. 97.
12. For Connolly's use of the phrase, see Donal Nevin, *James Connolly* (Dublin, 2006), p. 600.
13. Townshend, *Easter 1916*, p. 108.
14. O'Kelly/Ryan Papers, 'Talk No. 8', NLI MS 48,044/4.
15. BMH Witness Statement No. 399, p. 16.
16. Interview with Richard and Min Mulcahy, Mulcahy Papers, UCDA P7/D/30.
17. McGarry, *The Rising*, p. 165.
18. See especially Foy and Barton, *The Easter Rising*, pp. 167ff.
19. My thanks to Lauren Arrington for a very suggestive essay on this point.
20. Townshend, *Easter 1916*, p. 160.
21. Her diary for 25 Apr.: Hilary Pyle, *Cesca's Diary 1913–1916: Where Art and Nationalism Meet* (Dublin, 2005), pp. 203–4. 'Of course that will damn them. If they don't win, and it's impossible that they should, they'll all be shot.'

22. 'Ghosts' (Dublin, 1915), in *Collected Works of Padraic H. Pearse: Political Writings and Speeches* (London and Dublin, 1922), pp. 223–4.

23. The best of them are Townshend, *Easter 1916*, McGarry, *The Rising*, Foy and Barton, *Easter Rising*, and Clair Wills, *Dublin 1916: The Siege of the GPO* (London, 2009).

24. Grace Plunkett Papers, NLI MS 21,590.

25. Quoted in D. George Boyce, *Nationalism in Ireland* (London, 1991), p. 308.

26. Foy and Barton, *Easter Rising*, p. 36.

27. Ibid., p. 96.

28. Michael O'Flanagan's recollection, BMH Witness Statement No. 800, p. 25.

29. Ó Briain Papers, NLI MS 8,435/9. He also mentions Con Collins from Monagea, County Limerick, who followed the same trajectory through the London Post Office service and Gaelic circles there, before returning to Ireland, where he joined the Keating branch of the Gaelic League; he took dispatches to Kerry at Easter and was arrested with Stack over the Casement imbroglio. After the Treaty Debates in the Dáil (he opposed it) he retired and became a Post Office official once more.

30. A long interview in *New York Evening Post*, 11 Nov. 1915, Maloney Papers, NYPL, Box 6, is notably anti-British.

31. *Ireland Yesterday and Tomorrow* (Tralee, 1968), pp. 76–7.

32. See O'Kelly/Ryan Papers, 'Talk No. 8', NLI MS 48,044/4, and 'Talk No. 10', 48,044/2, for reiterated accounts of these events.

33. To Nina, 25 Apr. 1916, NLI MS 13,600, a copy.

34. The best guide to what did and did not happen in the provinces is Chapter 8 of Townshend, *Easter 1916*.

35. De Róiste's account in 1947 for Florence O'Donoghue, TCDA 10,539/274.

36. Quoted in McGarry, *The Rising*, p. 226. MacSwiney was obsessed by 'documents' and later arranged for certificates to be drawn up proving that Cork Volunteers had actually mobilized during the Rising.

37. McGarry, *The Rising*, p. 102; BMH Witness Statement No. 25 (Patrick Higgins), p. 5.

38. O'Hegarty, *The Victory of Sinn Féin*, p. 2.

39. See William Murphy, 'Enniscorthy's Revolution', in Colm Tóibín (ed.), *Enniscorthy: A History* (Wexford, 2010), pp. 399–433.

40. Quoted in McGarry, *The Rising*, p. 194.

41. Calculation of Foy and Barton, *Easter Rising*, p. 211.

42. McGarry, *The Rising*, pp. 254ff., for a discussion of this.

43. Reverend Bertram Carter, quoted in ibid., p. 194.

44. 9 May 1916, O'Kelly Additional Papers, NLI MS 47,974/1. During his initial incarceration, MacDermott nearly succeeded in slipping away with deportees, but was recognized by a 'G-man', John Barton, who ironically remarked, 'Ah, no, Johnny, you're not leaving us': a vivid indication of the intimate world of Dublin surveillance. McGarry, *The Rising*, p. 259.

45. Marie O'Neill, *Grace Gifford Plunkett and Irish Freedom: Tragic Bride of 1916* (Dublin, 2000), p. 43.

46. Edith Lyttelton, 'Notes from Ireland between January the Third and January the Fifteenth 1921', in Chandos Papers, Churchill College, Cambridge, 1.6/4. Lyttelton, who heard this from an Irish friend, added: 'My friend said this shewed great callousness, but I felt one could not tell. However, my friend's husband said that Plunkett was a degenerate and the story of his marriage was not at all a romantic one. It had been insisted upon by the priests. I heard this confirmed afterwards by the judge who tried him.' This is probably typical of the rumours circulating at the time.

47. McGarry, *The Rising*, p. 251.

48. Seán T. O'Kelly described a three-hour conversation with Con Markievicz after her release, where she talked of little else, and wanted to start a campaign to drive him from public life; to Mary Kate, 3 Aug. 1917, O'Kelly Additional Papers, NLI MS 47,974/2.

49. As he recorded in letters to his wife in the Maxwell Papers at Princeton University, Box 6, Folder 9. 'They are at me every moment not to overdo death sentences – I never intended to but some must suffer for their crimes' (9 May 1916); also a letter of Asquith's to him, 27 May (Box 2, Folder 8), urging him to practise restraint.

50. 25 July 1916, to Nina [copy], Casement Papers, NLI MS 13,600; for his trial speech, Ó Siocháin, pp. 458-9.

51. Ruth Dudley Edwards, *Patrick Pearse: The Triumph of Failure* (London, 1979), p. 318.

52. Gerard MacAtasney, *Seán MacDiarmada: The Mind of the Revolution* (Manorhamilton, 2004), p. 122.

53. *Indiana Catholic and Record* cutting, May 1916, in MAI, BMH CD 62/3/3.

54. To her aunt Frances Trench, 29 Apr. 1916, Pyle, *Cesca's Diary*, pp. 213-14.

55. Quoted in Leeann Lane, *Rosamond Jacob: Third Person Singular* (Dublin, 2010), p. 103.

56. Quoted in Margaret Ward, *Hanna Sheehy-Skeffington: A Life* (Cork, 1997), p. 198.

57. Entries in diary, 25 Apr., 30 Apr., 13 May, 26 Apr., 16 June 1916, NLI MS 32,582/29.

58. Official summons preserved in NLI MS 48,461/7.

59. In a letter to Agnes of 1 July 1916 (O'Kelly/Ryan Papers, NLI MS 48,446/2) she surmised that the charges arose from a meeting at Carrig-byrne the previous summer. Lewes was not a difficult confinement; a trip up to London to see her solicitor was 'a great day with some of the MPs; luncheon at the House and tea at Lyons', while the prison provided a good library and food, and smart clothes as well as food-parcels were sent from home, not to mention baskets of strawberries sent in by sympathetic local suffragettes.

60. 1 Sept. 1916, O'Kelly/Ryan Papers NLI MS 48,446/4.

61. To Nell, 2 Aug. 1916, O'Kelly/Ryan Papers, NLI MS 48,446/3.

62. Quoted in Risteárd Mulcahy, *Richard Mulcahy (1886–1971): A Family Memoir* (Dublin, 1999), p. 37.

63. Seán T to Mary Kate, 30 Dec. 1915, O'Kelly Additional Papers, NLI MS 47,974/2.

64. Quoted in MacAtasney, *Seán MacDiarmada*, pp. 139–40.

65. Seán T to Mary Kate, 11 June 1916, O'Kelly Additional Papers, NLI MS 47,974/1.

66. Father Mark O'Byrne to Mary Kate, 4 June 1916, O'Kelly/Ryan Papers, NLI MS 48,446/1.

67. Kathleen Browne to Nell, 13 Aug. [1916], O'Kelly/Ryan Papers, NLI MS 48,446/3: she planned to wear 'a completely Irish outfit of a sombre kind – purple tweed, trimmed with poplin. It does not seem to me right to wear anything bright or gay even at a wedding.'

68. 11 June 1916, O'Kelly Additional Papers, NLI MS 47,974/1 – a letter signed 'with love' for the first time.

69. To Mary Kate, 14 June 1916, 6 Aug. 1916, O'Kelly Additional Papers, NLI MS 47,974/1.

70. O'Kelly/Ryan Papers, NLI MS 48,044/3, 4.

71. Letters to Mary Kate, 4, 16 and 20 Mar. 1917, O'Kelly Additional Papers, NLI MS 47,974/2. Murray told Figgis that 'we had made a splendid impression everywhere by our gentlemanly behaviour, etc.' and cheeringly forecast the imminent demise of the Irish Party.

72. Liam Ó Briain to Piaras Béaslaí, [n.d. but 1917?], TS copy, Béaslaí Papers, NLI MS 33,970/6.

73. NLI MS 48,044/3, 4, and letter to Mary Kate, 20 Mar. 1917, 47,974/2.

74. Helena Molony and Winifred Carney (James Connolly's redoubtable secretary, who took his dictation amid the shelling of the GPO) were – according

to Molony – extremely sad to leave their internment. 'I really believe that whole household loved the three Irish ... If I had my choice I would rather have stayed over Christmas. They were all so overwrought that we both hated leaving them. Mrs Herbert played from 11 o clock and it was like a country pub to see them singing and shaking hands with us and their eyes flooded with tears the whole time you'd think we were their nearest relation. Miss Carney collapsed on the table sobbing and even I felt a bit damp. It was very sad, leaving them on Christmas Eve' (to Nell Ryan, 22 Jan. 1917, O'Kelly/Ryan Papers, NLI MS 48,447/1).

8 RECKONING

1. Translated by Robert Chandler (London, 2006), p. 828.
2. To Mary Kate, 22 Apr. 1917, O'Kelly Additional Papers NLI MS 47,974/2. The allegation against O'Flanagan is in the BMH Witness Statement of Leslie Price (Mrs Tom Barry), No. 1,754, pp. 33–4.
3. TS copy of letter to Pat McCartan, [n.d. but summer 1916], Maloney Papers, NYPL, Box 6; also Seán T to Mary Kate, 26 Apr. 1917, O'Kelly Additional Papers, NLI MS 47,974/2.
4. Ronan Fanning, *Fatal Path: British Government and Irish Revolution 1910–1922* (London, 2013), p. 144.
5. Quoted in Michael Laffan, *The Resurrection of Ireland: The Sinn Féin Party 1916–1923* (Cambridge, 1999), p. 116.
6. See Virginia Glandon, *Arthur Griffith and the Advanced-Nationalist Press in Ireland 1900–1922* (New York, 1985), p. 178, for a suggestive letter to Seán T. O'Kelly, 23 Jan. 1919; also Ronan Fanning, Michael Kennedy, Dermot Keogh and Eunan O'Halpin (eds.), *Documents on Irish Foreign Policy. Volume I: 1919–1922* (Dublin, 1998), No. 3/5, for his manifestoes from Gloucester Gaol.
7. Quoted in Laffan, *Resurrection of Ireland*, pp. 87–8.
8. Diarmaid Ferriter, *Judging Dev: A Reassessment of the Life and Legacy of Éamon de Valera* (Dublin, 2007), p. 91.
9. Laffan, *Resurrection of Ireland*, p. 260.
10. See Peter Hart, *The IRA at War 1916–1923* (Oxford, 2003), pp. 49–50; Charles Townshend, *The Republic: The Fight for Irish Independence 1918–1923* (London, 2013), pp. 26–9; Terence Dooley, 'IRA Veterans and Land Division in Independent Ireland 1923–48', in Fearghal McGarry (ed.), *Republicanism in Modern Ireland* (Dublin, 2003), pp. 86–107.

11. 7 Oct. 1918. For the full text of this letter see R. F. Foster, *W. B. Yeats: A Life. Vol. II: The Arch-Poet 1915–1939* (Oxford, 2003), pp. 131–2.

12. See Margaret Ward, *Hanna Sheehy-Skeffington: A Life* (Cork, 1997), pp. 225–6.

13. Máire Comerford, *The First Dáil* (Dublin, 1969), p. 51.

14. Laffan, *Resurrection of Ireland*, pp. 173, 185.

15. See correspondence in O'Kelly/Ryan Papers, NLI MS 48,448/1.

16. Townshend, *The Republic*, pp. 67ff.

17. This sweeping statement (part of an argument that instanced the Brehon Laws as 'the father of the Land Decree of the Russian Soviet Republic') was actually a statement drafted by Sinn Féin's American sympathizer Lincoln Colcord; see McCartan Papers, NLI MS 17,682.

18. This document, along with friendly letters from the Bolsheviks Santeri Nuorteva and L. A. Martens, is in NLI MS 17,682.

19. For McCartan's Russian adventures see Maloney Papers, NYPL, Box 7, Folder 72, for the TS report written later on (probably 1938); also McGarrity Papers, NLI MS 17,681, and his book *With de Valera in America* (Dublin, 1932).

20. 'Dynamics of Violence', in Hart, *The IRA at War*, and Joost Augusteijn, *From Public Defiance to Guerrilla Warfare: The Experience of Ordinary Volunteers in the Irish War of Independence 1916–1921* (Dublin, 1996).

21. 'The man who serves on an exemption tribunal, the doctor who treats soldiers or examines conscripts, the man who voluntarily surrenders when called for, the man who in any shape or form applies for an exemption, the man who drives a police-car or assists in the transport of army supplies, all these having assisted the enemy must be shot or otherwise destroyed with the least possible delay.' 14 Oct. 1918, quoted in Glandon, *Arthur Griffith and the Advanced-Nationalist Press*, p. 175.

22. *Round Table*, June 1921, quoted in Francis J. Costello, *The Irish Revolution and Its Aftermath, 1916–1923: Years of Revolt* (Dublin, 2003), p. 42.

23. See O'Kelly/Ryan Papers, NLI MS 48,044/2 for further details. According to O'Kelly, Johnston and William O'Brien sent in only rough notes, but their contribution was probably more decisive than that. The original draft had allegedly been contributed to by Eoin MacNeill, Robert Barton, Piaras Béaslaí, Michael Collins, Harry Boland, J. J. Walsh and Pádraic Ó Máille.

24. Comerford, *First Dáil, passim*.

25. Quoted in ibid., p. 75.

26. Rosamond Jacob to Hanna Sheehy-Skeffington, [n.d.], Sheehy-Skeffington Papers, NLI MS 22,689. Ní Bruadair would later devote

much of her efforts to building a hospital on the Kerry coast, unfortunately evicting some of her 'beloved people' from the surrounding land in
the process.

27. Townshend, *Republic*, p. 114.
28. 'The Geography of Revolution in Ireland', in Hart, *The IRA at War*; a
    subject opened up by David Fitzpatrick, 'The Geography of Irish Nation-
    alism 1910–1921', *Past & Present*, No. 78 (Feb. 1978), and illustrated by
    important local studies of Longford by Marie Coleman and of Sligo by
    Michael Farry, among others.
29. Cabinet minutes, 13 Aug. 1920, quoted in Costello, *Irish Revolution*,
    p. 204; for Warren Fisher report, Fanning, *Fatal Path*, p. 228.
30. Quoted in Costello, *Irish Revolution*, pp. 325–6.
31. See 'A Prayer' in Francis J. Costello, *Enduring the Most: The Life and
    Death of Terence MacSwiney* (Dingle, 1995), p. 151.
32. Costello, *Enduring the Most*, p. 76; the theory that this may have involved
    killing the anti-republican Bishop Daniel Cohalan seems improbable.
33. Ibid., pp. 128, 132, 134.
34. TS memoir by Muriel, Béaslaí Papers, NLI MS 33,914/11.
35. [n.d. but *c*. Oct. 1917], MacSwiney Papers, UCDA P48c/327. It is a very
    manic production, written from various Dublin locations, including the
    National Gallery. 'Don't any of you worry about my not sleeping, indeed
    my nights are not like the sleepless ones you had, they were frightful. I
    am perfectly happy awake – thinking of the most frightfully interesting
    things the whole time.' In a later letter, of late May or early June
    1918 (329), she charges him with care of her soul and confesses an over-
    whelming sense of sin and inadequacy, and worries about her ability to
    care for her coming child.
36. De Róiste to his wife, 24, 26, 28, 30 Aug., 8 Sept. 1920, TCDA
    10,539/493–510.
37. 29 Oct. 1920. See Foster, *The Arch-Poet*, p. 182.
38. Costello, *Enduring the Most*, p. 206; also see pp. 181–2 for resonant
    quotes.
39. Quoted in Leeann Lane, *Rosamond Jacob: Third Person Singular* (Dub-
    lin, 2010), p. 48.
40. Treaty Debates, 17 Dec. 1921, quoted in Costello, *Enduring the Most*,
    pp. 234–5.
41. Ernie O'Malley, *The Singing Flame* (Dublin, 1978), p. 16.
42. Wilfrid Ewart, *A Journey in Ireland in 1921*, Paul Bew and Patrick
    Maume (eds.) (Dublin 2008), p. 40.
43. Quoted in Costello, *The Irish Revolution*, p. 159.

44. 17 May 1919, quoted in Laffan, *Resurrection of Ireland*, p. 243.
45. Treaty Debates, 3 Jan. 1922, quoted in ibid., p. 243.
46. To Maloney, 31 Jan. 1922, Maloney Papers, NYPL, Box 6; TS copy in NLI MS 17,675/3. For Smuts see Costello, *The Irish Revolution*, p. 235.
47. Townshend, *The Republic*, pp. 384ff., for a lapidary exposition.
48. Tom Garvin, *1922: The Birth of Irish Democracy* (Dublin, 1996), pp. 32, 101.
49. Quoted in ibid., pp. 41–2.
50. 24 Apr. 1922, quoted in ibid., p. 151.
51. Quoted in John Regan, *The Irish Counter-Revolution 1921–1936* (Dublin, 1999), p. 182.
52. Garvin, *1922*, p. 25; for the threat to male members, ibid., p. 119.
53. *Free State*, 20 July 1922, quoted in Glandon, *Arthur Griffith and the Advanced-Nationalist Press*, p. 228.
54. Townshend, *The Republic*, p. 56.
55. [n.d.], Mulcahy Papers, UCDA, P7/D/42.
56. Quoted in Costello, *The Irish Revolution*, p. 294.
57. A statement of 1963, quoted as an epigraph to Garvin, *1922*.
58. Hart, *The IRA at War*, p. 78.
59. For their closeness see prison letters in O'Kelly/Ryan Papers, NLI MS 48,446/3; O'Kelly describes how disconsolate he was when 'Dinny' was released.
60. Quoted in Costello, *The Irish Revolution*, p. 314. For Lynch's 'Orders of Frightfulness' see P. S. O'Hegarty, *The Victory of Sinn Féin* (Dublin, 1924), Appendix. He ordered the assassination not only of Free State politicians but of supportive newspaper editors.
61. W. B. Yeats, *Explorations* (London, 1962), p. 413 (from *On the Boiler*, 1939).
62. Quoted in Regan, *Irish Counter-Revolution*, p. 87, a conversation with Mulcahy in 1965. For O'Higgins and 1916, see ibid., p. 84.

9 REMEMBERING

1. McCullough Papers, UCDA P120/17.
2. Important discussions of this theme are to be found in Ian McBride (ed.), *History and Memory in Modern Ireland* (Cambridge, 2001); Ann Dolan, *Commemorating the Irish Civil War: History and Memory 1923–2000* (Cambridge, 2003); Mary E. Daly and Margaret O'Callaghan (eds.), *1916 in 1966: Commemorating the Easter Rising* (Dublin, 2007);

Mark McCarthy, *Ireland's 1916 Rising: Explorations of History-Making, Commemoration and Heritage in Modern Times* (Farnham, 2012).

3. Annie MacSwiney to Sheila Humphreys, 29 Oct. 1928, quoted in McBride, *History and Memory*, pp. 193–4.

4. Peter Hart, *The IRA at War 1916–1923* (Oxford, 2003), p. 79.

5. Quoted in Clair Wills, *Dublin 1916: The Siege of the GPO* (London, 2009), p. 135.

6. See Dolan, *Commemorating the Irish Civil War*, pp. 73ff., and also her comments in Chapter 1 for the activities of the Free State Commemoration Committee, in which Desmond FitzGerald was a leading light. Also Deirdre MacMahon, '"A Worthy Monument to a Great Man": Piaras Béaslaí's Life of Michael Collins', *Bullán: An Irish Studies Journal*, Vol. 2, No. 2 (Winter/Spring 1996).

7. MacMahon, '"A Worthy Monument"', p. 59.

8. Review by 'W. J. W.' [Wylie?], *Studies*, Mar. 1927, quoted in Brian P. Murphy, *Patrick Pearse and the Lost Republican Ideal* (Dublin, 1991), p. 97.

9. To Gladys Hynes, 29 May 1937, FitzGerald Papers, UCDA P80/1693.

10. McCartan to William Maloney, 15 Nov. 1923, Maloney Papers, NYPL, Box 6.

11. See Hobson to McCartan, 24 Apr. 1936 and 1 Feb. 1937, Maloney Papers, NYPL, Box 6; and for an exhaustive treatment, W. J. McCormack, *Roger Casement in Death: Or Haunting the Free State* (Dublin, 2002).

12. 23 Oct. 1924, 12 Feb. 1928, Maloney Papers, NYPL, Box 6.

13. See Frances Flanagan's pioneering Ph.D. thesis '"Your Dream Not Mine": Nationalist Disillusionment and the Memory of Revolution in the Irish Free State' (Oxford, 2009), to which this chapter is much indebted.

14. O'Hegarty's high opinion of O'Duffy can be seen in the obituary he wrote in *Dublin Magazine*, Vol. 10 (1935), p. 92.

15. *Victory of Sinn Féin* (Dublin, 1924), p. 38.

16. Ibid., pp. 54–5.

17. To Maloney, 29 Dec. 1924, NYPL, Box 6. The reference is to AE's review in *Irish Statesman*, 20 Dec. 1924, signed 'Y. O.'.

18. To Stephen Gwynn, 16 Oct. 1929, NLI MS 8,600/13.

19. *Victory of Sinn Féin*, p. 91.

20. 'A View of Irish Culture', *Irish Statesman*, 20 June 1925. See also Frank Shovlin, *The Irish Literary Periodical 1923–1958* (Oxford, 2003), p. 32.

21. Nicholas Allen, *George Russell (AE) and the New Ireland 1905–1930* (Dublin, 2003), p. 201.

22. 'The Return to the Normal', *Irish Statesman*, 22 Dec. 1923.

23. Perceptively noted by Frances Flanagan. For analyses of *The Interpreters* see Allen, *George Russell*, Chapter 4, and Flanagan, '"Your Dream Not Mine"', Chapter 4.

24. Letters to St John Ervine, 5 Apr. 1933, quoted in Flanagan, '"Your Dream Not Mine"', p. 178, and to Yeats (23 May 1932), quoted in R. F. Foster, *W. B. Yeats: A Life. Vol. II: The Arch-Poet 1915–1939* (Oxford, 2003), p. 438.

25. 'Lessons of Revolution', *Studies*, Mar. 1923, quoted in Allen, *George Russell*, p. 138.

26. See Shovlin, *The Irish Literary Periodical*, Chapter 3.

27. Quoted in Flanagan, '"Your Dream Not Mine"', p. 192.

28. Ibid., p. 228.

29. Flanagan suggests that the landmark short-story collections of the early 1930s, O'Faolain's *Midsummer Night Madness* and O'Connor's *Guests of the Nation*, should be seen in this context.

30. 26 Feb. 1926, quoted in Robert Lowery (ed.), *A Whirlwind in Dublin: 'The Plough and the Stars' riots* (Westport, Conn., 1984), p. 82. See Foster, *The Arch-Poet*, pp. 304–9, for a full treatment.

31. Risteárd Mulcahy, *Richard Mulcahy (1886–1971): A Family Memoir* (Dublin, 1999), p. 261.

32. O'Faolain to James O'Donovan, 12 Aug. 1936, James O'Donovan Papers, NLI MS 21,987/xi.

33. Quoted by Diarmaid Ferriter in Daly and O'Callaghan, *1916 in 1966*, p. 208.

34. McCarthy, *Ireland's 1916 Rising*, p. 198.

35. Marnie Hay, *Bulmer Hobson and the Nationalist Movement in Twentieth-Century Ireland* (Manchester, 2009), p. 244.

36. The body was the Federation of IRA 1916–1921; quoted by Diarmaid Ferriter in O'Callaghan and Daly, *1916 in 1966*, p. 213.

37. Quoted in ibid., pp. 214–15.

38. For the BMH see Fearghal McGarry, *Rebels: Voices from the Easter Rising* (Dublin, 2011), Chapter 1; Diarmaid Ferriter, '"In Such Deadly Earnest"', *Dublin Review*, No. 12 (Autumn 2003), pp. 36–64; Evi Gkotzaridis, 'Revisionist Historians and the Modern Irish State: The Conflict between the Advisory Committee and the Bureau of Military History 1947–66', *Irish Historical Studies*, Vol. 35, No. 137 (May 2006), pp. 99–116; and Eve Morrison's Ph.D. thesis 'The Bureau of Military History: Separatist Veterans' Narratives of the Irish Revolution' (Trinity College, Dublin, 2011). For an elegant overview of the development of 1916 studies see Michael Laffan in Daly and O'Callaghan, *1916 in 1966*, pp. 323–42.

39. Ferriter, '"In Such Deadly Earnest"', p. 37.
40. *Sunday Independent*, 28 Apr. 1946, quoted in Gkotzaridis, 'Revisionist Historians', p. 105. O'Hegarty was probably thinking of R. M. Fox, who had been involved in the Citizen Army and indefatigably presented the revolution as a socialist revolt (see, for instance, *Green Banners: The Story of the Irish Struggle* (1938), *History of the Irish Citizen Army* (1943), *James Connolly: The Forerunner* (1946)). This analysis has recently been rediscovered by the English film-maker Ken Loach in *The Wind That Shakes the Barley*. O'Hegarty makes his feelings about the Citizen Army plain in his *History of Ireland under the Union 1801 to 1922* (London, 1952), p. 672.
41. De Róiste to Florence O'Donoghue, 5 Feb. 1955, O'Donoghue Papers, NLI MS 31,276/1.
42. Quoted in Ferriter, '"In Such Deadly Earnest"', p. 42.
43. Quoted in McGarry, *Rebels*, p. xvi.
44. Quoted in Ferriter, '"In Such Deadly Earnest"', p. 45.
45. O'Kelly's, No. 1,765, is particularly long and exigent. Hobson's was submitted (with a great deal of accompanying material) notably early – No. 30.
46. See O'Donoghue Papers, NLI MS 31,270/1–2.
47. Richard English, *Ernie O'Malley: IRA Intellectual* (Oxford, 1998), pp. 137ff., for O'Malley and O'Flaherty. The incident of killing a captured British soldier in *Guests of the Nation* bears a very close resemblance to an event in *On Another Man's Wound*.
48. English, *Ernie O'Malley*, p. 6.
49. These are collected in the O'Malley Papers, UCDA P17b, and partially published in Cormac O'Malley and Tim Horgan (eds.), *The Men Will Talk to Me: Kerry Interviews by Ernie O'Malley* (Cork, 2012), and Cormac O'Malley and Cormac Ó Comhraí (eds.), *The Men Will Talk to Me: Galway Interviews by Ernie O'Malley* (Cork, 2013).
50. *Kerry Interviews*, p. 277.
51. Ibid., pp. 68–9; some of this material, and his radio broadcasts, went into his book *Raids and Rallies* (London, 1982).
52. To Etáin O'Malley, 13 Mar. 1956; Cormac O'Malley and Nicholas Allen (eds.), *Broken Landscapes: Selected Letters of Ernie O'Malley 1924–1957* (Dublin, 2011), p. 363.
53. For a full consideration, see McCormack, *Roger Casement in Death: Haunting the Free State*.
54. Nina Newman to Gertrude Parry, Casement Papers, NLI MS 13,075/4.
55. To Maloney, 3 Dec. 1924, Maloney Papers, NYPL, Box 6.

56. BMH Witness Statements No. 588 (J. M. Cronin) and No. 253 (A. M. Sullivan).

57. Lucy McDiarmid, *The Irish Art of Controversy* (Dublin, 2005), pp. 205, 199.

58. *Life and the Dream: A Literary Life in Europe and America* (London, 1947), p. 281.

59. Margaret Ward, *Hanna Sheehy-Skeffington: A Life* (Cork, 1997), p. 262.

60. To Esther Roper, [n.d.], quoted in ibid., p. 305; also see p. 283.

61. Diary, quoted in Leeann Lane, *Rosamond Jacob: Third Person Singular* (Dublin, 2010), pp. 192, 255.

62. Quoted in Joanne Mooney Eichacker, *Irish Republican Women in America: Lecture Tours 1916–1925* (Dublin, 2003), p. 160.

63. Memo in Béaslaí Papers, NLI MS 33,914/11.

64. To E. Becque, 11 June 1937, MacSwiney Papers, UCDA P48c/41.

65. See Máire MacSwiney Brugha, *History's Daughter: A Memoir from the Only Child of Terence MacSwiney* (Dublin, 2005).

66. 2 Oct. 1925, 19 Feb. 1927, Maloney Papers, NYPL, Box 6.

67. To Maloney, 17 Nov. 1926, McCartan Papers, NLI MS 17,675/7.

68. Foster, *The Arch-Poet*, pp. 592–6.

69. He tried to run again in the presidential election of 1959, aged eighty-one, but failed to secure the requisite number of nominees.

70. To McGarrity, 16 Oct. 1925, McGarrity Papers, NLI MS 17,457/14. See John Regan, *The Irish Counter-Revolution 1921–1936* (Dublin, 1999), p. 187, for O'Higgins's part.

71. Regan, *The Irish Counter-Revolution*, p. 88.

72. Mulcahy, *Family Memoir*, p. 263.

73. Quoted in Flanagan, '"Your Dream Not Mine"', p. 11.

74. See Robert Wohl, *The Generation of 1914* (London, 1980), p. 210.

> What allowed European intellectuals born between 1880 and 1900 to view themselves as a distinct generation was that their youth coincided with the opening of the twentieth century and their lives were then bifurcated by the Great War. Those who survived into the decade of the 1920s perceived their lives as being divided into a *before*, a *during*, and an *after*, categories most of them equated with the stages of life known as youth, young manhood, and maturity. What bound the generation of 1914 together was not just their experiences during the war, as many of them came later to believe, but the fact that they grew up and formulated their first ideas in the world from which the war issued, a world framed by two dates, 1900 and 1914. This world was the 'vital horizon' within which they began conscious historical life.

75. 10 Apr. 1965, O'Kelly/Ryan Papers, NLI MS 48,044/1. The talk was to the Donegal Association on 6 Apr. Ó Briain also sent a series of notes robustly defending the Treaty.
76. See Dolan, *Commemorating the Irish Civil War*, p. 81.
77. De Róiste Papers, CCA 271/A/1.
78. 15 Apr. 1949, FitzGerald Papers, UCDA P80/1677(1).
79. Communication from Jennifer FitzGerald, 14 May 2012.
80. 26 May 1944, FitzGerald Papers, UCDA P80/1664.
81. Quoted in Regan, *The Irish Counter-Revolution*, p. 257.
82. To Maloney, 20 Mar. 1925, McCartan Papers, NLI MS 17,675/6.
83. R. D. Edwards, 'The Future of Fianna Fáil', *Leader*, 29 Jan. 1955, quoted in Gkotzaridis, p. 101.

CONCLUSION

1. Mark McCarthy, *Ireland's 1916 Rising: Explorations of History-Making, Commemoration and Heritage in Modern Times* (Farnham, 2012), p. 161.
2. John Marcus O'Sullivan, quoted in John Regan, *The Irish Counter-Revolution 1921–1936* (Dublin, 1999), p. 378.
3. 24 May 1905, CCA 271/A/7.
4. 20 Mar. 1906, CCA 271/A/10; he leant towards 'a Christian-Socialist-Democratic Republic . . . in which Irish educational capacity, intellectual attainments and the accepted Christian virtues of honesty, truth and integrity would be the best qualifications to success'.
5. 11 June 1917, McGarrity Papers, NLI MS 17,676.
6. 'Ireland: Past and Future', in William FitzGerald (ed.), *Voices of Ireland* (Dublin, 1923), p. 87, quoted in Frances Flanagan, '"Your Dream Not Mine"', p. 169.
7. Liam Brady, quoted in Fearghal McGarry, *The Rising: Ireland, Easter 1916* (Oxford, 2010), p. 62.
8. Sean O'Faolain, *Constance Markievicz; or, The Average Revolutionary* (London, [1934]; reprint London, 1987), p. 74.
9. 'From the Other Shore', quoted in Isaiah Berlin, *Russian Thinkers* (London, 1979), p. 89.
10. Quoted in R. F. Foster, *W. B. Yeats: A Life. Vol. II: The Arch-Poet 1915–1939* (Oxford, 2003), p. 63.

Bibliography

PRIMARY SOURCES

Collections in National Library of Ireland

Piaras Béaslaí
F. J. Bigger
Roger Casement
Casement Additional Papers
Tom and Kathleen Clarke
Coffey and Chenevix Trench families
Liam de Róiste
Geraldine Plunkett Dillon
Louise Gavan Duffy
Gaelic League of London minute-books
Alice Stopford Green
Stephen Gwynn
Bulmer Hobson
Rosamond Jacob
Patrick McCartan
Fionan MacColuim
Thomas MacDonagh
Joseph McGarrity
Art Ó Briain
Seán T. Ó Ceallaigh [O'Kelly]
Seán T. Ó Ceallaigh [O'Kelly] and the Ryans of Tomcoole
James O'Donovan
Seán O'Mahony
Grace Plunkett
Joseph Mary Plunkett

Hanna and Francis Sheehy-Skeffington
Sweetman family

Collections in UCD Archives

Michael Collins
Máire Comerford
Eithne Coyle
George Gavan Duffy
Denis and Mabel FitzGerald
Michael Hayes
Hugh Kennedy
Denis McCullough
Eoin MacNeill
Mary MacSwiney
Terence MacSwiney
Michael MacWhite
Richard Mulcahy
Kathleen O'Connell
Michael O'Rahilly
Desmond Ryan
W. P. Ryan

National Archives of Ireland

Bureau of Military History Witness Statements (also online at www.bureauof
militaryhistory.ie)
Crime Branch Special Files

Military Archives of Ireland

Bureau of Military History Contemporary Documents

Trinity College, Dublin, Archives

Liam de Róiste

Allen Library

Madeleine ffrench-Mullen, memoir/diary

Kilmainham Gaol Museum

Helena Molony

Pearse Museum

St Enda's Collection

Cork City and County Archives

Liam de Róiste

Boole Library, University College, Cork

Daniel Corkery

National Archives of Great Britain, Kew

Dublin Castle Special Branch Files: Sinn Féin and republican suspects 1899–1921

Churchill College, Cambridge

Chandos Papers

New York Public Library

William P. Maloney

Princeton University

Sir John Maxwell

Periodicals

An Claidheamh Soluis
Bean na hÉireann
Catholic Bulletin
Dana
Freeman's Journal

Inis Fáil
Irish Citizen
Irish Freedom
Irish Peasant
Irish Worker
Leader
National Student
Samhain
Shan Van Vocht
Sinn Féin
Uladh
United Irishman

Memoirs, Contemporary Writings and Published Letters

Andrews, C. S., *Dublin Made Me: An Autobiography* (Dublin, 1979, reprinted Dublin, 2011)

Birmingham, George A., *An Irishman Looks at His World* (London, 1921)

Breen, Dan, *My Fight for Irish Freedom* (Dublin, 1924, reprinted Dublin, 1981)

Briollay, Sylvain, *Ireland in Rebellion* (Dublin, 1922)

Brugha, Máire, *History's Daughter: A Memoir from the Only Child of Terence MacSwiney* (Dublin, 2005)

Clarke, Kathleen, *Revolutionary Woman: My Fight for Freedom*, Helen Litton (ed.) (Dublin, 1997)

Colum, Mary, *Life and the Dream: A Literary Life in Europe and America* (London, 1947)

Comerford, Máire, *The First Dáil* (Dublin, 1969)

Cousins, James and Margaret, *We Two Together* (Madras, 1950)

Czira, Sydney Gifford, *The Years Flew By: The Recollections of Madame Sydney Czira* (Dublin, 1974)

De Blácam, Aodh, *What Sinn Féin Stands For: The Irish Republican Movement, Its History, Aims and Ideals* (Dublin, 1921)

Dillon, Geraldine Plunkett, *All in the Blood: A Memoir of the Plunkett Family, the 1916 Rising and the War of Independence*, Honor Ó Brolcháin (ed.) (Dublin, 2006)

Ewart, Wilfrid, *A Journey in Ireland in 1921*, Paul Bew and Patrick Maume (eds.) (Dublin, 2008)

FitzGerald, Desmond, *Memoirs of Desmond FitzGerald* (Dublin, 1968)

Good, Joe, *Enchanted by Dreams: The Journal of a Revolutionary*, Maurice Good (ed.) (Dingle, 1996)

Good, J. W., *Ulster and Ireland* (Dublin, 1919)

Hackett, Francis, *The Green Lion* (New York, 1936)

Henry, Elsie, *The World Upturning: Elsie Henry's Wartime Diaries 1913–1919*, Clara Cullen (ed.) (Dublin, 1913)

Hobson, Bulmer, *Ireland Yesterday and Tomorrow* (Tralee, 1968)

Lyons, George A., *Some Recollections of Griffith and His Times* (Dublin, 1923)

MacBride, Maud Gonne, *Always Your Friend: The Gonne-Yeats Letters 1893–1938*, Anna MacBride White and A. Norman Jeffares (eds.) (London, 1992)

—, *Maud Gonne's Irish Nationalist Writings 1895–1946*, Karen Steele (ed.) (Dublin, 2004)

—, *A Servant of the Queen* (Dublin, 1938)

McCartan, Patrick, *With de Valera in America* (New York, 1932)

MacDonagh, Thomas, *When the Dawn is Come: A Tragedy in Three Acts* (Dublin, 1908)

MacEoin, Uinseann, *Survivors: The Story of Ireland's Struggle as Told through Some of Her Outstanding Living People* (Dublin, [n.d. but 1980])

McGarrity, Joseph, *The McGarrity Papers: Revelations of the Irish Revolutionary Movement in Ireland and America 1900–1940*, Seán Cronin (ed.) (Tralee, 1972)

MacSwiney, Muriel, *Muriel MacSwiney: Letters to Angela Clifford*, Angela Clifford (ed.) (Belfast, 1996)

Terence MacSwiney, *Principles of Freedom* (Dublin, 1921)

—, *The Revolutionist: A Play in Five Acts* (Dublin, 1914)

Milligan, Alice, *Poems by Alice Milligan*, Henry Mangan (ed.) (Dublin, 1954)

Nic Shiubhlaigh, Máire (with Edward Kenny), *The Splendid Years: Recollections of Máire Nic Shiubhlaigh's Story of the Irish National Theatre as Told to Edward Kenny* (Dublin, 1955)

O'Duffy, Eimar, *The Wasted Island* (New York, 1920)

O'Faolain, Sean, *Vive Moi!* (second edition, London, 1993)

Ó Gaora, Colm, *On the Run: The Story of an Irish Freedom Fighter* (a translation of Colm Ó Gaora's *Mise*), Mícheál Ó hAodha and Ruan O'Donnell (eds.) (Cork, 2011)

O'Hegarty, P. S., *The Victory of Sinn Féin* (Dublin, 1924, republished 1998)

O'Malley, Cormac K. H., and Allen, Nicholas (eds.), *Broken Landscapes: Selected Letters of Ernie O'Malley 1924–1957* (Dublin, 2011)

—, and English, Richard (eds.), *Prisoners: The Civil War Letters of Ernie O'Malley* (Swords, 1991)

—, and Horgan, Tim (eds.), *The Men Will Talk to Me: Kerry Interviews by Ernie O'Malley* (Cork, 2012)

—, and Ó Comhraí, Cormac (eds.), *The Men Will Talk to Me: Galway Interviews by Ernie O'Malley* (Cork, 2013)

O'Malley, Ernie, *On Another Man's Wound* (London 1936, reprinted Dublin 1979)

—, *The Singing Flame* (Dublin, 1978)

Paul-Dubois, L., *Contemporary Ireland* (Dublin, 1911; published in French, Paris, 1908)

Pearse, Patrick, *Collected Plays/Drámaí an Phiarsaigh*, Róisín ní Ghairbhí and Eugene McNulty (eds.) (Dublin, 2013)

—, *Collected Works: Political Writings and Speeches* (London and Dublin, 1922)

Plunkett, Joseph Mary, *The Poems of Joseph Mary Plunkett* (Dublin, 1919)

Ryan, Desmond, *The Invisible Army* (Dublin, 1932)

—, *Remembering Sion: A Chronicle of Storm and Quiet* (London, 1934)

Skinnider, Margaret, *Doing My Bit for Ireland* (New York, 1917)

Yeats, W. B., *The Collected Letters of W. B. Yeats. Vol. I: 1865–1895*, John Kelly and Eric Domville (eds.) (Oxford, 1986); *Vol. II: 1896–1900*, Warwick Gould, John Kelly and Deirdre Toomey (eds.) (Oxford, 1997); *Vol. III: 1901–1904*, John Kelly and Ronald Schuchard (eds.) (Oxford, 1994); *Vol. IV: 1905–1907*, John Kelly and Ronald Schuchard (eds.) (Oxford, 2005)

—, *Explorations* (London, 1962)

—, *Uncollected Prose: Vol. II*, John Frayne and Colton Johnson (eds.) (London, 1975)

Young, Ella, *Flowering Dusk: Things Remembered Accurately and Inaccurately* (London, 1945)

SECONDARY SOURCES

Unpublished Theses

Flanagan, Frances, '"Your Dream Not Mine": Nationalist Disillusionment and the Memory of Revolution in the Irish Free State' (Ph.D., Oxford, 2009)

Gannon, Darragh, 'Irish Republicanism in Great Britain 1917–1921' (Ph.D., National University of Ireland, Maynooth, 2011)

O'Neill, Ciarán, 'Rule Etonia: Educating the Irish Catholic Elite 1850–1900' (Ph.D., Liverpool, 2010)

Woods, Damien M. G., 'Doctor at the Mast-head: The Life and Political Career of Doctor Patrick McCartan 1876–1963' (M.S.Sc., UCD, 1994)

Works of Reference

McGuire, James, and Quinn, James (eds.), *Dictionary of Irish Biography from the Earliest Times to the Year 2002* (9 vols., Cambridge, 2009)

Books and Articles

Allen, Nicholas, *George Russell (AE) and the New Ireland 1905–1930* (Dublin, 2003)

Augusteijn, Joost, *Patrick Pearse: The Making of a Revolutionary* (Basingstoke, 2010)

—, *From Public Defiance to Guerrilla Warfare: The Experience of Ordinary Volunteers in the Irish War of Independence 1916–1921* (Dublin, 1996)

— (ed.), *The Irish Revolution 1913–1923* (Basingstoke, 2002)

Bartlett, Thomas, and Jeffery, Keith (eds.), *A Military History of Ireland* (Cambridge, 1997)

Béaslaí, Piaras, *Michael Collins and the Making of a New Ireland* (2 vols., Dublin, 1926)

Beiner, Guy, 'Revisiting F. J. Bigger: A Fin-de-Siècle Flourish of Antiquarian-Folklore Scholarship in Ulster', *Béaloideas*, Vol. 80 (2012), pp. 142–62

Bellenger, Dominic Aidan, 'An Irish Benedictine Adventure', in W. J. Sheils and Diana Wood (eds.), *The Churches, Ireland and the Irish* (Oxford, 1989), pp. 401–15

Bew, Paul, *Ideology and the Irish Question: Ulster Unionism and Irish Nationalism 1912–1916* (Oxford, 1994)

Bloxham, Donald, and Gerwarth, Robert (eds.), *Political Violence in Twentieth-Century Europe* (Cambridge, 2011)

Bowman, Timothy, *Carson's Army: The Ulster Volunteer Force 1910–1922* (Manchester, 2007)

Boyce, D. George, *Nationalism in Ireland* (London, 1982)

Boyle, Andrew, *The Riddle of Erskine Childers* (London, 1977)

Brinton, Crane, *The Anatomy of Revolution* (London, 1953)

Brustein, Robert, *The Theatre of Revolt: An Approach to Modern Drama* (London, 1965)

Campbell, Fergus, *Land and Revolution: Nationalist Politics in the West of Ireland 1891–1921* (Oxford, 2005)

Chaudhry, Yug Mohit, *Yeats, the Irish Literary Revival and the Politics of Print* (Cork, 2001)

Chevasse, Móirín, *Terence MacSwiney* (Cork, 1961)

Clare, Anne, *Unlikely Rebels: The Gifford Girls and the Fight for Irish Freedom* (Cork, 2011)

Coldrey, Barry, *Faith and Fatherland: The Christian Brothers and the Development of Irish Nationalism 1838–1921* (Dublin, 1988)

Coleman, Marie, *County Longford and the Irish Revolution 1910–1923* (Dublin, 2003)

Collins, Lorcan, *James Connolly* (Dublin, 2012)

Colum, Padraic, *Ourselves Alone! The Story of Arthur Griffith and the Origin of the Irish Free State* (New York, 1959)

Coogan, Oliver, *Politics and War in Meath 1913–23* (Dublin, 1983)

Coogan, Tim Pat, *De Valera: Long Fellow, Long Shadow* (London, 1993)

—, *Michael Collins: A Biography* (London, 1990)

Costello, Francis J., *Enduring the Most: The Life and Death of Terence MacSwiney* (Dingle, 1995)

—, *The Irish Revolution and Its Aftermath 1916–1923: Years of Revolt* (Dublin, 2003)

Cowell, John, *A Noontide Blazing: Brigid Lyons Thornton, Rebel, Soldier, Doctor* (Dublin, 2005)

Crowe, Catriona, *Dublin 1911* (Dublin, 2011)

Crowley, Brian, *Patrick Pearse: A Life in Pictures* (Cork, 2013)

Cunningham, John, *Unlikely Radicals: Irish Post-Primary Teachers and the ASTI 1909–2009* (Cork, 2009)

Curran, Joseph M., *The Birth of the Irish Free State 1921–1923* (Tuscaloosa, Ala., 1980)

Curtis, Kieron, *P. S. O'Hegarty 1879–1955: Sinn Féin Fenian* (London, 2010)

Daly, Mary E., and O'Callaghan, Margaret (eds.), *1916 in 1966: Commemorating the Easter Rising* (Dublin, 2007)

Davis, Richard, *Arthur Griffith and Non-Violent Sinn Féin* (Dublin, 1974)

Dolan, Anne, *Commemorating the Irish Civil War: History and Memory 1923–2000* (Cambridge, 2003)

Dudgeon, Jeffrey, *Roger Casement: The Black Diaries, with a Study of His Background, Sexuality and Irish Political Life* (Belfast, 2002)

Dunn, J., *Modern Revolutions: An Introduction to the Analysis of a Political Phenomenon* (Cambridge, 1989)

Edmunds, June, and Turner, Bryan S., *Generations, Culture and Society* (Buckingham, 2002)

Edwards, Owen Dudley, *Éamon de Valera* (Cardiff, 1987)

Edwards, Ruth Dudley, *Patrick Pearse: The Triumph of Failure* (London, 1979)

English, Richard, *Ernie O'Malley: IRA Intellectual* (Oxford, 1998)

—, *Irish Freedom: The History of Nationalism in Ireland* (London, 2006)

Fanning, Ronan, *Fatal Path: British Government and Irish Revolution 1910–1922* (London, 2013)

Farry, Michael, *The Aftermath of Revolution: Sligo 1921–1923* (Dublin, 2000)

—, *Sligo 1914–21: A Chronicle of Conflict* (Trim, 1992)

Feeney, W. J., *Drama in Hardwicke Street: A History of the Irish Theatre Company* (London, 1984)

Ferriter, Diarmaid, 'In Such Deadly Earnest"', *Dublin Review*, No. 12 (Autumn 2003), pp. 36–64

—, *Judging Dev: A Reassessment of the Life and Legacy of Éamon de Valera* (Dublin, 2007)

—, *Occasions of Sin: Sex and Society in Modern Ireland* (London, 2009)

FitzGerald, Jennifer, 'Desmond and Mabel FitzGerald', *Sentences: The Unofficial Journal for the Guides of Kilmainham Gaol*, Vol. 4, No. 1 (2005)

Fitzpatrick, David, *Harry Boland's Irish Revolution* (Cork, 2003)

—, *Politics and Irish Life: Provincial Experience of War and Revolution 1913–1921* (Dublin, 1977)

—, 'Militarism in Ireland 1900–1922', in Thomas Bartlett and Keith Jeffery (eds.), *A Military History of Ireland* (Cambridge, 1997)

— (ed.), *Revolution? Ireland 1917–1923* (Dublin, 1993)

— (ed.), *Terror in Ireland 1916–1923* (Dublin, 2012)

Fitz-Simon, Christopher, *'Buffoonery and Easy Sentiment': Popular Irish Plays in the Decade Prior to the Opening of the Abbey Theatre* (Dublin, 2011)

Foster, John Wilson, *Irish Novels 1890–1940: New Bearings in Culture and Fiction* (Oxford, 2008)

Foster, R. F., *W. B. Yeats: A Life. Vol. I: The Apprentice Mage 1865–1914* (Oxford, 1997); *Vol. II: The Arch-Poet 1915–1939* (Oxford, 2003)

Foy, Michael, and Barton, Brian, *The Easter Rising* (Stroud, 1999)

Frazier, Adrian, *Behind the Scenes: Yeats, Horniman and the Struggle for the Abbey Theatre* (London, 1990)

Garvin, Tom, *1922: The Birth of Irish Democracy* (Dublin, 1996)

—, *The Evolution of Irish Nationalist Politics* (Dublin, 1981)

—, *Nationalist Revolutionaries in Ireland 1858–1928* (Oxford, 1987)

Gibney, John, *Seán Heuston* (Dublin 2013)

Gkotzaridis, Evi, 'Revisionist Historians and the Modern Irish State: The Conflict between the Advisory Committee and the Bureau of Military History 1947–1966', *Irish Historical Studies*, Vol. 35, No. 137 (May 2006), pp. 99–116

Glandon, Virginia E., *Arthur Griffith and the Advanced-Nationalist Press in Ireland 1900–1922* (New York, 1985)

Graves, C. Desmond, *Liam Mellows and the Irish Revolution* (London, 1971)

Grene, Nicholas, *The Politics of Irish Drama: Plays in Context from Boucicault to Friel* (Cambridge, 1999)

Groth, A. J. (ed.), *Revolution and Revolutionary Change* (Aldershot, 1996)

Harp, Richard, 'The *Shan Van Vocht* (Belfast, 1896–1899) and Irish Nationalism', *Éire-Ireland*, Vol. 24 (1989), pp. 42–52

Hart, Peter, *The IRA and Its Enemies: Violence and Community in Cork 1916–1923* (Oxford, 1998)

—, *The IRA at War 1916–23* (Oxford, 2003)

—, *Mick: The Real Michael Collins* (London, 2005)

Hay, Marnie, *Bulmer Hobson and the Nationalist Movement in Twentieth-Century Ireland* (Manchester, 2009)

Hearne, Dana, 'The *Irish Citizen* 1914–1916: Nationalism, Feminism and Militarism', *Canadian Journal of Irish Studies*, Vol. 18, No. 1 (July 1992), pp. 1–14

Hepburn, A. C., *Catholic Belfast and Nationalist Ireland in the Era of Joe Devlin 1871–1934* (Oxford, 2008)

Herr, Cheryl (ed.), *For the Land They Loved: Irish Political Melodramas 1890–1925* (Syracuse, 1991)

Hogan, Robert, and Kilroy, James, *The Modern Irish Drama: A Documentary History. Vol. I: The Irish Literary Theatre 1899–1901* (Dublin, 1975); *Vol. II: Laying the Foundations 1902–1904* (Dublin, 1976); *Vol. III: The Abbey Theatre – The Years of Synge 1905–1909* (Dublin, 1978)

—, Burnham, Richard, and Poteet, Daniel P., *The Modern Irish Drama: A Documentary History. Vol. IV: The Abbey Theatre – The Rise of the Realists 1910–1915* (Dublin, 1979)

—, and O'Neill, Michael J., *Joseph Holloway's Abbey Theatre: A Selection from His Unpublished Journals* (Carbondale, Ill., 1967)

Hopkinson, Michael, *Green against Green: The Irish Civil War* (Dublin, 1988)

Horne, John, and Madigan, Edward (eds.), *Towards Commemoration: Ireland in War and Revolution 1912–1923* (Dublin, 2013)

Hughes, Brian, *Michael Mallin* (Dublin, 2012)

Hutchinson, John, and O'Day, Alan, 'The Gaelic Revival in London 1900–1922: Limits of Ethnic Identity', in Roger Swift and Sheridan Gilley (eds.), *The Irish in Victorian Britain* (Dublin, 1999)

Jeffery, Keith, *Ireland and the Great War* (Cambridge, 2000)

Kelly, Matthew, 'The End of Parnellism and the Ideological Dilemmas of Sinn Féin', in D. George Boyce and Alan O'Day (eds.), *Ireland in Transition 1867–1921* (London, 2004), pp. 142–58

—, *The Fenian Ideal and Irish Nationalism 1882–1916* (Woodbridge, 2006)

—, 'The Irish Volunteers: A Machiavellian Moment?', in D. George Boyce and Alan O'Day (eds.), *The Ulster Crisis 1885–1921* (London, 2005)

Kissane, Bill, *The Politics of the Irish Civil War* (Oxford, 2003)

Kumar, Krishan, 'Twentieth-Century Revolutions in Historical Perspective', in *The Rise of Modern Society: Aspects of the Social and Political Development of the West* (Oxford, 1988)

Laffan, Michael, *The Resurrection of Ireland: The Sinn Féin Party 1916–1923* (Cambridge, 1999)

Lane, Leeann, *Rosamond Jacob: Third Person Singular* (Dublin, 2010)

Levitas, Ben, *The Theatre of Nation: Irish Drama and Cultural Nationalism 1890–1916* (Oxford, 2002)

Lewis, Gifford, *Eva Gore-Booth and Esther Roper: A Biography* (London, 1988)

Lowery, Robert G. (ed.), *A Whirlwind in Dublin: 'The Plough and the Stars' Riots* (Westport, Conn., 1984)

Lyons, F. S. L., *Culture and Anarchy in Ireland 1890–1939* (Oxford, 1979)

Macardle, Dorothy, *The Irish Republic 1911–1923* (London, 1937)

MacAtasney, Gerard, *Seán MacDiarmada: The Mind of the Revolution* (Manorhamilton, 2004)

McBride, Ian (ed.), *History and Memory in Modern Ireland* (Cambridge, 2001)

McCarthy, Cal, *Cumann na mBan and the Irish Revolution* (Cork, 2007)

McCarthy, Mark, *Ireland's 1916 Rising: Explorations of History-Making, Commemoration and Heritage in Modern Times* (Farnham, 2012)

McConnel, James, *The Irish Parliamentary Party and the Third Home Rule Crisis* (Dublin, 2013)

McCoole, Sinéad, *Guns and Chiffon: Women Revolutionaries and Kilmainham Gaol 1916–1923* (Dublin, 1997)

—, *No Ordinary Women: Irish Female Activists in the Revolutionary Years 1900–1923* (Dublin, 2003)

McCormack, W. J., *Roger Casement in Death: Or Haunting the Free State* (Dublin, 2002)

McDiarmid, Lucy, *The Irish Art of Controversy* (Dublin, 2005)

McGarry, Fearghal, *Rebels: Voices from the Easter Rising* (Dublin, 2011)

—, *The Rising: Ireland, Easter 1916* (Oxford, 2010)

— (ed.), *Republicanism in Modern Ireland* (Dublin, 2003)

McGee, Owen, *The IRB: The Irish Republican Brotherhood from the Land League to Sinn Féin* (Dublin, 2007)

MacMahon, Deirdre, '"A Worthy Monument to a Great Man": Piaras Béaslaí's Life of Michael Collins', *Bullán: An Irish Studies Journal*, Vol. 2, No. 2 (Winter/Spring 1996)

McMahon, Timothy G., *Grand Opportunity: The Gaelic Revival and Irish Society 1893–1910* (Syracuse, 2008)

McNulty, Eugene, 'The Place of Memory: Alice Milligan, Ardrigh and the 1898 Centenary', *Irish University Review*, Vol. 38, No. 2 (2008), pp. 203–21

—, *The Ulster Literary Theatre and the Northern Revival* (Cork, 2008)

Mannheim, Karl, 'The Problem of Generations', in *Essays on the Sociology of Knowledge*, Paul Kecskemeti (ed.) (London, 1952)

Matthews, Ann, *The Kimmage Garrison 1916: Making Billy-Can Bombs at Larkfield* (Dublin, 2010)

—, *Renegades: Irish Republican Women 1900–1922* (Cork, 2010)

Maume, Patrick, *Life that is Exile: Daniel Corkery and the Search for Irish Ireland* (Belfast, 1993)

—, *The Long Gestation: Irish Nationalist Life 1891–1918* (Dublin, 1999)

Maye, Brian, *Arthur Griffith* (Dublin, 1997)

Meleady, Dermot, *John Redmond: The National Leader* (Dublin, 2013)

Mitchell, Angus (ed.), *The Amazon Journal of Roger Casement* (Dublin, 1997)

— (ed.), *Sir Roger Casement's Heart of Darkness: The 1911 Documents* (Dublin, 2003)

Mitchell, Arthur, *Revolutionary Government in Ireland: Dáil Éireann 1919–1922* (Dublin, 1995)

Mooney, Joanne Eichacker, *Irish Republican Women in America: Lecture Tours 1916–1925* (Dublin, 2003)

Morris, Catherine, *Alice Milligan and the Irish Cultural Revival* (Dublin, 2012)

Morrison, Eve, 'The Bureau of Military History and Female Republican Activism', in Maryann G. Valiulis (ed.), *Gender and Power in Irish History* (Dublin, 2009)

Morrissey, Conor, 'Albinia Brodrick: Munster's Anglo-Irish Republican', *Journal of the Cork Archaeological and Historical Society*, Vol. 117 (2011)

Morrissey, Susan K., *Heralds of Revolution: Russian Students and the Mythologies of Radicalism* (Oxford, 1998)

Mulcahy, Risteárd, *My Father, the General: Richard Mulcahy and the Military History of the Revolution* (Dublin, 2009)

—, *Richard Mulcahy (1886–1971): A Family Memoir* (Dublin, 1999)

Murphy, Brian P., *Patrick Pearse and the Lost Republican Ideal* (Dublin, 1991)

Murphy, William, 'Enniscorthy's Revolution', in Colm Tóibín (ed.), *Enniscorthy: A History* (Wexford, 2010)

Nelson, Bruce, *Irish Nationalists and the Making of the Irish Race* (Princeton, 2012)

Nevin, Donal, *James Connolly* (Dublin, 2006)

Nic Dháibhéid, Caoimhe, '"This is a case in which Irish national considerations must be taken into account": The Breakdown of the Gonne–MacBride Marriage 1904–1908', *Irish Historical Studies*, Vol. 37, No. 146 (Nov. 2010)

Norstedt, Johann, *Thomas MacDonagh: A Critical Autobiography* (Charlottesville, Va., 1980)

Novick, Ben, *Conceiving Revolution: Irish Nationalist Propaganda during the First World War* (Dublin, 2001)

Ó Broin, Leon, *Revolutionary Underground: The Story of the Irish Republican Brotherhood 1858–1924* (Dublin, 1976)

O Brolchain, Honor, *Joseph Plunkett* (Dublin, 2012)

O'Faolain, Sean, *Constance Markievicz; or, The Average Revolutionary* (London, [1934]; reprint London, 1987)

Ó hÓgartaigh, Margaret, *Kathleen Lynn: Irishwoman, Patriot, Doctor* (Dublin, 2006)

O'Neill, Marie, *From Parnell to de Valera: A Biography of Jennie Wyse Power 1858–1941* (Dublin, 1991)

—, *Grace Gifford Plunkett and Irish Freedom: Tragic Bride of 1916* (Dublin, 2000)

O'Rahilly, Aodogán, *Winding the Clock: O'Rahilly and the 1916 Rising* (Dublin, 1991)

Ó Siocháin, Séamus, *Roger Casement: Imperialist, Rebel, Revolutionary* (Dublin, 2008)

Owens, Rosemary Cullen, *Smashing Times: A History of the Irish Women's Suffrage Movement 1889–1922* (Dublin, 1984)

Pašeta, Senia, *Before the Revolution: Nationalism, Social Change and Ireland's Catholic Elite 1879–1922* (Cork, 1999)

—, *Irish Nationalist Women 1900–1918* (Cambridge, 2013)

—, *Thomas Kettle* (Dublin, 2008)

Pyle, Hilary, *Cesca's Diary 1913–1916: Where Art and Nationalism Meet* (Dublin, 2005)

—, *Red-Headed Rebel: Susan L. Mitchell, Poet and Mystic of the Irish Cultural Renaissance* (Dublin, 1998)

Regan, John M., *The Irish Counter-Revolution 1921–1936* (Dublin, 1999)

Reid, Colin, *The Lost Ireland of Stephen Gwynn: Irish Constitutional Nationalism and Cultural Politics, 1864–1950* (Manchester, 2011)

Rumpf, Erhard, and Hepburn, A. C., *Nationalism and Socialism in Twentieth-Century Ireland* (Liverpool, 1977)

Shovlin, Frank, *The Irish Literary Periodical 1923–1958* (Oxford, 2003)

Sisson, Elaine, *Pearse's Patriots: St Enda's and the Cult of Boyhood* (Cork, 2004)

Steele, Karen, *Women, Press and Politics during the Irish Revival* (Syracuse, 2007)

Thompson, William Irwin, *The Imagination of an Insurrection: Dublin, Easter 1916* (London, 1967)

Tierney, Michael, *Eoin MacNeill: Scholar and Man of Action 1867–1945*, F. X. Martin (ed.) (Oxford, 1980)

Townshend, Charles, *The British Campaign in Ireland 1919–1921: The Development of Political and Military Policies* (Oxford, 1975)

—, *Easter 1916: The Irish Rebellion* (London, 2005)

—, *The Republic: The Fight for Irish Independence 1918–1923* (London, 2013)

Trotter, Mary, *Ireland's National Theatres: Political Performance and the Origins of the Irish Dramatic Movement* (Syracuse, 2001)

Valiulis, Maryann, *Portrait of a Revolutionary: General Richard Mulcahy and the Founding of the Irish Free State* (Dublin, 1992)

Van Voris, Jacqueline, *Constance de Markievicz in the Cause of Ireland* (Amherst, Mass., 1967)

Venturi, Franco, *Roots of Revolution: A History of the Populist and Socialist Movements in Nineteenth-Century Russia* (London, 1960)

Ward, Margaret, *Hanna Sheehy-Skeffington: A Life* (Cork, 1997)

—, *Maud Gonne: Ireland's Joan of Arc* (London, 1990)

—, *Unmanageable Revolutionaries: Women and Irish Nationalism* (London, 1989)

Wheatley, Michael, *Nationalism and the Irish Party: Provincial Ireland 1910–1916* (Oxford, 2005)

Wiel, Jérôme aan de, *The Catholic Church in Ireland 1914–1918* (Dublin, 2003)

Wills, Clair, *Dublin 1916: The Siege of the GPO* (London, 2009)

Wohl, Robert, *The Generation of 1914* (London, 1980)

Yeates, Padraig, *A City in Wartime: Dublin 1914–18* (Dublin, 2011)

—, *A City in Turmoil: Dublin 1919–21* (Dublin, 2012)

—, *Lockout: Dublin, 1913* (Dublin, 2001)

Biographical Appendix

C. S. ['Todd'] Andrews (1901–85): born in Dublin; educated at St Enda's; politicized by the 1916 Rising; joined the Irish Volunteers, 1917; fought in the War of Independence, 1919–21; opposed the Treaty; interned during the Civil War; graduated from UCD; worked with state companies, the Irish Tourist Association, the ESB, and Bord na Móna; married Mary Coyle, 1928; Executive Chairman with CIE, 1958; Chairman of RTÉ Authority, 1966; father of Fianna Fáil TDs David and Niall Andrews.

Thomas Ashe (1885–1917): born in County Kerry; Principal of a Dublin National school, 1908–16; member of the IRB; joined the Irish Volunteers, 1913; active member of the GAA and the Gaelic League; led successful attack on Ashbourne RIC barracks, Easter 1916; sentenced to life imprisonment; released June 1917; Sinn Féin propagandist and organizer of de Valera's election campaign in Clare, 1917; rearrested and imprisoned in Mountjoy; organized a hunger-strike among the Sinn Féin prisoners to campaign for political status; died after being force-fed by the prison doctor.

Robert Barton (1881–1975): born in County Wicklow; educated at Oxford; progressive landlord; converted to Home Rule nationalism, 1908; joined the Irish Volunteers, 1913; accepted British Army commission, 1914; posted to Dublin prior to the Easter Rising; deeply affected by events; resigned his commission and joined the republican movement, as did his sister Dulcibella; elected Sinn Féin MP for Wicklow West, 1918; Minister for Agriculture in the first Dáil, 1919; arrested but escaped from Mountjoy; rearrested 1920 but released 1921; co-signed the terms of the truce, July 1921; Minister for Economic Affairs in the second Dáil, 1921–23; part of the Treaty delegation; reluctantly signed; rejected the Treaty in the Dáil and took the anti-Treaty side; occupied the Hammam Hotel with Brugha and Stack; lost seat in

1923 election; Chairman of Agricultural Credit Corporation 1933–59; Director of the *Irish Press*; Chairman of Bord na Móna, 1946.

Piaras Béaslaí (1881–1965): born in Liverpool; a journalist by profession (his father edited the *Catholic Times*); prominent in Gaelic League from 1896; moved to Dublin, 1906; heavily involved in staging Irish-language drama; became Manager of Na hAisteoirí, a travelling group of amateur Irish actors, 1912; joined the Irish Volunteers, 1913; initiated into the IRB, 1914; involved in the coup which saw the removal of Hyde from the Gaelic League, 1915; fought in the Four Courts during the Rising, 1916; imprisoned but released June 1917; elected TD for East Kerry, 1918; edited *An tÓglách* and *Fáinne an Lae*, 1917–20; took the pro-Treaty side; official biographer of Collins; continued writing until his death. Wrote poems *Bealtáine 1916 agus Dánta Eile*, 1920; short stories *Earc agus Áine agus Sécealta Eile*, 1946; plays *An Sgaothaire agus Cuig Dramaí Eile*, 1929, and *An Dánar*, 1929; and books *Michael Collins and the Making of a New Ireland*, 1926, and *Astronár*, 1928.

Francis Joseph Bigger (1863–1926): born in Belfast; educated at QCB, where he qualified as a solicitor; joined the Belfast Naturalists' Field Club, where he learnt Irish; revived the *Ulster Journal of Archaeology*, 1894; elected Fellow of the RSAI, 1896; joined the Gaelic League and became member of its Executive Committee; promoter of all things Irish, including processions, pageants, *céilidhe* and *feiseanna*; co-organized the Belfast Gaelic League pageant to commemorate 1798; founder member of the Ulster Literary Theatre; helped to organize the Irish Harp Festival, 1903; founded Feis na nGleann, 1904; contributed to radical journals and befriended many republicans, but his political career was curtailed after 1916; continued to carry out conservation works around Ulster; remembered as a pioneer antiquarian and local historian. Wrote *The Holy Hills of Ireland*, 1907, *Four Shots from Down*, 1918, and *Crossing the Bar*, 1926.

Ernest Blythe (1889–1975): born in County Antrim to Protestant parents; locally educated; moved to Dublin, 1905; moved in Gaelic League circles with Seán O'Casey; joined the IRB, 1906; co-edited *Irish Freedom*, 1910; joined the Irish Volunteers, 1913; became full-time Volunteer Organizer, 1914; gaoled in 1915 and again in early 1916; subsequently missed the Easter Rising; released Christmas 1916; elected to Sinn Féin Executive, 1917; elected MP for Monaghan North, 1918; Minister for Trade and Commerce in the first and second Dáil, though he opposed the Belfast Boycott and many of his colleagues' policies towards Northern Ireland; supported the Anglo-Irish Treaty, 1921; Minister for Finance, 1923–32; lost seat in 1933; elected to the Seanad, 1934; Blueshirt activist, 1932–5; Managing Director of the Abbey Theatre, 1941–67.

Harry Boland (1887–1922): born in Dublin; son of Fenian James Boland; CBS educated; joined the IRB, the Gaelic League and the GAA; founding member of the Irish Volunteers, 1913; fought at the GPO, 1916; released from imprisonment, June 1917; elected to Sinn Féin Executive, 1917; orchestrated Sinn Féin victory in 1918 elections; elected TD for Roscommon South, 1918; President of the IRB Supreme Council, 1918; sent as a Dáil and IRB envoy to the US, 1919; opposed the Treaty; took up arms against the government; killed following a gun battle with Free State forces at the Grand Hotel, Skerries, 1922.

Robert Brennan (1881–1964): born in County Wexford; CBS and RUI educated; journalist by profession; founder member of the Wexford branch of the Gaelic League, and close friend of the Ryan family of Tomcoole; Sinn Féin County Secretary; IRB Organizer; one of the leaders of the planned Wexford rebellion in 1916; death sentence commuted; released from prison, June 1917; in charge of Sinn Féin Publicity Bureau and appointed Director of Elections, 1918; arrested over the 'German Plot', released 1919; produced the *Irish Bulletin* during the Anglo-Irish War, 1919–21; opposed to the Treaty, 1922; supported de Valera's Fianna Fáil Party following the Sinn Féin split, 1926; helped to establish the *Irish Press*, appointed its first general manager, 1931; appointed Irish Minister to the USA, 1938–47; continued to contribute to the *Irish Press* until his death. Father of the writer Maeve Brennan.

Cathal Brugha (Charles William St John Burgess) (1874–1922): born in Dublin; educated at Belvedere College; joined the Gaelic League, 1899; joined the IRB, 1908; co-founded a candle-manufacturing business; married Kathleen Kingston in 1912; joined the Irish Volunteers, 1913; involved in Howth gun-running, 1914; Second-in-Command to Ceannt in the South Dublin Union during the Rising; badly wounded and permanently crippled; elected to Sinn Féin Executive, 1917; IRA Chief-of-Staff, October 1917–April 1919; elected TD for Waterford, 1918; elected Acting President of the first Dáil, 1919; appointed Minister for Defence; proposed swearing an oath of loyalty to the republic and the Dáil, April 1919; strongly opposed to the Treaty; fought for the anti-Treaty forces; died from wounds received in action early in the Civil War.

William Bulfin (1863–1910): born in Birr, educated locally and at Galway grammar school, emigrated to Argentina 1884 and followed various occupations until his contributions (as 'Che Buono') to the Irish-Argentine *Southern Cross* made him its editor and eventually proprietor; passionate Irish-Irelander, Gaelic Leaguer and Sinn Féiner, in touch with Hyde, Griffith and others, and helped to promote *United Irishman* abroad; made frequent return visits to Ireland, his bicycle tour of 1902–3 producing the bestselling articles and eventually book, *Rambles in Eirinn*, 1907; returned to Ireland in 1909 intending to settle but died of pneumonia the next year.

Roger Casement (1864–1916): born in Dublin but grew up in County Antrim; left school at fifteen and worked as a shipping clerk, ship's purser and surveyor; joined British Colonial Service in Africa, 1892; received knighthood in 1911 for heroic campaigns on behalf of exploited natives in Africa and South America; retired from colonial service, 1912; joined Gaelic League, 1904; wrote in nationalist press under the pseudonym of 'Sean Bhean Bhocht'; joined the Irish Volunteers, 1913; went to Berlin, where he attempted to secure German arms and enlist Irish prisoners of war; secured arms in 1916, but realized German aid would not be enough for a successful enterprise and went to Ireland to try to stop the Rising; captured after landing in Kerry; tried and found guilty of high treason; knighthood annulled; clemency campaign derailed by the deliberate government circulation of his 'Black Diaries', which revealed his homosexuality and turned public opinion; converted to Catholicism; hanged 3 August; remains returned to Ireland and reinterred at Glasnevin Cemetery, 1965.

Áine Ceannt (*née* ní Bhraonáin) (1880–1954): born in Dublin; educated at the Dominican College, Eccles Street; joined the Gaelic League, where she met her future husband, Éamonn Ceannt; married June 1905; became member of Cumann na mBan on its inception, 1914; wrote and delivered dispatches during the Easter Rising; Vice-President of Volunteer Dependants' Fund; Vice-President of Cumann na mBan, 1917–24; member of Sinn Féin's Standing Committee, 1917–24; served on Sinn Féin courts; took the anti-Treaty side; appointed to General Council of the Irish White Cross; General-Secretary of the Children's Relief Association, 1922–47; served on the Executive Committee of the Irish Red Cross, formed in 1939.

Éamonn Ceannt (Edward Kent) (1881–1916): born in County Galway; son of an RIC officer; CBS educated; became a Clerk of Dublin Corporation; joined the Gaelic League, 1899; elected to governing body 1909; founded the

Dublin Pipers' Club 1900; married Áine ní Bhraonáin, 1905; joined Sinn Féin, 1907, elected to its National Council; led Irish athletes to Rome for the jubilee of Pope Pius X; organized resistance to the visit of George V in 1911; joined the IRB, 1911; founder member of the Irish Volunteers, 1913; participated in Howth gun-running; member of IRB Supreme Council, 1915; member of the IRB Military Council; signatory of the 'Proclamation of the Irish Republic'; held the South Dublin Union during the Rising; executed, 8 May 1916.

Robert Erskine Childers (1870–1922): born in London; reared in County Wicklow with his cousins the Bartons; educated Cambridge; Clerk in the House of Commons, 1895–1910; served in the Boer War; converted to Home Rule, 1908; resigned from the House of Commons, 1910; involved in Howth gun-running, 1914; served in the British Navy, 1918–19; awarded a DSC, 1917; Secretary of the Irish Convention, 1917; Home Rule sympathies hardened into full support for the Republic of Ireland; elected to Dáil Éireann as TD for County Wicklow, 1919–21; appointed Minister for Propaganda; served as Principal Secretary to the Treaty delegation; opposed the Treaty and fought on the republican side; captured, court-martialled, 1922; executed, 24 November 1922. Wrote *The Riddle of the Sands*, 1903; *The Framework of Home Rule*, 1911.

Thomas James ['Tom'] Clarke (1858–1916): born on the Isle of Wight of Irish parentage; moved to Dungannon at an early age; educated St Patrick's National school; joined the IRB before emigrating to New York; arrested in London and sentenced to penal servitude for life for possession of explosives; released in 1899, returned to America, where he married Kathleen Daly, niece of Limerick Fenian John Daly; returned to Ireland in 1907 and was co-opted on to the Supreme Council of the IRB; ran a newsagent's which became a centre of IRB organization; presided over the Dublin Wolfe Tone Clubs Committee and organized a visit to Tone's grave to counter the King's visit to Ireland in 1911; published *Irish Freedom*, 1910–14; dismissive of politics, heavily involved in setting up the Military Council in 1915; first to sign the 'Proclamation of the Irish Republic' in 1916, fought in the GPO during the Easter Rising; executed, 3 May.

Kathleen Clarke (*née* **Daly**) (1878–1972): born in Limerick; niece of Fenian John Daly; married Tom Clarke in New York, 1901; returned to Dublin, 1907; involved in the production of *Irish Freedom*, 1910; Vice-President of Cumann na mBan; chosen as a confidante by the IRB Supreme Council,

1916; briefly imprisoned after the Easter Rising; husband Tom executed; established the Volunteer Dependants' Fund, 1916; member of the Sinn Féin Executive; central in the party's adoption of equal rights for women, 1917; imprisoned May 1918–February 1919; Dublin Corporation Councillor, 1919; founder member of the Irish White Cross, 1920; elected to Dáil, 1921; opposed the Treaty; member of Fianna Fáil; entered the Dáil, 1927; accepted nomination to the Senate, 1928; Lord Mayor of Dublin, 1939–41; split with Fianna Fáil, 1941; lost seat on Dublin Corporation; unsuccessful Clann na Poblachta candidate, 1948; concentrated on humanitarian work subsequently.

Diarmuid Coffey (1888–1964): born in Dublin; TCD educated; called to the Bar, 1912; joined the Irish Volunteers, 1913, and worked on the staff at their HQ; involved in the Howth gun-running, 1914, but not in the 1916 Rising; a member of the Secretariat of the Irish Convention, 1917–18; advocated a scheme of Dominion Home Rule, 1917; worked at the Co-operative Reference Library and edited its quarterly, *Better Business*, 1917–21; married Frances Georgina Trench ('Sadhbh Trinseach'), 1918, who died later that year (Coffey married her cousin Sheela Fitzjohn Trench in 1929); took the pro-Treaty side; served as a lieutenant in the National Army, 1922–3; attached to the Oireachtas staff as Clerk to the Seanad, 1923–36; Assistant Keeper of the PROI, 1936–56. Wrote *Douglas Hyde: An Craobhín Aoibhinn*, 1917; *Douglas Hyde: President of Ireland*, 1938.

Cornelius ['Con'] Colbert (1888–1916): born in Newcastlewest, County Limerick, to a family of strong-farmers with a Fenian tradition; educated by CBS in Dublin; worked as a clerk and joined Gaelic League and Fianna (from inaugural meeting in 1909), rising high in the organization and teaching drill, small arms, scouting techniques, etc., specialities which he also instilled in St Enda's pupils (where he worked for free). Head of an IRB circle by 1912 and on Provisional Committee of Irish Volunteers in 1913, to which organization he devoted most of his efforts thenceforth. Notably pious, abstemious and dedicated, he led the occupation of Watkins' Brewery and then Jameson's Distillery in 1916 Rising; reluctantly surrendered and was executed on 8 May, despite his youth and the relatively small part he had played in hostilities.

Michael Collins (1890–1922): born in County Cork; educated locally; worked as a clerk in London; sworn into the IRB, 1909; active in GAA and Gaelic League activities; joined the Irish Volunteers, 1914; returned to Ireland, 1915; fought in the GPO; interned in Frongoch but released December

1916; took up work with the Irish National Aid and Volunteer Dependants' Fund; instrumental in rebuilding the IRB; elected to Sinn Féin Executive, 1917; organized intelligence system; elected MP for Cork South, 1918; Minister for Home Affairs, 1918; Minister for Finance, 1919–22, in the first Dáil; organized the National Loan; President of Supreme Council of the IRB, 1919; IRA Director of Intelligence; Acting President of the Dáil, 1920; prominent role in War of Independence; reluctant member of the Treaty delegation, 1921; Commander-in-Chief of the government forces during the Civil War; shot and killed in County Cork, 22 August 1922.

Padraic Colum (1881–1972): born in County Longford; poet and dramatist; contributed poetry to the *United Irishman*; wrote *The Saxon Shillin'*, 1902, *Broken Soil* (also known as *The Fiddler's House*), 1903, *The Land*, 1905, *Thomas Muskerry*, 1910; co-founded the *Irish Review*, 1911; married Mary Maguire, 1914; moved to the USA; published *Collected Poems*, 1953; *Our Friend James Joyce*, 1959.

Máire Comerford (1893–1982): born in County Wicklow; privately educated; moved to Wexford; involved with the local co-operative movement and the United Irishwomen; joined Sinn Féin, 1916; joined Cumann na mBan, 1917; active during War of Independence; opposed the Treaty; acted as courier to IRA units during the Civil War, 1922–3; imprisoned but released after hunger-strike; sent on a fundraising tour to the USA; elected to Sinn Féin Executive, 1926; gaoled for jury intimidation; edited the women's page of the *Irish Press*; continued in journalism until 1964; remained active in republican protest until her death. Published *The First Dáil*, 1969.

James Connolly (1868–1916): born in Edinburgh to Irish parents; received a basic education but read widely; joined the British Army at fourteen and probably served in India and Ireland before deserting; married Lillie Reynolds in 1890; active trade unionist; moved to Dublin 1896; became Organizer for the Dublin Socialist Club; founded the Irish Socialist Republican Party, 1896; founded the *Workers' Republic* journal, 1898; moved to America, 1902; continued socialist and trade unionist activity; founded the Irish Socialist Federation in New York, 1907; established its journal the *Harp*, 1908; co-founded the International Workers of the World; returned to Dublin, 1910; Ulster Organizer of the Irish Transport and General Workers' Union; led the workers during the lockout after Larkin's imprisonment, 1913; Acting Secretary of the ITGWU, 1914; Commander of Irish Citizen Army, 1913; against trade union involvement in the war; approached by the

IRB and joined with militant nationalists, 1915; agreed on joint uprising; one of the signatories of the 'Proclamation'; fought in the GPO; badly wounded; executed 12 May 1916. Wrote *Erin's Hope*, 1897, *Labour in Irish History* and *Labour, Nationality and Religion*, 1910, *The Reconquest of Ireland*, 1915.

Seán Connolly (1882–1916): born Dublin, to a docker's family; educated CBS; worked as a dispatch clerk at Eason's stationers; strikingly handsome and with a good tenor voice; trained as an actor in Inghinidhe na hÉireann drama class; learnt Irish, and appeared in Gaelic League productions before joining the Abbey in 1913; active in ITGWU and Citizen Army (in whose Liberty Players productions he also participated); commanded ICA contingent (which included his sister and three brothers) in Dublin Castle area at Easter 1916, where he shot dead the Duty Constable at the Castle; led the brief occupation of the City Hall and was shot dead by a sniper. A friend of Seán O'Casey, he may have partly inspired Jack Clitheroe in *The Plough and the Stars*.

Daniel Corkery (1878–1964): born Cork City, son of a master carpenter; educated Presentation Brothers South Monastery School and became a teacher; joined Gaelic League; became prominent in various cultural activities in Cork, and a guru-figure to young nationalists such as Terence MacSwiney; founder member of Cork Dramatic Society, 1908, which put on plays of his such as *The Embers*, 1909; also published collections of short stories, notably *A Munster Twilight*, 1916, and *The Hounds of Banba*, 1920, and an impressive novel, *The Threshold of Quiet*, 1917. Mentored the younger writers Frank O'Connor and Sean O'Faolain, who later turned against Corkery's fervent and exclusivist type of nationalism, which infused his important work of historical-cultural criticism, *The Hidden Ireland*, 1924, and the polemical *Synge and Anglo-Irish Literature*, 1931. Professor of English at UCC, 1931–47, and nominated by the Taoiseach as member of the Seanad, 1951–4.

William T. Cosgrave (1880–1965): Sinn Féin member of Dublin Corporation, 1909; Captain, 4th Battalion, Dublin Brigade, Irish Volunteers, in South Dublin Union, 1916; death sentence commuted to life imprisonment; Sinn Féin MP for Kilkenny, 1917; Minister for Local Government in Dáil cabinet, 1919; President of the Executive Council [Prime Minister], Irish Free State, after death of Michael Collins in 1922; leader of Cumann na nGaedheal Party, 1922–33, and Fine Gael Party, 1934–44.

Sydney Czira (*née* Gifford) (1889–1974): born in Dublin; educated Alexandra College; contributed articles to *Sinn Féin*; member of Inghinidhe na hÉireann; co-founded *Bean na hÉireann*, 1908; elected to Sinn Féin Executive, 1911; contributed to IRB paper *Irish Freedom*; used the pseudonym 'John Brennan' in her writings; involved in the suffrage campaign; moved to America, 1914; immediately involved in US republican circles; returned to Ireland, 1922; involved in the Women Prisoners' Defence League; resumed work as a journalist and broadcaster.

Liam de Róiste (1882–1959): born in County Cork; educated locally; a teacher by profession; joined the Gaelic League, 1899; became its Secretary in Cork, 1902; helped found Coláiste na Mumhan, an Irish-language college in Ballingeary, 1904; co-founded the Cork Celtic Literary Society, 1901, and the Cork Dramatic Society, 1904; published the *Shield*, August 1906–July 1907; co-founded the Cork branch of Sinn Féin, 1906; married Nóra ní Bhriain, 1909; helped form the Cork branch of the Irish Volunteers, 1913; involved in events surrounding Easter 1916 but took no active part; elected to the first Dáil, 1918; took the Treaty side; involved in the Irish Christian Front, which supported Franco in the Spanish Civil War; otherwise devoted himself to the International Trading Corporation and other projects of industrial and commercial development in Cork. Active in the study of Irish history and culture until his death. Wrote the plays *The Road to Hell*, 1908; *Fodhla*, 1908; and a collection of poetry *Voices of the Past*, 1915.

Éamon de Valera (1882–1975): born in New York, reared in County Limerick; CBS, Blackrock and UCD educated; joined the Gaelic League, 1908; married Sinéad Flanagan, 1910; joined the Irish Volunteers, 1913; participated in the Howth gun-running, 1914; occupied Boland's Mill during the Rising, 1916; spared from execution; released from prison, June 1917; Sinn Féin MP for East Clare from 1917; President of Sinn Féin, 1917–26; President of the Volunteers, 1917–22; gaoled 1918 but escaped 1919; President of the first Dáil, 1919; toured America in the hope of gaining US recognition for the republic and to raise funds; elected President of the Republic of Ireland, August 1921; resigned over his opposition to the Treaty, December 1921; re-enlisted in his old IRA unit but as a private; arrested by Free State troops, August 1923; resigned the presidency of Sinn Féin, March 1926; established Fianna Fáil, November 1926; entered the Dáil, June 1927; President of the Executive Council, 1932–7; abolished the oath of allegiance, 1933; removed all reference to the monarch and the Governor-General from his Irish constitution, 1937; Taoiseach, 1937–48: Minister for External Affairs, 1937–47;

Minister for Education, 1939–40; maintained Irish neutrality during Second World War; suppressed the IRA; defeated in 1948 elections; returned as Taoiseach, 1951–4 and 1957–9; President of the Republic of Ireland, 1959–73.

Sinéad de Valera (*née* Flanagan) (1878–1975): born in Dublin; qualified as a National school teacher at Baggot Street College; joined the Gaelic League and Inghinidhe na hÉireann; enthusiastic amateur dramatist; taught Irish for beginners at Gaelic League College, where she met Éamon de Valera, 1909; married him the following year; gave up career to rear family; settled in Greystones post-1916; saw little of husband during this period; home frequently raided during the Civil War; continued with Gaelic League activities, writing and adapting plays and children's stories; made few public appearances in later life; buried in Glasnevin Cemetery. Wrote *Coinneal na Nodlag agus Sgealta Eile*, 1944, and *Áilleacht agus an Beithidheach*, 1946.

Geraldine Plunkett Dillon (1891–1986): born in Dublin into the wealthy Plunkett family; UCD educated; married UCD lecturer Thomas Dillon (later Professor of Chemistry at UCG), Easter 1916; brother Joseph executed, May 1916; social campaigner; member of the Irish-language Taibhdhearc Theatre; wrote a caustic account of her life as daughter of Count and Countess Plunkett and sister of Joseph Plunkett, posthumously published; mother of writer Eilís Dillon.

George Gavan Duffy (1882–1951): born in Cheshire, son of the Young Irelander (and Premier of Victoria) Sir Charles Gavan Duffy; raised in France; educated at Stonyhurst College and in France; qualified as a solicitor, 1907; married Margaret Sullivan, 1908; solicitor for Roger Casement during his treason trial, 1916; called to the Bar, 1917; elected Sinn Féin MP for Dublin South, 1918; travelled Europe in search of support for the Irish cause, 1919–21; part of the Treaty delegation; last to sign; reluctantly recommended it to the Dáil; appointed Minister for External Affairs in the Provisional government, 1922; resigned in protest when Dáil courts were summarily disbanded, July 1922; resigned from the Dáil over the treatment of captured republican forces; Judge of the High Court, 1936; heavily influenced by the values of de Valera's 1937 constitution; President of the High Court, 1946.

Louise Gavan Duffy (1884–1969): born in France; daughter of Sir Charles Gavan Duffy; moved to Ireland, 1907; joined the Gaelic League and became fluent in Irish; graduated from UCD, 1911; taught at St Ita's, 1911–12; joined Cumann na mBan, 1914; present in the GPO, Easter 1916; involved with prisoner associations, 1917; re-elected to the Executive of Cumann na mBan, 1917; opened Scoil Bhríde, an Irish-speaking school for girls, 1917; supported the Treaty, 1922; taught in UCD until her retirement.

Francis John ['Frank'] Fay (1870–1931): born in Dublin, attended Belvedere College and became secretary to an accountant, but always passionately interested in theatre, and in theatrical history; in 1891, with his brother William, set up Ormonde Dramatic Company; also worked with Inghinidhe na hÉireann's dramatic productions; ardently nationalist at this stage of his life; became drama critic for *United Irishman*, 1899–1902, advocating an Irish-speaking theatre and attacking Yeats's theatrical vision (*Cathleen ni Houlihan* may have been an implicit response to these onslaughts); moderated his stance, and advocated a more inclusive national theatre movement; the Fay brothers' National Dramatic Society merged with the Irish Literary Theatre to form the Irish National Theatre Society in 1902, out of which the Abbey would eventually grow; acted tragic parts for Yeats, notably Cuchulain in *On Baile's Strand*, and became a vitally important voice coach; when the Abbey became a limited company and the Yeats–Gregory–Synge triumvirate assumed control, 1905, disagreements mounted, and the Fays left in 1908. Frank worked in America and Britain before returning to Ireland in 1921, where he resumed his elocution work.

Darrell Figgis (1882–1925): born in Dublin; worked as a tea merchant while becoming a regular literary contributor to various journals; play *Queen Tara* staged at the Gaiety, 1910; became politically active following visit to Achill Island, 1913; joined the Volunteers, 1913; involved in 1914 gun-running; not active during the Rising but arrested nonetheless; interned at Reading Gaol, released December 1916; elected Secretary of the reorganized Sinn Féin, 1917; arrested following the 'German Plot', 1918; released March 1919; acted as a judge in the Dáil courts; edited the *Republic*, June–September 1919; supported the Treaty, 1921; elected to the Sinn Féin Executive, 1922; Vice-Chairman of the committee to draft the constitution; elected as an independent TD for Dublin County, 1922 and 1923; generally unpopular, fell from political and social favour following a number of scandals; committed suicide in London, 1925. Poetry collections *A Vision of Life*, 1909; *The Crucibles of Time*, 1911; published *A Chronicle of Jails*, 1917; *The Gaelic State in the Past and Future*, 1917; *Children of Earth*, 1918; *The Paintings of William Blake*, 1925; *Recollections of the Irish War*, 1927.

Desmond FitzGerald (1888–1947): born (as Thomas Joseph FitzGerald) and educated in London, to an emigrant family from Cork and Kerry; as a young journalist and poet became friendly with the Imagist movement (T. E. Hulme, Richard Aldington) and particularly with Ezra Pound; with his marriage to Mabel McConnell became more ardently nationalist, living in Brittany and Kerry, joining the IRB and working as a Volunteer organizer; convicted and imprisoned for seditious speeches in 1915; involved in the Rising and subsequently imprisoned; active in the Dáil as a TD and as Director of Publicity, making a notable success of the *Irish Bulletin*; supported the Treaty (unlike his wife) and was Minister for External Affairs in both the Provisional government and the first government of the Free State, and eventually Minister for Defence. Became progressively detached from politics from the 1930s, though supported right-wing Catholic groups, the Blueshirts and Francoist Spain; continued to write poetry and to study and lecture on Thomistic philosophy.

Mabel FitzGerald (*née* **McConnell**) (1884–1958): born in Belfast; daughter of a Presbyterian unionist; attended Victoria College and Queen's University; became a convinced nationalist and Irish-language enthusiast in college; married Desmond FitzGerald, 1911; moved to France, then to Kerry, 1913; with Desmond, organized Volunteers in Kerry; joined the garrison at the GPO, 1916; active in prisoner-release groups; managed Desmond's successful election campaign while he was imprisoned, 1918; Executive member Cumann na mBan, 1918–22; opposed to her husband's endorsement of the Treaty; gave birth to future Taoiseach Garrett, 1926; converted to Catholicism, 1943.

Madeleine ffrench-Mullen (1880–1944): born in Malta; moved to Dublin at an early age; with her brother Douglas, became an active nationalist and Gaelic revivalist; contributor to *Bean na hÉireann*; active during the 1913 lockout; joined the Citizen Army; served during the Easter Rising; co-founded St Ultan's (Teach Ultáin), the first hospital for infants in Ireland, 1919; joined Sinn Féin; elected to Rathmines District Council, 1920; advocated social and economic improvements; worked for the remainder of her life at St Ultan's with her partner Kathleen Lynn.

Maud Gonne *see* **Maud Gonne MacBride**

Alice Stopford Green (1847–1929): born in County Meath; educated at home; moved to England in 1874, mixed with leading liberals and married the bestselling historian J. R. Green, who died young; questioned British imperialism and favoured Home Rule; campaigned on behalf of Boer prisoners during the Boer War; questioned the manner in which Irish history was presented; rewrote the history of medieval Ireland in *The Making of Ireland*

and Its Undoing, 1908; through the publication of various historical works, argued that the Irish were well capable of governing themselves; helped to fund the committee set up to import arms, 1914; shocked, however, at the 1916 Rising and at Casement's approaches to Germany; campaigned for his reprieve nonetheless; moved to Dublin, 1918; her house on Stephen's Green used by leading nationalists during the War of Independence; supported the Treaty; became member of the Free State Senate until the failure of her health.

Arthur Griffith (1871–1922): born in Dublin; educated CBS and then became a printer; founded Celtic Literary Society, 1893, with William Rooney, and was an IRB member into the early 1900s as well as active in the Gaelic League and a prominent pro-Boer; founded newspapers *United Irishman*, 1899, and *Sinn Féin*, 1906; organized the Irish Transvaal Committee, 1900, and Cumann na nGaedheal, which later developed into the rather amorphous Sinn Féin movement; *The Resurrection of Hungary*, 1904, suggested a blueprint for self-sufficiency in an autonomous Ireland, but from about 1910 he seemed to be moving towards a dual-monarchy arrangement for Ireland rather than a separatist republic. Supported Volunteers and attacked the 1912 Home Rule Bill, but the war gave him an opportunity to readopt a radical stance with anti-war 'mosquito' publications; inactive in 1916 but was interned and became influential as Sinn Féin changed to a republican party; MP for East Cavan, 1918; Acting President of Dáil, 1919; headed the Irish delegation in the Treaty negotiations; elected President of the Dáil in 1922 and died of a cerebral haemorrhage in the same year.

Michael Hayes (1889–1976): born in Dublin; CBS and UCD educated; teacher by profession; joined the Irish Volunteers, 1913; did not advocate armed revolt but nonetheless fought at Jacob's Biscuit Factory during the Rising; married Margaret Kavanagh, 1917; became immersed in Sinn Féin politics; interned 1920–21; elected to the second Dáil, 1921 while in prison; supported the Treaty; appointed Minister for Education in the Provisional government, 1922; Minister for Foreign Affairs, 1922; Ceann Comhairle of the Dáil, 1922–32; member of the Seanad, 1937–65; head of the Irish Department, UCD, 1951–9.

Bulmer Hobson (1883–1969): born in Belfast; educated at the Friends' school, Lisburn; Quaker parents involved in the Home Rule and suffragette movements; became a republican, 1898; joined the Gaelic League and the GAA; co-founded the Ulster Literary Theatre, 1904; involved in literary magazine *Uladh*, 1904–5; sworn into the IRB, 1904; co-founded the

Dungannon clubs, 1906; established the *Republic*, December 1906; Vice-President of Sinn Féin, 1907; moved to Dublin, 1908; co-founded Fianna Éireann, 1909; resigned from Sinn Féin, 1909; founded *Irish Freedom*, 1910; member of the IRB Supreme Council, 1911; Secretary of the Volunteers Executive, 1913; lost faith of many IRB leaders after persuading MacNeill to comply with Redmond's demands regarding the Volunteers, 1914; involved in Howth gun-running, 1914; opposed to the Rising, instead advocating a guerrilla campaign, 1916; detained by a suspicious IRB until the outbreak of the Rising; took no part in action; ostracized from nationalist politics thereafter; embittered at his treatment; worked with the Revenue Commission until his retirement in 1948. Wrote a history of the Irish Volunteer Force, 1918; a life of Wolfe Tone, 1919; and an autobiography, *Ireland Yesterday and Tomorrow*, 1968.

Richard ['Dick'] Humphreys (1896–1968): nephew of Michael 'The' O'Rahilly; moved with his widowed mother and family to Dublin, 1909; radicalized by his O'Rahilly aunt, a fierce nationalist; educated St Enda's and Clongowes; joined Volunteers and assisted in Asgard gun-running; with Pearse in the GPO, interned in Wakefield Gaol, then studied law at King's Inns; fought in Anglo-Irish War and took anti-Treaty side, helping to shelter Ernie O'Malley at the family home; motor-racing enthusiast who later worked in automobile industry.

Sighle Humphreys (1899–1994): born in Limerick city; niece of the O'Rahilly; family moved to Dublin, 1909; studied at the University of Paris; participated in pre-1916 Volunteer activities; joined Cumann na mBan, 1919; active throughout War of Independence; opposed the Anglo-Irish Treaty; imprisoned 1922–3, released after a hunger-strike; Director of Publicity for Cumann na mBan, 1926; participated in republican protests against Seán O'Casey's *The Plough and the Stars*, 1926; imprisoned for sending jurors intimidating letters, 1928; co-founder of Saor Éire, 1931; leading member of the Boycott British League, 1932; married IRA activist Donal O'Donoghue, 1935; disillusioned with de Valera, joined Clann na Poblachta; opposed Irish entry to the EEC, 1973; supported IRA hunger-strikers, 1981 and the republican campaign in Northern Ireland.

Douglas Hyde (1860–1947): born in County Roscommon; TCD educated; co-founded the Irish Literary Society in London, 1891; became President of the National Literary Society, 1892; co-founder and first President of the Gaelic League, 1893; wrote the first all-Irish play, *Casadh an tSúgáin*, to receive theatrical production, 1901; first Professor of Irish at UCD, 1909; held post until 1932; led successful Gaelic League campaign to make Irish compulsory for matriculation in the new NUI; resigned as Gaelic League President over its politicization, 1915; Irish Free State Senator, 1925–6; first President of Ireland, 1937. Major works: *Love Songs of Connacht*, 1893, and *A Literary History of Ireland*, 1899. An autobiography, *Mise agus an Connradh*, 1931.

Rosamond Jacob (1888–1960): born in Waterford to Quaker parents with nationalist sympathies; educated at home and at 'Miss Smith's' in Waterford; joined the Gaelic League, the National League and Inghinidhe na hÉireann, 1900; co-founder of Sinn Féin in Waterford, 1906; joined the Irish Franchise League, 1908; joined Cumann na mBan, 1914; sided with the republicans during the Civil War; Secretary of the Irishwomen's International League, 1920–27; joined Fianna Fáil, 1926; reported favourably on social conditions in the USSR, 1931; remained politically active until her death. Wrote *Callaghan*, 1915, *The Rise of the United Irishmen 1791–1794*, 1937, *The Troubled House*, 1938, *The Rebel's Wife*, 1957.

Anna Johnston ('**Ethna Carbery**') (1866–1902): born in County Antrim; daughter of the prominent Fenian Robert Johnston; regularly contributed poetry to publications such as *United Ireland*, *O'Donoghue's Magazine*, *Young Ireland*, the *Nation* and the *Catholic Fireside*; founded the *Northern Patriot* with Alice Milligan, 1895; founded the literary magazine the *Shan van Vocht*, 1896; played an active role in the 1798 Centenary commemorations; member of Inghinidhe na hÉireann, 1900; assisted Maud Gonne in organizing children's protest against the visit of Queen Victoria to Dublin, 1900; wrote and staged patriotic plays around the country with Gonne; married Séumas MacManus, 1901; died of gastritis, April 1902. Work posthumously published as *The Four Winds of Éireann*, 1902, *The Passionate Hearts*, 1903, and *In the Celtic Past*, 1904.

Hugh Kennedy (1879–1936): born in Dublin; educated at the Jesuit University College in Dublin; graduated from the RUI and called to the Bar, 1902; Honorary Secretary of the Central Committee of the Gaelic League; legal adviser to the Department of Local Government in the first Dáil, 1919; Law Officer of the Provisional government, 1921; co-drafted the constitution of the new state; helped secure finality and supremacy for the Irish courts; involved in drafting the draconian measures adopted by the Free State against members of the IRA; elected TD for Dublin West, 1923; appointed Attorney

General of the Free State, 1923; involved in the establishment of a new court system; first Chief Justice of the Free State, 1924.

Thomas ['Tom'] Kettle (1880–1916): born in Dublin, son of Parnellite and Land Leaguer Andrew Kettle; educated at Clongowes Wood and University College; highly active in student politics; called to the Bar, 1905, but pursued a career in political journalism; co-founded the Young Ireland branch of the United Irish League, 1904; editor of the *Nationist*, 1904–5; elected MP for Tyrone East, 1906; appointed first Professor of National Economics, UCD; supporter of Home Rule, women's suffrage and the strikers of 1913; joined the Irish Volunteers, 1913; backed Redmond's call for Irishmen to join the war effort, 1914; given the rank of Lieutenant and Recruiting Officer; recognized changing opinion in Ireland post-Easter 1916 but insisted on taking up a combat role on the Western Front; killed at Ginchy, September 1916.

James Larkin (1874–1947): born in Liverpool (though he claimed otherwise in later life) to emigrants from Ulster; left school aged eleven and worked at many trades, including as a seaman, in USA and Britain; joined ILP and became an active figure in Dockers' Union, becoming General Organizer in 1906. Posted to Belfast in 1907, he organized a brief but legendary general strike; moving to Dublin, he developed his epic oratorical qualities and founded the ITGWU, whose headquarters at Liberty Hall became the centre for a vibrant syndicalist counter-culture. His aggressive journalism and flamboyant oratory, notably through the *Irish Worker*, made him a famous though divisive figure within labour politics as well as a hate-figure for the employers. A Labour Councillor on Dublin Corporation and President of the ITUC by 1913, in the same year he confronted Dublin's premier capitalist, William Martin Murphy, which resulted in the epic lockout, drawing international opinion but eventually collapsing. (The British TUC's suspicion of Larkin played a part in this.) Always sympathetic to nationalist politics, he had by now developed the Irish Citizen Army into a small but effective militia. However, his lengthy absence in the USA from 1914 sidelined him from revolutionary events in Ireland. Much involved in internecine socialist politics in America, he became an outspoken advocate of communism and spent time in gaol for 'criminal syndicalism'; on his return to Ireland in 1923 he battled for control of the ITGWU, lost and formed his own political party and (later) union; he retained his Moscow connections (where he spent much time in the early 1920s) until 1929, and was elected three times to the Dáil, once as a communist; he returned to the Labour Party in the 1940s. He remained an iconic figure for Dublin's working classes.

Fionan Lynch (1889–1966): born in County Kerry; educated at Blackrock College and at UCD; a teacher by profession; taught in Wales, where he formed a branch of the Gaelic League, 1911; moved to Dublin, sworn into the IRB, 1912; joined the Irish Volunteers, 1913; co-founded Na hAisteoirí, 1912; given charge of guarding Hobson during the Rising, also fought at North King Street, 1916; subsequently gaoled but released after hunger-strike, 1917; rearrested during the 'German Plot', 1918; elected Sinn Féin TD for Kerry South, December 1918; married Brighid Slattery, 1919; served as Assistant Secretary to the Treaty delegation, 1921; took the pro-Treaty side; Minister for Education, January–August 1922; Commandant-General in pro-Treaty forces during the Civil War, 1922–3; Cumann na nGaedheal TD for Kerry and Kerry South, 1923–44; Minister for Fisheries, 1922–8; Minister for Land and Fisheries, 1928–32; spoke at Blueshirt meetings, 1933; Ceann Comhairle of the Dáil, 1938–9; retired from politics, 1944; served as a Circuit-Court Judge, 1944–59.

Liam Lynch (1893–1923): born in County Limerick; apprenticed to hardware trade in Mitchelstown, Cork, 1910; joined Gaelic League, 1910; Irish Volunteers, 1913; Adjutant, Fermoy Battalion, 1918; Officer Commanding, North Cork (Cork No. 2) Brigade, 1919; Officer Commander, 1st Southern Division, IRA, 1921; opposed Treaty, 1922; Chief-of-Staff, IRA, 1922; killed in action, 1923.

Kathleen Lynn (1874–1955): born in County Mayo; medical practitioner; suffragist, socialist and nationalist; assisted the strikers during the lockout, 1913; joined the Citizen Army; medical officer during the Rising, 1916; Honorary Vice-President of the Irish Women Workers' Union, 1917; Vice-President Sinn Féin Executive, 1917; imprisoned, 1918; active in south Tipperary during the War of Independence; took the anti-Treaty side; elected TD for Dublin South, 1923; lost seat, 1927. In 1919 founded St Ultan's Hospital for Infants (Teach Ultáin) with her lifelong partner, Madeleine ffrench-Mullen, a pioneering enterprise aimed at helping impoverished children and their mothers, both medically and educationally; continued to campaign for better housing, disease prevention and the eradication of tuberculosis (the BCG inoculation was introduced at St Ultan's in 1937); remained in medical practice until her death.

John MacBride (1865–1916): born in Westport, County Mayo; studied medicine; joined the IRB at an early age; undertook a mission to the USA, 1896; emigrated to South Africa; organized the 1798 Centenary celebrations there;

joined an Irish Brigade to fight on the Boer side against Britain, 1899; married Maud Gonne in Paris, 1903, and separated from her, 1905; returned to Dublin, worked for City Council; member of the IRB Supreme Council; not involved in planning of Easter Rising but offered his services to MacDonagh; fought at Jacob's Biscuit Factory; executed 5 May.

Maud Gonne MacBride (1866–1953): born in Aldershot; daughter of a British Army officer of Irish descent; educated in France; began working for Irish freedom after falling in love with French politician Lucien Millevoye; edited *La Patrie* and published *L'Irlande libre*, 1897; founded and became first President of Inghinidhe na hÉireann ('The Daughters of Ireland'), 1900; organized counter-attractions for children during Queen Victoria's visit, 1900; converted to Catholicism; took the lead role in Yeats's play *Cathleen ni Houlihan*, 1902; married Major MacBride, Paris 1903; separated 1905; contributed to *Bean na hÉireann*, 1908; remained in Paris until her return to Dublin in 1917; arrested in connection with the 'German Plot', interned for six months, 1918; worked with the White Cross during the War of Independence; opposed the Anglo-Irish Treaty; first Secretary of the Women's Prisoners' Defence League, 1922; published autobiography *A Servant of the Queen*, 1938; buried Republican Plot, Glasnevin Cemetery.

Patrick McCartan (1878–1963): born in County Tyrone; educated at St Malachy's College, Belfast, and at UCD; joined the IRB; established Dungannon clubs among students in Dublin; joined Sinn Féin; elected member of Dublin Corporation, 1909; qualified as a medical doctor, 1910; responsible for purging the IRB of many older members; organized the Irish Volunteers in Tyrone, 1914; toured America to raise funds, 1914; co-opted on to the IRB Supreme Council, 1915; plans to link Ulster and Connacht Volunteers failed, Easter 1916; elected MP for King's County, 1918; returned to the US, involved in the Clan na Gael split, 1919; accompanied de Valera on his US tour, 1919–20; undertook a secret mission to Russia to seek recognition for the Irish republic from the Soviet government, 1921; reluctantly supported the terms of the Treaty; lost Leix–Offaly seat, 1922; returned to America until 1937; remained left wing and republican in his views, co-founded Clann na Poblachta, 1946; member of Seanad, 1948–51. Published *With de Valera in America*, 1932.

Denis McCullough (1883–1968): born in Belfast; CBS educated; piano-tuner by trade; joined the Gaelic League in the 1890s; joined the IRB, 1901; Chairman of the Ulster Provincial Council, 1905; co-founder of the Dungannon clubs, 1906; Ulster representative on the Supreme Council, 1907–16; member of Irish Volunteers Executive, 1913; imprisoned, August–November 1915; elected President of the IRB Supreme Council, 1915; not kept informed of final details of the Easter Rising; attempted with 132 Volunteers to unite with Connacht Volunteers but failed; imprisoned, May 1916; married Agnes Ryan, August 1916; fought as an ordinary Volunteer during the War of Independence; supported the Treaty; moved to Dublin, 1922; elected Cumann na nGaedheal TD for Donegal, 1924; resigned soon afterwards and continued in business until his death.

Tomás MacCurtain (1884–1920): born in County Cork; Secretary of Blackpool branch of Gaelic League, 1902; joined Sinn Féin and IRB, 1907; Fianna Éireann Organizer, 1911; Commander, Cork Brigade, Irish Volunteers, 1916; imprisoned in Wakefield, Frongoch and Reading, 1916–17; Sinn Féin Councillor for Cork North-West in 1920 local elections; elected Lord Mayor of Cork, January 1920; assassinated in his home, 20 March 1920. Coroner's jury found verdict of murder against the RIC and the Prime Minister, Lloyd George.

Seán MacDermott (Seán MacDiarmada) (1883–1916): born in County Leitrim; emigrated to Edinburgh before moving to Belfast; joined the AOH and Hobson's Dungannon clubs before being sworn into the IRB in 1906; became a Sinn Féin Organizer, travelling the country, founding local branches; appointed IRB National Organizer, 1908–16; Manager of *Irish Freedom*; active in the Gaelic League, the GAA and the Celtic Literary Society; stricken with polio in 1911; elected to the Provisional Committee of the Irish Volunteers, 1913; involved in the Howth gun-running, July 1914; imprisoned, May–September 1915; co-opted on to the secret Military Council of the IRB upon his release; anxious for the Rising to occur at the earliest possible date; most likely to have instigated the 'Castle Document'; signed the 'Proclamation of the Irish Republic'; fought at the GPO with Connolly; executed, 12 May.

Muriel MacDonagh (*née* **Gifford**) (1884–1917): born in Dublin; member of the Women's Franchise League and Inghinidhe na hÉireann with her sisters Helen, Grace and Sydney; married Thomas MacDonagh, 1912; activities curtailed due to poor health; husband executed, May 1916; Officer and Committee Member of the Volunteer Dependants' Fund, 1916; received into the Catholic Church, 1917; drowned in a swimming accident, July 1917.

Thomas MacDonagh (1878–1916): born in County Tipperary; educated at Rockwell College and UCD; a teacher by profession; joined the Gaelic

League in 1901; assisted Pearse in the foundation of St Enda's in 1908; first play, *When the Dawn is Come*, produced at the Abbey, 1908; on leaving St Enda's became a Lecturer in UCD, 1911–16; married Muriel Gifford, 1912; co-founded the *Irish Review*, 1911; managed the Irish Theatre, 1914; founder member of the Irish Volunteers, 1913; appointed to the Provisional Committee; sworn into the IRB, March 1915; organized the funeral of O'Donovan Rossa, 1915; given overall command of the Dublin Volunteer battalions; co-opted on to the IRB Military Council, April 1916; signed the 'Proclamation of the Irish Republic'; occupied Jacob's Biscuit Factory; executed, 3 May.

Joseph McGarrity (1874–1940): born Carrickmore, County Tyrone; emigrated to the USA 1892, and made money in the liquor trade and as a hotel-keeper in the Philadelphia region; joined Clan na Gael in 1893 and became a key figure in Irish-American nationalism, giving money and support to Irish nationalist causes and keeping closely in touch with Irish affairs through intense correspondences such as that with his old friend and fellow Carrickmore man, Patrick McCartan, and Éamon de Valera; instrumental in raising a million dollars for Friends of Irish Freedom in 1919 and placing five million dollars' worth of bond certificates. After initial doubts he opposed the Treaty and raised much money for the republican cause; continued to advocate uniting Ireland through physical force and disapproved of de Valera's shift to constitutionalism from 1926.

Patrick McGilligan (1889–1979): born in County Derry; educated at Clongowes Wood and UCD; graduated as a teacher; studied law, called to the Bar, 1921; Leeson Street home used as a meeting place and safe house for militant republicans, 1918–19; member of the economic commission established in connection with Anglo-Irish negotiations, 1921; appointed Secretary to Kevin O'Higgins, Minister for Home Affairs, 1922; won UCD Dáil seat, 1923; Minister for Industry and Commerce, 1924–32; implemented the Shannon hydroelectric scheme and oversaw the founding of the ESB, 1927; Minister for External Affairs, 1927–32; played a leading role in the passing of the Statute of Westminster, 1931; appointed Professor of Constitutional Law, International Law, and Criminal Law and Procedure at UCD, 1934; active member of the opposition party in the Dáil, 1932–48; continued to pursue a legal career; Minister for Finance in the first inter-party government, 1948–51; Attorney General in the inter-party government, 1954–7; retired from politics after losing Dáil seat, 1965.

Eoin MacNeill (1867–1945): born in County Antrim; educated at St Malachy's College, Belfast, and at TCD; took up a position in the civil service; co-founder of the Gaelic League, 1893; first editor of *An Claidheamh Soluis*, 1899–1901; Vice-President of the Gaelic League, 1903; took up position at UCD, 1909; co-founder of the Irish Volunteers, 1913; manipulated by the IRB into organizing a mobilization of Volunteers, Easter 1916; issued counter-orders too late to halt the Rising; arrested and sentenced to life imprisonment; released June 1917; elected to the first Dáil, 1918; Minister for Finance, 1919; elected Ceann Comhairle to the second Dáil, 1921; presided over the Treaty Debates; Minister for Education, 1922–5; Irish Free State representative on the Boundary Commission, 1924–5; subsequently returned to academic life. Wrote *Phases of Irish History*, 1919, and *Celtic Ireland*, 1921.

Mary MacSwiney (1872–1942): born in London; moved to Cork at an early age; UCC educated; founder member of the Munster Women's Franchise League, 1911; founded a Cumann na mBan branch in Cork, 1914; arrested following the Easter Rising; set up own Irish school, Scoil Íte, 1916; elected to Cumann na mBan's National Executive, 1917; maintained a public vigil at Brixton Gaol with her sister Annie while brother Terence fasted to death, 1920; elected TD for Cork City, 1921; bitterly opposed the Anglo-Irish Treaty; refused to join de Valera's Fianna Fáil, 1926; lost seat, 1927; resigned from Sinn Féin, 1934; backed the IRA campaigns of the late 1930s.

Muriel MacSwiney (*née* Murphy) (1892–1982): born in County Cork to the wealthy Murphy brewing and distilling dynasty; convent educated in England; joined the Gaelic League and Cumann na mBan; married Terence MacSwiney, 1917; uncertain over the wisdom of her husband's hunger-strike, 1920; travelled to America delivering lectures on British rule in Ireland; received the Freedom of New York, 1921; opposed the Treaty; part of the republican Hammam Hotel garrison with Cathal Brugha; became strongly left wing and atheist in her views; moved to Germany, 1923; estranged from her daughter Máire, 1934; worked for various socialist causes for the rest of her life.

Terence MacSwiney (1879–1920): born in Cork, CBS educated; an accountant by trade; co-founded the Celtic Literary Society, a member of the Gaelic League and the Cork Dramatic Society; wrote *The Holocaust* and *The Revolutionist*, plays which reflected his beliefs of self-sacrifice and political idealism; co-founded the Cork Volunteers in December 1913; published *Fianna Fáil*, 1914; dispersed southern Volunteers on MacNeill's orders, Easter 1916; imprisoned on separate occasions 1916–19; elected as TD for West Cork, entered the first Dáil, 1919; became Lord Mayor of Cork, 1920; arrested while chairing a Sinn Féin court; commenced a hunger-strike in Brixton Gaol; died after a 74-day fast.

Michael Mallin (1874–1916): born in the Liberties of Dublin; spent fourteen years in the British Army before returning to Dublin to work as a silk-weaver as well as trying several other ways to earn a living; became Secretary of the Silk Weavers' Union and an influential figure in the Irish Citizen Army; active in the Rising as Commandant of the Stephen's Green garrison, with Constance Markievicz as his Second-in-Command; executed, 8 May 1916.

Constance Markievicz (*née* **Gore-Booth**) (1868–1927): born in London; daughter of Sir Henry Gore-Booth, a leading progressive landholder in Sligo; privately educated, later studied at the Slade School of Art in London and in Paris; took up the cause of women's suffrage; met fellow art student Casimir Markievicz (1874–1932), married, 1900; with her husband, wrote and acted in plays for the Theatre of Ireland; joined Sinn Féin, 1908; launched Fianna Éireann, joined Inghinidhe na hÉireann, 1909; regular contributor to *Bean na hÉireann*, which she co-founded, 1908; wrote *A Call to the Women of Ireland*; Executive Member of Sinn Féin, 1911; supported the trade unionists during the lockout, 1913; Honorary Treasurer of the Citizen Army, 1913; instrumental in merging Inghinidhe na hÉireann with Cumann na mBan; co-founded the Irish Neutrality League, 1914; fought in the College of Surgeons building during the Rising; death sentence commuted because of her sex; received into the Catholic faith, 1917; President of Cumann na mBan, 1917; elected Sinn Féin MP for Dublin, 1918; first woman to be elected to Westminster but refused to take her seat; gaoled 1920–21; Minister for Labour in the first Dáil, 1919–21; opposed to the Treaty; Sinn Féin abstentionist TD, 1923–7; joined Fianna Fáil, 1926; elected TD for Dublin South, 1927.

Liam Mellows (1892–1922): born in Lancashire; returned to Ireland to live in Wexford at an early age; educated at Royal Hibernian Military School; employed as a clerk; joined Fianna Éireann, 1911; appointed full-time Fianna Organizer, 1913; sworn into IRB, 1912; elected to the Executive Committee of the Volunteers, 1914; influenced by James Connolly's socialism; led a minor insurrection in Galway, Easter 1916; escaped to New York; worked with Devoy on *Gaelic American*; elected MP Galway East and for Meath, 1918; agent for de Valera's US tour, 1920; opposed the Treaty; fought at the Four Courts; imprisoned but appointed Minister for Defence in the republican government; executed by firing squad in retaliation for the assassination of Seán Hales, 8 December 1922.

Alice Milligan (1866–1953): born in County Tyrone; educated at Methodist College, Belfast, and King's College, London; wrote *A Royal Democrat*, 1892; co-formed branches of the Irish Women's Association throughout Ulster; founding editor of the *Northern Patriot* and the *Shan Van Vocht*, 1895–6; Secretary of Belfast 1798 Centenary Committee, elected to Dublin Centenary Executive, 1897; pioneer director and producer of dramatic pageants and tableaux, which toured Ireland and Britain; wrote the plays *The Green upon the Cape*, 1898, *The Ossianic Trilogy*, 1899, and *The Escape of Red Hugh*, 1901; travelling lecturer for the Gaelic League, 1904–9; joined in fundraising campaigns for 1916 prisoners; opposed the Treaty; continued to contribute poems and articles to nationalist publications.

Seán Milroy (1877–1946): born in Cumberland, moved to Cork as a young man; became friendly with Arthur Griffith, joined Sinn Féin, 1909; joined the Irish Volunteers; imprisoned June–September, 1915, for delivering an inflammatory speech; fought during the Rising, 1916; subsequently imprisoned; upon release elected to the Standing Committee of Sinn Féin, 1917; rearrested but escaped from Lincoln Gaol with de Valera and Seán McGarry, 1919; elected Sinn Féin TD for Cavan, 1921; supported the Treaty; resigned from the Dáil over government policy, 1924; member of the Seanad, 1928–36.

Helena Molony (1883–1967): born Dublin, to a grocer's family, orphaned young and was converted to nationalist activism by hearing Maud Gonne speak; active member of Inghinidhe na hÉireann; edited *Bean na hÉireann*, 1908–11; known as 'Emer' within the movement. Also closely involved in trade union movement and Fianna, sharing lodgings with Constance Markievicz; arrested and gaoled for demonstrating against royal visit, 1911; an accomplished actress, and worked with the Abbey as well as the Markieviczes' Independent Dramatic Company (from 1911 Independent Theatre Company); General Secretary of Irish Women Workers' Union, 1915, and Secretary of Irish Citizen Army's women's section; organized first-aid section at City Hall in 1916 Rising; interned and imprisoned; briefly on Sinn Féin Executive, 1917, opposed the Treaty and remained an IWWU official for twenty years, playing an active role in various disputes within the movement, remaining a syndicalist and an advocate of workers' control; also active in republican causes, and a founder of Saor Éire in 1931, though shortly afterwards resigned. Her last stage appearance was in 1922.

David Patrick Moran (1869–1936): born in Waterford; educated Castle-knock College; emigrated to London, 1887, active in Gaelic League, returned to Ireland to edit *New Ireland Review*, 1898, and then founded the *Leader*, 1900, which advocated cultural and economic nationalism and Catholic exclusivism, while excoriating the pretensions of 'physical-force nationalism', satirizing the social snobberies associated with aspirant Anglicization, and violently attacking the Literary Revival. Though associated with the Volunteers he was sidelined during the revolution, and the *Leader*, though long-lived, never regained its influence.

Seán Moylan (1889–1957): born in County Limerick; locally educated; involved in the Gaelic League and the GAA; nationalism further rationalized upon moving to Dublin, 1909; returned to Limerick, 1914; joined the local Volunteers company; moved to Cork, where he set up a Volunteers company in Newmarket; mobilized his men in 1916 but stood down due to counter-manding orders of MacNeill; heavily involved in subsequent reorganization of the Volunteers and Sinn Féin; led his company on an arms raid at an RIC barracks, 1918; arrested but escaped, remaining on the run until 1921; Com-mandant of the No. 2 Cork Brigade of the IRA; captured, 1921; elected to the second Dáil, 1921; opposed the Treaty; active on the anti-Treaty side during the Civil War, 1922–3; joined Fianna Fáil, 1926; TD for Cork North, 1932–57; Minister for Lands, 1943–8; Minister for Education, 1954–7; lost his seat in 1957 but immediately appointed to the Seanad; Minister for Agri-culture from 1957 until his sudden death in 1957.

Josephine Mary ['Min'] Mulcahy (*née* Ryan) (1884–1977): born in County Wexford; studied at the Royal University and at London University; estab-lished a branch of Cumann na mBan in London University; returned to Ireland in 1914; taught German in Rathmines Technical School; enjoyed a close relationship with Seán MacDermott, spending the hours before his exe-cution with him in his prison cell, 1916; acted as a courier during the Rising; subsequently sent to America to report on events to Devoy; married Richard Mulcahy, 1919; residence in Ranelagh subjected to frequent raids during the War of Independence; supported the Treaty, as Mulcahy was one of its lead-ing advocates, despite the fact that her sister Mary Kate and brother James opposed it strongly; nonetheless family relations held firm and Civil War bitterness was not continued.

Richard Mulcahy (1886–1971): born in Waterford; CBS educated; Post Office clerk; Gaelic League member; joined the IRB, 1907; joined the Irish Volunteers, 1913; fought in north County Dublin as Second-in-Command to Thomas Ashe during the Rising; released from Frongoch, December 1916; stage-managed the funeral of Ashe, 1917; made Commandant of the Dublin Brigade, Irish Volunteers, 1917; IRA Chief-of-Staff, 1918; elected MP for Clontarf, 1918; sat in the first Dáil, appointed Minister for Defence, 1919; married Josephine Mary ('Min') Ryan, 1919; TD until 1961; supported the Treaty; General Officer Commanding of Military Forces of the Provisional government, 1922–3; Minister of Defence, 1923–4; Chairman of Gaeltacht Commission, 1925–6; Minister for Local Government and Public Health, 1927–32; Leader of Fine Gael, 1944–59; Minister for Education, 1948–51 and 1954–7.

Gobnait ní Bruadair (Albinia Brodrick) (1861–1955): born in London, daughter of the eighth Viscount Midleton; privately educated; trained as a nurse; wrote articles for the *St James Gazette*; moved to Kerry, 1907; established an agricultural co-operative, 1908; joined Cumann na mBan and Sinn Féin following the Rising, 1916; Sinn Féin member on Kerry County Council, 1919–21; worked with the Irish White Cross; opposed the Treaty, 1922; arrested but released after hunger-strike, 1923; owner of *Irish Freedom*, 1926–37; left Cumann na mBan to co-found Mna na Poblachta, 1933.

Máire nic Shiubhlaigh (1883–1958): born in Dublin, to an Irish-speaking family with radical and Fenian traditions (her printer father later founded the Tower Press). Joined Gaelic League and Inghinidhe na hÉireann, acted in their tableaux, and took part in the Fay brothers' Ormonde productions (Willie Fay lodged in the Walker house). A founder member and star of the Irish National Theatre Society, playing in Yeats's early plays with marked success, notably on the 1903 tour; also worked with Yeats's sisters in Dun Emer industries. Leading lady in important early Abbey productions (in which her brother Frank and two of her sisters also appeared) but became alienated from the theatre's management over political issues, and the control exerted by Yeats and Gregory. Resigned and joined Theatre of Ireland, where she never achieved the same fame apart from in Séumas O'Kelly's *The Shuiler's Child*; returned from time to time to the Abbey. Active in Cumann na mBan, served in Jacob's Biscuit Factory during 1916 Rising, and remained active in republican politics; married General Éamonn Price in 1928; her last stage appearance was in 1948.

George Noble, Count Plunkett (1851–1948): son of a rich builder, educated Congowes and Trinity; studied law but was more interested in poetry, architectural history and Renaissance art; Director of the National Museum of Ireland, 1907. His donations to the Little Company of Mary earned him the papal title of 'Count'. His Parnellite nationalism was radicalized by his children, particularly Joseph; after the 1916 Rising and his son's execution he was sacked from the Museum, and took a leading part in the republicanized Sinn Féin movement, being elected as MP for Roscommon North in 1917. Briefly appearing as a possible leader, he was Minister for Foreign Affairs in the Dáil until January 1922, but followed a strict republican line and was marginalized from politics thereafter.

Arthur Patrick Donovan ['Art'] Ó Briain (1872–1949): born in London; educated St Charles College, studied civil engineering in Paris; joined the Gaelic League in London, 1898; President, 1914–35; spearhead of Irish nationalist community in London; joined the IRB and the Irish Volunteers; founded the National Aid Front, 1916; campaigned for republican prisoners including Casement; President of Sinn Féin in England and Wales; served as a representative of the Dáil in England; co-founder of the Irish Self-Determination League of Great Britain (ISDL), 1919; organized various demonstrations and meetings in London; worked closely with Collins during the Anglo-Irish War; opposed the Treaty; dismissed from position as an envoy of the Provisional government by the Department of Foreign Affairs, 1922; continued to campaign for the republican cause; gaoled on various occasions, 1922–4; became editor of the *Music Trades Review*; Irish Minister to France and Belgium, 1932–8.

Liam Ó Briain (1888–1974): born Dublin (as William O'Brien); educated CBS and gained a scholarship to UCD, achieving a first-class degree in Languages in 1909; a committed Gaelic Leaguer and French scholar, subsequently studied in Germany, returning to Ireland in 1914, joining Volunteers and working in UCD with Mary Kate Ryan, at whose wedding to Seán T. O'Kelly he was best man; helped print 'Proclamation of the Irish Republic' in Liberty Hall and served under Michael Mallin with ICA in Rising; after imprisonment joined University College, Galway, where he was Professor of Romance Languages for the rest of his long career. Sinn Féin candidate in 1918, served as a republican judge, involved in arms-running during Anglo-Irish War and was arrested; supported Treaty, stood for Senate in 1925 and then left politics; much involved in theatrical movements in Galway, and translated many European classics into Irish.

Edward Conor Marshal O'Brien (1880–1952): born in Limerick; a grandson of Young Irelander William Smith O'Brien; attended university at TCD and Oxford; developed an interest in Irish nationalism through the influence of the Gaelic League; chief patron of the Irish College at Carrigaholt, County Clare; leader of the Irish Volunteers in Clare; part-financed and took part in a plan with Figgis and Childers to land 600 rifles in Wicklow, 1914; enlisted as a lieutenant in the Royal Navy; returned to Ireland, 1919; appointed Inspector of Fisheries for the second Dáil; took part in numerous sailing expeditions around the world.

Francis Cruise O'Brien (1885–1927): born in Dublin; educated at CBS and University College; editor of student magazine *St Stephen's*, 1906; elected to the Executive of the Literary and Historical Society, 1905–7; frequently clashed with college authorities; politically active in the Young Ireland branch of the UIL; editor of the *Wexford People*, 1910; married Kathleen Sheehy, 1911; supported Redmond's endorsement of Britain's First World War involvement, 1914; condemned the Easter Rising but opposed the executions that followed; involved with Horace Plunkett in drawing up plans for future government, 1916–17; deputy editor of the *Irish Statesman*, 1919–20; worked for the *Freeman's Journal* and the *Irish Independent*; suffering from tuberculosis, he collapsed and died on Christmas Day 1927. Co-edited W. E. H. Lecky's *Clerical Influences*, 1911, from the first edition of his *Leaders of Public Opinion in Ireland*; collaborated on two pamphlets, *Ireland's Food in Wartime*, 1914, and *Starvation in Ireland*, 1917.

Kathleen Cruise O'Brien (*née* **Sheehy**) (1887–1938): born in Tipperary but moved to Dublin at an early age; daughter of MP David Sheehy, a leading member of the IPP; educated in France and at the University College, St Stephen's Green, where she studied Irish; founding member of the Irish Women's Franchise League, 1908; elected Vice-President of the Young Ireland branch of the UIL, 1910; married Francis Cruise O'Brien, 1911; lost three brothers-in-law, 1916, including Tom Kettle and Francis Sheehy-Skeffington; taught Irish at Rathmines Technical School; wrote an Irish grammar and a textbook in the 1920s; her play *Apartments* performed at the Abbey, 1923.

Seán T. Ó Ceallaigh (O'Kelly) (1882–1966): born in Dublin; CBS educated; joined the Gaelic League, 1898; Junior Assistant at the NLI, 1898–1902;

joined the IRB, 1901; co-founder of Sinn Féin, 1905; member of Dublin Corporation, 1906; Business Manager of *An Claidheamh Soluis*; founder member
of the Irish Volunteers, 1913; supervised the landing of arms in Wicklow,
1914; sent on IRB mission to secure US funds, 1915; took part in the Easter
Rising at the GPO, 1916; subsequently gaoled, released December 1916;
prominent in the reorganization of Sinn Féin; Acting Chairman of Sinn Féin
National Executive, 1918; elected to the first Dáil, 1919; elected Ceann
Comhairle; sent to Paris to represent the Dáil at the Peace Conference, and
subsequently acted as Sinn Féin representative in Rome, forging many relationships with the Vatican; opposed the Treaty but favoured constitutional
opposition; detained during the Civil War; founding Vice-President of Fianna
Fáil, 1926; maintained a devoutly Catholic standpoint in parliamentary
opposition; Minister for Public Health and Government, 1932–9; served as
Vice-President of the Executive Committee, 1932–7; and as Tánaiste, 1938–
45; appointed Minister for Finance, 1939; elected President of Ireland, 1945;
re-elected unopposed, 1952; married Mary Kate Ryan, 1918; married her
sister Phyllis following her death; buried in Glasnevin Cemetery.

J. J. ['Ginger'] O'Connell (1887–1944): born in County Mayo; educated at
Clongowes Wood and UCD; Chief Inspector of the Irish Volunteers, 1915–
16; travelled the country organizing Volunteer corps and lecturing on military
tactics; conveyed the countermanding order of MacNeill to Cork Volunteers,
1916; took no part in the fighting but imprisoned at Frongoch; released,
December 1916; organized Sligo Volunteers; rearrested and imprisoned for
alleged involvement in the 'German Plot', 1918; Director of Training during
the War of Independence; supported the Treaty; Deputy Chief-of-Staff in the
Free State Army, 1922; kidnap by anti-Treaty IRA forces a major factor in
the outbreak of Civil War; released upon rebels' surrender; held rank of Colonel in the army for the rest of his military career.

Rory O'Connor (1883–1922): born in Dublin; educated at Clongowes Wood
and UCD; prominent in militant student circles; worked as a railway engineer in Canada, 1911–15; returned to Ireland reputedly at the behest of the
IRB, 1915; involved with the Gaelic League and Irish Volunteers; trained
members in bomb-making; involved in the production of the forged 'Castle
Document', 1916; wounded during the Rising; Director of Engineering during the War of Independence; Director of Military Operations in England;
opposed the Treaty; occupied the Four Courts with republican forces, 1922;
imprisoned in Mountjoy; executed by government forces in retaliation for
the killing of Seán Hales, 8 December 1922.

Eimar O'Duffy (1893–1935): born in Dublin, to a 'Castle Catholic' background, which gave him much material for his satirical novels. Educated Stonyhurst and UCD, where he was a prominent student journalist, honing talents later employed on the *Irish Volunteer*; became a socialist and joined the IRB but thought the 1916 Rising a mistake. Involved in dramatic productions with Joseph Plunkett and Thomas MacDonagh. After the revolution worked as a teacher, a dentist, and in the Department of External Affairs before moving to Paris and London, where he died. His satiric novels such as *King Goshawk and the Birds*, 1926, sustained his reputation for a while, though they are less illuminating than his *Bildungsroman* of 1919, *The Wasted Island*.

Sean O'Faolain (1900–1991): born (as John Whelan) in Cork, to an RIC family; became an enthusiast for the Irish language and while a student at UCC was involved in republican activities; under Daniel Corkery's influence supported the republicans in the Civil War but became disillusioned and rejected pietistic Irish nationalism and (largely) Catholicism. His landmark short-story collection, *Midsummer Night Madness*, 1932, was banned but established him at the forefront of his generation of Irish writers, a position he maintained not only through his fiction-writing but through his editing of the pluralistic (and often subversive) literary magazine the *Bell* from 1940, and his imaginative biographies of figures such as Daniel O'Connell and Hugh O'Neill.

Michael O'Flanagan (1876–1942): born (as 'Flanagan') to a small-farming family with a Fenian tradition near Castlerea, County Roscommon; ordained in 1900 after a brilliant career at Maynooth and returned to teach Irish at Summerhill College, Sligo, where he had gone to school; active in Gaelic League and co-operative movement, and a celebrated preacher; frequently visited USA on fundraising tours; on Executive Committee of Sinn Féin from 1911, and wrote separatist articles for journals such as the *Spark* and the *Leader*, frequently clashing with his clerical superiors; preached at O'Donovan Rossa's funeral, 1915; prominent in reorganized Sinn Féin from 1918 and a tireless election campaigner; the shift to violent tactics worried him and he lost influence from 1919, though he continued active in the movement (and was Chaplain to Dáil Éireann in 1919). Although he apparently favoured a dominion settlement at one stage, he opposed the Treaty and the foundation of Fianna Fáil, remaining in Sinn Féin (and being elected President of the organization in 1933), though his relations with the movement were mercurial.

Patrick Sarsfield ['P. S.'] O'Hegarty (1879–1955): born in County Cork; CBS educated; entered employment in the Post Office and transferred to London;

active in Irish circles, joining the Gaelic League, the GAA and the IRB along with other prominent future revolutionaries; became a member of the IRB Supreme Council; contributed to *Irish Freedom*, 1910–14; advocated a strict separation between Church and state, and firmly secularist in religious views, but moderate in his militarism; inactive in the Easter Rising; refused to take oath of loyalty in 1918 and lost his civil service position; took the pro-Treaty side in 1922; appointed Secretary for the Department of Posts and Telegraphs, 1922. Wrote *The Victory of Sinn Féin*, 1924, and *A History of Ireland under the Union*, 1952.

Michael O'Hickey (Micheál Ó Hiceadha) (1861–1916): born in County Waterford; educated at CBS and at St John's College; ordained to the priesthood, 1884; spent early priesthood in Scotland; member of the Gaelic Union; contributed poetry to the *Nation* and the *Gaelic Journal*; member of the London Irish Literary Society, 1892; on return to Ireland used position of diocesan Inspector of Schools to promote the use of the Irish language; appointed Professor of Irish at St Patrick's College, Maynooth, 1896; member of the RAI and Fellow of the RSAI, 1897; Vice-President of the Gaelic League, 1898–1903; active supporter of agitation seeking compulsory Irish for matriculation to the newly established NUI, 1908; removed from his Chair at Maynooth for condemning Irish bishops for their stance on the matter, 1909; appeal dismissed by Rome, 1912; returned to Waterford, where he died of blood poisoning in 1916.

Kevin O'Higgins (1892–1927): born in Queen's County (County Leix); educated at Clongowes, St Mary's Christian Brothers', Portlaoise, and St Patrick's College, Maynooth; studied law at University College, Dublin; joined Irish Volunteers, 1915, Sinn Féin MP for Queen's County, 1918; Assistant Minister for Local Government, 1919; TD for Leix–Offaly, 1922, re-elected, 1923; Minister for Home Affairs, 1922 (renamed Justice, 1924); Assistant Adjutant-General on army general staff, 1922; Minister for External Affairs, 1925; assassinated, 1927. A ruthless advocate of draconian policies towards republican dissidents during and after the Civil War, he subsequently showed an interest in reviving a dual-monarchy approach to Anglo-Irish relations.

John Joseph O'Kelly ('Sceilg') (1872–1957): born Valentia Island, County Kerry; learnt Irish from his father and became a devout Irish-Irelander; did not attend secondary school but through his own efforts became a teacher and journalist in Dublin from 1897; passionate Gaelic Leaguer, much involved in producing Dineen's *Dictionary*, co-founder of the notably republican Keating branch, and leading spirit in acrimonious disputes over language policy and the editorship of *An Claidheamh Soluis*; edited *Banba*, 1901–6; founder member of Sinn Féin, and editor of the *Catholic Bulletin*, 1911–22, which under his guidance powerfully and influentially endorsed the Easter Rising; treasurer of Irish National Aid and Volunteer Dependants' Fund; deported, 1917; Sinn Féin TD for Louth, 1918, and deputized as Ceann Comhairle for first Dáil; President of Gaelic League from 1919, and Minister for Irish and then Education; opposed Treaty, campaigning against it in the USA and Australia; broke with de Valera over the latter's recognition of the Free State, remaining a republican purist and member of Sinn Féin, and continuing to publish books and pamphlets on Irish politics and religion.

Ernie O'Malley (1897–1957): born in County Mayo; educated CBS and UCD, where, at the latter, he began to study medicine; joined the Irish Volunteers, 1917; highly active during the War of Independence, serving under Richard Mulcahy and Michael Collins; captured, December 1920, but escaped, February 1921; took the rank of Commandant General in the IRA's Southern Division; rejected the Treaty; appointed to the IRA Army Council, October 1922; fought in the Four Courts, June 1922; badly wounded and captured in Dublin, November 1922; elected TD for Dublin North during his incarceration, 1923; went on a 41-day hunger-strike; released July 1924; spent much of his time travelling Europe and North America and developing his interests in literature and the visual arts; married the American sculptor Helen Hooker, 1935; later life spent documenting his role in the IRA. Published classic and highly 'literary' autobiographies *On Another Man's Wound*, 1936, and *The Singing Flame*, posthumously, 1978.

O'Rahilly, Michael ('The O'Rahilly') (1875–1916): born in Ballylongford, County Kerry, to an influential shop-owning dynasty; educated at Clongowes and UCD, leaving to take over the family business, which he subsequently sold; lived off a private income in Bray and Dublin and temporarily moved to England and America but became a passionate Irish-language enthusiast and separatist nationalist, adopting a Gaelic 'title' around 1904 and returning to Dublin in 1909; involved in nationalist journals such as *Sinn Féin* and *Irish Freedom* and, most of all, *An Claidheamh Soluis*, which he revitalized. An early advocate of the Volunteering movement, he was much involved in obtaining arms for it; supported MacNeill in countermanding the order to rise on Easter weekend 1916, but took part in the fighting and died in action.

Kevin O'Shiel (1891–1970): born in County Tyrone; CBS and TCD educated; called to the Bar, 1913; member of the Irish Volunteers until it split, 1914; disillusioned by the postponement of Home Rule; joined the Anti-Partition League, 1916; joined Sinn Féin, 1917; Judicial Commissioner of the newly established Dáil Land Commission, 1920; supporter of the Treaty; Assistant Legal Adviser to the Provisional government, 1922–3; Director of the government's North-Eastern Boundary Bureau, 1922–5; served as a Commissioner with the Irish Land Commission, 1923–63. Wrote *The Rise of the Irish Nation League*, 1916, *The Making of a Republic*, 1920, and *The Land Problem in Ireland and Its Settlement*, 1954.

Patrick Henry Pearse (1879–1916): born in Dublin; educated at the CBS and the Royal University; joined the Gaelic League, 1896; called to the Bar, 1901; convinced of the centrality of the Irish language in cultivating nationalism; edited *An Claidheamh Soluis*, 1903–9; involved in theatrical and literary circles; founded St Enda's School, 1908, and St Ita's girls' school, 1910; adopted a militant tone after early support for Home Rule, 1912; admitted to the IRB, 1913; founder member of the Irish Volunteers, 1913; undertook a fundraising trip to the USA on behalf of St Enda's and the Volunteers, 1914; took charge of the Volunteers who refused to side with Redmond's call to join the British Army; IRB Director of Military Operations; delivered the graveside oration at the funeral of O'Donovan Rossa, 1915; delivered the 'Proclamation of the Irish Republic', Easter 1916; head of the Provisional government of the Republic of Ireland; surrendered, 19 April; executed, 3 May. Wrote the plays *The Singer*, 1910; *An Rí*, 1911; *Eoin*, 1915; and published *Songs of the Irish Rebels*, 1914.

William ['Willie'] Pearse (1881–1916): born in Dublin; CBS educated; entered the Metropolitan School of Art, 1897; studied sculpture under Oliver Sheppard; followed his brother Patrick into the New Ireland Literary Society and the Gaelic League; member of the Executive of the Wolfe Tone and United Irishmen Memorial Committee, 1898; continued his studies in London and Paris before returning to Ireland in 1906; exhibited work at the RHA and Oireachteas exhibitions between 1906 and 1913; taught art and English at St Enda's; co-established the Leinster Stage Society, 1912; joined the Irish Volunteers, 1913; took part in the Easter Rising but had little authority and was not involved in its planning; executed most likely because of his sibling relationship with Patrick, 4 May 1916.

George Noble Plunkett *see* **George Noble, Count Plunkett**

Grace Plunkett (*née* **Gifford**) (1888–1955): born in Dublin; studied at the Slade School of Fine Art, London, 1907–8; joined Inghinidhe na hÉireann, 1910; contributed to the *Irish Review* and the *Irish Citizen*; engaged to Joseph Plunkett, 1915; converted to Catholicism; married Plunkett hours before his execution, 1916; appointed to the Sinn Féin Executive, 1917; opposed the Treaty, 1922; imprisoned, 1923; concentrated on work as a cartoonist and artist following the Civil War.

Joseph Mary Plunkett (1887–1916): born in Dublin, son of Count and Countess Plunkett; educated at Belvedere College, Stonyhurst, in Paris, and by tutors; ill from childhood with recurrent glandular tuberculosis; inclined towards mysticism and theatricality, and interested in Orientalist subjects after his travels in North Africa; published *The Circle and the Sword*, 1911; edited the *Irish Review*, 1913–14; joined the Irish Volunteers, 1913; elected to Provisional Committee; co-founded the Irish Theatre Company, 1914; named in the twelve-man Executive of the Volunteers, 1914; appointed Director of Military Operations, 1914; inducted into the IRB, 1915; travelled to Germany to help Casement secure aid for the Rising, and probably chief strategist in its military planning; travelled to America to brief Clan na Gael on progress; signatory of the 'Proclamation of the Irish Republic'; fought in the GPO during the Rising; married Grace Gifford in prison on the eve of his execution, 4 May 1916. *Collected Poems* published posthumously.

Jennie Wyse Power (*née* **O'Toole**) (1858–1941): born Baltinglass, County Wicklow; active in Ladies' Land League, and remained a strong Parnellite; opened the Irish Farm and Produce Company shops and restaurant at 21 Henry Street, Dublin, 1899, a central meeting place for nationalists; committed Gaelic Leaguer and on the board of management of Ring College; active suffragist, co-founder of Inghinidhe na hÉireann, member of Sinn Féin Executive, and active in Dublin politics; founder member and President (in 1915) of Cumann na mBan; supported 1916 rebels and helped to organize Volunteer Dependants' Fund; supported Treaty and continued to be prominent in Dublin Corporation politics as well as Cumann na nGaedheal, but resigned from that party in 1925 and later became a Fianna Fáil Senator.

John Redmond (1856–1918): born Dublin, to a mixed Catholic gentry and Protestant family with deep Wexford roots; educated Clongowes and (briefly) Trinity College; followed his father into Parnellite politics in 1881; active though not in the inner circle, and supported Parnell during the split; an impressive orator with pluralist instincts, he became head of the reunited party in 1900, holding the party together despite challenges from mavericks, and helping to bring about a series of ameliorative measures to do with land, education and housing, before Home Rule came back to the forefront of politics after 1909. His instincts were conservative (he opposed women's suffrage and was unsympathetic to labour) and increasingly imperial, and he initially underestimated the strength of Ulster resistance to Home Rule; the Bill introduced in 1912 was decried by many as insufficient. By this stage, the rhetoric of advanced nationalism, and brilliant publicists such as Arthur Griffith, had portrayed the Irish Parliamentary Party scornfully as collaborationist, ineffectual and clientelist – and, since Redmond's alliance with Joseph Devlin of the Ancient Order of Hibernians, deeply in thrall to atavistic Catholicism. However, he managed to take over much of the Volunteer movement after 1913, and his decisive support for the war effort looked at first like an effective ploy. But his exclusion from Irish policy-making in London, the favour shown to leaders of Ulster unionism by the government and the inexorable progress of the war towards a bloody stalemate helped to destroy his credibility. Attempts to bring off a Home Rule settlement after the Rising were undermined partly by the unacceptability of Partition, and partly by unionist objections. He died in March 1918, nine months before the destruction of his party by Sinn Féin in the December election.

William Rooney (1873–1901): born in Dublin; CBS educated; a railway clerk by trade; early member of the Irish Fireside Club, where young people took Irish-language lessons and were introduced to the works of Irish nationalist authors; met Arthur Griffith through the club; joined the Leinster Literary Society, contributing to its journal *Eblana*; established the Celtic Literary Society, 1893; edited the Society's journal, *An Seanachaidhe (The Storyteller)*; joined the Gaelic League despite his dissatisfaction with its non-political stance; travelled the country promoting the Irish language; leading member of the 1798 Centenary Committee; persuaded Griffith to return from South Africa to edit the *United Irishman*, 1899; developed Sinn Féin policy with Griffith; founded Cumann na nGael as an umbrella nationalist organization, 1900; died from TB, 1901.

George Russell ('AE') (1867–1935): born Lurgan, educated Dublin, met his 'oldest friend and enemy', Yeats, when a fellow student at Metropolitan School of Art; mystic, poet, painter, but also a passionate co-operativist and the efficient and tireless Secretary of Irish Agricultural Organisation Society from 1897, editing the eclectic *Irish Homestead* (which published, among much else, the early work of James Joyce) with his close friend Susan

Mitchell; published as 'AE' from 1893, both books of poetry and many visionary pamphlets on the Irish future; closely involved in early years of Irish National Theatre Society, his Rathgar salon attracting a circle of young writers (often disapproved of by Yeats); idealistically nationalist, oscillated in his support of advanced politics, but was unequivocally on the workers' side in the 1913 lockout (the *Irish Homestead* carried an important series of articles in dialogue with James Connolly). Powerfully affected by the 1916 Rising, Russell was much involved in the Irish Convention of 1917, which attempted to bring about an agreed devolutionary solution; after its failure he campaigned against British policies in Ireland, flirting with republicanism while following his own path; he endorsed the Treaty and from 1923 edited the *Irish Statesman*, a sophisticated, pluralist and often subversive journal of literature and current affairs, widely read until its demise after a libel case in 1928 and the withdrawal of backers after the 1929 stock-market crash; at odds with the clerical and pro-censorship tone of Irish public life, he spent much of his peripatetic last years in the USA and England.

Desmond Ryan (1893–1964): born in London, son of W. P. Ryan, moved to Ireland in 1906; much influenced by his father's left-wing nationalism, and by his own education at St Enda's and an early devotion to Pearse, whom he served in the GPO in 1916; after internment attended UCD and became a journalist for *Freeman's Journal* and edited Pearse's works, as well as writing a biography of James Connolly; disillusioned by the Civil War, moved to London, continuing to work as a journalist and historian of the revolution; returned to Ireland at outset of Second World War, where he farmed, wrote many books on labour history and Fenianism, and a *roman à clef*, *The Invisible Army*, 1932, and occupied himself with labour politics.

James Ryan (1891–1970): born in County Wexford, brother of Mary Kate, Min, Agnes, Nell and others of the Tomcoole Ryan family; studied at the Royal College of Surgeons; joined the IRB, 1914; served as Chief Medical Officer at the GPO during the Rising; imprisoned at Frongoch, released during the summer of 1916; went into medical practice in Wexford; Commandant of the Wexford Battalion of the Volunteers, 1917; elected MP in South Wexford, 1918; married Máirín Cregan, 1919; arrested and interned on Spike Island, 1920; opposed the Treaty; provided medical aid during the government shelling of the Four Courts and later in the Hammam Hotel, 1922; arrested and interned in Mountjoy and the Curragh; participated in a 36-day hunger-strike; re-elected as a Sinn Féin TD for Wexford while in prison, 1923; founding member of Fianna Fáil, 1926; later held the posts of Minister for Agriculture, Minister for Health and Social Welfare, and Minister for Finance; on retiring from the Dáil, nominated to the Seanad; served until 1969.

Mary Kate Ryan (1878–1934): born in County Wexford; educated by Loreto nuns in Wexford and Dublin; graduated from the Royal University and Cambridge; her nationalism emerged during her time in London; returned to Ireland, 1910; worked at the National University as a language teacher; temporary Professor of French, 1913–18; her home at Ranelagh Road used as a frequent meeting place for republicans; arrested after the Easter Rising but released in June 1916; married Seán T. Ó Ceallaigh, 1918; continued teaching during his long absences as an international envoy; initially supported the Treaty but soon turned against it; the Treaty split the Ryan family, as her sisters Min and Agnes were married to pro-Treaty supporters Richard Mulcahy and Denis McCullough; continued to lecture at UCD until her death from heart problems in 1934.

William Patrick ['W. P.'] Ryan (1867–1942): born in County Tipperary; emigrated to London and became a journalist, 1886; active Irish revivalist; prominent member of the Gaelic League; returned to Ireland, 1905; edited the *Irish Peasant*; his fierce criticism of the Catholic Church forced the paper to close under pressure from Cardinal Logue, 1906; kept the paper alive under various titles but lost support for his socialist stance and for having fallen out with Sinn Féin; returned to London to work with the *Daily Herald*, 1911. Remained with the paper until his death. Wrote *The Plough and the Cross*, 1910, *The Pope's Green Island*, 1912, *The Celt and the Cosmos*, 1914, *The Irish Labour Movement*, 1919.

Francis ['Frank'] Sheehy-Skeffington (1878–1916): born in County Cavan; UCD educated; committed to women's rights and pacifism; married Hanna Sheehy, 1903; co-founded the Young Ireland branch of the United Irish League, 1904; assistant editor of the *Nationist*, 1906; freelance journalist, contributed to the *Irish Peasant* and the *Irish Nation*; published a biography of Michael Davitt, 1908; co-founded the Irish Women's Franchise League, 1908; co-founded the *Irish Citizen*, 1912; supported the strikers during the 1913 lockout; imprisoned for making anti-recruitment speeches, 1915; released after hunger-strike; organized a civilian defence force to prevent looting during the 1916 rebellion; arrested by the military and shot without trial, 26 April 1916.

Hanna Sheehy-Skeffington (1877–1946): born in County Cork; daughter of Nationalist MP David Sheehy; educated at the Royal University of Ireland;

married Francis Skeffington, 1903; both committed to feminism, pacifism, socialism and nationalism; co-founded the Irish Women's Franchise League, 1908; arrested for suffragette activities, 1912; released after hunger-strike; edited the *Irish Citizen*, 1913–20; Francis shot without trial during Easter Rising, 1916; toured USA to publicize the case, 1916–18; Director of Organization for Sinn Féin, 1921; opposed the Anglo-Irish Treaty; campaigned for prisoners' rights, 1922–3; Vice-President of the Women's International League for Peace and Freedom; split with Fianna Fáil when de Valera entered the Dáil, 1927; contributed to the *Irish Word* and *An Phoblacht*; opposed the 1937 constitution; formed the Women's Social and Progressive League, 1937; unsuccessful candidate in the 1943 general election.

Edward ['Ned'] Millington Stephens (1888–1955): born in Dublin; TCD educated; called to the Bar, 1912; occupied various legal offices in the civil service; sympathetic to Sinn Féin; accompanied Collins during the Anglo-Irish Treaty negotiations, 1921; Secretary for the North-East Boundary Bureau and prominent in the Free State's bid to redraw the border, 1922–6; served as Assistant Registrar of the Supreme Court until his retirement in 1950. Nephew of the playwright J. M. Synge, of whom he wrote an absorbing memoir, *My Uncle John*, posthumously published, 1974.

John Francis Sweetman (1872–1953): born in County Wexford; entered Downside Abbey, 1891; ordained a priest, 1899; Catholic Chaplain to British forces during the Boer War, 1899–1902; adopted a nationalist viewpoint because of his Boer War experiences; appointed Superior and Headmaster of the Benedictine school in Enniscorthy, 1905; moved the school to a larger establishment near Gorey, which he christened 'Mount St Benedict', 1907; the school with its unorthodox regime attracted students such as James Dillon and Seán McBride; after 1916 became strongly anti-British and pro-Sinn Féin; attended the funeral of Thomas Ashe, 1917; publicly supported the anti-conscription campaign, 1917; accused of harbouring Sinn Féiners at Mount St Benedict; school forced to close as parents removed pupils in response, 1925; placed under ecclesiastical ban, 1925–39; allowed to return to Mount St Benedict when his priestly faculties were restored, 1939; buried in the grounds of the school.

Cesca Trench ('Sadhbh Trinseach') (1891–1918): born in Liverpool to an Anglo-Irish clerical family; educated in England and Switzerland; learnt Irish from 1907 (taught by her cousin Dermot Trench, who is satirized in the opening chapter of *Ulysses*), joined Gaelic League, 1908, and became a passionate *Gaeilgeoir* and Sinn Féin supporter; studied art in Paris, 1912–14, and Metropolitan School of Art, Dublin, from 1914; involved in Cumann na mBan and Executive of Gaelic League, and produced much art-work for the nationalist movement; married Diarmuid Coffey in April 1918 and died in influenza epidemic that October.

William Butler Yeats (1865–1939): born in Dublin to an artistic family, who lived largely in London during his youth, spending inspirational summers in Sligo; influenced by the old Fenian John O'Leary, and by Maud Gonne, and spent much time in neo-Fenian circles in Dublin from the mid-1880s; sought to inspire a national literature for Ireland (in English), through landmark volumes such as *The Celtic Twilight*, 1893, and *The Wind Among the Reeds*, 1899, as well as through plays such as *The Countess Cathleen*, 1892, and the Abbey Theatre, which he founded with Augusta Gregory in 1904 and dominated for the next thirty years; distanced himself from advanced nationalism from about 1906 but reinserted himself into the nationalist narrative after 1916, through poems, plays and public speeches, returning to Dublin to live in 1922 and becoming a Senator of the Free State; awarded Nobel Prize for Literature in 1923.

Ella Young (1867–1956): born in County Antrim, moved to Dublin, 1880; graduated from the RUI; published poems on Celtic mythology and mysticism; joined Sinn Féin, 1912; co-founded Cumann na mBan, 1914; opposed the Treaty, 1922; Secretary of the Irish Republican Memorial Committee, 1922; moved to America, 1925; lectured at Berkeley. Published *The Coming of Lugh*, 1909, *Celtic Wonder Tales*, 1910, *The Wonder-Smith and His Son*, 1927, *The Tangle-Coated Horse*, 1929, *The Unicorn with Silver Shoes*, 1932, and her autobiography *Flowering Dusk*, 1945.

Acknowledgements

My first thanks must be to the Wolfson Foundation and the British Academy; by electing me to a Research Professorship for 2009–12, they made the writing of this book possible. I owe much to Tim Wilson and Colin Reid, who not only took over my teaching duties while I was on leave, but contributed materially to this book with stimulating ideas and suggestions. I am also grateful to the Electors of the James Ford Lectures in British History at Oxford, who elected me Ford's Lecturer for 2012, a challenge which helped to concentrate my mind and produced the nucleus of this book.

I am also very grateful to Darragh Gannon and Daragh Curran, who provided valuable research assistance in Dublin, and to Tom Dunne, who helped with sources in Cork; to my secretary, Jules Iddon, who characteristically put in efforts far beyond the call of duty; and to Gill Coleridge, Cara Jones and Peter Straus at my agents, Rogers, Coleridge & White. My publisher Simon Winder at Penguin must be thanked for his encouragement, patience and perceptiveness about what this book tries to do. Marina Kemp worked wonders during the production process. At W. W. Norton I am equally grateful to Steve Forman for his support and to Justin Cahill for his close, stimulating and suggestive reading. As with every other book of mine she has edited, Donna Poppy contributed infinitely more than the term 'copyeditor' suggests.

I owe much to the staffs of various libraries and archive collections, especially Seamus Helferty at the marvellous Archives Department in University College, Dublin, and Orna Somerville; and many people in the National Library of Ireland, notably James Harte, Bernie Metcalfe, Keith Murphy, Nora Thornton and above all Mary Broderick in the treasure-trove of Prints and Drawings, who went to endless trouble on my behalf. Brian Crowley at the Pearse Museum and Niall Bergin at the Kilmainham Gaol Archives were immensely helpful and generous with illustrative material. For conversations, advice, suggestions, hospitality and help with tracing material, I owe much to

Nicholas Allen, Susan Barr, Guy Beiner, Catherine Berney, Robin Blake, Susan Brigden, Cathal MacSwiney Brugha, Jeffrey Dudgeon, Owen Dudley Edwards, Marianne Elliott, Diego Fasciati, Jennifer Fitzgerald, Frances Flanagan, Andrew Gailey, Conor Gearty, Robert Gerwarth, Mary Hickman, Anne Hodge, Sam Hynes, Alvin Jackson, Lar Joye, Catriona Kelly, John Killen, Cormac Kinsella, Roger Kirker, Hermione Lee, Ben Levitas, Eve Morrison, Conor Morrissey, John McBratney, Ian McBride, Padraig McCartan, Fearghal McGarry, Catherine Morris, Marc Mulholland, Pat Murphy, Richard Murphy, Caoimhe nic Dháibhéid, Daithí Ó Corráin, Julia O'Faolain, Eunan O'Halpin, Margaret Ó hÓgartaigh, Cormac O'Malley, Ciarán O'Neill, Hilary Pyle, Lucy Riall, Frank Shovlin, Anthony Tierney, Donal Tinney, Colm Tóibín, Phil Twomey and Charles Townshend. Senia Pašeta, who was writing her own path-breaking study of Irish nationalist women at the same time, shared many of her insights, and I am profoundly grateful to her. Richard English was a constant source of encouragement and suggestions. Elizabeth Berney and Risteárd Mulcahy gave me vivid insights into their parents' world. Catriona Crowe provided many insights and imaginative suggestions about 'complicating the narrative'. Joseph Hassett contributed much of insight, and persuaded me to lecture on this subject at Canisius College during an early stage of my research. The symposia organized by the European Network on Theory and Practice of Biography, based at the University of Valencia, were a regular source of interest and stimulation, particularly from my friend Isabel Burdiel, founder of the Network; inspiration was also provided by the Oxford Centre for Life-Writing at Wolfson College, Oxford, and by the sustaining friendship and challenging ideas provided by its founder and director, Hermione Lee. My wife, Aisling, has made sharply perceptive contributions throughout, and has put up with this book, and its author, with exemplary fortitude; I owe her more than I can say. I am also profoundly grateful to those who read the whole manuscript in first draft: Tom Dunne, Selina Hastings and Matt Kelly. Their advice and support mean an immense amount to me. The errors and obscurities that survived their readings are all my own.

The book is dedicated to Jay Tolson – fine writer, close reader and old friend of my youth, who understands 'the problem of generations'.

I am grateful for permission to make direct quotations of unpublished material in their possession from the National Library of Ireland, the Archives of University College, Dublin, and the Cork City and County Archives. I am also grateful to the family of the late Máire MacSwiney Brugha for permission to reproduce photographs in their possession, as well as material in the

ACKNOWLEDGEMENTS

MacSwiney Papers at UCD, to Padraig McCartan for permission to reproduce the photograph of his father, to Risteárd Mulcahy for permission to reproduce Patrick Tuohy's portrait of Richard Mulcahy, and to Cormac O'Malley for permission to reproduce his mother's photograph of Ernie O'Malley. Material from the Maloney Collection of Irish Historical Papers is quoted with the permission of the Manuscripts and Archives Division, the New York Public Library, Astor, Lenox and Tilden Foundations. The extract from 'In Memory of Eva Gore-Booth and Con Markievicz' on p. 231 is reprinted with the permission of Scribner Publishing Group, a division of Simon & Schuster, Inc., from *The Collected Works of W. B. Yeats. Volume I: The Poems*, revised by W. B. Yeats, edited by Richard J. Finneran, copyright © 1933 by The Macmillan Company, renewed 1961 by Bertha Georgie Yeats; all rights reserved. Every effort has been made to establish contact with the holders of original copyrights; in cases where this has not been possible I hope this general acknowledgement will be taken as sufficient.

Index

Pages upon which text illustrations appear have been set in italic.